GOTHICKA

VICTORIA NELSON

The dream avatar Paprika swallows the corporate patriarch and his dark dream. From the anime film *Paprika* (2006), directed by Satoshi Kon.

VICTORIA NELSON

GOTHICKA

Vampire Heroes,
Human Gods,
and the New Supernatural

HARVARD UNIVERSITY PRESS
CAMBRIDGE, MASSACHUSETTS & LONDON, ENGLAND ▪ 2012

The verse translation from *The Danse Macabre of Women* by Ann Tukey Harrison
is reprinted by permission of The Kent State University Press.
"My Father's Wedding" from THE MAN IN THE BLACK COAT TURNS
by Robert Bly. Copyright © 1981 by Robert Bly. Reprinted by permission of
Georges Borchardt, Inc., for Robert Bly.

Library of Congress Cataloging-in-Publication Data
Nelson, Victoria.
   Gothicka : vampire heroes, human gods, and the new supernatural / Victoria
Nelson.
      p. cm.
   ISBN 978-0-674-05014-3 (alk. paper)
   1. Gothic fiction (Literary genre)—History and criticism.   2. Gothic revival
(Literature)—History and criticism.   3. Horror tales—History and criticism.
4. Spirituality in literature.   5. Horror films—History and criticism.
6. Horror comic books, strips, etc.—History and criticism.   7. Goth culture
(Subculture)—History and criticism.   I. Title.
   PN3435.N45 2012
   700'.415—dc23   2011041651

For Frank, who likes the Gothick,
and his bright future

CONTENTS

A

WINTER'S TALE.

IN FOUR VOLUMES.

BY

J. N. BREWER,

AUTHOR OF THE MANSION HOUSE, &c.

" Oh, it is wondrous fweet
" To wile away the tedious wintry night
" By fome furprifing tale of true love's hap,
" And fheeted fpectre, that thro' midnight aifle
" Glides dreadful!"

VOL. IV.

LONDON:

PRINTED AT THE
Minerva-Prefs,
FOR WILLIAM LANE, LEADENHALL-STREET.

1799.

Title page of a Gothick novel in the Hammond Collection.
Courtesy of the New York Society Library.

PREFACE

The boy's novelette may be ignorant in a literary sense, which is only like saying that a modern novel is ignorant in the chemical sense, or the economic sense, or the astronomical sense; but it is not vulgar intrinsically—it is the actual centre of a million flaming imaginations.

—G. K. Chesterton, "A Defence of Penny Dreadfuls"

In 1811, a Newport, Rhode Island, dry goods merchant named James Hammond founded a lending library upstairs from his shop that quickly grew to 8,000 volumes of popular fiction with a scattering of playscripts and poetry. And this fiction, the ancestor of the modern mass paperback, was very popular indeed; a single novel, usually printed in three volumes, circulated as many as 400 to 500 times. Hammond's clients devoured the nineteenth-century equivalent of airport novels not in economy-class coach but in real coaches and in sitting rooms up and down the northeastern seaboard of the new country. They also wrote and drew on the inside front and back covers, tore out illustrations that caught their eye, and generally read the books to pieces. Today the bindings of these volumes literally fall apart when they are opened, leaving a trail of shredded orange pigskin on the surface of the Rare Book Room reading table at the New York Society Library.

What manner of literary fare were the good folk of Newport so eagerly consuming? Sensational Gothick fiction full of violence, sexual assault, and assorted other outrages and titillations, hot off the press from London and quickly reprinted, often in a matter of a month or two, in American editions. Packed with equal portions of sex, gore, and high-flown sentimentality, the contents of these tattered volumes still hold their power to enthrall the modern reader, a fact that partly explains how this book came to be written. I first encountered Matthew Lewis's *The Monk*, the best-known exemplar of this venerable shock genre, in a suitably Gothick architectural space: the then unretrofitted bowels of Doe Library at the University of California, Berkeley, nine floors of stacks compressed *Being John Malkovich*–style into a four-story sandwich. As a senior with a prized stack pass, I should have been engaged in research on my honors thesis on Chaucer. Instead I sat cross-legged on the cold metal floor enthralled by this salacious tale of lustful monks, evil abbesses, complaisant nuns, and a baby's corpse decaying in an underground crypt. I gulped down its 400-odd pages in one go, staggering out of the stacks a few head-spinning hours later stiff and disoriented but eager for more.

Abandoning Gothick novels as such while I pursued a very brief graduate school career in medieval studies (like Lewis and his fellow Gothick writers, I loved the Middle Ages), I stayed immersed in the Gothick tradition without knowing it through my instinctive love of stories of the supernatural. With very few exceptions I found them only in popular fiction and B movies—ghost stories, horror films, and the like. There was always Henry James's *The Turn of the Screw*, of course, but the critic Edmund Wilson had interpreted this work so magisterially through the favored twentieth-century psychological lens of erotic obsession (i.e., the apparitions of Quint and Miss Jessel are the governess's fevered projections driven by sexual repression) that no room was left, if you will, for the undead.

My own orientation remained more or less that of Wilson's until I began the series of essays that resulted in *The Secret Life of Puppets* ten years ago. Ground zero for this study of the Western supernatural grotesque was an essay on the horror writer H. P. Lovecraft and the Polish Jewish fabulist Bruno Schulz, two contemporaries who embodied the different destinies of the fantastic tale in Europe and America. Noting his father's death from syphilis and the striking resemblance of his monsters' deformities to the physical disfigurations caused by that disease, I fashioned my initial take on Lovecraft as a by-the-book (the book being the bible of mental health professionals, the *Diagnostic and Statistical Manual of Mental Disorders*) psychological reading. All the while I was dogged by the feeling that despite the obvious pathology, despite his own express position as materialist and atheist, Lovecraft—like many other writers of scary stories—was reaching for some kind of dark transcendence. But what, exactly, did this transcendence consist of?

Because its tracks were much more visible in what I call the "sub-Zeitgeist"—the grab-bag mass market popular culture lying beneath or around or on top of the secular-materialist mainstream—than in high art of any sort, once again Lovecraft showed me the way. In *The Secret Life of Puppets* I argued that a historically distorted supernaturalism, configured after the Protestant Reformation as a free-floating "demonic" loosely attached to a Christian belief system, has long been an important dimension of American popular culture. This unbalanced worldview has characteristically emphasized the dark side: ghosts, monsters, and other assorted creatures of the imaginary grotesque. The result has been that outside the purview of organized religion, the genre of supernatural horror has been the preferred mode, or even the only allowed one, a predominantly secular-scientific culture such as ours has had for imagining and encountering the sacred, albeit in unconscious ways. That book's analysis ended in the last decade of the twentieth century, when the unconscious religiosity carried by the demonic seemed to be reaching a peak at the same time as it was seeking broader avenues of expression.

In the years since *The Secret Life of Puppets* was published, this trend has emerged as a much more explicit spirituality expressed in performance and practice as well as in fiction and film. Where that book tracked, through the end of the twentieth century, the nature of the supernatural in the post-Reformation popular imagination, *Gothicka* attempts to describe the surprising new turn toward the light taken in the increasingly transformed subgenres of the Gothick. Still accessed through the grotesque and monstrous but displaying some striking new features, the twenty-first-century Gothick is showing signs of outgrowing the dark supernaturalism it inherited from its eighteenth-century ancestor.

As part of a broader movement toward reincorporating gnosis in the episteme-dominated worldview of high intellectual culture in the West, the Gothick is rehabilitating supernaturalism as an aesthetic mode—brighter, more Romantic, and more culturally heterodox within the framework of postcolonial global popular culture. The change in sensibility from twentieth- to twenty-first-century Gothick (in the words of Stephenie Meyer's *Twilight* heroine Bella Swan) is a journey from horror story to fairy tale. At the same time as it nostalgically reinvents key elements of a premodern Catholic worldview fused with new elements of popular culture cum folklore from other parts of the globe, I argue, the Gothick is serving as a vehicle for developing the frameworks of new religious movements.

For some, this book will be more notable for its omissions than its inclusions. I can already hear my readers asking: "Where's the X-Men, the Silver Surfer, the Fantastic Four? Where's the in-depth discussion, surely relevant, of Michael Chabon's *The Amazing Adventures of Kavalier & Clay* or Neil Gaiman's *American Gods?* China Miéville and urban fantasy? Is that *all* you have to say about Goths? Where's the extended treatment of videogame narrative this book clearly calls for? Where's the *music*, for heaven's sake?" On the other side of the fence, readers who aren't familiar with the films, novels, and graphic novels discussed here will miss, with one exception, treatment of many contemporary high literary exemplars of the Gothick, such as Iris Murdoch, Thomas Pynchon, and Joyce Carol Oates. Nor is any space devoted to the subgenre known as American or Southern Gothic, a synonym for what might be called the realist psychological grotesque, and its proponents.

Instead, following a thread of logic more intuitive than analytical, tracing a few strands but leaving out many others in the still-mighty tradition of old-fashioned Gothick, I've chosen to focus on a curious sprinkling of bright nodes in the Gothick darkness and, using the foundational arguments laid down in *The Secret Life of Puppets*, tried to connect them in a way that makes sense to me. It may be overgeneralizing to see these works in a range of Gothick subgenres as early warning signals of a growing tide of religiosity, one that is perhaps not as threatening as secular humanists (who traditionally connect religious belief of any sort with fundamentalism) might fear, but I leave that determination to the *disputandum* of the scholars whose work I am so indebted to.

Which brings me to still another omission: I have made no attempt to survey the present state of Gothick scholarship and position my own thinking within it, thereby omitting mention of many current key thinkers in this vast, rich, and exciting field. Had I expended the necessary time and space to do so, I would not have had room, either mentally or on the page, for the explorations presented here. I have learned an enormous amount from the scholars whose work I do cite and am acutely aware of the large negative space left by those I omitted.

Missing, finally, are any real judgment calls on all the writers and filmmakers I have discussed. I will simply say that delivering literary-critical evaluations felt somewhat beside the point here. Once again I must invoke G. K. Chesterton and his great essay "A Defence of Penny Dreadfuls," a work I also called upon in *The Secret Life of Puppets*. "Literature is a luxury; fiction is a necessity," Chesterton declared. "People must have conversation, they must have houses, and they must have stories."[1]

Chesterton was right. In the rhythms of Story every human being finds primal solace. Young or old, educated or illiterate, we must have Story. Gothick writers and filmmakers may not be masters of sophisticated style or characterization, but they do know Story. The Story of Terror has a different resonance than the Quest Story or the Story of Love Lost and Found, but it is still a Story. The fascinating transformations this Story is undergoing today, in line with larger transformations in our culture, is the subject of my study.

Metaphysics is a branch of fantastic literature.

—JORGE LUIS BORGES

St. Dominic at his desk, with attendant animals. Master of James IV of Scotland, Spinola Hours. Bruges and Ghent c. 1510–1520. JPGM ms Ludwig IX 18, fol. 260v. Courtesy of the J. Paul Getty Museum, Los Angeles.

ONE

WHITE DOG, THE PREQUEL

Between Imagination and Belief

Take—

An old castle, half of it ruinous.

A long gallery with a great many doors, some secret ones.

Three murdered bodies, quite fresh.

As many skeletons, in chests and presses.

An old woman hanging by the neck; with her throat cut.

Assassins and desperadoes *"quant suff."*

Noises, whispers, and groans, threescore at least.

Mix them together, in the form of three volumes to be taken at any of the watering places, before going to bed.

—Anonymous, 1797

What does a Tokyo teenage girl dressed in a demure but mildly sinister Little Bo Peep outfit known as "Elegant Gothic Lolita Vampire Romance" ("Goth Loli" for short) have in common with London's St. Pancras train station or virtually any midwestern U.S. college building erected in the 1880s, male strippers performing at a romance writers' convention, *Pride and Prejudice and Zombies* (a 2009 mash-up of the Austen classic), a Lovecraftian secret society called the Bate Cabal, Dan Brown's *The Da Vinci Code*, any horror movie you watch on late-night television, Nathaniel Hawthorne's *The House of the Seven Gables*, the heavy metal band Black Sabbath, the television series *Lost* (about a group of airplane crash survivors on an island, whose storyline became increasingly metaphysical as the seasons wore on), and, last but not least, roadside memorials to accident victims?

All partake of a distinct sensibility with a 250-year-old English literary ancestor, dubbed *le genre noir* by the French but more commonly known as the Gothic, and rendered here as *Gothick* to distinguish it from the medieval cultural period its first practitioners drew inspiration from. Aptly described by Fred Botting as "an invented amalgam of pre-Enlightenment forms," a Gothick novel or "romance" composed in England in the late eighteenth or early nineteenth century might be loosely described as a sensationalistic, intricately plotted tale set in pre-Reformation (ergo Catholic) England or the Continent and featuring despotic aristocrats, sinful clerics of both sexes, illicit passion, incest, ghosts or things that look like ghosts, secret mysteries, and murder, all enfolded in the suffocating embrace of an ancient abbey, castle, or ancestral home, the classic charged Gothick space linked to an oppressive past that generally goes up in flames by story's end.[1]

The traditional bookends for this literary shock genre, also the first to boast a substantially female authorship, are Horace Walpole's anomalous 1764 novelette *The Castle of Otranto*, followed by the more substantial novels of Ann Radcliffe (most notably *The Mysteries of Udolpho* in 1794), and ending more or less with Charles Maturin's *Melmoth the Wanderer* in 1820.[2] Walpole himself, son of a prime minister and designer-builder of Strawberry Hill, a faux-medieval architectural fantasia on the Thames, was right at the forefront of a mid-eighteenth-century anticlassical reaction to Enlightenment rationalism that included the Graveyard school of poetry exemplified by Thomas Gray and Edward Young, the cultivation of "feelings," and an antiquarian passion for medieval religious architecture, literature, and folklore, all of which helped lay the foundations for the Romantic aesthetic as well as the Gothick genre.

Gothic without the -*k*, in turn, was the insulting label, redolent of nasty barbarian Huns, bestowed on the European Middle Ages by Italian architects of the Rinascimento anxious to distinguish their own work, inspired by Greek and Roman antiquity, from what they regarded as the follies of a certain style of medieval sacred architecture. In these pages *Gothic*, or simply *Old Goth*, will refer primarily to the late medieval period in England.[3] For Horace Walpole and his contemporaries, the Gothic-medieval era ran straight through to the year 1600; in their eyes, Shakespeare was a writer of supremely Old Goth plays whose supernatural elements, notably the ghost of Hamlet's father, served as inspiration for the otherworldly flourishes that ornamented their self-described Gothick novels. In a separate strand of the Gothick, the novelist Ann Radcliffe made famous a technique, destined to become a major strand in the Gothick, that came to be known as the "explained supernatural," in which bizarre events were first presented as otherworldly and later rationalized or revealed as hoaxes.[4]

Reading Radcliffe, Lewis, or Maturin is like being dumped into a turbulent ocean with only a puny life vest to keep you afloat. Wave after giant wave of catastrophic plot turns break over your head as a strong undertow of dread pulls you ever farther from solid ground. Catharsis, when it comes, never fully dissolves the accumulated tension. By the time you surface, gasping for breath, at the story's end, the air that's available is insufficient to recover from the anxiety of almost drowning. The characters, of course, take a much heavier beating than readers do. Those who aren't dead by the end are pretty thoroughly wrung out, as Charlotte Dacre's scene of an (ostensibly happy) father-son reunion in *The Libertine* (1807) amply demonstrates: "Their arms entwined, their throbbing hearts met, and beat in tremendous agony against each other's bosoms. . . . The tears of Felix covered his cheeks—sighs and groans rent his breast, but still Angelo wept not—his brain and heart were bursting—he tore himself from the arms of his son, and rushed from the dungeon."[5] As imagined by their equally youthful authors, the teenage heroes and heroines of these early Gothick novels were not—in lifestyle terms—the first Goths, but they were almost certainly the first Emos.[6]

The kind of reading experience such novels induce—one of high-pitched and unremitting anxiety—was distinctly new in English literature and a very different effect from that, say, produced by the calculated manipulations of later writers such as Dickens, who yank the heartstrings in ways still safely contained within the great sentimental plot machinery in whose gears injustice and bad behavior are slowly but inexorably ground to bits. By the end of a typical Gothick novel, the dark has almost swallowed up the light; a heavy pall of death still lingers. The perpetration of multiple violent crimes is scarcely balanced by a perfunctory meting out of justice that is likely to produce, as with the proud cleric Ambrosio's death in *The Monk*, further mayhem in the form of a gory execution performed by Lucifer himself. The survivors' putative happy future, tossed out as a meager bone in a formulaic concluding paragraph, is always overshadowed by lasting melancholy from the memory of a lost loved one.[7] Heart still pounding, you put the novel down, exhausted. (And then, because this kind of fright is also pleasurable, you go out for the eighteenth-century equivalent of pizza.)

The readerly sensation of riding a runaway horse carries straight through into the works of the two most famous Gothick writers of the late twentieth century. The novels of Anne Rice and Stephen King gallop at the same fevered, incantatory pace as outrage is piled on violent outrage and an ending twist often triggers a plunge into further darkness. In contemporary action-adventure videogaming, where many of the scenarios are constructed as Gothick narrative, the shift in roles from passive reader to interactive participant as first-person shooter produces an exponential rise in intensity and attendant anxiety, pushing the Gothick feeling experience into a whole new territory.

From its inception, the Gothick was regarded as the disreputable but wildly popular black-sheep older sibling of English Romanticism even as Romantic poets such as Coleridge, Byron, and Keats indulged in writing Gothick specimens of their own, and Mary Shelley, wife to Romantic poet Percy Shelley, wrote the most famous late Gothick novel, *Frankenstein* (1818).[8] German and English Romantics alike made important contributions to the Gothick (notably to the German genre of "terror novel," or *Schauerroman*), and it is generally recognized now that the two literary movements/sensibilities, once severely separated by critics, actually made up a single continuum[9] that initially shared the same literate middle-class readership.[10] The Gothick is now often dubbed "dark Romanticism," though no one so far, to my knowledge, has had the temerity to call Romanticism "bright Gothick." Besides sharing a complex cluster of reactions against the Neoclassical aesthetic, Romantic and Gothick modes had common roots in political progressivism. The salaciously anticlerical English Gothick novels, a product of Protestant bias, were wildly popular in revolutionary France, whose ideals and failures in turn deeply influenced both the English Romantic poets and later Gothick storytellers.

Two centuries after its heyday, Romanticism by name alone is long gone—though we will see it surfacing again in a high-end Gothick mode

I call New Expressionism—but its evil older twin is bigger than ever.[11] As David Punter first recognized three decades ago, the genre has shown an uncanny ability to adapt over time to radically different social and cultural matrices.[12] Then as now a consummate violator of boundaries, the down-and-dirty Gothick moved on to colonize a far greater empire than its original circumscribed territory. Much as each level of a fourteenth-century Old Goth cathedral replicates itself geometrically from the one beneath it in an infinitely divisible fractal sequence, the Gothick has kept on reproducing its overarching form in a staggering array of new subgenres.[13] Over the course of the nineteenth century these included not just the new fiction of ghost stories and theatrical melodrama but also the architecture and visual arts (the Gothic Revival, Pre-Raphaelite, and Arts and Crafts movements).

Historically, the rapidly proliferating Gothick quickly subdivided into overlapping subgenres of supernaturalism, anticlericalism, psychological horror, and sentimental romance. Old Goth–style supernaturalism became more prominent, less apologized for or rationalized, in nineteenth-century ghost stories featuring the mostly menacing spirits of individuals who survived death. In these tales, notably English but also widespread on the Continent (e.g., the French *contes fantastiques* of Charles Nodier, Prosper Mérimée, and others), the nasty depiction of Catholic clerics was gone. Instead, the old Church casts a nostalgic shadow over the ruined abbeys of Victorian Protestant writers such as Joseph Sheridan Le Fanu and the meticulously accurate historical settings of Edwardian Montague Rhodes James's ghostly tales. In his *Dracula* (1897), set partly in Catholic eastern Europe, the Irish Protestant Bram Stoker introduced the crucifix and holy water as amulets for warding off vampires in this nineteenth-century Gothick subgenre based on south Slavic folklore.

Supernaturalism also resurfaced, this time from the Romantic side of the Gothick-Romantic equation, in Victorian fantasy and children's literature. Drawing on shared roots in ballad and folklore revival, proponents of this genre such as the fantasist George MacDonald and the folklorist Andrew Lang laid the foundations for twentieth-century writers such as J. R. R. Tolkien and J. K. Rowling, whose works in turn helped fuel the immense fantasy literature industry of the late twentieth and early twenty-first centuries. In this hybrid subgenre, dark Gothick characters and themes are typically subsumed within a brighter Romantic folktale matrix in which "good" supernatural creatures such as fairies and elves counterbalance the forces of evil.

In North America—where, as Leslie Fiedler liked to say, the haunted forest replaced the ruined castle as the Gothick charged space[14]—the genealogy of supernaturalism runs from Charles Brockden Brown and Nathaniel Hawthorne through Edgar Allan Poe (in whose detective stories the "explained supernatural" plays out as a mad caricature of rationalism) and his twentieth-century literary successor H. P. Lovecraft.[15] High literary culture, meanwhile, remaining almost exclusively realist through the twentieth century, acknowledged an American or Southern Gothic school of the psychological grotesque starting in the 1940s. The influence of this tradition, which included the writers William Faulkner, Tennessee Williams, Carson McCullers, and Flannery O'Connor, is visible in contemporary realist writers such as Cormac McCarthy and Joyce Carol Oates.

Through the twentieth century, the great tidal bore of the Gothick—from the blue-covered chapbooks hawked on street corners in New York and London and moving up, in ascending inflationary order, to penny dreadfuls, shilling shockers, and dime novels—swelled into pulp fiction, comic books, and B movies, which morphed downriver into a range of new media from animated cartoons to videogaming to interactive fan fiction and virtual reality role playing. The emerging subgenre of science fiction, heir of the Gothick through Mary Shelley's seminal *Frankenstein* and H. G. Wells's "scientific romances" of the later nineteenth century, put a new twist on the concept of "explained supernatural" by introducing scientific technology and futurist fantasy as a rationalizing frame for an imaginary otherworld made magically possible by machines—"Gothicizing the future," in Alexandra Warwick's phrase, as the haunted Gothick space shifted from abbeys and mansions to asylums and ultimately to spaceships in the twentieth century.[16]

The 1960s marked the new prominence of these marginal entertainments with a supernaturalist slant as they moved out of the pulps and B movies into mainstream popular culture, along with a not coincidental spike in alternative spirituality, dominated almost through the end of the century by a wide range of groups and movements known as "New Age." Supernaturalism also began to play a much more dominant role in children's literature. Werewolves loped into the venerable Hardy Boys series in 1979, clones and resurrection of the dead by 1987—themes that would have been unthinkable in children's mystery novels of two decades earlier.[17] In the 1990s, Rowling's fabulously successful Harry Potter series, about a boy wizard and his classmates at a school for sorcerers, triggered a surge of young adult fantasy fiction. This body of work quickly jumped the fence into adult blockbuster movies that, along with sagas of comic book superheroes, dominated the big-screen movie market of the first decade of the twenty-first century.

The final Gothick strand, the sentimental romance written by and for women, enjoys enormous popularity today both in its classic forms and in highly hybridized new ones. Building on the work of Radcliffe and the other early women Gothick novelists, this subgenre did not find its own distinctive identity until the mid-nineteenth century. Straight through the late twentieth century, writers of Gothick romances typically presented, just as Poe had, the teasing hint of haunting or the supernatural; true to Radcliffe's template, however, all mysteries were revealed, by story's end, to have a rational explanation.

Today the dynamic, ever-expanding Gothick flourishes in a huge array of subgenres, most obviously as endless permutations of horror stories linked with supernaturalism (including tales of vampires, werewolves, and other imaginary denizens of the dark side that were first introduced as fictional characters in the eighteenth and nineteenth centuries). Still carrying many of its original defining characteristics, the Gothick has its tentacles in so many pop culture products at the dawn of the new century that Maurice Lévy has dubbed the phenomenon "a spreading process and imperialist conquest of the whole human experience." Proposing finally that the greatest Gothick writer of the twentieth century was Sigmund Freud and that the "Gothic has left the realm of fiction and begun to invade our lives, our brains, even our bodies," Lévy asks if there's anything left that's "*not* Gothic."[18]

Drawing on a complex layering of sources, the diverse subgenres of twenty-first-century Gothick share at least four common features. First, they borrow from—or more accurately, simply belong to—the Anglo-American Gothick literary tradition that nominally starts with Walpole. Gothick motifs of the haunted architectural space that combusts by story's end, the imperiled young woman menaced by a dangerous older man, the manmade monster, and the supernatural shape-shifter are still reproduced with remarkable consistency in the global Gothick.

Second, they borrow from the Old Goth historical period of the Middle Ages, usually through the filter of nineteenth- and twentieth-century "medievalisms." The original Gothick novels and Romantic poetry imitated the form and content of medieval romances and ballads; current Gothick subgenres also borrow from such Old Goth art forms as the dream vision and the morality play. Moreover, many of today's subgenres affirm an underlying and pervasive supernaturalism that paradoxically exceeds that of the original eighteenth-century genre, thereby bringing them closer in spirit to the cultural products and popular religious imagination of the medieval Gothic period, even more so as analogous folk beliefs of Japan, other Asian countries, and Catholic Europe move to the foreground in the new global Gothick.

Third, they are amazingly hybrid. The Gothick was and is the ultimate mongrel form. Walpole's declaration that he was combining "ancient and modern romances" in *Otranto* set the template for today's genre-combining stories and half-breed human-supernatural characters.[19] Proliferating across all storytelling media, Gothick horror has mated with noir, science fiction, comedy, romance, and erotic fiction; within individual narratives Gothick characters flip their sex, species, and deep nature (most conspicuously, from evil to good). When the half-human, half-vampire heroes of *Blade* (a graphic novel–movie hybrid) and *Blood: The Last Vampire* (a manga–live action hybrid) hunt down old-style "bad" vampires to kill them, it's a perfect parable of the way new Gothick subgenres simultaneously embed and destroy older conventions.

Fourth, as they have moved increasingly from the margins to the mainstream over the last twenty years, many Gothick subgenres display—in a variety of provisional and eclectic ways—an implicit heterodox spirituality that grows directly out of their robust supernaturalism.[20] The most striking characteristic of the new Gothick's spiritual framework is what René Girard calls "the metamorphosis of the maleficent into the beneficent," in which antagonist-villains (vampires, werewolves, assorted demons and imps of hell) have become protagonist-heroes who struggle with their darkness even as they incarnate on earth as gods.[21] This heterodoxy in turn has moved a small but significant portion of fans out of the territory of imagination and into that of belief.

Faced with the continuity and unquenchable vitality of the Gothick, the temptation to look no further back in historical time for the genre's origin story than the eighteenth century is strong. Yet what Erich Auerbach argued more broadly about the arc of Western literature—that twentieth-century literary conventions were the historical fulfillment of the medieval vernacular mixing of high and low styles—surely applies with even greater force to the Gothick, a genre that continues to draw from the worldview of the Middle Ages as well as its literary styles and stories.[22] Medievalist and film scholar Carol Clover argues that we can never fully grasp modern American popular culture without first understanding the popular culture of the European Middle Ages. Medieval literature, Clover points out, "is a world of the formulaic. A world of cycles, in which there is no original, no real or right text, but only variants. A world in which texts can be shortened, lengthened, imitated, disguised, sequeled, prequeled, changed from verse to prose or prose to verse, and so on. A world in which, to fall back on an old but useful distinction, character is more a function of plot than vice versa."[23]

This description could be applied equally to the contemporary graphic novel and many others of the magpie subgenres of the Gothick, past and present. From its radical (to us) notions of artistic originality to its heavy underpinning of folk religion, the medieval Gothic cultural era of the Catholic European West—whose denizens believed in a material world deeply penetrated by the supernatural as manifested in everyday miracles, saints with superpowers, a feminine divine embodied in the Virgin Mary, a devil with a real tail, and an array of hybrid monsters—provides a richer subtext to contemporary Anglo-American Protestant popular culture than we might first imagine. "The past is that Other which we seek to idolize more than anything else," the art historian Michael Camille once said, asking: "Is this what makes the Middle Ages so fascinating for us today—because it appears (or is so often represented as) a period when people not only understood their place in the world but had access to symbols and signs that granted them access to the world to come?"[24]

I am not making a simple historical analogy between our times and the Middle Ages, though in recent decades that parallel has begun to replace the time-honored fall-of-the-Roman-empire trope. Rather, I would like to suggest that besides sharing the aesthetic of a kind of mad pantextuality, Gothick writers, filmmakers, gamers, and Goth kids of the twenty-first century (who live in an utterly different world than, say, Paris in the year 1206 C.E.) are moving intuitively toward an image-based, animistic, supernaturalist orientation that has some common features with the world-view that fueled this older historical substratum of our culture. This remains an exceedingly complicated effect to pin down, not least because characterizing that very long period of European cultural history in any sort of meaningful way is just about impossible. The Middle Ages, as Leslie J. Workman states flatly, "are virtually unique among major periods or areas of historical study in being entirely the creation of scholars."[25]

Is it even possible, then, to distinguish between a "true" medieval and the rampant medievalisms that people in every later historical period have projected onto this era in the Western past? The answer must be no, but then and now it's a spectrum. The Society for Creative Anachronism and other medieval reenactor groups are an example of self-conscious, nostalgic medievalism in our time.[26] So are the Gothick story lines of videogames from *Myst* and *Adventure* to *Castlevania*. But mash-ups such as Bill Willingham's graphic novel series *Fables* (2002–), featuring Snow White and other fairy-tale characters living in a secret Manhattan community called Fabletown that is ruled by Old King Cole, represent, if you will, a "deep" medievalism in their layering of different story contexts and characters. Where Dan Brown's ersatz tidbits of Templar, Cathar, and Grail lore represent a familiar strand of Gothick-style ornamental medievalism, in her *Twilight* vampire romances Stephenie Meyer creates (with, one feels, no totally conscious intention to do so) a radically different effect: a sculptural pantheon of demigods and -goddesses who glitter like haloed saints and act like Hindu deities or the divine-human *anthropoi* of late antiquity. Finally, participating in the topographic allegories of supernaturalist videogames positions a modern gamer more actively in the dual-reality universe that premodern Europe shares with traditional cultures around the world than reading Clara Reeve's *The Old English Baron* ever did for her late eighteenth-century audience.

But why the difference—in amount and kind of supernatural content— between the eighteenth century and now? Scholars have regarded the original Gothick as the first Western literary genre operating implicitly in the vacuum left by the departure of religious belief among large portions of the educated classes. "Viewing Gothick mystery as a substitute for discredited religious mystery," says Lévy, "we may consent to recognize that, despite its wild extravagance and puerile heresies, *le genre noir* represented for its producers and consumers alike a genuine expression of profound religious malaise."[27] Victor Sage has defined the Gothick not just as a narrow literary genre featuring "a decorative metaphysical or graveyard feeling" but as "a whole complex of popular theological ideals of a predominantly, if not exclusively, Protestant variety."[28] Robert Geary sees the Gothick novel in its beginnings not just as an expression of Protestant anticlericalism or as a simple reaction to eighteenth-century rationalism but as part of the process of the secularization of literature in which the supernatural moves out of the traditional religious framework to be cultivated as a sensation in itself.[29]

By the eighteenth century any supernaturalism outside the firmly drawn boundaries of orthodox religious belief was labeled "superstition" and firmly (if nostalgically) linked via Gothick entertainments either to exotic Catholic countries on the Continent or to England's own Catholic past.[30] Belief in ghosts and witches was no longer a matter of public record among the educated classes but rather was displaced, for a reader's guilt-free enjoyment, into the imaginary of fiction. As Alex Owen has shown, it was just this shift in register from belief to imagination, which she views as part of the modernizing quest for consciousness, that carried forward the process of secularization in nineteenth-century England.[31]

Yet the supernatural remained a charged subject for Gothick writers of the classic period, who were alternately attracted and repulsed by it. Even as they rebelled against the neoclassic rationalism of the mid-eighteenth century and laid the foundations for Romanticism, the early Gothick novelists presented apparitions and the appurtenances of pre-Reformation Catholic Christianity as window dressing rather than living belief. In his second preface to *Otranto*, Walpole felt the need to apologize for the presence of the supernatural in the form of oversized statue parts that drop from the sky, ancestral portraits that come to life, and the castle itself cloven in two as divine punishment for evildoing. "Belief in every kind of prodigy was so established in those dark ages," he tells his readers, "that an author would not be faithful to the manners of the times who should not omit all mention of them. He is not bound to believe them himself, but he must represent his actors as believing them."[32] Diane Hoeveler argues, on the matter of the "explained supernatural" in the Gothick, that "explaining away the supernatural in the gothic discourse is another way of privileging its talismanic force. . . . Because this culture could not turn away from God, it chose to be haunted by his uncanny avatars: priests, corrupt monks, incestuous fathers, and uncles."[33]

In Anglo-American Protestant culture the desacralized supernatural was of a very specific kind: dark. The Protestant Reformation and the scientific revolution had set in motion the first stage of this process in seventeenth-century western Europe. As the supernatural was being excluded from the natural world, any lingering manifestations were demonized. Whereas the medieval Catholic world, for example, sanctioned belief in ghosts as the manifestation of souls trapped in Purgatory who could only return to show themselves to the living if God permitted it, the official Protestant line eventually became: There is no such thing as ghosts, but if you actually see one, it was sent by the Devil to deceive you.[34] The new argument went something like this: If divine intrusions into our lives such as miracles ended with the age of the patriarchs (that is, around the sixth century c.e.) and if natural wonders such as lightning, earthquakes, and floods were not God's punishment but had their causes in the material world, then anything perceived in the material world that could not be explained rationally must belong to the dark side.[35]

The figure of the Devil or Satan, consequently, is central to the Gothick imaginary, past and present.[36] To understand the role this figure plays in the contemporary Gothick requires jumping back to a time in western Europe when Satan was neither a humorous conceit (as in many twentieth-century Gothick subgenres), a melodramatically imaginary being (as for Matthew Lewis and his eighteenth-century colleagues), nor simply theologically real (as for John Milton in the seventeenth century and a considerable number of Christian faithful through to the present day), but part of a belief system in which both Satan and his opposite number, God (through Jesus and Mary as well as angels and saints), made open and frequent interventions in everyday life—the belief system, in short, of the Old Goth Middle Ages.

Historically, Satan had not always been a major player in Christian dogma. After relatively little prominence for more than a millennium, the Father of Lies moved abruptly to center stage around the beginning of the fourteenth century, producing what one scholar has called "three centuries of demonic obsession" that deeply impacted western European culture and led to the witch hunts that swept the region (and the Americas, in its wake) from the end of the fifteenth century through the mid-seventeenth century.[37] Where Church statements on doctrine in earlier times had been devoted to denouncing heretics, the late medieval period produced the new clerical discipline of "demonology," designed to investigate the relationship between demons and their human pawns.

This unholy connection, it was thought, could take one of two forms: voluntary pact or involuntary possession. For relationships falling into the first category, the *Malleus Maleficarum* (1486, "Hammer of Witches [Evildoers]"), by the Dominican inquisitor Heinrich Kramer, became the foundational Church treatise on sorcery and witchcraft. The practice of magic, regarded in earlier medieval Christian times as mere superstition, was now deemed real—and suspect. The Islamic sciences of alchemy and astrology, coming to Europe via Moorish Spain, also fell under the shadow of theological suspicion. By the sixteenth century, the cautionary legend of Faust, the doctor of philosophy who trades his soul to the Devil in exchange for unlimited knowledge and power, was widely staged in theaters across Europe and the British Isles.

The voluntary pact was a heavily gendered transaction. Whereas men "sold" their souls to the Devil in a legal contract, those women who made this choice did so with their bodies, in sexual congress, since women were considered to be more vulnerable to what one scholar calls "a penetrative, interiorizing union" with divine and demonic forces alike. For a female saint, ecstatic union with God was considered to be the prime initiatory experience; for a witch, it was sexual intercourse with the Devil.[38] With the new focus on the Devil in the later Middle Ages, attention shifted from the divine possession of female saints to witches' matings with Satan. The conscious choice witches exercised in this transaction made them culpable and worthy of punishment.

But the Devil could also take over people without their consent, and this form of coerced possession could be accomplished either directly, in the form of demons, incubi, or succubi, or through another person's curse. As a spiritual and bodily invasion, involuntary possession was likewise recorded most commonly with women. Just as they did with reports of sightings of Mary or angels, however, clerics made a serious effort to distinguish between possession by the Devil and garden-variety madness, which even by the fourteenth century was already becoming a secular medical diagnosis.[39] Accusations of either sorcery or possession were also, of course, a classic tactic of the Church to discredit heterodoxy. The obsession with demonic possession made a late and final appearance in seventeenth-century France, when the priest Urbain Grandier, possibly for political reasons, was held responsible for the mass possession of nuns by demons at a convent in Loudon and was burned at the stake.

The new Protestant movements latched on to the Devil even more relentlessly than their Catholic counterparts, producing an almost Gnostic obsession with Satan, whom Martin Luther declared to be lord and master of the living world as well as the source of any unexplainable occurrences taking place in it. Satan was widely regarded among Protestant thinkers as "God's hangsman" (in James I's phrase), second cause to God's first cause, extracting divine punishment in a material world where God no longer directly intervened.[40] This, as we have already seen, was part of the move from belief in supernatural agencies capable of doling out both beneficence and maleficence to belief in a magical universe that was uniformly dark, and ultimately to belief in neither. During this transitional period mysterious events in nature could still be attributed to devilish influence simply because their causes were unknown or uncertain.

In the pivotal seventeenth century God's divine intervention was no longer believed to be manifest in everyday life, while Satan's was. In England, where Henry VIII's drastic break from the Church of Rome had caused a social and intellectual upheaval equivalent to Mao's socializing of China, this shift in thinking took a very long time to take root. For the first 150 years of Protestantism in England (along with its colonies in America and elsewhere), God was still the causal agency for everything that happened in the world, including "providences" such as material prosperity as well as natural disasters.

But many of the practices accreted for more than a millennium in Latin Christendom that Protestants deemed imagistic and hence idolatrous were retained in Radical Reformation sects. Many of these early dissenting groups clung conservatively, to a greater or lesser degree, to a number of tenets of the Old Goth medieval cosmology that the intertwined worldviews of mainstream Protestantism and the emerging new scientific disciplines were rapidly rendering obsolete. Foremost among these increasingly heretical notions was a belief in a deep interconnection between the worlds of spirit and matter, the primacy of spirit, and its ever-present intrusion into our world of the senses. This older notion of a hierarchy of "signatures" or correspondences connecting the celestial realm with the inferior natural world had come increasingly under attack in the pivotal seventeenth century, most obviously from the new empiricism that disassociated naturally occurring events from divine or otherworldly intervention.[41]

The Calvinist view of a cosmos from whose physical workings the Deity was increasingly detached had helped lay the groundwork for the mechanistic universe of eighteenth-century Newtonian physics. Many of the dissenting English sectarians of this time, however, claimed to possess "that supernatural solution to earthly problems which the makers of the Protestant Reformation had so sternly rejected," and, as Keith Thomas points out, they "revived the miracle-working aspect of medieval Catholicism without its Roman and hierarchical features."[42]

As the first Gothick novels were being written, metaphysicians turned philosophers were interested in identifying the sources of aesthetically experienced terror in the natural world now that it was disconnected from sacred awe. Walpole's contemporary Edmund Burke said that terror comes from a triggering agency, known simply as the sublime, that is the diametrical opposite of the beautiful. The fear or terror produced by the sublime is a big, grand feeling, "the strongest emotion of which the mind is capable of feeling," and often comes in reaction either to entities perceived as supernatural or to wild mountain landscapes.[43] This was the moment in Western cultural history when transcendence shifted from being an attribute of God to being an attribute of nature, with the suggestion that humans having this experience in consciousness were able to connect with a desacralized transcendent themselves. As Thomas Weiskel put it, "The sublime revives as God withdraws from an immediate participation in the experience of men"—and he adds, significantly, "The essential claim of the sublime is that man can, in feeling and speech, transcend the human."[44] Just this sense of self-divinization, as we will see, became central to the evolving spirituality of the Gothick.

As a generator of terror, the sublime after Burke was linked with the Gothick sensibility as much as with the Romantic.[45] The Gothick sublime, says Vijay Mishra, the scholar who coined this term, is a kind of void ("an absence, a lack in the structure itself") that attracts "the unthinkable, the unnameable, and the unspeakable," making it "anti-analytic, supra-sensible, and beyond the grasp of our cognitive faculties."[46] Though he argues that this brand of sublimity lies completely outside a religious framework, the very vocabulary of ineffability, and the vacuum these words create, tends to suck the transcendental, acknowledged or not, right back in. Other commentators have also noted in the Gothick the historical shift in the sense of the sacred that I have called the transition from "full of awe" to "awful." The cultivation of feelings of terror or dread in the face of evil forces serves as a flawed vehicle to the transcendent—a dark transcendent shorn of the larger metaphysical context that embraces the divine as well as the demonic.[47]

Taking Rudolf Otto's classic definition of the religious experience as fear in the presence of the numinous, we might say that it shifted, in the post-Enlightenment framework of the Gothick, into a much more narrowly defined sensation of horror provoked by the imaginary rather than the metaphysical.[48] Beyond the framework of Protestant Christianity, supernaturalism was the one remnant of the rejected sacred, in the spiritual vacuum created by secularized intellectual culture, that could safely travel out of religious belief into the as-if world of the imaginary. In this way a limited genre with a small and almost exclusively dark vocabulary was overweighted with a great deal of displaced numen. This strange quirk of cultural and religious history would set the Gothick's curiously distinctive tone through the end of the twentieth century, when the long-mounting internal pressure blew open this constricted vessel with a more expansive reinvention of the supernatural.

For me a single miniature found in the Spinola Book of Hours that is the frontispiece to this chapter says it all. An illuminated Scottish devotional of the early sixteenth century, the Spinola Hours depicts St. Dominic, founder of the Dominican order, a friar who, impressed by the simplicity of the Cathar heretics in southern France (a group that would loom large in the later fictive Gothick), attempted to scale down his order of mendicant preachers accordingly but whose descendants in the order included Torquemada, founder of the Inquisition. In this image Dominic sits engrossed in a manuscript, blissfully unaware of a dreadful creature with the wide flat whiskery face of a catfish and a reptile's long tail whose scaly arm has stretched under the chair to claw at the hem of his white robe.

With one important omission, this pairing of oblivious scholar with floor-scuttling monster could just as easily serve as an illustration for "The Stalls of Barchester Cathedral" or "The Diary of Mr. Poynter," Gothick ghost stories written some 400 years later by the medievalist M. R. James. The difference between James's desanctified Gothick monsters and the Old Goth Catholic sensibility is exemplified by the presence of a second animal in the Spinola Hours miniature: a little white dog crouching under Dominic's lectern. Clasped in its jaws is a flaming torch signifying the saint's ultimate victory over temptation as he carries the light of God into the world.[49]

The presence of the monster, and absence of the dog, defines the Gothick supernatural from the years 1764 through 1999: sheer terror, with no prospect of salvation. By the end of the twentieth century, the severe and obvious limitations of the dark Gothick as the only vehicle for the supernatural outside organized religion finally reached a tipping point. Chafing at what in most traditional human cultures would be an unnatural distortion and stigmatization of the world of spirits, the sub-Zeitgeist responded with a kind of unconscious imperative to transform this dark template into a sunnier, more all-embracing spiritual framework.

And transform it did. Though the Mississippi of traditional "bad" Gothick still runs broad and steadfastly black, a surprising number of its postmillennial tributaries are letting a bit of Romantic sunlight in. This trend shows itself in "good" monsters such as Swamp Thing, Hellboy, and Bella the human turned vampire demigoddess. Hybrid heroes such as Perseus or "Percy," the demigod descendant of Zeus in Rick Riordan's Percy Jackson series; Red Riding Hood as a superhero in a steampunk magical world in Nick Percival's *Legends;* and God as a middle-aged African American woman named "Papa" in William P. Young's *The Shack* all break the Protestant post-Enlightenment mold of the dark Gothick as they evoke under-the-table folk religious beliefs that are present in many other cultures besides the European Middle Ages.

In the Gothick subgenres of the twenty-first century, as we will see, the dark sublime's antithesis—the beautiful—begins to surface, uniting Gothick and Romantic traditions as this hybrid sensibility continues to morph to meet the changing consciousness of our culture. These key new tributaries of the twenty-first-century Gothick no longer promote supernaturalism as an evil and imaginary dimension outside ordinary human existence, but rather (in the words of Alan Ball, creator of the HBO vampire series *True Blood*) consider it to be "deep nature," integral to our daily lives in the way it was (or we believe it was) in premodern Europe.[50] This trend toward a kind of normative supernaturalism in the Gothick mutually reinforces an equally subliminal activity of new religion building in its contemporary subgenres.

"Religion building" is a fancy assertion to make about popular entertainments, but here I follow William James's simple definition of religion as "belief in the reality of an unseen order."[51] And I argue, along with Philip K. Dick, that particularly when the divine has been exiled from the table of serious art and intellectual discussion for well over a century, you have to look for it in what elite culture thinks of as the trash. That is, in the sub-Zeitgeist, that disreputable realm of popular culture, B movies, pulp fiction, and folk belief where, modernity or no, the line between belief and imagination is often erased, a shadowy territory where—to give Northrop Frye's notion of "secular scripture" a slightly different twist—a certain kind of low-level but potent theological rumination is constantly taking place.

Large numbers of young people around the world who have been raised essentially outside institutional religion have their only experience of fear and trembling before the supernatural through global popular entertainment, and it leaves them thirsty for more. At least two American-based new world religions, Mormonism and Christian Science, were cooked in this cauldron; the creator of Scientology, L. Ron Hubbard, moved seamlessly from writing science fiction novels to founding a science fiction religion; and other new religious movements have also blossomed from notions that conflate the fictional extraterrestrial with the formerly celestial. As we will see in the following pages, belief and imagination also merge in the quasi-religions and magic cults that have sprung up around individual works of fantasy and science fiction.

Carrying its own brand of "spilt religion" (as the critic T. E. Hulme famously dubbed the Romantic movement), for 250 years the Gothick has served as one of secular society's disavowed back doors to the world beyond appearances. By presenting an array of imaginary immortals and humans with paranormal powers that blend monstrous with good and light with dark, the twenty-first-century Gothick offers a weird subliminal corrective to Protestant Christianity's three male gods of light. It's as if, in those realms of the Western popular imagination where the horrific has held sway for hundreds of years, the scaly monster that menaces St. Dominic in the Spinola Hours has shape-shifted into his little dog, reconfiguring the sacred through the formerly monstrous and evil in ways that transform our conceptions of both. The new "bright" Gothick in its many forms makes the radical suggestion that if we want to get to heaven, monsters and demi-goddesses can help show us it is right here on earth.

Ambrosio hoodwinked by the demon Matilda in *The Monk*. From the 1822 New York edition published by William Borradaile, engraving by Jean François Eugène Prudhomme. Courtesy of the New York Society Library.

TWO

FAUX CATHOLIC

A Gothick Genealogy from
Monk Lewis to Dan Brown

Scarcely had the abbey-bell tolled for five minutes, and already was the church of the Capuchins thronged with auditors. . . . But very few were influenced by [motives of piety or desire for information]; and in a city where superstition reigns with such despotic sway as Madrid, to seek for true devotion would be a fruitless attempt.

—Matthew Lewis, *The Monk*

We have seen it on the big screen any number of times: the possessed woman writhing, screaming, face morphing (courtesy of computer-generated imagery) into a hideous leer as despairing relatives edge prudently away from the imminent prospect of projectile vomiting.

Demon possession, open-and-shut case. Who you gonna call?

Not your rabbi, imam, or Methodist minister. No, you want that Roman Catholic priest with his collar, cross, holy water, and Vulgate Bible—all the papist trappings that Protestant Americans shun in real life but absolutely demand for a convincing onscreen exorcism. A mild-mannered Episcopal reverend or a megachurch preacher in a track suit reciting the Lord's Prayer in English over that tormented soul? I don't think so. Nothing less, or other, than the sting of holy water, the hiss of the cross against burning flesh, will make the demon depart, wailing in agony.

And what about that secret office, always housed deep in the bowels of the Vatican, laboring over the centuries to keep the parchment containing secrets threatening to orthodoxy from falling into the wrong hands, or stop an incarnation of a rebel angel, even Satan's own child born to a mortal woman, from wreaking havoc on the world? What a letdown if the headquarters of this agency so crucial to the salvation of humankind turns out to be down the corridor from the bingo room in the local Lutheran church basement! The narrator of Elizabeth Kostova's 2005 vampire novel *The Historian* voices just these doubts: "The hospitable plain Protestant chapels that dotted the university . . . didn't look qualified to wrestle with the undead. I felt sure those big square Puritan churches in the [New England] town green would be helpless in the face of a European vampire."[1]

After the incense clears, this is the central paradox in movies and books such as *The Exorcist, Stigmata, The Omen, End of Days, The Order, The Rite,* and countless others: that an exoticized, patently fictional, and some would say anticlerical fantasy about Catholicism strangely empowers and elevates the very religious denomination it seems to slander. The Catholic League and other religious organizations decry these movies and novels but, understandably, fail to appreciate their implicit subtext: first, that this fantasy pop culture religion I like to call faux Catholic provides the *only* effective defense against the forces of evil as embodied in the Judeo-Christian figure of Satan or vampires and other supernatural creatures, and second, that the battle between good and evil is most effectively waged not with the Church of Rome's real-life theological doctrine but with its perceived magical talismans—talismans that continue to exert a strong but guilty fascination for Protestants and other non-Catholics around the world.

The film adaptation of *The Exorcist* (1973), from the novel written by a conservative Catholic, William Henry Blatty, with the full blessing of the Catholic Church, was the seminal story that set in motion the twentieth-century faux Catholic subgenre of male priests chasing the Devil out of possessed females, a subgenre still going strong forty years later in such films as *The Exorcism of Emily Rose* (2005), *The Last Exorcism* (2010), and *The Rite* (2011).[2] *The Last Exorcism* is the first movie in this tradition, interestingly, to substitute a Louisiana tent preacher for the Catholic priest, but in the end the self-confessed phony exorcist Cotton Marcus and his beige three-piece suit prove no match for the possessed girl and the Devil cult she belongs to, headed by the kindly local pastor now got up in a scarlet faux

Catholic hooded robe of Satan.[3] In *The Rite*, the exorcist priest himself is possessed, a twist of convention that further demonstrates that the functionaries of the Catholic Church, in faux Catholic logic, are effective against the Devil only because they somehow remain connected to him.[4] The possibility always lurks that in the end they may reveal themselves as emissaries of the very evil they claim to be fighting against.

Furthermore, as we will see in the case of Dan Brown, even an idea heretical to all Christian denominations—that Jesus was only mortal, mated with Mary Magdalene, and had human descendants—is one seen by his readers as well as the author himself to be most effectively combated by the institution of the Catholic Church.

Why the implicit bestowal of greater authority and power by mostly non-Catholic writers and filmmakers on a religion they don't belong to or believe in? The specific historical reason for this ambiguous valorization lies in the literary source of this fare: the Protestant anticlerical Gothick novels of the late eighteenth and early nineteenth centuries. Their creators' obsessive fascination with what the Puritans before them liked to call "egregious popish impostures"—aka the European medieval Catholic past with its magical relics and rites, its credulity-straining miracles, its idolatrous statuary, its corrupt clergy and ecclesiastical hierarchy—initiated this enduring and endlessly reinvented theme into international popular culture. For the early Gothick novelists, this love-hate affair with Catholicism featured a certain amount of secret nostalgia, of two kinds. The first was for the ruins and living vestiges of the Middle Ages they could see with their own eyes in southern European Catholic countries such as Italy or Spain or (as in the case of Ann Radcliffe and, later, Poe) simply imagine from their own reading.

Beneath their ridicule of past ages' "superstitious" practices, however, lay another, more uneasy nostalgia for the comfort and security these rites offered. The medieval Catholic Church had drawn down God's power and blessings into daily life through many rituals, most of which were performed by the priest, and consecrated objects had magical power. Once all these rituals and holy objects were dispensed with, what protective powers did Protestants have against the Devil? It boiled down to external ritual versus internal resolve: if amulets and the holy supernatural powers invested in the figure of the priest could no longer be used, that put the burden of exorcism on individual prayer, which all denominations seemed to agree was not guaranteed to work.[5] As late as 1725, an English Protestant divine could report, in a sentiment that would echo through centuries of Anglo-American popular entertainments right down to Kostova: "It is common for the present vulgar to say, none can lay a spirit but a *Popish priest*."[6] Even today U.S. Catholic priests report being overwhelmed by requests for exorcism from people of all denominations.[7]

I take as my foundational text Matthew Lewis's *The Monk*, published in March 1796 when its author was not quite twenty-one. By the traditional measure *The Monk* belongs to the "middle" period of the original Gothick—with Horace Walpole and his *Castle of Otranto* marking the genre's beginning, followed by an avalanche of novels and chapbooks penned by a host of mostly female writers and culminating in the works of Radcliffe by the end of the century. It was Lewis more than any previous Gothick writer, however, whose work took England and Europe by storm. Like *The Da Vinci Code* two centuries later, *The Monk* created an international sensation and made its author an overnight celebrity. Like Brown, "Monk" Lewis, as he came to be known, was accused of copying other sources, and by its fourth edition *The Monk* had also been expurgated of some of its more scandalous sexual material.[8]

Precociously astute about human nature and the temptations of vaulting careerist ambition, Lewis fashioned a narrative whose mad eroticism, over-the-top gore, and pell-mell pace keep *The Monk*—as my own experience shows—a lively read even today. In the course of a long and convoluted plot set mostly in sixteenth-century (i.e., Old Goth) Madrid, two young gentlemen, Lorenzo and Raymond, lose their lady loves to evil clerics—Agnes, Lorenzo's sister and Raymond's lover, and her baby to the wrath of the abbess of the convent where she has been unfairly confined (but from which she, but not the baby, is eventually rescued), and Antonia, whom Lorenzo hopes to marry, to the lust of the ambitious and newly fallen abbot Ambrosio. We also meet a third young woman, Matilda, who masquerades as a male novice to gain access to Ambrosio and is the first to tempt him down the path of perdition. Matilda tells Ambrosio she has made a pact with the beautiful "fallen angel" Lucifer, and eventually the proud abbot does too, so that he may fulfill his lustful desire for the innocent Antonia after murdering her mother to keep her from exposing him.

Ambrosio's Faustian pact with Satan, unlike the involuntary possession of females, is typically voluntary and masculine. Once he has killed Antonia as well to conceal his crime, he makes another pact with Lucifer (in his less attractive winged, horned, and taloned form) to escape further torture from the Inquisition. Now Lucifer lets Ambrosio know that Matilda is not human but an agent of Hell, and that Ambrosio's two victims, Antonia and her mother, were his own sister and mother. Lucifer flies the hapless monk into the sky and drops him thousands of feet onto a rocky precipice where, after six days of having his eyeballs pecked, flesh bitten, and blood extracted by various natural predators, Ambrosio expires—only to be catapulted instantly into eternal damnation.

Though Lewis serves up the obligatory moldering vaults and gloomy medieval atmosphere of earlier Gothick tales, this faux Catholic story is all about sexual repression unleashed. *The Monk* focuses obsessively on the Roman clergy's sexual transgressions, abuses of power, and hypocritical cruelty toward confessed sinners. This theme stands in striking contrast to today's mainstream faux Catholic films and books, which, in an interesting reversal of focus, studiously avoid cleric-lay sexuality in spite of (or perhaps because of?) ongoing revelations about sexual abuse of minors by priests, concentrating instead on demonic possession and heretical doctrine.[9] As we will see, heresy (*heterodoxy* is the correct word these days, but it lacks that Gothick zing) is the twenty-first-century Gothick's great subject and subtext.

The anticlerical strand of the Gothick carried on in England by works such as Maturin's *Melmoth the Wanderer* flourished in Catholic countries on the Continent as well, especially France during the Revolution and after. Where Maturin's character Melmoth, like Ambrosio in *The Monk*, sells his soul to the Devil and must suffer the tortures of the Inquisition, the evil Jesuit of Eugène Sue's *The Wandering Jew* (1844) covets the Wandering Jew's fortune, which has been collecting interest all those centuries since the death of Jesus.[10] Here the clerical transgression is not lust but covetousness, and this Gothick theme of an undead capitalist amassing great wealth thanks to prudent investment over the centuries would translate easily into the vampire subgenre in years to come.[11] In Italy, both Garibaldi in the nineteenth century and Mussolini (in his pre-Fascist socialist phase) in the twentieth wrote anticlerical Gothick historical romances.[12] Anti-Catholic exposés masquerading as nonfiction but cast in Gothick fictional conventions—such as the Montreal prostitute Maria Monk's lurid *Awful Disclosures of the Hotel Dieu Nunnery in Montreal* (1836)—were best sellers in nineteenth-century America.[13]

Today the global Gothick has produced a certain cognitive dissonance between, to name only one example, the mildly anticlerical thrillers of the Spanish writer Arturo Pérez-Reverte, on one hand, and the Japanese manga (comic book) series *Hellsing*, on the other.[14] The latter features the Holy Order of Protestant Knights, a group formed by Dracula's old foe Abraham van Helsing and led by his female descendant "Sir" Integra Hellsing to protect England from vampires; their rivals, in a nice faux Catholic touch, are a corresponding secret group, Iscariot, deployed by the Vatican.[15] Korean graphic novelist Hyung Min-woo's *Priest* series (2002–), set in time periods ranging from the Crusades to the Old West to the present day, features a former Holy Knight and priest who has sold his soul to a demon in order to combat a powerful fallen angel; in its 2011 U.S. movie incarnation, set in the future, the fallen angels became vampires. The role of warrior-priest has migrated back to at least one U.S.-designed videogame, *Warhammer*.[16] (How the Anglo-American classic Gothick feeds into a new global Gothick vernacular with its own distinctive features is a topic that will be taken up in chapter 9.)

Last but not least is a classic example of Protestant anti-Papism from the underbelly of American pop culture, a self-published but fairly widely circulating novel of the 1990s with many sequels called *The Last Days of Christ the Vampire*, in which that secret department deep in the bowels of the Vatican is dedicated to concealing just this central fact about Jesus' true identity.[17] In the shape-shifting, genre-crossing Gothick of the late twentieth century, Christ as vampire was the logical consequence of the long historical displacement of the divine by the demonic in Western Protestant popular culture.

As the twentieth century drew to a close, the faux Catholic Gothick moved from simple anticlericalism to the exploration of alternative Christianity and other spiritualities. A harbinger of this shift was James Redfield's *The Celestine Prophecy* (1993), a novel cum spiritual manifesto presenting a New Age meditative discipline purportedly recorded on "parchments" dating from 600 B.C.E. that were discovered by (who else?) Catholic priests in Peru.[18] Initially self-published by the author, this *Da Vinci Code* of the 1990s became a best seller that eventually sold upwards of 20 million copies.

Which brings us to the twenty-first century and Dan Brown, the first 900-pound gorilla of this millennium's Gothick novelists. Brown's Apollonian, tightly paced novels *Angels and Demons* (2000), *The Da Vinci Code* (2003), and *The Lost Symbol* (2009) deliver the dense plotting, if not the fever-pitch emotional excitement, of the classic Gothick. While his most famous novel gave the venerable faux Catholic its distinctive new heterodox twist, *Angels and Demons* hews most closely to the classic Monk Lewis model of the Luciferan rise and fall of a supremely ambitious, power-mad Roman Catholic cleric. This novel also marks the first appearance of Brown's signature character Robert Langdon, the Harvard "symbologist" who will return in *The Da Vinci Code* and *The Lost Symbol*.

In *Angels and Demons*, Langdon is flown to a top-secret Swiss research laboratory when one of its chief scientists is murdered. Langdon's task is to decode the word *Illuminati* branded on the dead man's chest, which he authoritatively asserts is the name of a centuries-old but now defunct anti-Catholic secret society of philosophers and scientists, including Galileo, that gradually morphed into "the world's oldest and most powerful satanic cult."[19] Meanwhile, the scientist's adopted daughter, Vittoria, herself a scientist, has discovered that a portion of the antimatter her father has succeeded in isolating has disappeared. When the news arrives that an anonymous caller has stashed the antimatter somewhere in the bowels of the Vatican, Robert and Vittoria rush to Rome on the lab's private jet. The bomb threat has come just as the cardinals have convened to elect a new head of church after the death (actually murder) of the previous pope. But now the four main candidates have disappeared, and one by one their mutilated bodies appear in locations across Rome as Robert and Vittoria vainly attempt to decipher the Illuminati-laden historical clues the caller phones in. As the body count climbs, the truth finally emerges: the real terrorist is not a member of the Illuminati but rather a high Vatican official possessed by a mad desire for power.

In the character of Carlo Ventresca, the *camerlengo* (cardinal who functions as the pope's private secretary), we clearly see the lineaments of Lewis's spectacularly sinful monk Ambrosio. Cardinal Ventresca is described as having "the air of some mythical hero—radiating charisma and authority," but he also proves to be the novel's villain.[20] Following the more prudish conventions of the modern faux Catholic Gothick, Ventresca commits no sexual crimes, but in his murderous quest to become pope he shares the monk Ambrosio's overweening ambition, justifying his assassination of the four cardinals in line for the papacy on the grounds that they were too liberal. Ventresca's soul is not carried away by Satan, but there's a nostalgic whiff of brimstone in the air when he sets himself alight on a high balcony overlooking Vatican Square and burns to death.

Angels and Demons also features a racist, stereotypical portrait of a Middle Eastern "Hassassin," a dark creature with "an appetite for hedonistic pleasure . . . bred into him by his ancestors" (a reference to the Muslim sect founded by al-Hassan ibn al-Sabbah, to whose warriors legend attributes the conversion of the term *hashish* to *assassin*).[21] The Hassassin believes he is taking his orders from an "ancient brotherhood" when all along he has been under the control of the rogue cardinal Carlo Ventresca. Much like the hapless Hassassin, however, readers are more likely to take away the impression they labored under for most of the novel—that the murders were orchestrated either by the so-called Illuminati or by the organized bureaucracy of the Vatican itself—than to remember the last-minute exposure of the true villain. It's an unintentional effect that recalls Ann Radcliffe's revelation in *The Mysteries of Udolpho* that the images in a castle's marvelous mirror are an optical effect, not a haunting, entailing a complicated explanation that fails to completely erase the indelible impression of the supernatural the mirror has left on the reader.

Brown employs the same time-honored tactic of bait and switch among "Manichaean others" (to use Umberto Eco's useful phrase) in *The Da Vinci Code*, whose story goes briefly like this: The night before he is to meet with Jacques Saunière, senior curator at the Louvre, Robert Langdon is summoned to the museum by the Paris police. Saunière's murdered body has just been found, ritually posed, in the museum's Grand Gallery, but the curator has managed to leave a string of coded enigmatic clues that hold the secret of his death and much more. Both Langdon and Saunière's granddaughter, cryptologist Sophie Neveu, become suspects as a tangled story unfolds of an ancient society called the Priory of Sion, of which Saunière was grandmaster, and the great secret the society has guarded against millennia-long assaults by the Catholic Church: documents revealing that Jesus was mortal, not divine, that he married Mary Magdalene, who escaped to France with their child, and that the bloodline of Jesus and King David has carried through via the founding dynasty of France, the Merovingians, to the present day.

Unraveling two thousand years of suppression of the "sacred feminine" by the patriarchal church, Robert and Sophie leapfrog across England and Scotland seeking the answers to the coded messages left by Sophie's grandfather, Leonardo da Vinci, the Knights Templar, and assorted others. The pair are pursued both by law enforcement and by the blind albino assassin monk Silas, who seems to be working for his Opus Dei masters but turns out to be, like the prelate who heads Opus Dei himself, the dupe of the wealthy English Grail scholar Leigh Teabing. At the novel's end, Sophie herself and her brother are revealed to be the direct descendants of Jesus and Mary Magdalene, and she and Robert enjoy a romantic tryst.

Structural similarities between this novel and *Angels and Demons* include the following: Langdon hooks up professionally and romantically with the granddaughter (*A&D:* adopted daughter) of the murdered wise man, a museum curator (*A&D:* priest turned scientist), who is also head of a secret society, and the two must follow a path of coded historical clues across France and England (*A&D:* Rome). In both, four wise men are murdered (here, higher-ups in the Priory of Sion instead of Roman Catholic cardinals). In both, the murders are committed by a simpleminded or crazed assassin and appear to be the work of a secret society (Illuminati, Opus Dei) but turn out to be masterminded by a single person operating entirely on his own (Cardinal Ventresca, Leigh Teabing). But even though, as Robert Langdon declares at the end of *The Da Vinci Code*, the Vatican and Opus Dei are "completely innocent," once again it's likely that this last-minute plot reversal is lost on the vast majority of readers, who take away with them the idea, foregrounded for most of the story, that Opus Dei really was behind it all.

On his former website (refashioned since the publication of *The Lost Symbol*) Brown affirmed that he is a Christian, but he did not specify which denomination.[22] He said that he didn't read much fiction except the "classics" and the works of Robert Ludlum, whose low-grade, densely plotted thrillers have obviously influenced his work. *The Da Vinci Code*, however, belongs to a sub-subgenre of the faux Catholic Gothick inspired by the 1983 nonfiction *Holy Blood, Holy Grail* by Michael Baigent, Richard Leigh, and Henry Lincoln.[23] The first two of these authors unsuccessfully sued Brown for plagiarism, though they did not sue any other of the less spectacularly successful fictions before and after *The Da Vinci Code* that incorporate their pseudohistorical thesis: that Jesus was a mortal man, he

29

FAUX CATHOLIC

married Mary Magdalene, and their descendants founded the Merovingian dynasty of France.[24]

The Da Vinci Code has a number of fictional antecedents as well: David Morrell's *Fraternity of the Stone* (1985) boasted a secret society of Crusaders who recruit fighters against those same "dark ancestors" of Dan Brown's Hassassin and a modern Opus Dei that is a supremely organized covert information-gathering agency of the Vatican. Pérez-Reverte's *The Flanders Panel* (1996) featured an Old Master painting (fifteenth century, Flemish) that conceals a murderer's identity in coded chess-game visual symbols and a hidden written message revealed in ultraviolet light. Brown may have also drawn some inspiration from Eco's *Foucault's Pendulum* (1988) without recognizing that this novel was intended to be a parody of occultist conspiracy theory, including that found in *Holy Blood, Holy Grail* (whose main thesis, that "Holy Grail" is the coded image for Mary Magdalene's womb, is rendered as one of *Foucault's Pendulum*'s later chapter epigrams). There is a resonance between the opening of Eco's novel, in which a ritual murder is about to be enacted in a famous historical space in Paris (the vault of the Conservatoire National des Arts et Métiers, Saint-Martin-des-Champs, where the pendulum of Léon Foucault is located), and Brown's situating of his character's murder with ritual overtones in the Louvre, followed by a second murder in the Church of Saint-Sulpice, which contains another artifact of early science, an astronomical sun marker that Brown misidentifies, intentionally or not, as the "Rose Line," a so-called older version of the prime meridian that also supposedly runs through the Rosslyn Chapel in Scotland and the Louvre.

Foucault's Pendulum and *The Da Vinci Code* each proceed—one sophisticated and tongue in cheek, the other in deadly earnest—with a manic and completely specious connect-the-dots romp through two thousand years of Western esotericism. Eco, a fervent anti-occultist, conflates too much of the esoteric tradition into a single bulky punching bag, but he is dead on in his satiric take on those whose paranoid desire to find connections overwhelms their common sense and ability to deal fairly with the historical record. Taken in the context of *Foucault's Pendulum*, the conflated occult history presented in Brown's novel reads like the good semiotician's worst nightmare. As displayed in *Angels and Demons, The Da Vinci Code*, and *The Lost Symbol*, Brown's knowledge of Church history, art history, and Western esoteric societies has the stretched-thin feel of an undergraduate term paper. You don't see a sophisticated understanding here, but rather some earnest and copious note taking from various secondary sources delivered with the sort of emphatic assurance only a Harvard "symbologist" can muster. (In *The Da Vinci Code* Robert Langdon's scholarly bibliography for his new book is proudly described as containing no fewer than fifty entries, "many of them academic best-sellers.")[25]

But from the Gothick perspective none of this matters, just as it doesn't matter that vampire folklore didn't originate in Hungary or Transylvania. In the end it's all grist for the Gothick mill. Gothick fiction accepts borrowings in an almost folkloric way; elements laid down by one author (such as Anne Rice's sculptural metaphor for vampires) are picked up and extended by the next in line (White Wolf's vampire videogame, then Stephenie Meyer in her *Twilight* series), and only the really famous ones get accused, usually unfairly, of plagiarism. The case of *Holy Blood, Holy Grail* is a bit different, however. Though it is clear Brown believed he paid his primary source sufficient homage by playfully introducing two of its authors' names in anagrammatic form as the villain "Leigh Teabing" and including an afterword in later printings explicitly citing the book, readers of *Holy Blood, Holy Grail* understand that its authors were correct in asserting that Brown did appropriate, in considerable detail, what they called the "architecture" of their theory about Mary Magdalene and the Merovingian line. The awkward point legally was that Brown took their ersatz scholarship at face value as historically true, and a historical fact cannot be plagiarized, only transmitted.

The relationship of *Holy Blood, Holy Grail* to fact, however, had been exposed as extremely problematic long before Brown drew from this book. In 1993, Pierre Plantard, the self-proclaimed direct descendant of the Merovingians (and thus of Jesus) prominently featured in *Holy Blood, Holy Grail*, confessed that he had made up the whole genealogy and deposited the "secret documents" himself in the Bibliothèque Nationale.[26] The authors of *Holy Blood, Holy Grail* may have already had their suspicions about Plantard's veracity when they first wrote their book, which was based on an earlier BBC program. It doesn't seem, though, that Brown knew of Plantard's confession when he wrote *The Da Vinci Code*—and in any event he gave the Merovingians (and Jesus) a different line of descent in his character

Sophie Neveu. Since Baigent and Leigh, the litigants, could not possibly win if their book were judged entirely factual and could equally not confess to a hoax, Baigent tried to backpedal by saying their book presented "evidence, not proof." The judge, however, was having none of this and ruled against them, even to the point of concealing a *Da Vinci Code*–like secret code of his own devising in his written judgment.[27] A subsequent appeal was turned down.

The industry of more than ninety books on the subject of all the things Dan Brown got factually wrong will not be examined here simply because *The Da Vinci Code*'s power operates in the realm of myth making and religious speculation, where the factual is irrelevant. The Gothick subgenre spawned by *The Da Vinci Code*, its predecessors, and its imitators is noteworthy among contemporary faux Catholic fictions in making the tenets of Christianity an explicit topic and proposing a new religious mystery to take the place of the discredited old one.[28] The stated goal of the murdered curator Jacques Saunière, and of Brown himself, is the restoration of the principle of the "sacred feminine." As Robert explains to Sophie, the Priory of Sion "believes that Constantine and his male successors successfully converted the world from matriarchal paganism to patriarchal Christianity by waging a campaign of propaganda that demonized the sacred feminine, obliterating the goddess from modern religion forever."[29] In one of many interviews, Brown elaborated further: "Prior to two thousand years ago, we lived in a world of gods and goddesses. Today, we live in a world solely of God. I simply wrote a story that explores how and why this shift might have occurred, what it says about our past and, more importantly, what it says about our future."[30]

At first glance, it might seem that *The Da Vinci Code* indeed mainstreamed the notion of the sacred feminine out of the margins of New Age pop culture, and at a culturally auspicious moment for doing so. In a decade in which the "Goddess Mary" was featured on a *Time* magazine cover with an accompanying article devoted to the new "Protestant Mary," along with the trickle-down effect of popular works on the Gnostic Gospels and newly discovered texts such as the Gospel of Judas that chip away at the façade of the New Testament, "people are looking for a different kind of religious understanding," Karen King, Harvard professor of ecclesiastical history, says of *The Da Vinci Code*.[31] Women, King believes, "find comfort in the idea of a married woman with a baby as an alternate figure to the polarized female models of virgins and prostitutes in Christianity."[32]

The Da Vinci Code, however, presents no actual goddess character to its readers, no representation of a divinity. We are told that the Priory of Sion worships Mary Magdalene as "Goddess" and "Divine Mother," but this happens offstage, taking a backseat to the dominant issue of Jesus' nondivinity. What's more, if Jesus is a mere mortal, how precisely is Mary Magdalene divine? Whatever her iconic links to goddesses such as Isis, Mary Magdalene is portrayed in the novel as a woman who marries, bears a child, and dies; she is given no ascension-to-heaven moment. There is also very little mention of Jesus' mother, Mary, who some would argue has served, far more than in any Protestant denomination, as the Catholic Church's own female principle. The story is told from the perspective of the traditional thriller's male protagonist, and the Priory of Sion's hilariously fictitious list of grandmasters taken from *Holy Blood, Holy Grail* (which includes Victor Hugo and Jean Cocteau) has not a single woman in it. The only inadvertent whiff of the goddess in either novel occurs in *Angels and Demons*, when the statuesque scientist Vittoria Vetra provokes outrage by striding through the Vatican in her short shorts. And since no "real" angels and demons are depicted in the story, the novel's title turns out to be a metaphoric label, the "explained supernatural" frame, for the good and evil humans who struggle with each other in the story.

This novel's greatest attraction for its readers, I believe, is not goddess culture or the sacred feminine, but rather the assertion that Jesus was no divinity but a man like everybody else. For those first coming across this heterodox notion (one that was openly embraced by several of America's Deist-oriented Founders in the eighteenth century), packaged as empirical "fact" in a very palatable fictional form by an enthusiastic popularizer, it's heady stuff. Yet as recently as twenty years ago, Martin Scorsese's 1988 film adaptation of the Greek writer Nikos Kazantzakis's midcentury novel *The Last Temptation of Christ*, which did no more than assert the human side of Jesus and his own doubts about his divinity, generated an enormous outcry from Christian groups and was more or less buried by the protest. Why, then, was *The Da Vinci Code* able to bulldoze the opposition of organized religion at every turn?

Not all the reasons for this novel's staggering success, it turns out, had to do with its content. Despite its folkloric elaboration of themes, popular culture is a complex dialogue between mass market content providers and heterogeneous global audiences, a dialogue that took a quantum leap in interactivity once the World Wide Web was created. *The Da Vinci Code* had been groomed for best-sellerdom long before it ever saw print, and it was a canny top-of-the-line marketing plan, not the book's controversial theology, that initially put the novel within reach of the maximum possible number of readers.

Determined to hit it big with this book, Brown was rightly convinced of the need to compress his rather complicated historical argument and accompanying narrative into very short sound-bite chapters that a much wider audience than dedicated thriller readers would be able to digest easily and understand. Unlike Kazantzakis's deeply literary work, *The Da Vinci Code* is full of zingy one-liners on the order of "The greatest story ever told is the greatest story ever *sold*" and throwaway references to such personages as Walt Disney, who, Brown tells us, "had made it his quiet life's work to pass on the Grail story to future generations."[33] For the 200-page detailed plot synopsis he submitted, Brown received a two-book contract and an advance of $400,000, an amount that basically signals a publisher's commitment to do everything necessary to make a book a best seller. After the book's success proved even greater than projected, this figure was quickly renegotiated upward. Three months before publication, 10,000 advance reader copies of *The Da Vinci Code* were sent to booksellers (a larger number than the first print run of any of Brown's previous three novels), and the book had a first printing of 230,000.[34]

Yet it is equally clear that neither Brown nor his publisher was at all prepared for the juggernaut that followed. After ten weeks, a million copies were in print. The book sold 6.5 million in the United States in its first year; after the second year, the total was 10 million.[35] As of the end of April 2006, the book had sold more than 40 million copies in hardback and more than 1 million in the recently released paperback.[36] The release of the movie version the following month spiked those numbers even higher. By the end of the decade, *The Da Vinci Code* had sold a total of 80 million copies and been translated into more than forty languages.[37]

In the meantime, objections from Christian leaders were immediate and vociferous, though the first official denunciation by the Catholic Church did not come until March 2005, two years after publication, when Cardinal Tarcisio Bertone, archbishop of Genoa, spoke out against the book and urged Catholics not to buy or read it.[38] Though Opus Dei refrained from boycotting the movie, bravely declaring it would "generate interest in Christianity," a few weeks before the film version's release Archbishop Angelo Amato, the second-ranking official in the Vatican's doctrinal office and a close associate of Pope Benedict XVI, called on Roman Catholics to boycott the film, declaring the novel to be "full of calumnies, offenses and historical and theological errors regarding Jesus, the Gospels and the church," according to Reuters. "If such lies and errors had been directed at the Koran or the Holocaust, they would have justly provoked a world uprising," the archbishop said. "Instead, if they are directed against the church and Christians, they remain unpunished."[39]

But nobody listened. Promoted in the United States by no less than ten History Channel programs exploring aspects of the novel with the help of dubious "experts" (including Baigent and Leigh) and kitschy soft-focus reenactments, the movie opened to record box office profits worldwide, including in predominantly Catholic countries. As Thomas Doherty noted in the *Washington Post*, this outcome would have been unthinkable for the previous generation of American Catholics, who had exerted real influence by observing the church's boycott and proscription orders. Hollywood's first Production Code of censorship, written in 1930 by a Catholic publisher and a Jesuit priest, inspired the establishment of the Legion of Decency, the forerunner of today's Catholic League. "When the Catholic hierarchy lost the power to energize millions of parishioners for some real Catholic action," Doherty notes, "when American Catholics responded to calls to boycott Hollywood blockbusters with approximately the same obedient deference they accorded the Vatican's advice on birth control, then Catholic dominion over Hollywood lapsed." Today, he concludes, "the only Code that Hollywood adheres to is the kind authored by Dan Brown."[40]

Tellingly, after the record opening (surpassed, ironically, only by Mel Gibson's conservative Catholic *The Passion of the Christ* in 2004), the Vatican newspaper *L'Osservatore Romano* dubbed the movie "much ado about nothing" and the uproar around it nothing but a clever marketing strategy designed to promote interest in a dull movie and a dull book.[41] When the film of *Angels and Demons* was released in 2009, there was considerably less flurry. The script, by David Koepp and Akiva Goldsman, made significant sanitizing changes to the story: Vittoria Vetra does not wear short shorts in the Vatican, the assassin is not Arab but indeterminate Eurotrash, Robert Langdon does not have sex with a descendant of Jesus, and a soothing coda is appended in which Cardinal Strauss says to Robert Langdon as the new Pope is installed, "Thanks be to God for sending someone to save this church." When Langdon expresses polite doubt, the cardinal affirms, "You know He did." Having learned its lesson about bestowing free publicity, the Church wisely declared *Angels and Demons* "harmless entertainment which hardly affects the genius and mystery of Christianity."[42]

Which brings us back full circle to the Gothick's charged relationship with the desanctified supernatural. Following in the tradition of the early Gothick, *The Da Vinci Code*'s function is simply the unmaking of a godhead, not the putting forward of a goddess or any other deity in its place. The supernatural is not present as an active agency in any of Brown's five novels, all of which, along with *The Lost Symbol* and his two earlier technothrillers, *Digital Fortress* (1998) and *Deception Point* (2001), belong structurally to the conspiracy theory genre. Despite its professed thesis, *The Da Vinci Code* is a profoundly secular book, to which Peter Brooks's comment on the radical Gothick message of *The Monk* and Mary Shelley's *Frankenstein*—that "the Sacred in its traditional Christian form, even in the more purely ethical version elaborated by Christian humanism, is no longer operative"—equally applies.[43] As we will see in chapter 11, it would be left to Gothick Christian writers such as William P. Young to embody the "sacred feminine" in his characters Papa, Sarayu, and Sophia in his neo-Christian allegory *The Shack*.

Even so, the fact that classic Gothick fiction did not include a married Jesus indicates just how much closer Christianity stood to Western intellectual life two hundred years ago, when heresy was a much more taboo subject than fornicating monks and nuns, than it does today. The Catholic Church has reason to be upset about *The Da Vinci Code* because the function it serves in secularizing Jesus is not really to promote a dialogue about Christianity, as both Brown and its apologists have rather ingenuously argued, but rather to help deliver a death blow to the Christian Trinity as it has been understood by all denominations, not just Catholics. Even with its discourse displaced one remove, the book's amazing popularity is an indication of the deep interest among the cultural descendants of the Protestant Reformation (not to mention the rest of the world) in developing alternative religious narratives in a secular society where the penalty for heresy is merely controversy, not torture followed by dreadful and prolonged death.

On this issue central to all Christianity, we return again to the question: Why construct this fictional heresy around the Catholic Church in particular? First and most obviously, as all writers of faux Catholic narratives know, it is more convenient to represent somebody else's religious denomination engaged in scheming, suppression, and conspiracy across the ages than one's own. A plot point that would provoke far greater outrage in U.S. audiences, for example, would be to identify close associates of Billy Graham and John Calvin in the historical cover-up around Jesus and Mary Magdalene.

More than simply deflecting criticism away from Protestant Christianity, however, in Brown's hands the faux Catholic genre still reveals its supremely unconscious deference to the Catholic Church as the most enduring and powerful standard-bearer of a Christianity that no longer seems entirely relevant. Despite all the polls showing that this or that number of Americans regularly attend church, believe in the Rapture, and so forth, many who profess to be Christian believers are simply *imaginatively* distant from the precepts of the religion they grew up with. I suspect a large number of Americans share the confusion of an elderly midwesterner who once told me that he and his wife were raised Methodist but had started attending the Catholic Church across the street from their retirement home because the choir was so much better. He stopped to consider a moment. Then, brow furrowed, he leaned forward. "You know, the Catholics and the Protestants?" he whispered. "Which came first?" And he still seemed troubled after I told him, as if some larger, more important question behind this one had been left unanswered—as, indeed, it had.

Statistics, themselves a kind of peculiarly American secular scripture, always constitute a dubious proof, but sometimes they can accurately reflect certain of these dissonances in belief. One recent poll that records 78 percent of people in the United States as believing in the resurrection of Jesus also shows the rather astounding number of 13 percent now believing that Jesus' death on the cross "was faked" and, as represented in *The*

Da Vinci Code, that Jesus was married and had a family.[44] The Canadian pollster himself expressed shock at this result in such a religiously conservative country as the United States. A similar poll in the United Kingdom (commissioned, notably, by Opus Dei), where no fewer than one out of five adults had read *The Da Vinci Code*, revealed that 60 percent of people who had read the book believed Jesus had children by Mary Magdalene, as did 30 percent—a significant figure in itself—of those who had *not* read the book.[45] Christopher Partridge has described what he calls the growing "occulture" of new religious movements derived from popular culture. Against the secularization thesis, which argued that the twentieth century saw the decline of religious belief in Western societies, he notes that dominant religious institutions are becoming weaker as alternative religions thrive in a massive shift from organized religion to what is euphemistically called spirituality.[46]

After Christianity, then, whither the Gothick, as channeled by Dan Brown?

Making what we will soon see is an archetypal twenty-first-century move from classic Gothick faux Catholic to consciousness-based "divine human" spirituality, Brown's third Langdon novel, *The Lost Symbol* (2009), offers a provocative answer. At first glance the novel seems to focus on another old-fashioned obsession of the classic Gothick—the Freemasons—and it presents a plot that again is structurally almost identical to the previous two: a mutilation of a high priest of a secret organization (Freemasons instead of Illuminati or Priory of Sion) discovered in a national public space (Capitol Rotunda in Washington, D.C.), a crime committed by an implausible villain with a putative ethnic identity (Middle Eastern again) that is later overturned, complication upon complication unfolding within the intellectual frame of a grab bag of esoteric ideas once again mistakenly conflated into a single monolithic tradition.[47]

Brown's passion for his project is unmistakable. An ambitious effort, *The Lost Symbol* is a blend of Wikipedia-type historical sound bites and intricately layered flashbacks within flashbacks. This time, however, with his characteristic flair for identifying the sub-Zeitgeist's newest preoccupations, he has grafted his familiar mélange of plot elements to a strand of twenty-first century spirituality and new physics that posits the primacy of human thought and intention over the world of matter.[48] This new science of consciousness, Brown says, is actually very old because the ancients studied the human mind far more deeply than modern science has. All the religions of the world have been seeking a lost symbol, "the symbol we all shared . . . the symbol of all the mysteries of life that we could not understand."

What is this symbol? None other than God, Brown tells us. But who or what is God? All sacred texts of all religions also contain a secret subtext of truths meant to be shielded from the unworthy: that humans, with sufficient training, possess their own godlike powers to shape matter and the world around them. But all the functionaries of all the religions on earth have lost their primal connection to these universal "Ancient Mysteries," as Brown calls them (the label and the concept come from Theosophy); they "no longer knew the Source from which their potent wisdom had once flowed."[49] What is happening now, he says, is the dawning awareness that God lies inside humans rather than outside.

The rediscovery of this ancient secret—which Brown boils down into a trademark sound bite, *"Mind over matter"*—began after the cataclysmic events of 9/11 and puts us on the brink of a paradigm shift, a "vast coalescing of human intention," that the new discipline of noetic science is investigating. We now understand that God is a single universal consciousness, "a mental energy that pervades everything," and most especially humans. As his character Katherine Solomon, a noetic scientist, puts it, "The Second Coming is the coming of *man.* . . . The Word of God is really the word of Man." We are all man-gods now, Brown says. Humans who train their minds to tap into this energy become the creators, not the created, and will "be able to *Design* the world rather than merely create it."[50]

Reviewers of *The Lost Symbol* made little mention of its central spiritual thesis, which of course lacks the immediate shock value that "Jesus as mortal" possessed. As in Brown's previous novels also, the relentless thriller structure overwhelms the theoretical subtext, and his old-fashioned conspiracy theory plot, with its code puzzles and diagrams, remains very male-centric despite the presence of the obligatory female scientist. Just as *The Da Vinci Code* offers no female gods as characters to embody its thesis, *The Lost Symbol* never quite makes its point because no human character turns into a god, or at the least displays godlike powers, in its pages. Brown's smoke, however, always portends fire. His nose for cutting-edge trends is unerring, and we will find man-gods emerging as a dominant theme throughout the twenty-first century Gothick, including children's literature and comic-book/graphic-novel narrative as well as adult fiction and film. As later chapters will show, in her *Twilight* series Stephenie Meyer embodies both the divine human and the "sacred feminine" in her vampire demigoddess Bella; so does Guillermo del Toro in the character of Ofelia, the child martyr and underworld princess of his film *Pan's Labyrinth*.

Though the notion of humans as gods in their own right failed to arouse any noticeable outrage, deification or theosis has been a disputed doctrine since Christianity began. In late antiquity the ubiquitous figure of the divine human went by the names Jesus (for Christians), Adam Kadmon (for Jews), and Anthropos (for Hermetic philosophers). As the Gnostic "great light man," he was the intermediary between God and humankind, representing a level of conscious awakening and godlike powers that humans could aspire to. As the Hermetic tradition was revived in the Italian Renaissance, natural philosopher Giordano Bruno believed he could make himself the equal of a god by meditating on inner images animated by astral powers.

A current doctrine of the Eastern Orthodox Church and the Church of Jesus Christ of Latter-day Saints, deification was revived in Western Christianity by the Protestant Theosophist mystic Jakob Boehme in the seventeenth century and was carried to North America during the Radical Reformation. Groups such as the eighteenth-century Immortalists declared themselves capable of becoming gods on earth, and the Freemasons emphasized the divine human in their Rite of Perfection. Such "Perfectability" during a person's lifetime became an important principle not only of Mormon and Christian Science belief in the nineteenth century—as Mary Baker Eddy pronounced, "Man *is*, not *shall be*, perfect and immortal"— but also, in the next century, of the breakaway Christian New Thought movement, which encouraged its followers to harness divine powers within themselves.[51]

In its day a sizeable transatlantic organization, New Thought has unspooled in a variety of religious and secular versions of the "Mind-cure" philosophy (as William James dubbed it), starting with its own surviving denominations, including the Unity and Religious Science churches, the spiritually based Alcoholics Anonymous organization, various nonaffiliated forms of "prosperity Christianity," and secularized self-help philosophies as expounded in the minister Norman Vincent Peale's 1952 best seller, *The Power of Positive Thinking*, all of which stress every person's ability to create his or her own reality and physical environment through conscious intent.[52]

New Thought is thus the direct ancestor of the current "intention-setting" spiritual practices that Brown cites. Rhonda Byrne's 2006 best-selling self-help book and documentary *The Secret*, however, brought a form of reinvented New Thought to a much larger global audience.[53] A lifestyle metaphysics program based on the Old Goth law of correspondence between levels of reality (also known as the "law of attraction"), *The Secret* also drew heavily on Brown's *Da Vinci Code* Gothick atmospherics for the look of its website and film: candlelit rooms hung with velvet curtains, chests full of scrolls (and "Secret Scroll" emails to its subscribers), History Channel–style "reenactments" of murky legends around faux medieval Knights Templar and Roman centurions, and the now obligatory list of Western male power figures over the ages (Plato, Shakespeare, Leonardo, Emerson, Einstein, etc.) to whom the Secret is said to have brought success. In fact, as Byrne explains, the "century-old book" containing the wisdom that produced this marketing package with high production values was none other than *The Science of Getting Rich*, a classic New Thought treatise by the Christian Socialist Wallace Wattles.[54] In an ironic twist of mutual referencing (though he never mentions the book directly), *The Secret* seems to have made its mark in turn on Dan Brown's marketing team as he wrote *The Lost Symbol*, whose cover design of a thick red wax seal oddly resembles the seal that decorates the cover of *The Secret*.

Meanwhile, the populace retains its strong appetite for heresy that these works of new Gothick fiction help to feed. This is no new phenomenon under the American sun, where transcendental movements and Great Awakenings war ceaselessly with pragmatic empiricism for hegemony in the national spirit. The crowd searches, restlessly, for spiritual ideas that capture its imagination. In examining the way movies rewrite Christian theology and fabricate new versions, Douglas Cowan has noted that sacred narratives themselves adapted and mutated in much the same way.[55] What the secularization of Jesus (and the fictional elevation of assorted female gods and divine humans) simply means in terms of the sub-Zeitgeist of popular culture, where fantastic literature and religion building have a long history of cross-fertilizing each other, is that the gradual departure of the Christ figure from the category of the divine leaves room for something else to move in and take its place. Or as Maurice Lévy once said of the horror writer H. P. Lovecraft, "To formulate sacrilege is to recover the sacred."[56]

Byrne's lifestyle metaphysics and Brown's noetic science of consciousness in *The Lost Symbol* belong, in fact, to the wider new phenomenon of ·"personal gnosis" that reflects a widespread turn from organized religion to individually determined spirituality under the sometimes misleading umbrella label "New Age." Catherine Albanese points out the American preference for unmediated spiritual experience in what she calls the "metaphysical religions" that constitute New Age spirituality, a potent syncretic mix of "Transcendentalism and spiritualism, mesmerism and Swedenborgianism, Christian Science and New Thought, Theosophy and its ubiquitous spinoffs, and especially metaphysical Asia" that have blended in turn with quantum physics, parapsychology, and "an astrological dispensationalism that parallels the Protestant fundamentalist vision."[57] In spite of the many Old Goth elements evident in New Age spirituality, however, Wouter Hanegraaff cautions that New Age religions "cannot be characterized as a return to pre-Enlightenment worldviews"; they are, rather, eminently syncretic (some might say Gothick) medievalisms that mix esoteric and secular elements.[58]

The multiplatform success of *The Da Vinci Code* occurred in a realm that is simultaneously a fertile field and an intellectual vacuum—that curious ahistorical, apocalyptic world of the American pop culture sub-Zeitgeist in which Brown can be called "one of the best-selling authors of all time" just as Elvis is the greatest rock-'n'-roll star of all time and Hank Aaron (or Barry Bonds) is the greatest home run hitter of all time. The prevailing culture is unlikely to be swept away anytime soon by a New Age goddess religion—recall that Balzac's mystical potboiler *Seraphita* took Paris by storm in 1835 yet failed to produce a country of Swedenborgian converts—but we should expect other forms of religious speculation packaged in fictional form (most probably some hybrid of Gothick, thriller, science fiction, and fantasy) to keep arriving on our doorsteps. In another ten years *The Da Vinci Code*, *The Lost Symbol*, and *The Secret* will have faded from memory as completely as *The Celestine Prophecy* already has. But they count among any number of faint tremors indicating how far the ground of orthodoxy has shifted under our feet. Religion has not so much declined as migrated in Western societies today. Especially in the United States, not places of worship or theological seminaries but dog-eared paperback fiction and the Web are the true early warning signals of religious upheavals to come.

Cthulhu mask. Courtesy Bob Basset Workshop, bobbasset.com.

THREE

GOTHICK GODS

The Worshipful World of Horror Fandom

Ann Radcliffe's *The Mysteries of Udolpho* to M. G. Lewis' *The Monk* to C. R. Maturin's *Melmoth* to Edgar All[a]n Poe's tales and poetry to R. W. Chambers' *The King in Yellow* to Bram Stoker's *Dracula* and on to Hanns Heinz Ewers, H. P. Lovecraft and Anne Rice . . . all in their own ways, wittingly or unwittingly, have contributed to the descent of the Gothick God of Darkness in popular culture.

—Sir Stephen E. Flowers, Ph.D., GME

I.

Picture a deserted Montauk beach on a hot summer's night. The year is 1965. A teenage boy prostrates himself on the sand and prays to Cthulhu, monstrous "Great Old One" from outside space and time, fictional creation of the Gothick horror writer H. P. Lovecraft. Reciting the only sentence Lovecraft provided in the entity's tongue Aklo—*Ph'nglui mglw'nafh Cthulhu R'lyeh wgah'nagl fhtagn*—the boy cries, "Cthulhu! Cthulhu! Appear to me!"[1]

"And then?" I ask, listening to this tale some decades later.

"I went home and went to bed," said the distinguished scholar telling me the story.

With his cephalopod head, scaly body, claws, and wings, Cthulhu reminds me of nothing so much as a *babewyn*, one of those hybrid monsters who appear in the margins of medieval illuminated manuscripts.[2] A gargoyle demon, a humanoid Blemmye or Sciopode of the thirteenth-century Hereford map, the catfish-headed creature menacing St. Dominic in the Spinola Hours.[3]

A monster god, a *babewyn*. Following the trail of Cthulhu leads to the strange territory where these equivocal creatures still breed today, the place where the American "secular scripture" of the Gothick has spawned new religions for hundreds of years, where the strange unions between readers and writers, the real and the imaginary, the imaginary and the spiritual, works of fiction and sacred scripture, worshippers and fans have spawned metaphorical monsters of their own. My point of departure is that last unlikely hybrid, between worshippers and fans, and a convergence in twenty-first century American popular culture between a certain subgroup of Gothick fiction fandom and post-1960 new religious movements. My focus is Cthulhu's creator Howard Phillips Lovecraft, whose work not only is plentifully populated with hybrid monsters but also has helped propagate many of these paradoxical modes.

H. P. Lovecraft's initial circumscribed reputation as a purveyor of squishy monster stories for boys has gradually given way, since his death in 1937, to a belated recognition of an exceptional literary sensibility, at once unique yet falling very much within both the Gothick tradition and the broader tradition of American literature. Out of the wide range of Lovecraft's admirers and literary imitators, I want to single out that special subgroup of fans for whom his fictions have assumed an ontological and even theological authority.

Together, Lovecraft and the New England city to which he felt symbiotically bound—as witness the famous line "I am Providence," which was drawn from one of his letters and now adorns the tombstone that fans erected at his grave in the 1970s—provide an emblem of this larger cultural phenomenon for two reasons: first, because Lovecraft boasts one of the oldest still flourishing congeries (to use a favorite word of his) of fan groups and second, because old Providence—which he dubbed "that universal haven of the odd, the free, and the dissenting"—was an important site in the development of various new American religions that trace their ancestry back to the Protestant heterodoxies of the seventeenth-century

Radical Reformation.[4] And these two elements join in an even more shadowy union: between Providence's historical association with religious dissension and the fact that its most famous literary son was a writer of Gothick horror stories.

Let us make a quick detour through the long and dynamic process of religion building in the New World. The postindigenous society known as "America" began, of course, as a Western religious idea initiated by English Puritans, and since these ideological beginnings it has remained a culture periodically swept by religious fervor. The eighteenth century saw the first in a series of Great Awakenings (a disputed term used here for convenience), galvanic episodes of religious revitalization and populist evangelism that periodically disturbed the Euro-American dream of reason for the next three centuries.

If we follow William McLoughlin's classic and much deconstructed interpretation of this phenomenon, this first grand upheaval was preceded by a similar upheaval in England—namely, the Puritan revolution, resulting in the migration in large numbers of these dissenters to North America in the first half of the seventeenth century. It was followed by at least three more, depending on which commentator you believe: a second at the turn of the nineteenth century, spilling over into Transcendentalism in high culture as well as countless popular manifestations, including new religious groups such as the Mormons, Christian Scientists, Shakers, and Spiritualists. A third shake-up took place between 1890 and 1930, which included Theosophy; a fourth began in the 1950s and 1960s, and the fifth we may now be in the midst of.[5]

Part of the initial thrust of populist religion in North America stems from the fact that the beliefs of the early sects of the Radical Reformation mentioned in chapter 1 found more open expression in the relatively freer arena of the New World, where dissenters could simply pull up stakes and move to a new territory. Commentators such as John L. Brooke, Arthur Versluis, and D. Michael Quinn have convincingly traced the dissemination of Renaissance Hermetic and alchemical traditions among the European settlers in America via the revolutionary Protestant religious sects of seventeenth-century England, including the Quakers, Baptists, Pietists, Methodists, Universalists, and Immortalists—groups that found a home outside the pale of Puritan orthodoxy in what Brooke identifies as a "sectarian coast" stretching from Cape Cod through Rhode Island to the

Connecticut river.[6] The eighteenth and early nineteenth centuries brought further esoteric influences from the other side of the Atlantic, including Freemasonry, the Swedenborgian church, and the Gothick/Romantic revival of Old Goth medieval esotericism.[7]

Some of these radical Protestant sects of colonial America placed an almost Gnostic emphasis on the primacy of the spiritual over the evil, illusory material world. Many, including the Shakers, the Perfectionists, and the Quakers, also shared a belief in the potential of humans to become like gods during their life on earth. Where Emerson was waxing eloquent about the divinity of man, Joseph Smith was devising a religion around it. The doctrine of human divinity would resurface in Scientology's notion of the "Operating Thetan," a perfected being exempt from the cycles of birth and death, and in the teachings of many other esoteric societies, from the early twentieth-century Hermetic Order of the Golden Dawn through New Age religious groups such as the Neopagans, Wiccans, and the Course of Miracles, all of which subscribe to some form of the belief that the "Christed" or Higher Self is capable of manifesting in the earthly body to produce a "divine human." It is a concept, as we will see, also central to twenty-first-century Gothick religion building.

Since the time that Bibles were first printed in vernacular languages (not coincidentally, at the onset of the Protestant Reformation), mass media publication of scripture helped fuel radical reinterpretations of Christianity. Then as now, a person's ability to read and reflect on his own copy of a scripture guaranteed privacy of worship and encouraged as well the development of a highly individualistic "personal gnosis" as a means of accessing the transcendental. By the nineteenth century, the religious manifestos of the two "American heresiarchs" Joseph Smith and Mary Baker Eddy, written by the founding individuals themselves rather than by later commentators, were published and distributed to a mass audience within a relatively short time after they were written.[8] This instant scripture, moreover, was partially shaped by conventions of popular nonfiction and Gothick fiction as well as esoteric folklore (wonder and providence narratives, the romance of gold tablets written in a secret celestial language, and the self-improvement tradition begun by Benjamin Franklin, respectively).

In nineteenth-century America, wide distribution of the new scriptures had the subliminally powerful effect of further underlining similarities between their story lines and those of popular fiction.[9] In a popular culture infused with mystic "visions, dreams, and voice," Swedenborg's *Heaven and Hell*, for example, was a best seller along with the novels of James Fenimore Cooper and Sir Walter Scott.[10] This structural congruence was dramatically extended in the twentieth century, when individual works of science fiction or fantasy would be used as the scriptural-narrative basis of new religious groups, either by their authors (e.g., L. Ron Hubbard and Scientology) or by a portion of their audience (the fans we will meet in the next section of this chapter).[11]

Just as Mormonism (wittily dubbed "a modern Pelagianism in a Puritan religion" by one commentator) promised Christ's reappearance in the New World and Mary Baker Eddy injected Christianity with "Science," the twentieth century's new religious movements updated and recontextualized religion's ground.[12] Many of them drew their inspiration both from the dominant scientific worldview and from the science fiction literature that uses technology as its great rationalizing device for the supernatural, often fashioning their gods as extraterrestrials possessing advanced powers.[13] In a transference process Christopher Partridge has called the "sacralization of the extraterrestrial," for these groups outer space has become the Gnostic realm whose Archons possess the power to create, control, and destroy earth and its inhabitants.[14] Typically these deities are said to have traveled to earth in their spacecraft at a distant time in the planet's past and set in motion the events that produced humans—either by leaving some of their own kind here with limited or no memory of their extraterrestrial (read "divine") past, or by endowing a select group of humans with special powers.[15]

Since the Great Awakening that began in the 1960s, an enormous magpie energy has been poured into the creation of new religious movements (NRMs) from all kinds of sources. Evoking images of berobed Druidists shuffling around Stonehenge on the eve of summer solstice, New Age religious movements tend to inspire ridicule from the mainstream, which has its own nervous issues around spirituality. Some of the NRMs incorporate the latest scientific advances, notably in DNA and string theory; other "research-based" religions, such as Wicca, draw on Celtic and Nordic folklore, feminist archaeology, Reichian psychology, comics, movies, and novels.[16] Much like the proliferating sects of Late Antiquity, the current deeply syncretic new religious movements overlap and borrow from each other. Following the trend toward personal gnosis, individual practitioners also characteristically pick and choose among elements of different religions old and new.[17]

At the turn of the twenty-first century, the advent of the World Wide Web has created an even greater syncretism in these new movements, along with the disappearance of anything resembling single authoritative texts.[18] A prime example is the Neopagan/Wiccan *Book of Shadows* (first composed by British Wiccan Gerald Gardner in the 1950s, then adapted by Stuart and Janet Farrar in the 1970s), which spawned countless adapted versions and eventually became the generic name for individual magicians' journals. Likewise, the "dreaded *Necronomicon*," a made-up grimoire Lovecraft liked to allude to in his stories, now exists in many faux versions that, like the *Book of Shadows*, are often quoted as scriptural authority, a nebulous but unchallengeable sourcing reminiscent of the very stretchable medieval concept of *auctorite*.[19]

Even though the Internet especially has created an almost infinitely replicating, untrackable intertextuality, written scripture still remains important in NRMs.[20] But Erik Davis, among others, has also observed that most post-1960 New Age religious movements "owe their existence to what was in some sense a *literary* resonance"—that of earlier commentators such as Margaret Murray, Robert Graves, and Ashley Montagu and later ones such as the archaeologist Marija Gimbutas.[21] Harold Bloom has also noted the curiously literary sensibility—in terms of both direct influence and general aura—of some of the older radical Protestant sects turned respectable religions. "As a gnosis," Bloom comments, what he calls the "American Religion"—an unconsciously Gnostic celebration of the self unique to this country that he finds triangulated in the faiths of Mormons, Southern Baptists, and Pentecostalists—"has much in common with the American romance, a peculiar literary genre that includes narratives as diverse as Hawthorne's *The Scarlet Letter* and Pynchon's *The Crying of Lot 49*." This hybrid trifecta, which Bloom describes as a "blend of ancient heresies and nineteenth-century stresses," has cast off the Protestant sensibility even as it continues to declare itself Christian and counts an unmediated personal relationship between the individual and a divinity, "walking and talking with Jesus," as its paramount religious experience.[22]

Along with these Christian denominations, most of the new religious movements known as "New Age" also emphasize the primacy of the personal relationship between the individual and the sacred. These varied forms of personal gnosis again reflect the trend toward individually determined spirituality. Carried to the extreme, personal gnosis can mean, as Douglas Cowan has pointed out about the freewheeling, mix-and-match personal pantheons of most modern Pagans, that "subjective experience at the individual level has been raised to the status of personal ontology" and the simple criterion of personal inner certainty becomes proof of divine revelation, a tenet that obviously carries a number of doctrinal consequences.[23]

2.

Enter the fans.

The twentieth century marked the appearance of the second element in our hybrid union of acolytes and aficionados. This was the organized groups of admirers, under the wide umbrella of mass commercial entertainment, attached to specific entertainers, works of literature or film, or sports clubs and players. *Fan*, of course, is the short form of *fanatic*, a word current in English since the sixteenth century to describe a person "characterized, influenced, or prompted by excessive and mistaken enthusiasm, especially in religious matters," as the *Oxford English Dictionary* puts it. *Fanatic* derives in turn from Latin *fanaticus*, "temple attendant," from *fanus*, "temple."[24] In late antiquity, the Romans condescendingly applied *fanaticus* (in its sense of going a bit overboard in religious observance) to members of marginal and orgiastic sects such as those dedicated to Isis and the Magna Mater; for Christians, it was a synonym for *pagan*.[25] In English the word is used as early as the seventeenth century in reference to religious zealots.[26] For almost two thousand years, then, *fanatic* has been a word that Western mainstream religious orthodoxy applies pejoratively to members of marginal and potentially threatening religious groups.

The first modern nonreligious usage of the short form *fan* appears in U.S. newspapers of the late nineteenth century in reference to sports devotees. By the early twentieth century it was stretched to include ardent enthusiasts of the new mass entertainment genres of movies and science fiction, fantasy, and horror literature. The emergence and growth of fan groups in these new areas was an extremely rapid phenomenon: science fiction, fantasy, and horror grew out of the matrix of Gothick pulp fiction that had thrived in America since the late 1800s, and movies had swept this country by the teens of the new century. During the 1920s sci-fi and horror enthusiasts, like their movie counterparts, abandoned their roles as solitary admirers and actively banded together; columns devoted to reader discussion in the science fiction pulps spawned organized groups who began to correspond independently with one another.[27] These reader communications became so lively and insistent that they soon spilled over into their own journals, known as fanzines.

Curiously, while the sci-fi and horror genres spawned fanzines, other genres well represented in the pulps, such as mysteries and westerns, did not.[28] One reason may well lie precisely in the religious roots of the word *fan* and the state of heightened emotion or devotion the word connotes, as reflected in the title of Francis T. Laney's fanzine *The Acolyte* (1942–1946), an amateur publication that concentrated on Lovecraft.[29] What science fiction, fantasy, and supernatural horror of the Lovecraftian type offer that the other genres don't is the attraction of a fully realized alternate world or universe.[30] Movies, in turn, offer the images of *stars* (a celestial, divinizing term), entities whose media-enhanced larger-than-life personalities and love lives create a shifting pantheon very like that of the minor Greek deities—and, like them, encompassing a broader spectrum of good and bad behavior than Catholic saints, who fulfill a not dissimilar pantheistic function.

Lovecraft himself began his writing career not as a fan exactly, but as a member of a kind of group that preceded fan clubs—the amateur journalists' societies that were created in America in the mid-nineteenth century. Still a fixture in Lovecraft's day, these groups published journals for private distribution containing a wide array of essays, fiction, poetry, and opinion. But a number of resemblances unite the "ajas," as they were called, with the essentially fan-oriented amateur press associations, or "apas," that followed them. In fact, the first known unofficial sci-fi fan magazine in America, *The Recluse* (1927), was published by a New York club to which Lovecraft belonged, and his famous essay "Supernatural Horror in Literature" appeared in its only issue.[31]

One scholar of fandom has noted the "curious blend of distance and intimacy" inherent in fan groups, commenting that they include people more at ease communicating in print than in person.[32] Lovecraft, who is estimated to have written more than 75,000 letters in his short lifetime, fits this psychological profile almost too neatly.[33] His membership in the United Amateur Press Association (of which he was president for a time) provided him with valuable social outlets and even the courage to continue with his own writing.

The United Amateur Press Association also gave Lovecraft his first opportunities not only to practice his own art but also to engage in another kind of literary hybridizing: rewriting and extending other amateur writers' stories. Lovecraft himself little imagined that after his death in 1937 other professional writers, such as August Derleth, and then a sizeable body of fans would rewrite, extend, and stretch his body of work into an unimaginably large and ever-growing *babewyn* of globe-circling proportions.

Historians of sci-fi, fantasy, and horror fandom nostalgically regard the 1930s as its golden age. A number of fan associations and their magazines burst on the scene during this decade, which also witnessed the beginning of a very important phenomenon of fandom: conventions. The first World Science Fiction Convention or "Worldcon" was held in 1936 in Philadelphia, followed by two more in 1940. At the 1942 convention held in Chicago, it is reported, fans barely old enough to drink alcohol sang "everything from 'Popeye the Sailor' to 'The Internationale.'"[34] Conventions were important in adding greater interactivity and strengthening personal bonds among fans, which in turn led inevitably to a plethora of feuding, merging, and splitting among the primarily male members of these groups in a way fondly reminiscent of the various socialist and communist groups of this highly politicized decade.

As fans continued to band together in ever larger and more organized groups, they began writing and distributing not just opinion and appreciation but also works of fiction (known as "faaanfiction" or "sercon faaanfiction," meaning serious, not parodic) in the spirit of, or using the framework and characters of, their literary heroes' work.[35] The foundational premise of this ultimate *babewyn*, as articulated by fan scholar Henry Jenkins, is deeply hybridizing: "Fandom recognizes no clear-cut line between artists and consumers; all fans are potential writers whose talents need to be discovered, nurtured, and promoted and who may be able to make a contribution, however modest, to the cultural wealth of the larger community."[36] There is a Gramscian air here of shared "meaning production" as a collective, not individual, effort—or as Lovecraft put it in a pamphlet he wrote extolling the virtues of amateur journalism: "There are no limits of age, sex, education, position, or locality in this most complete of democracies."[37] This does not prevent present-day fandom from being a fraught and feuding landscape of middle-class, college-educated competitors, however, as revisionist fan scholar Milly Williamson has pointed out.[38]

Fan scholar Rich Brown sees this early "faaanfiction" peaking in the late 1950s, declining in the 1970s, and reemerging in the beginning of the 1990s, when it began a fin de siècle sea change into its present, supremely interactive new golden age.[39] The 1960s was the decade that marked a real turning point in the social organization of fandom, however. Synchronous with psychedelics, communalism, and new spirituality came the mainstreaming of science fiction and the supernatural out of the tripartite ghetto of pulp fiction, B movies, and comic books. With the television series *The Twilight Zone* (1959–1966), followed by the series *Star Trek* (1966–1969) and then *Star Wars* (1977) on the big screen, this genre gained new legitimacy in popular culture and a much wider audience. The *Star Trek* series in particular produced an enormous base of fan groups that is still expanding today. Starting in 1997, J. K. Rowling's seven-volume Harry Potter phenomenon did the same for fantasy fiction and was further mainstreamed via the big-budget movies of the Potter series, as were other fantasy classics.

The current extreme fan interactivity in Gothick genres began in the early 1970s with fantasy-oriented role-playing games such as *Dungeons & Dragons* (not to mention the *Dungeons & Dragons* poetry that quickly sprouted in the wake of the popular game). Though players initially sat around a table casting dice and simply visualized the Old Goth medieval characters and story line they were enacting, these exercises in active imagination made role-playing games part of a larger participatory trend that would quickly blossom into actual performance. The next step, of course, was videogames that translated these in-your-head fantasy scenarios into actual visual settings. Earlier works such as those of Lovecraft and the medieval scholar J. R. R. Tolkien's 1953 trilogy *Lord of the Rings*—the latter a prime influence on the faux medieval story line and general ambience of *Dungeons & Dragons*—were quickly retranslated into these new interactive modes. They were and are heavily Gothick, from the early and relatively innocent *Myst* (still the top-selling computer adventure game franchise) and *Castlevania* to *BloodRayne*, *Gothic*, and many, many more.

As fandom became increasingly a "mythmaking microcosm," role playing and videogames joined the rising tide of interactivity by establishing a much more dynamic relationship with the targeted story than ever before: from live, full-dress role playing in Renaissance Faires and groups such as the Society for Creative Anachronism to the increasing prominence of costumers (people outfitted as, and playing the part of, characters from a television show, movie, or book) at sci-fi conventions, which had mushroomed after 1970 into much bigger and wilder events that in turn helped fuel the reenactment phenomenon around historical events ranging from the American Civil War to the Crusades.[40]

With this spurt of post-1960s growth, finally, women entered the formerly almost exclusively male subculture of fandom, especially in the crucial area of fan writing. Female fans, and soon all-female fan groups, quickly made their influence felt in writing narratives that expanded on, and substantially departed from, the mother narratives of their favorite authors or TV shows. Since the 1990s these fannish narratives, long and short, have become complex stories featuring what are for outsiders unexpected and sometimes shocking themes: starting in the 1970s, *Star Trek*, for example, has produced a huge body of fan writing, known as "Treklit," with a range of specific story types, most notoriously "K/S" (for Captain Kirk and Mr. Spock) or "slash" fiction, which imagines homoerotic relations, romantic and sexual, between these two characters. Supernormal traits of telepathy and psychological merging are also presented as key elements of relationship in many of these stories.[41]

As a fan fiction genre, erotic slash fiction (in the words of one blogger) spread "faster than herpes" into every conceivable fictional venue (Harry/Draco, Frodo/Bilbo) but most interestingly into Judeo-Christian religious narrative: David/Jonathan, Jesus/Judas, Moses/God, Lucifer/God.[42] Unthinkable even twenty years ago, this fannish sexualizing of scripture is scarcely a sign of sublimated spiritual longing, though using God as a fictional character, however louche, does underscore the perception of the Bible as simply another piece of Gothick fiction to be riffed on. The lack of consequences, legal or otherwise, for the authors of these playful stories says more about the splintering of Christianity's hegemony in our culture than does any amount of academic theological analysis. Graffiti artists, after all, have a keen nose for the impending demolition/renovation of a venerable public building. They don't have to wait until it's been vacated to start tagging; they just *know*, somehow.

Meanwhile, the sci-fi, fantasy, and horror subgenres carry on their role as Gothick hypothesis-generating engines, if only because they are the only venues available for presenting realities other than the one we experience with our five senses. Here cosmogonies and gods can be created and just as quickly forgotten, with only a select few having the resonance to attract a body of initiates. "Fiction, as a vehicle, has often been used by occultists," Kenneth Grant, acolyte of the twentieth-century esoteric practitioner Aleister Crowley, once commented. "Ideas not acceptable to the everyday mind, limited by prejudice and spoiled by a 'bread-winning' education, can be made to slip past the censor, and by means of the novel, the poem, the short story be effectively planted in soil that would otherwise reject or destroy them."[43] The religion-making impulse, which remains a deep part of American culture no matter how denigrated it continues to be by the intellectual elite, is just as strong among those who grew up outside organized religion or are alienated from it as it is for the orthodox faithful. These seekers grasp eagerly at any scraps of the Gothick supernatural, however spiritually meager they may be, and in attempting to build a temple on them return the word *fan* to its original meaning.

The deep spiritual allure of fandom's alternate world for a culture divided between religious orthodoxy and a secular mainstream cultural elite was pinpointed by one of its prime apologists, J. R. R. Tolkien, who openly declared that in *The Lord of the Rings* trilogy he wanted to create an alternate mythology for England. In "On Fairy-Stories"—his very Gnostic essay styling fantasy writers as demiurges or world creators—Tolkien describes the way in which what he calls a "Secondary World," that is, "storymaking in its primary and most potent mode," brought into being by "subcreators" such as himself, can command the response of "Secondary Belief" from a reader.[44] In a letter to a friend, Tolkien further asserted that *The Lord of the Rings* was "fundamentally a religious and Catholic work. That is why I have not put in, or have cut out, practically all references to anything like 'religion,' to cults and practices. . . . For the religious element is absorbed into the story and the symbolism."[45]

A co-creator of the main Tolkien fan website sums up this appeal of Secondary Worlds, especially to those large numbers of readers raised with no religious training at all: "People want to participate in the universe they love." This "True Believer," as Tolkien acolytes only half ironically call themselves, goes on to say: "A hundred years ago people all went to church. Even if they didn't believe it, they bought into the overarching story that was involved. Today there is no meta-story. One reason people like Tolkien is because they want a myth that's true, and they see it there."[46]

The experience of Secondary Belief that separates a fan from the ordinary reader or moviegoer is an intensity of engagement that accepts the content of the reading or viewing experience as real, not fantasy. Fans approach a film or work of fiction by their hero in the spirit of one Tolkien amateur researcher who said simply, "What I do is treat Middle-Earth as if it were a real thing."[47] Fans engaged in Secondary Belief include, for example, those who accepted as documentarian and true the faux "found footage" horror film *The Blair Witch Project* (1999) and the *Paranormal Activity* series that began in 2009. This kind of experience stands in contrast to the more typical Coleridgean "suspension of disbelief" we are presumed to have during most aesthetic experiences—or, more laterally, the aesthetic "hesitation" that Tzvetan Todorov identifies as "experienced by a person who only knows the laws of nature, confronting an apparently supernatural event" in a work of fiction.[48]

Secondary Believers come in what I see as two distinct types. On what is not necessarily a slippery slope to cultdom, what might be called the committed consumers are followed by the supercommitted performers. These are fans who attempt to re-create the experience of the alternate world in their own lives. Some *Star Trek* fans have adopted the identity of one or another of the imaginary species represented in this program, such as the Klingons and the Vulcans, to actively fashion their own way of life. More than forty years later, there are still self-identified *Enterprise* officers who live the series, in uniform, every day of their lives.[49] Davis recounts how members of the Swedish orcish rock group Za Frumi ("The Righteous Spirits" in the corrupted elvish tongue spoken by the orcs) and hundreds of other fans go into the woods in midsummer "garbed in elaborate costumes featuring latex, prosthetics, and Orientalist armor," enacting mock raids, speaking orcish, and performing shamanistic rituals. In the course of these gatherings, one participant told Davis, "sometimes it's very difficult to remember it's not really happening."[50]

In the same way, inspired by the ten-foot-tall blue-skinned indigenous humanoids of the planet Pandora, online Na'vi communities sprang up quickly after the movie *Avatar* appeared in 2009. One site defines "Na'vi 'Kin" as "those who are Na'vi in human form. Be it reincarnated Na'vi, Na'vi on a mental level, or spiritual Na'vi, we have one thing in common— we are Na'vi, truly, in our hearts and at our cores."[51] Tutorials in the invented tongue, constructed by a retired professor, are popular, too. Na'vi are one of the life-forms claimed in the heterogeneous online Otherkin community, in the words of one website "an assortment of people who have come to the somewhat unorthodox, and possibly quite bizarre, conclusion, that they identify themselves as being something other than human." The true self, though currently reincarnated as human, may be vampire, angel, werewolf, or other supernatural entity, and one's physical shape may show deformities indicating this secret identity ("back muscle problems from 'supporting' wings"). A number of explanations for this conviction, including "mental aberration," are put forward; in the end, says the writer, invoking the mantra of personal gnosis, "it comes down to personal belief."[52]

Having brought their favorite author's world out of a book and then into their own lives, the Na'vi 'Kin and the blue-skinned orcs are right at the edge of, and close to erasing, that critical line between imagination and belief. Even so, between these two groups of Secondary Believers and a third group we might call the Primary Believers yawns a particularly large gap. The step from consuming and/or performing to creating a spiritual practice or worship that attempts to connect to a nonmaterial dimension of reality is a big one, and only a small minority attempts it. Beyond those subcommunities that have formed a worshipful relic- and talisman-based relation to the stars of the TV show *Star Trek* (strands of hair and blood samples from the actors in the series sell at conventions for thousands of dollars) lies, for example, the thirty-year-old Church of All Worlds, taken from the pages of Robert E. Heinlein's *Stranger in a Strange Land* and turned into a bona fide religious organization with the New Age adjuration of human divinity: "Thou Art God! Thou Art Goddess!"[53]

The transformation of Secondary Belief from a temporary state of mind into an enduring experience of Primary Belief is the bridge that allows certain individuals to leave behind not just the world of the Muggles but also the realm of fandom as they enter a brand-new, but also very old, territory.

3.

Now to Lovecraft. What kind of Secondary World did he create, and how do his fans inhabit it?

Along with the city of Providence, a deeply Gothick-tinged New England past served as Lovecraft's *locus inspirationis*. His story "The Case of Charles Dexter Ward," a dark-mirror history of Providence, includes many features of the Old Goth worldview shared by the seventeenth-century New England dissenting sects, notably the interpenetration of the material and immaterial worlds and the quest for immortality during life.[54] Sorcerers and the occasional witch (women characters are few and far between in his stories) represent token nods to the more notorious aspects of New England's Puritan past, but these figures seem perfunctory next to Lovecraft's true and deeply original subject, those misshapen horrors from "beyond the stars" he called the Great Old Ones.

In a typical Lovecraft story, the protagonist (who is also often the narrator) either encounters or discovers he is related by blood to, or descended from, a ghastly horror of distorted size and form. This encounter or realization either triggers or is coincident with his own regression into the antihuman creature. By story's end he is either mad (and, conventionally, writing from an asylum) or engulfed and metamorphosing into an alien creature himself. In the context of his non-Christian but Puritan-influenced cosmos, hellfire has been replaced with oozing slime.

Framing this simple narrative pattern was an elaborate cosmogony of extraterrestrial beings—what his fans (not Lovecraft himself) called the "Cthulhu mythos," after the entity we have already met, who lies in a state of suspended animation in his ruined city deep beneath the Pacific Ocean. They also include the blind idiot god Azathoth, the demiurge Nyarlathotep, and Yog-Sothoth, another mediating entity who wanders in space and is capable of assuming various loathsome forms in our reality. By the merest accident, through developing the simple cellular organisms that became their slave species the Shoggoths, the Great Old Ones are responsible for the creation and evolution of life on earth, including humankind. As our detached and indifferent creators, these monstrous entities stand in relation to humans as Dr. Frankenstein did to his own Gothick monster, which from their point of view is us.

That's the pure, unadulterated, stand-alone Lovecraft. Multiple hybrid *babewyn* Lovecrafts also survive in the revisions he performed on aspiring writers' stories, in effect turning them into part of his own oeuvre. In addition to these symbiotic collaborations, over the last eighty years Lovecraft's distinctive matrix of deities, hapless humans, and horrific predicaments (not to mention all those fake *Necronomicons*) has provided the raw material for a dizzying spectrum of spinoffs. Today's Lovecraftiana is an immense uncharted territory that, like some of his monsters, just keeps on getting bigger. Commercially sold literary knockoffs—especially the dense cluster of fake scholarship around Lovecraft's invented grimoire the *Necronomicon*—are legion.[55] In the global arena, the Japanese pop concept of *kawaii* or "cute" was translated by an American toy company into an infamous "cute Cthulhu" blood-spattered plush doll, one of many markers of the twenty-first-century shift to the good (or at the least harmless) monster.

In 1981, Chaosium Press, a major purveyor of Lovecraft-associated wares, brought out the popular role-playing game *The Call of Cthulhu*, which now enjoys a multinational audience of players. The rules follow the narrative arc of a typical Lovecraft story, but with the distinctively different goal of defeating the Great Old Ones via brainpower and scholarship, thereby avoiding physical and/or psychic disintegration (as in the original), or by employing the impressive array of magical and mundane weaponry customary in other role-playing games. Another twist on usual gaming rules is the substitution of losing "Sanity points" instead of gaining physical punishment points during encounters with Lovecraft's monsters. "An increase in an investigator's Cthulhu Mythos points," the rulebook tersely states, "always lowers his or her maximum possible Sanity points."[56]

The Call of Cthulhu has its own fan convention, the Cthulhucon, and is available in French, German, Spanish, and Japanese as well as English. Chaosium's twenty-year commemorative edition of this game in 2001 was bound in leather and printed in sienna ink on high-quality paper; by its thirty-year mark the game was still thriving along with a sizeable stable of spinoff games. For the aspiring writer of Cthulhu mythos fiction as well as the role player (a distinct overlapping of functions is apparent here), encyclopedias, reference and character lists, and guidelines are plentifully available. In 1996 the Lovecraft mythos was translated into an action videogame, *Quake*, and the phenomenon shows no signs of slowing down in the new century.[57]

The vast domain of cinematic influence exerted by the Lovecraft mythos stretches far beyond the handful of Lovecraft stories that have been directly adapted to the movies with middling success: from H. R. Giger, the Swiss painter and production designer whose work includes the Lovecraftian monster that shares top billing with Sigourney Weaver in Ridley Scott's *Alien* (1979), and Guillermo del Toro to countless other horror directors, screenwriters, and production designers who pay homage to his dark universe.[58] The drowned spirit Davy Jones in the popular *Pirates of the Caribbean* series, to name only one example, sports Cthulhu's octopus face. Lovecraft's presence in comics and graphic novels is equally ubiquitous, including an homage in Alan Moore's *Watchmen* and the writer's own fictionalized story in the graphic novel series *The Strange Adventures of H. P. Lovecraft*, also adapted to film.[59] Davis argues that Lovecraft is that rare beast among writers, a true "genre originator" whose "narrative tropes, atmospheric imagery, and monster lore [have been elaborated] into an intertextual web that, like all realized genres, congeals into an archetypal reality more powerful than any specific instantiations of the material."[60]

If we divide the world of Lovecraft fandom into the same three groups of consumers and performers (Secondary Believers) followed by spiritual practitioners (Primary Believers), some similarities and differences with the continuum of other fan groups emerge. Even though his monsters owe nothing to Christian theology and Lovecraft himself was vehemently atheistic, his fictional universe follows the post-Reformation Protestant pattern of restricting the supernatural exclusively to that which provokes terror and fear. Unlike, for example, the vampire subgenre, which has followed the new twenty-first-century arc of evil villains morphing into sympathetic heroes and, ultimately, guardian angels and beneficent gods, the Lovecraft opus and its proliferating offspring (with the notable exception of the "cute Cthulhu" toy and its offspring) have proved mostly resistant to this millennial sentimentalizing of the demonic, staying true instead to the classic dark Gothick tradition. Consequently, many Lovecraft aficionados from all three groups—consumers, performers, and spiritual practitioners—conflate his Great Old Ones with the dark side of Christianity, though practitioners, as we will see, commit to shamanic energy rather than Satanic powers in the usual sense.

The Lovecraft consumer fan base has also resisted some other post-1970 transformations in the fan world. Unlike other sci-fi gatherings, up through

2001 the principal Lovecraft convention, the NecronomiCon (since disbanded and reorganized as a general fantasy-horror convention in Florida), remained 80 to 90 percent male, no doubt because of the almost exclusively masculine universe, monsters included, his characters inhabit.[61] That's the respectable center of Lovecraft fandom, the committed consumers: an initially adolescent male culture of literate, sensitive boys who often, though not always (based on my own informal survey), grow up to be scholars or filmmakers. Further down the continuum of Secondary Belief among group two, the performers, are the lifestyle emulators, in this case young men who imitate the writer rather than his creatures: they dress like Lovecraft in cheap suits, eat canned food (the frugal Lovecraftian diet), and only ride the bus (as he did) on their frequent hejiras to Providence.[62]

Many ardent Lovecraft fans participate in the annual graveside ceremonies at the Swan Point Cemetery marking the author's birthday in August and his death date in March; another ceremony takes place at Halloween. An astounding ten to fifteen people per day visit Lovecraft's grave, often leaving flowers, books, trinkets, and masks. Such visits and ceremonies constitute what I would call an unconscious religious rite, as opposed to a conscious one; it's the gray zone between groups two and three, performers and believers. A darker interactive note, however, was struck by a real-life event with an eerie echo of a Lovecraft story. "The Case of Charles Dexter Ward" contains the fictitious news headline "Nocturnal Diggers Surprised in North Burial Ground," after the eponymous main character returns to Providence and begins digging up cemeteries looking for his ancestor's grave. On December 4, 1997, under the headline "Lovecraft's Grave Disturbed at Swan Point," the *Providence Journal* recounted an episode in which persons unknown tried unsuccessfully to dig up the family burial site.[63] There is no way of knowing if this attempt at grave robbery was a prank or an actual attempt to retrieve Lovecraft's bones for ritual purposes.

The most flamboyant "performers," in both senses of the word, have been, first, the postpunk rock musicians of the early 1980s and, second, the enormous Goth subculture that grew out of this music and is still with us more or less in its original form thirty years after that style of rock morphed into other directions. The original Goth bands drew their aesthetic and style of self-presentation directly from Gothick horror movies.

They wore scary costumes and death's-head makeup and decked out their performances with fog effects and faux bats, a style that quickly caught on with their fans and spread to rock nightclubs. Starting in the later 1980s, the internationally known rock musicians who made Lovecraft their muse not only drew lyrics, titles, and overall inspiration from his works but also pushed the Goth-Satanic link to its limit. Along with bands explicitly named H. P. Lovecraft, Yog-Sothoth, Azathoth, and NecronomicoN (described as a Canadian "spiritual occult death metal" band) are many, many others inhabiting a specific Goth/Satanic/Lovecraft-framed sensibility. The group GWAR's lead singer, Oderus Urungus, reportedly wore "a spiked prosthetic appendage nicknamed 'The Cuttlefish of Cthulhu,'" and their 1990 album *Scumdogs of the Universe* has a track called "Horror of Yig."[64]

Fans began to imitate the look of these bands, and Goth quickly morphed into a lifestyle that was also fed by the burgeoning Gothick vampire fiction and film of the late 1970s. The self-conscious irony of the original Goth musicians turned more serious and occult among their followers. Because it figures prominently in Bram Stoker's *Dracula*, the town of Whitby became the site of the biggest Goth festival in the United Kingdom in 1993, a celebration that is still being held annually.[65] That same year saw the publication of Poppy Z. Brite's novel *Lost Souls*, featuring the androgynous male Goth vampires Zillah, Molochai, and Twig, who "outlined their features in dark blots of makeup" and "teased their hair into great tangled clumps."[66] Post-2000, Goths divided into many new sub-subcultures as the scene leaped to the Internet and proliferated there.[67]

As Secondary Believers, Goths "believe that the dark parts of the soul are just as important as the bright parts," in the words of a carefully neutral work on Goths directed at mainstream teens and available at your local public library. "They focus on those dark parts because they see beauty in them," the author says, going on to say that Goths' attraction to darkness includes "moonlit nights, haunted houses, cobwebs, graveyards, and candle-lit rooms." They are deeply into music and feelings, frequent graveyards for the tranquility these places offer, and believe we must understand death before we can fully appreciate life.[68] All these qualities could be equally ascribed to Thomas Gray or any other poet of the late eighteenth-century Graveyard school of poetry, though Gray, so far as is known, did not indulge in piercings or tattoos.

Like the Lovecraft practitioners and the vampire subculture, the Goths themselves don't see their world as dark. As a Goth fan/filmmaker, Blair Murphy, says: "The entire Goth/vampire/pop funerary subculture is actually about rebirth, and what we are seeing is actually a phoenix rising from the grave."[69] Amazingly durable for over thirty years, overall the Goth scene appears to have fallen off somewhat since the turn of the millennium. Former Goths have cited the 9/11 bombings in New York and the shootings at Columbine High School in Colorado as key turning points that damaged the credibility of the lifestyle.[70]

A few of the original rock bands (such as Tool, whose members are Ordo Templis Orientis initiates and declare the group itself and its music as a religion) belong to the Primary Believers in the Lovecraft fan spectrum. These are the small number of dedicated individuals who take this writer's fictional universe entirely seriously and attempt to harness its perceived powers for their own ends. These spiritual groups and magic practitioners share a hundred-year-plus genealogy that starts from late nineteenth- and early twentieth-century self-described occult groups, heirs of a cultural Victorianism that had previously embraced Theosophy and Spiritualism.[71] Though Theosophy in particular drew from Hindu and Buddhist esoteric traditions, the famous Hermetic Order of the Golden Dawn, which counted W. B. Yeats as a member, incorporated the same strands of Western esotericism that had been carried to the New World by the seventeenth-century dissenting Protestant sects. Like so many others, Golden Dawn initiates subscribed to the idea of the "Divine Self" and the ability of human consciousness to control the material world. Alex Owen parses their magical practices involving astral travel adventures (which William James aptly dubbed "inner romances") as "an extraordinary and controlled performance of the conscious 'I' . . . [as] a shaper of individual psychic reality."[72] As we saw in chapter 2, this early twentieth-century doctrine of shaping reality through consciousness carried straight through to the "intentional" spiritual communities of a hundred years later.

A key figure in these early groups, Aleister Crowley (1875–1947), broke away from the Golden Dawn to join Theodor Reuss's Ordo Templis Orientis (or OTO), a group that was influenced in turn by the rituals of Freemasonry and Carl Kellner's Hermetic Brotherhood of Light. Here he created the template for twentieth-century "magick," as he termed it, in his Thelema ("Do what thou wilt") creed: developing "powers of will and imagination" with the goal of projecting them into another dimension and thereby becoming oneself a kind of divinity.[73] Crowley's disciple Kenneth Grant made up a chart drawing parallels between Lovecraft's universe and Crowley's (for example, Lovecraft's Yog-Sothoth and Crowley's Satthoth), claiming they experienced the same inner reality with no knowledge of each other's work.[74] Grant also discusses Crowley's technique of "barbarous names of evocation," simplistic repetition of a language with no meaning by which the magus connects to the other world, a tool that would be widely adopted by the Lovecraftian covens.[75] Grant's New Isis Lodge, by his own account, performed sex rites involving a priestess and eight prosthetic feelers, a scenario that would have had the notoriously proper Lovecraft spinning in his grave at Swan Point.

Also following closely in Crowley's footsteps and helping to cement the notion of a "Lovecraft/Crowley Axis"[76] was the American showman-charlatan Anton LaVey (1930–1997, real name Howard Stanton Levey), who founded the Church of Satan in San Francisco during the tumultuous 1960s, naming his Order of the Trapezoid after Lovecraft's "Shining Trapezohedron," the magic stone featured in the story "The Haunter of the Dark."[77] Pointing out that Lovecraft's "theme of a constant interrelationship between the constructive and destructive facets of the human personality is the keystone of the doctrines of Satanism," LaVey (or rather, his disciple Michael Aquino, who actually wrote the piece) asserts that the rites around Lovecraft's monster gods show an egalitarian advance over those of other religions:[78]

> The concept of worship is strikingly absent from the Cthulhu mythos. . . . [The gods'] relationship to their followers is invariably that of teachers to students. Compare the description of a Lovecraftian ceremony to a Christian mass or a Voodoo rite and it is clear that the element of servility is definitely lacking in the first.[79]

Aquino (at LaVey's request) composed two Lovecraftian rites included in *The Satanic Rituals*, titled "Ceremony of the Nine Angles" and "The Call to Cthulhu." Billed as "translations," what Aquino in LaVey's voice has come up with here is a not-bad imitation of Lovecraft's Aklo, which he dubbed Yuggothic after Yuggoth, a planet Lovecraft invented as a stand-in for Pluto.[80] Both rites conflate Cthulhu with Satan, who, following the

Crowley tradition, is not the "evil scarecrow of Christian myth" but positive cosmic energy, "a being not evil but rather independent, assertive and creative."[81] The Nine Angles rite calls upon all the Lovecraftian gods as well as the "gaunts" (a reference to the "night gaunts," specters Lovecraft claimed had haunted him in nightmares since childhood). The purpose of both rites is somewhat vague except as an affirmation of a path through this "World of Horrors," but Nine Angles avers that in the course of human deification "the time shall come when the gaunts will bow before us, and man shall speak with the tongues of the hornless ones."[82]

Though the Church of Satan, as channeled through its charismatic leader, was as much showbiz as it was a new religion, it did spawn (if I may use this word) the breakaway Temple of Set, founded by Michael Aquino. On the Temple's webpage an essay by Dame Patricia Hardy, GME, makes reference to the Church of Satan rituals written by her husband, Michael Aquino, and further describes their purpose ("to destroy old horizons and bring new ones into being") as well as useful mood-enhancing devices, including lighting and music, for practicing "Lovecraftian Workings."[83] It is from this Temple of Set that some current Lovecraft magic sects, still calling themselves the Order of the Trapezoid (OTr), trace their ancestry and share grandmasters (such as Aquino and Hardy).

One of these groups, Starry Wisdom (under the umbrella of the Order of the Trapezoid but calling themselves Setians after Aquino's Temple of Set), is named after the invented cult that is the subject of Lovecraft's story "The Haunter of the Dark." The cult in Lovecraft's story, as the OTr official website explains, "possessed a stone, the Shining Trapezohedron, through which they received hidden and unearthly knowledge."[84] These Setians declare that "the ability to build an objective foundation is vital to the exploration of subjective/receptive states," and they are dedicated to studying academic subjects related to their pursuits: everything from quantum mechanics (for manipulating the physical world) to comparative anthropology (for shaman and dream states). Knights and Dames of the Trapezoid devote themselves to pursuing goals that include "comprehension of the ideas of eternity and infinity; survey of the methods and tools born of the night sky; probing of the boundaries of Self linked to ideas of space and time; mastering the creation of universes into which the Self may manifest."[85] In all, the members of the Order of the Trapezoid strive to "further the Aeon"—that is, the anticipated New Age that twentieth-century NRMs variously called the Age of Aquarius, the Aeon of Horus (after Crowley), the Aeon of Maat, and other names, sometimes adopting their own dating system from whatever point year 1 is designated to be.[86]

The Lovecraft groups' debt to the larger Neopagan/Wiccan religious movements is also reflected in a treatise posted by the practitioner-scholar Stephen Flowers on the OTr website concerning the "Gothick God of Darkness." This Hidden God, he tells us, "who dwells in a spiraling tower fortress and who has guided and overseen our development from time immemorial . . . has remained concealed but very close to us awaiting the [approaching] 'future' time of reawakening." He is a "wise and dark communicator" whose legacy can help "those chosen by him" achieve "a permanent (immortal) consciousness" which is free to act or not act in the material world as it desires." Flowers's Gothick God is a familiar syncretic entity drawn from Neopagan traditions around the Visigoths, a so-called master race whose "secret traditions" have been passed down through the ages by "some as yet unknown paraphysical process" encoded in human DNA.[87]

The Lovecraft groups also fall under another umbrella category, that of Chaos magic (or magick, as its practitioners prefer, after Crowley), a late twentieth-century amalgam of practices defined by its practitioners as "the cutting edge of the occult sciences" that seeks to create a "synthesis so that science will become more magical and magic more scientific."[88] The founder of Chaos magick is generally recognized as Austin Osman Spare, a former disciple of Crowley's, and its major practitioner another Englishman, Peter Carroll, among others, but the practice of Chaos magick, with its strong Lovecraftian undercurrents, is now widely spread among all kinds of occult groups and individual practitioners.[89]

Chaos mages believe that reality is simply a construct of consciousness; to access extradimensional realities, they can draw freely from any and all belief systems in their magic ritual and still get "replicable" results. Erik Davis dubs Chaos magick "postmodern" because of the characteristic way in which it "erodes the distinction between legitimate esoteric transmission and total fiction." Chaos magicians such as Peter Carroll reject traditional esotericism; Carroll, for example, "gravitates towards the Black, not because he desires a simple Satanic inversion of Christianity but because he seeks the amoral and shamanic core of magical experience—a core that Lovecraft conjures up with his orgies of drums, guttural chants, and screeching horns." This kind of hybridized Lovecraftian magic, Davis concludes, is "not a pop hallucination but an imaginative and coherent 'reading' set in motion by the dynamics of Lovecraft's texts, a set of thematic, stylistic, and intertextual strategies" that mirrors Lovecraft's own distinctive "web of intertextuality."[90] One of the Lovecraft-based groups, the Bate Cabal, for example, describing itself on its website as a "group of media oriented, anarchistic occultists," declares that "every reality is authentic in terms of the system within which it is created."[91]

The Bate Cabal's mission statement, like those of the other groups, bears more than a passing resemblance to the rule manual of *The Call of Cthulhu* in some elements but departs from it strikingly in others.[92] Gamers and mages concur in their basic perception of the Lovecraft pantheon and the goal of gaining entry to the nonsensory realm "between the planes" (also called the "spaces" or the "angles," roughly equivalent to dimensions). The difference lies in the fact that in the game the Great Old Ones are—as they were for Lovecraft—the old-fashioned enemy to be shunned or conquered, though (because of their superior powers) never destroyed. For the mages, however, who have taken the crucial last step from Secondary to Primary Belief, they are most fervently sought out and prayed to.[93]

All the Lovecraftian rites seem to involve what the pioneer psychic researcher Frederic Myers noted as the efficacy of "devolutive" states and trauma for inducing an extradimensional experience.[94] Another magic cult based on Lovecraft and contained within the Bate Cabal is the Esoteric Order of Dagon, named after the local fraternal lodge run by the sinister amphibious half-humans in Lovecraft's great story "The Shadow over Innsmouth." An archived rite of the Esoteric Order of Dagon directed at attracting the "Great Old Ones" who live "between the spaces," proposed by a "Soror" of the Yig Lodge in Cincinnati, involves taking a "victim" chosen randomly from the group to the woods, a basement, or a pit at night. The victim was to be bound and tied, blindfolded, and subjected to a recording of "a soundtrack of bestial, barbarous and unhuman noise" for between twenty and forty-five minutes, depending on his or her endurance level. This rite is based on the principle that fear creates an empty space "or a 'hole,' as it were, which can be filled, and generally is, by the thing it is afraid of." The intense fear generated by the victim during this rite should create a "psychic vacuum" that the other members can use "to attract those Denizens of the spaces 'between' the spaces we know. These

Denizens surround us at all times, but are screened from our senses by the euclidian spatial structures which we inhabit." The rite allows the entities to break through these structures and communicate directly with participants.[95]

Beyond the specifically Lovecraftian groups, individual spiritual practitioners of all kinds have absorbed the Lovecraft mythos into their syncretic practices. In his *Pseudonomicon* Phil Hines, a well-known Chaos magician, vividly describes the sensory experience of rite-induced "Cthulhu Madness": "I felt a pressure inside my head building up—something huge trying to pour itself into me. Sensations of geological time—layers sleeting through my awareness. The heat of magma; slow grinding of continents shifting; the myriad buzz of insects. Nothing human. . . . It sounds so simple to say I heard [Cthulhu's] call—but I did. Gods do not, generally, have a lot to say, but what they do say, is worth listening to."[96]

Another individual practitioner, John L. Smith, posts an invocation on his "Lovecraftian Qabalah" webpage called "The Star Onyx, Being a Ritual to invoke the Great Old Ones, suitable for regular use by the Magician," that uses both Lovecraft's Aklo language and Enochian (the language of the angels the Elizabethan natural philosopher John Dee reported recording, taken up by the Hermetic Order of the Golden Dawn and replicated through Crowley by many magical practitioners today), the purpose of the ritual being to "activate the Spirit-Vision."[97] Still another posts a "Lovecraftian Banishing Ritual," echoing the older terminology of the Golden Dawn and mixing Lovecraft's Aklo and Michael Aquino's Yuggothic with Egyptian and astrological languages.[98]

Other practitioners have attempted esoteric dreaming techniques based on Lovecraft's invented cultic practices, also having as their goal the breakdown of rationality/sanity, the better to access other dimensions. Lovecraft himself dreamed copiously, as he related to friends in letter after letter; often these dreams contained the seeds of stories.[99] And in the stories his characters also dream, often to ill effect since their dreams open them up to the dire influence of the Great Old Ones. The "knowledge and formulae" needed to open the path to the Great Old Ones were denied to Lovecraft himself, one recent practitioner asserts, because "in waking life [he] vehemently denied the veridical nature of the material with which he was dealing" and so "the process of appropriation was almost completely subconscious, occurring through the medium of dream-experiences. As would be expected," the writer rather shrewdly concludes, "the visitation of such unhuman and ultracosmic revelations took the form of the most hideous nightmares."[100] But when I asked my friend the scholar the outcome to his youthful prayer to Lovecraft's Great Old One on the beach at Montauk, he said, "I had a very positive dream in which Cthulhu appeared to me. And after that some very nice things unfolded in my life."

So here we have a number of highly intelligent imaginations that have fastened themselves to the work of a Gothick writer dead seventy years to produce what manner of hybrid spiritual experience? Precious access, they might tell you, to a transcendental dimension of reality that the prevailing secular worldview refuses to acknowledge and that organized religion denounces outside its own doctrinal terms. Or the liberation achieved from the confines of the individual ego into "cosmic immensity," as Kenneth Grant puts it, that produces "a divine madness, an inebriation of the senses which is nonetheless perfectly and exquisitely controlled."[101]

As heirs of the nineteenth- and twentieth-century spiritual movements, the new fan-based magic and spiritual groups have gone far beyond what their forebears in the Radical Reformation dreamed of by way of restoring what Protestant Christianity stripped away.[102] Somehow, between the efforts of the Lovecraft groups and those of their sunnier counterparts the Neopagans, some modest foundation laying took place in the 1990s for broader-based new religious movements yet to come, whose scriptural-narrative source may well be a work of popular fiction or film and whose tenets will probably fit within the outlines of Harold Bloom's post-Christian American religion, as do those of many of the sects I have considered here. Now, since the turn of the century, the Gothick Gods of Darkness are undergoing a further paradigm shift as new religion builders struggle to widen their narrow palette from black and gray to more colorful hues.

Yet given a choice of transcendences—as today's spiritual arena certainly allows—the simple question must still be asked: Why would you want to worship a squid-headed entity who cares nothing about you and the mere sight of whom is likely to drive you insane?[103]

As counterintuitive as it seems to the secular imagination, monstrous deities have a long history in human religious experience, particularly in religions, such as Hinduism, that lack the strict dualism of Christianity. Within Christianity itself, outside the austerely image-free kingdom of post-Reformation Protestantism and its three bright male Gods there is a long tradition of the *via negativa* as a superior way of knowing, and chapter 10 will explore some of the Old Goth Christian monsters and monster gods.

The worship of fictional monster gods cum teachers, the quest for the divine via the transformed demonic, is part of a deep shift in sensibility that started in the late twentieth century. For those outside the pale of orthodoxy, Gothick pop culture products such as Great Old Ones, vampires, Klingons, and orcs offer the only easily accessible bridge to the transcendental. As the filmmaker Guillermo del Toro has said about watching horror movies, "Believing in supernatural things allows you to actually have a spiritual experience in a time when you cannot do that in . . . [an] uplifting way without sounding somewhat foolish."[104] And fan-critic Kirk J. Schneider further testifies: "To a large extent, I arrived at a spiritual understanding of life through horror—*my own* as well as that which I witnessed in books and movies. Although this may not be the traditional path to such a sensibility, it is a much more common one, I believe, than is ordinarily acknowledged."[105]

Small wonder, then, that when the gods speak, their language is Aklo.

An archangel mates with a female demon to produce Genesis, the entity that inhabits Jesse Custer's soul. *Preacher: Proud Americans.* Artist: Steve Dillon. Writer: Garth Ennis. © DC Comics. Used with permission.

FOUR

DECOMMISSIONING SATAN

In Favor of His Man-God Whelps

"God is dead. Meet the kids."

—Jacket blurb, Neil Gaiman's *The Anansi Boys*

I.

"A monster of vaguely anthropoid outline, but with an octopus-like head whose face was a mass of feelers, a scaly, rubbery-looking body, prodigious claws on hind and fore feet, and long, narrow wings behind"—so the horrified narrator describes a stone statuette of the entity Cthulhu in H. P. Lovecraft's "The Call of Cthulhu."[1]

Substitute snakes for octopus feelers and you have the unpleasantly transformed Lucifer in the final pages of Matthew Lewis's *The Monk*, whose "hands and feet were armed with long talons . . . over his huge shoulders waved two enormous sable wings; and his hair was supplied by long snakes, which turned themselves round his brows with frightful hissings."[2]

Thanks to the Gothick womb Lovecraft's highly original imagination inhabited, this avowed materialist's Great Old Ones carry the unmistakable stamp of Christian demonology, and it was certainly one reason so many of the Lovecraft-derived rituals discussed in the previous chapter were linked with the twentieth-century alternative religious movement of Satanism. As Christopher Partridge has argued, the "dark spirituality" of contemporary popular culture is deeply rooted in the highly dualistic iconography of the Christian church.[3] But in the decade before and after the turn of the millennium, the familiar figure of the Devil and his traditional realm have undergone a radical transformation.

There's a tangled thread to follow here. Lovecraft himself regarded his inventions as terrifying to behold and madness-inducing but supremely indifferent to humans, a position Church of Satan founders Anton LaVey and Michael Aquino would finesse thirty years later when they declared that Lovecraft's entities "are never stereotypes of good or evil; they vacillate constantly between beneficence and cruelty. . . . Critics who consider the Old Ones as Aristotelian elementals—or as a collective influence of malignancy which man must destroy if he is to prevail—suggest a philistine disposition."[4]

This doctrinal position of the Church of Satan was a harbinger of a growing trend in the Gothick imaginary and in New Age spirituality alike: neutralizing the traditionally demonic, repositioning it as an odd but equally sincere way of turning toward the divine, then handing off its transcendent powers to the Christian Devil's *babewyn* human offspring. Down in the sub-Zeitgeist, where the boundary between belief and imagination is highly permeable, Satan was undergoing the same paradigm shift that was turning vampires into undead human gods who walk the earth.

Let us pick up the story of Satan from chapter 1 at the time the youthful Matthew Lewis was writing his most famous work. In the late eighteenth century the metaphysical division of territory instituted at the time of the Protestant Reformation—heaven for God, earth for Satan— was already being abandoned by scientists and theologians alike and the stereotyped figure of Lucifer, aka Satan, aka the Devil, was growing ever so slightly camp. In *The Monk*, God doesn't manifest in the physical world; only Satan does, and grandly, first as the beautiful young fallen angel Lucifer, then taking the form of the lovely Matilda, and finally as winged monster.

Only twenty-five years later, a far more modern Satan appears in the Scotsman James Hogg's Gothick novel *Private Memoirs and Confessions of a Justified Sinner* (1824), in which the Devil, following Celtic folk tradition rather than Christian iconography, is a shape-shifter who manifests as an attractive person or a double.[5] In this story there is no pact as such, but the theological framework is that of extreme Calvinism, notably the belief that only certain people have been elected for salvation and these people will be saved regardless of the sins they commit in life. The main character's moral weaknesses are cleverly exploited by his "elevated and dreaded friend" the external tempter, causing the deluded man to commit murder after murder while still believing himself to be one of the righteous. Hogg's rendering of the hapless Mr. Wrigham's downfall, one of the most psychologically nuanced portraits of a religious fanatic in English literature, marks an important step in the move toward the interiorization of evil as a subjective state. At the end of the nineteenth century Henry James would nicely allegorize the split between these two worldviews, and literary sensibilities, in his ambivalent portrait of the governess in *The Turn of the Screw*: is the evil inside her, or is it outside? The "inside" position would come to dominate mainstream literature of the following century.

Back on the Gothick low road, however, the next big move toward subjectivizing the supernatural was Robert Louis Stevenson's *The Strange Case of Dr. Jekyll and Mr. Hyde* (1886). In this novella, aptly dubbed "Stevenson's rationalized werewolf tale," temptation has been downloaded from a supernatural agency to a material drug, a chemical accessed through a character's body instead of his soul.[6] The male body, while less vulnerable to devilish possession, is open to metamorphosis. Stevenson's twist on the Old Goth/Gothick tropes of possession and transformation would be heavily mined in superhero comics of the next century, in which physical agents (nuclear radiation, chemical pollution, etc.) are capable of transforming a male character's physical shape and abilities along with his psychological identity (the Hulk, Spider-Man), sometimes even of elevating him to a transcendental level of existence (the godlike Dr. Manhattan in Alan Moore's *Watchmen*). Unlike Mr. Hyde, however, the transformed/deformed twentieth-century superhero is usually on the side of good, not evil, and works to protect humankind.

The Adversary himself, meanwhile, banished from mainstream intellectual culture along with God, still stayed firmly entrenched in the popular imagination for the next 200 years. Satan's pacts with men, and possession of women, have endured in Gothick entertainments into the present day in more or less the same form in which they were laid down in the late Middle Ages. The difference lay in the fact that by the twentieth century deals with the Devil were embedded in an imaginary universe where Dominic's white dog was absent—that is, they were divorced from any kind of religious context in which redemption and absolution were possible. As Anne Rice's vampire Armand remarks, "People who cease to believe in God or goodness altogether still believe in the devil."[7]

In Anglo-American popular entertainments the Devil reemerged as a quasi-comic figure, a trickster who either outwits or is outwitted by his human prey. A separate subgenre of comic tales about turning the tables on the Devil by finding loopholes in his legal contract, in fact, dates back to medieval popular storytelling.[8] We see this strand of folktale tradition taken up in Stephen Vincent Benét's "The Devil and Daniel Webster" (1937–1938), a staple of mid-twentieth-century high school literature anthologies and clearly modeled on "The Devil and Tom Walker," Washington Irving's story of a century earlier. Irving's Devil, called "Old Scratch" after local New England slang, appears to the miserly no-account seeking Captain Kidd's treasure as a dark, exoticized ruffian "neither Negro nor Indian."[9] Tom Walker himself is a comic caricature of evil, and his eventual departure to Hell with attendant thunderbolts has nothing particularly tragic about it.

Benét's reworking has Webster, the famed lawyer and statesman of Irving's time, helping out an unlucky farmer who makes a vow to sell his soul to the Devil merely as an exclamation of despair. The next day "a soft-spoken, dark-dressed stranger" with eyes that glow like a fox's shows up, a deal is struck, and what follows is a balloon mortgage on the man's soul that falls due all too soon. Daniel Webster is forced to argue the case before a judge and jury of American villains chosen by the Devil himself. In the end Webster gets both his man and America acquitted by virtue of sheer oratorical excellence.[10]

John Collier, a literary writer who published in mainstream glossy magazines such as *The Saturday Evening Post* rather than the pulps, often used the Devil as a comic manipulator of fate in his midcentury cosmopolitan fantasies. In the story "The Devil George and Rosie," the Devil is a "smart and saturnine individual . . . who had the repulsive look of a detective dressed up in evening clothes for the purpose of spying in a nightclub."[11] No scaly hybrid monster, the new Devil is a trickster figure on the order of Faust's Mephisto, well educated and nattily dressed, a master of witty Shavian discourse who often nabs his male victim by exciting greed or lust and deftly outwitting him (or, in the Irving strand, getting outwitted in turn), sending him to the flames of that same mock Hell whose gaping mouth lies under the town of Sunnyside, California, where Buffy the vampire slayer will later take up residence.

Underneath comedy, of course, lies the time-honored psychological principle of converting hidden anxiety triggers (such as the physical existence of a real Satan and a real Hell and/or the prospect of life, or no life, after death) into humor to cushion their impact. Alongside these representations is the stark fact, as a 2004 Gallup poll editor states bluntly, that "regardless of political belief, religious inclination, education or region, most Americans believe that the Devil exists."[12] Christopher Partridge notes that the number of those who believe in the Devil has risen sharply since 1968 and remains consistently higher in North America than in the United Kingdom and Continental Europe. Still, he says, "the evidence suggests that such beliefs are particularly resilient and fascinating to Westerners" as compared to the rest of the world.[13]

And so it was left to the far less mainstream fare of Gothick horror to keep churning out stories of the Devil's possession of females—stories that, unlike male pact stories, are never played for laughs. Until recently, only women were depicted as possessed, and only the rite of exorcism performed by a Roman Catholic priest could expel the demon/Devil. After horror became mainstreamed in best-selling novels and films during the 1960s, this theme played out over and over again in the big-budget Hollywood exorcism films discussed in chapter 2. Even in the post-2000 *Paranormal Activity* series, each story so far has located demonic possession in the woman, not the man. *The Rite* features two possessed males, a priest and a little boy, but they remain physically intact and entirely rational while their female counterpart writhes in stereotypical agony.

Along with exorcism, another twentieth-century wrinkle on the theme of involuntary demonic possession was the motif of women as unwilling or unwitting mothers of the new Antichrist. Adapted from the Ira Levin novel, the Roman Polanski film *Rosemary's Baby* (1968), on which the ever self-publicizing Anton LaVey managed to score "technical advisor" status, famously combined pact and possession in a tale of a woman impregnated by the Devil during a Black Mass as payment for the deal her ambitious husband has struck with him.[14] *The Omen* (1976), once cleverly dubbed "*The Exorcist* for Protestants," tells the story of a baby switched at birth into the home of an American ambassador and his wife; various sequels follow this son of Satan through murder and mayhem on his quest to become president of the United States.[15] In *End of Days* (1999) Satan tries to mate with a human female by the last hour of the last day of the old millennium so that he may reign over the earth for the next thousand years.[16] Fortunately, thanks to Arnold Schwarzenegger in the role of a valiant ex-policeman, his plan is foiled.

It was a foregone conclusion, however, that sooner or later this venerable Gothick theme would circumvent the female human vessel entirely and jump straight to the twentieth-century transcendent, that is, outer space. In John Carpenter's *Prince of Darkness* (1987), Satan has undergone the twentieth-century sci-fi metamorphosis and is now a 7-million-year-old alien male organism who buried his "son," a viscous green "prebiotic fluid," in a sealed container on earth that Christ, also an extraterrestrial but from a humanlike race, discovers. Christ's disciples, and by extension the Catholic Church, decide to keep the container a secret, choosing to characterize evil as a strictly spiritual phenomenon until science can deal with Satan and putting the container under permanent guard (that secret department in the Vatican again). Unfortunately, science can't deal with Satan because he lives, it turns out, on the subatomic level, where empirical laws do not work. "Say goodbye to classic reality," a professor at the film's "University of the Sciences" observes, "because our substance collapses on the subatomic level into ghosts and shadows." Satan escapes from his container to parasitically possess a female student, who in turn infects other students; ultimately another female student pushes the possessed woman through a mirror into antispace, a charged Gothick territory where by story's end Satan lurks in a new female body, waiting to wreak havoc on the world again.[17]

With all this deviltry afoot, are there any signs of the other side of the good-evil equation? It is a direct heritage of the Protestant Gothick that in supernatural horror films and novels dark energy is vanquished by brute force, by a spell, or by some other technical means, never (or very rarely) by Satan's opposite number.[18] On the infrequent occasions when this entity makes an appearance, it's never in horror and usually in a big-budget Hollywood film, where he's always played for laughs—vide the cutesy God in innumerable comedy films, from George Burns in *Oh God!* (1977) to Morgan Freeman in *Bruce Almighty* (2003). (As yet, however, no jokey Jesus has taken a bow on the big screen, probably because Americans take him more seriously than they do God.) And as with the pact-with-the-Devil stories, the plots of these films often turn on a legal contract or promise the human (always male) must fulfill.

In the meantime witches, the Devil's familiars, have turned from bad to good, thanks in no small part to the surge in Paganism, Wicca, and similar alternative religions in the second half of the twentieth century. But this shift was also prefigured by such pantheistic fantasy fictions of the early twentieth century as L. Frank Baum's Oz books and even E. M. Forster's strangely prescient, goddess-invoking "Story of the Siren" (1920). Starting with the *Bewitched* television series (1964–1972), the "good witch" is now as familiar a trope as the bad witch used to be, and even the bad witches of Baum's Oz have turned sympathetic protagonists in the twenty-first-century revisionist *Wicked* (2003).

St. Dominic's dog, aka God's redemption, also wags its tail in the less common Gothick subgenre of the female character who learns she is carrying not the Devil's spawn but the Messiah and is consequently forced to fight off the gathering dark "angels" (usually not outright demons) who don't want the Second Coming to happen. In *The Seventh Sign* (1988), Jesus makes a rare appearance (in this kind of film, that is) to judge mankind in the midst of apocalyptic signs the world is ending, while a human woman about to give birth must decide if she is ready to give up her own soul to stop Armageddon.[19] In *Legion* (2010), a shiftless woman at a desert truck stop is pregnant with the Messiah just as God is about to end the world; the archangel Michael, defying God's orders, defends her and the small group she is stranded with against the horde of warrior angels, led by Gabriel, sent to annihilate the baby.[20]

Perhaps in observance of still-felt taboos, neither devil babies nor divine ones ever appear on-screen (the infamous yellow eyes at the end of *Rosemary's Baby* being Satan's, not the child's). Big-screen birthing of divine and devil children, however, was part of a late twentieth-century shift away from the former principals, Satan and God, to a new generation of hybrid offspring, incarnate demons and gods in human bodies, that were busy grabbing center stage.

These half-human *babewynes*, including Hellboy, Spawn, and assorted demigods (mostly male and mostly sired by the Devil), were born in a different medium that has arguably, thanks to its stories' wholesale conversion into major Hollywood blockbusters, become the major Gothick medium and mythmaking engine of the twenty-first century. Flying under the radar of the cultural mainstream for much of the twentieth century, comic books and graphic novels have now come into their own in contemporary American popular culture. Thanks to the deep influence of American comic book culture across all its subgenres, the postmillennial Gothick shows more ambiguous shadings between good and evil, angels have fallen very hard indeed, demons are well on the way to readopting their pre-Christian status as morally neutral daimones, and monsters turn out to be heroes.

2.

Comic books of the mid-twentieth century had much in common with the blue-covered Gothick chapbooks hawked on London and New York street corners 150 years earlier. Aimed at the lower classes, cheap and crudely printed, blue books and comics alike were crammed with the same lurid violence deplored by the middle classes of both eras, who feared (in the same way that generations before them feared servants' ghost stories) that their children's minds would be forever damaged by the contact.[21]

Historically, the origin of comic books lies in pulp fiction "picture novels" of the early twentieth century. The comics, however, quickly carved out their own distinct territories, the most famous of which was the unique alternate universe populated by men and women possessing colossal supernatural abilities. The comic books of the Golden and Silver Ages (approximately the late 1930s to the mid-1950s and the mid-1950s to the mid-1970s, respectively) gave American children and teenagers a rich pantheon of monstrous and beautiful divine humans—superheroes, superheroines, and supervillains either transplanted from other worlds (such as Superman's planet, Krypton) or alchemically transfigured through trauma linked to manmade disaster (nuclear radiation, environmental pollution, etc.), all of whom successfully concealed their demigod natures behind a regular-citizen persona. As historian of religion Jeffrey Kripal argues, in the comic book superheroes from Superman to the X-Men "divinity is relocated squarely in humanity, the miraculous is refigured as the paranormal, and traditional religion is exposed to a harsh critical light."[22] Unlike the saints and siddhis of religious tradition, the superheroes of the Golden Age gained only enhanced physical and mental abilities without the accompanying spiritual vision; they performed miracles but lacked sanctity, a situation that would change in the Silver Age of the 1960s and 1970s.

Christopher Knowles has identified Edward Bulwer-Lytton's novel *The Coming Race* (1871), with its race of superhumans residing inside the hollow earth, together with Theosophy's Ascended Masters and Nietzsche's superman, as a hybrid template for the comic book superheroes.[23] Battling megafoes using their talismanic powers, however, Superman and his cohorts could equally trace their lineage from the heroes of Old Goth chivalric romances, as Laura Miller has noted.[24] But the comics were also, as the psychologist Fredric Wertham's famous treatise *Seduction of the Innocent* (1954) pointed out in damning detail, violently, outrageously lurid, bloody, and over the top.[25] The fifties horror comics in particular, as comic book historian Jim Trombetta put it delicately, "slap[ped] the raw archetype on the reader's plate."[26]

In a word, the comics were Gothick.

Like the old Gothick chapbooks, the comics and their graphic novel successors have byzantine story lines crammed with subplots, backstory flashbacks, and rambling digressions of the sort Monk Lewis would surely appreciate. Like the recent TV serials *Lost* and *True Blood*, they show what Linda Williams calls "horizontal suspension," characteristic of a form of melodrama in which time and space have been slowed to accommodate the massive overlapping of stories and characters.[27] Alan Moore, the originating James Joyce of a later generation of graphic novelists, describes the comics' crazy-quilt Gothick supernatural universe as "jeweled with alien races ranging from the transcendentally divine to the loathsomely Lovecraftian, where whole dimensions are populated by anthropomorphic funny animals. Where Heaven and Hell are demonstrably real and even accessible, and where angels and demons alike seem to walk the earth with impunity."[28]

A further layer of hybridity was simply the by-product of canny marketing tactics as the principal comics publishers, DC and Marvel, ensured that all their series characters made promotional appearances in one another's stories. Moore again: "Try to imagine Dr. Frankenstein kidnapping one of the protagonists of *Little Women* for his medical experiments only to find himself subject to a scrutiny of a team-up between Sherlock Holmes and Hercule Poirot." Authorship became a moot point as editors created story lines, gave assignments, and otherwise erased the lines demarcating "originality." As a result, many of these amazingly complex stories had longer lives than either their human creators or readers: "Anyone picking up a comic book for the first time is almost certain to find themselves in the middle of a continuum that may have commenced before the reader's birth, and will quite possibly continue long after her or his demise."[29]

Comic books of the Golden and Silver Ages drew from the same well of Christian demonology and "occulture" that the traditional Gothick did. As part of the trend already noted, the American comics featured many more devils and demons than their European counterparts.[30] Fueled by New Age metaphysics, however, the increasingly sophisticated Silver Age comics of the 1960s and 1970s helped give Satan some new and distinctively heterodox forms. In another significant move that was a harbinger of the new Gothick, they also drew their superhero characters (such as Spider-Man, Thor, and Dr. Strange) from the monster comics of the 1950s. In *Tomb of Dracula*, a Marvel series that ran from 1972 to 1979, Dracula is usually the conventional antagonist, but sometimes he is not. In one story he goes up against Satan brandishing a cross even as it burns his hands. The last line reads: "The dark ones attacked us . . . but there was a good man here. He told us to believe in the power of God."[31] Batman, likewise, ensconced in a very Gothick Gotham City, might look like a vampire, but he is a force for the good.[32]

By this time many comic writers had become speculative natural philosophers rather on the order of John Dee or Robert Fludd and much preferred making up new cosmologies to reproducing the orthodox one. The comic book illustrators, many of whom were sophisticated artists with training in art history, followed suit. In the creative symbiosis that resulted, medieval Christian images of Hell, the Devil, demons, and marginal grotesques epitomized in the works of Dante and Bosch radically morphed into complex extended multicultural pantheons balancing good and evil gods, immortal beings, and humans with superpowers.[33]

Thus, for example, not Satan but "Shathan," a horned antithesis of God who lives in a self-created antiuniverse called Dis (named after a level in Dante's Hell), makes his appearance in the comic *Beyond the Sinister Barrier* (1966), by Gardner Fox and Murphy Anderson.[34] In Todd McFarlane's *Spawn* series (1992–), the master of Hell is not Satan but a demon called

Malebolgia, described as "the supreme master of the dark netherworld who gathers souls in preparation for Armageddon."[35] Satan is also given a wide array of demigod children begotten with humans or angels (usually sons, though with the occasional Satana, Madame Satan, or Lady Satan thrown in) whose nondemonic half can have a mitigating effect on the Satanic DNA. The pan-Gothick theme of genetic hybridity so rampant after the year 2000 (human-vampire, human–Olympic god, etc.) started in the comics.

The hero of Marvel's 1970s *Son of Satan* series is a character named Daimon Hellstrom.[36] His blond hair combed in hornlike waves, his super-hero costume emblazoned with a pentangle, Daimon makes his first appearance brandishing a trident as he drives a fiery chariot across the sky. He is, we are told in the stylized lettering that so perfectly replicates the fever-pitch breathlessness of the eighteenth-century Gothick: "MORE than man—half-human, half-fallen angel—neither MORTAL nor IMMORTAL—adversary of evil and sometimes of GOOD."

Son of Satan and a mortal woman, Daimon must recharge his soulfire in the fiery lake of Hell at the end of every night and then, vampirelike, re-treat inside his Gothick Victorian mansion on the family estate in Massa-chusetts before daybreak. There he morphs into his human form, lament-ing: "Am I always to be both heir to HELL—and—man of GOD?" (a reference to his time in a faux Catholic seminary, studying for the priesthood). Wanting desperately to be free of his "infernal heritage," Daimon has de-voted his life to exorcising demons, but he is still branded by the pentangle on his chest and is subject to fits of infernal rage.

In "The Shadow of the Serpent" episode an Atlantean priestess (replete with metal cone-cup bra and bikini) summons the astral form of Daimon and takes him on a "metaphysical junket" outside the universe so that he can see that natural cataclysms threatening the earth are actually brought on by men. Sounding eerily like the goddess Philosophia explaining the universe to the sixth-century Christian philosopher Boethius in his dream vision *The Consolation of Philosophy*, the priestess lays out to Daimon the Old Goth notion of the animistic universe that was actively being revived in the New Age metaphysics of the 1960s and 1970s.[37] "Few realize it," she states, "but the earth itself is highly RESPONSIVE to the psychic emana-tions of the creatures that INHABIT it. When those vibrations grow overly VIOLENT . . . the planet REBELS! And the STRESS is felt throughout the COSMOS as a weakening of the bonds of the PRIMAL MATRIX—the 'model' on which the universes are structured." She shows Daimon the "foundation of all life," a pentangle-shaped energy matrix of the universe that is guarded by Spyros, a giant with a hooded face and a double-edged axe. When Daimon wonders if this matrix is God, she replies that it is "not Valka himself" (presumably the Atlantean name for God), but Valka's creation.

Daimon has the choice to stand by and let the cataclysms on earth happen as a cleansing and purging, but he declares, asserting the constant theme of self-determination that is the essence of his struggle against his father (and is the mantra of the comic superheroes generally), "Man must be free to purge HIMSELF!" and steps in to save the city of St. Louis from the fiery serpent hovering above it. Then he unmasks the giant Spyros to expose the ravaged face of Adam, the first human and the first human to sin—the first victim of Daimon's father, Satan. Daimon spares Adam, whose axe strikes the serpent and dissipates it. But as Daimon warns Byron, "Earth has not been *truly* safe since the day ADAM was placed upon it." In a 1990s reincarnation of the series, featuring a twist typical of that decade, Daimon decides he must fight both Heaven and Hell for humanity's sake, and ultimately he assumes the throne of Hell himself.[38]

Daimon's last reverse apotheosis took place after the great morphing of comics into graphic novels that began in the late 1970s. With their larger format, better paper for reproducing color, and durable binding, graphic novels could be sold in bookstores and preserved in libraries. As a result, they shifted into a higher market niche that reached a wider and older (but initially still primarily male) audience. Early examples such as Will Eisner's *A Contract with God* (1978) told real-life stories of ordinary people, but the wild metaphysical virus of Silver Age comics soon invaded this new form along with a new crop of English and Scottish writers, notably Alan Moore, Garth Ennis, Warren Ellis, Jamie Delano, Neil Gaiman, and Grant Morrison. These story creators injected—as modeled by Moore's groundbreaking *Watchmen* series—a political and apocalyptic edge to their stories and a noirish tarnish on their superheroes' souls in the shadow of the approaching millennium.[39] Jettisoning orthodox Christianity in favor of the same syncretic Theosophist-oriented cosmology favored by Dan Brown and the Chaos magicians that posits the ability to inhabit divine consciousness while on earth, the 1990s graphic novel renaissance helped shape the future direction of the commingled realms of the Gothick and alternative spirituality.

The first thing to notice about the Satan of the post-1980 graphic novel is that he looks noticeably more glamorous, in a tortured Miltonian sort of way, than his comic book predecessors. In *John Constantine: Hellblazer*, Satan first appears as a muscular dark-skinned rock star with long black hair and a Byronesque shirt who is arbitrating two demons' argument over which of them possesses Constantine's soul.[40] In Neil Gaiman's *Sandman* series he appears as a similarly Romantic fallen angel, Lucifer Morningstar the Light Bringer, a reference to the literal meaning of *Lucifer*, echoing the character's first appearance in Alan Moore's *Swamp Thing*. A handsome fellow decked out in a Greek tunic and wings, this Lucifer bears a startling (and intentional) resemblance to David Bowie.[41]

More than Satan, it was his male offspring who came to dominate the graphic novels of this decade. Taking a page from *Son of Satan*, they are quite literally a mixed bag: half infernal deity on one hand and half human, angel, or whatever on the other. Demonic and human elements clash inside these half-breed protagonists in a manner congruent to the external battles they wage against the forces of destruction around them, usually accompanied by Christian-shaded apocalyptic rumblings about the end of the world and the ultimate fight between good and evil.

The character John Constantine, a down-and-dirty London magician whose job description is "to conjure and oppose demons," was also first introduced by Alan Moore in the series *Swamp Thing* in 1985. The spinoff series, *John Constantine: Hellblazer*, written first by Jamie Delano (artist John Ridgeway) and then by others, began in 1988 and became the longest-running graphic novel to date; a feature film, *Constantine*, appeared in 2005. Disillusioned and cynical, Constantine is a classic noir character embedded in the sociopolitics of 1980s Thatcherite England, a morally questionable man who still suffers guilt over harm he's (usually unwittingly) caused others and whose physical appearance was modeled on that of the rock singer Sting.[42] Early on in the series, however, John Constantine becomes a hybrid man-demon when he is forced to accept a blood infusion from his nemesis, the demon Nergal, after a failed suicide attempt arising from his guilt over the death and damnation of a girl child in a cult bust-up in Newcastle when he was a young man.[43]

Following his death, John Constantine reincarnates as an astral body zooming down from the outer spheres to a city street as he cries, "We are all gods or demons . . . exerting the energy of WILL to squeeze the anarchic creativity of nature into our image." The astral realms are rendered here in visual puns (an "astral plane" is an airplane) and other surreal images, with an explanatory note: "All these visuals are constructed by me to rationalize the essential world." There is also an undercurrent, taken up in other graphic novels, that Heaven and Hell don't leave a lot to choose from: both realms are authoritarian and flaky by turns, archaeological remnants of a fading religion. By averting a ceremony to mate a woman named Zed to angels in this episode, for example, Constantine further foils a divine attempt whereby "humanity would've become the slaves of heaven."[44]

Neil Gaiman's *Sandman* (1989–1996) features a main character named Morpheus or Dream, the personification/god of dreams who boasts a bevy of *D*-named allegorical sibling gods: Destiny, Death, Desire, Despair, and Delirium. In one episode, Dream must journey to Hell to right the injustice he inflicted on his lover Nada when he sentenced her to 10,000 years there for defying him. First, however, he sends his red-bearded emissary Cain to meet with Lucifer, who injects a bit of Christian heterodoxy when he asks Cain if he has ever heard about his followers the Cainites: "Gnostic sect, second century, they rejected the books of the New Testament in favor of the Gospel of Judas . . . They believed that *we* [Lucifer] created the heaven and the earth . . . and that the way to heaven and salvation was to give way to *lust* and *temptation* in *all* things. And no greater percentage of them turned up [in Hell]," he concludes, "than of any other religion."[45]

After 10 billion years, however, Lucifer has gotten bored with ruling Hell and wants to close it down. "Hell is over," he says, sending all its residents away. Giving a hearty French kiss goodbye to a female ghoul with a face that is half living human, half rotting corpse (yet another hybrid), Lucifer has Dream cut off his wings and departs for earth, eventually surfacing on a beach in Australia. (Later Lucifer would gain his own series with a different writer chronicling his escapades after leaving Hell.)

Gaiman was not the only graphic novelist to float the notion of Satan getting bored with ruling Hell. In Kaz's 1990 graphic story "The Tragedy of Satan," the Devil gets fed up with God for making him administer Hell and travels to earth to get a heart.[46] The comedy film *Little Nicky* (2000) picks up the *Sandman* idea with a Satan bored after 10,000 years and wanting to pass on the throne to one of his three sons. When the two older brothers fight over the succession and escape to earth, Satan sends the youngest, Nicky (another hybrid, this time with a mother who is an angel, not human), to get them back.[47]

All this is one way of saying, in sub-Zeitgeist speak, that some people, not Satan, were getting bored after 2,000 years of the same setup—and it was time for a change. What that change might be gets worked out very directly in a number of 1990s graphic novels. *Spawn* (short for "Hell-spawn"), a series created by Todd McFarlane that began in 1992 and is still running (it was also an animated TV series and a 1997 movie), is the story of Al Simmons, an African American ex-marine turned CIA operative and hit man who's murdered by his CIA director. Sent to Hell because he was a murderer himself, Al makes a deal with his new boss, the demon Malebolgia: his human soul in exchange for the chance to return to earth to see his wife one last time. Al is double-crossed again, of course, and like Daimon Hellstrom before him, he struggles—with a metal face mask, a swirly red Venetian cloak, and gloves to conceal his demon's body—to stay human and not demonic in his fights against evildoers. "For someone who didn't believe in religion," Spawn complains, "I sure got thrown into a biblical nightmare. Demons. Souls. Deals. Lies. THAT's what's in the great beyond, not some cute old man in a beard."[48]

What he got, of course, was the classic Protestant Gothick supernatural. But over the course of an impossibly complex story line that I now turn over to the anonymous wisdom of a Wikipedia summary, the traditional dark universe turns into something else entirely:

> Spawn, now given the powers of a god and the protection of the Mother, gains the power to recreate Earth, restoring everyone to life, but leaving humanity every memory of the Rapture. Both God and Satan have no role in the "new" Earth, because they're trapped in their perception of a barren Earth until they cease their seemingly endless fight, and Spawn, with his last act as a god himself, closes every door between Hell, Heaven and Earth.[49]

Following the trajectory of Daimon Hellstrom, *Spawn*'s mortal hero, Al Simmons, ends up a man-god: the immortal, morally ambiguous ruler of the universe.

In 1994 Mike Mignola created *Hellboy*, another still-current series featuring a half-human, half-demon hero in a new Gothick hybrid genre Mignola dubbed "film noir monster detective."[50] (Hellboy's reincarnation in film will be taken up in chapter 10.) In many ways a pivotal figure in the Gothick journey from dark to light, Hellboy is the offspring of a dead witch and a demon, summoned in 1944 by a resurrected Rasputin brought back from death by the goddess Hecate in league with Nazi occultists. Rasputin and the Nazis intend Hellboy, "born of human woman in hell, reborn of human design on earth," to be none other than the Great Beast, brought forth in the world to usher in the Norse era of chaos known as Ragna Rok.[51]

Instead of manifesting to the evildoers, however, the rebirthed juvenile Hellboy jumps the fence and appears in a fireball to the good guys channeling him in a ruined abbey elsewhere in England. From this classic faux Catholic setting, in which medieval sacred murals and a large crucified Jesus figure prominently, Hellboy is taken to America and raised by his loving English scientist surrogate father in the secret government Bureau for Paranormal Research and Defense. Grown to manhood, he's a bright red Hulk-sized muscular demon with sawed-off horns, a right hand made of stone, and a devil's tail. Though he can't rid himself of his great stone Hand of Doom, he protests, "If I am from Hell, I have no memory of it! I don't know what it looks like."[52]

Displaying the blurring of traditional boundaries between good and evil, antagonist and protagonist so prominent in the new Gothick, Hellboy is simultaneously inverted Jesus and fighter of evil, son of Satan in Hell and direct descendant of Arthur, king of Britain, through his human mother. Bred to be the Beast of the Apocalypse, brought up as a cigar-smoking, wisecracking American tough guy, he rewrites his destiny to remain steadfastly on the side of good. A triumph of nurture over nature, Hellboy is one of many sacred monsters to populate the twenty-first-century Gothick pantheon of demigods and demigoddesses.

In this magic, shifting world where a mongrel dog transforms from one frame to the next into the fifty-foot monster-god Anubis, Mignola, like Gaiman, has folded a syncretic brew of Lovecraft and Norse, Greek and Egyptian mythologies into his own invented mythos, which has its share of nonmale dark divinities. His Lovecraftian seven-bodied collective dragon, Ad-Jahad, is neither male nor female. The witches of Thessaly are women who "call down the moon" and change into monstrous birds and animals; their ruler is the "hellish, heavenly, and earthly Hecate, goddess of crossroads, witch queen, gorgon-eyed terrible dark one . . . thirsty for blood and the terror of mortal men."[53]

The sophisticated, irreverent, and gross-out gorefest series *Preacher*, created in the mid-1990s by Garth Ennis, a northern Irish writer who had worked on the Constantine series, and the artist Steve Dillon, is the story of Jesse Custer, a car thief turned preacher (both occupations thanks to his fraught childhood in the clutches of a demonically Gothick grandmother in Louisiana). One Sunday, while delivering a scathing sermon in church, Jesse has the fortune or misfortune to be possessed by Genesis, an infantile hybrid creature, half demon and half angel, just escaped from heaven. Genesis's cometlike entry into Jesse's body obliterates his congregation in a nuclearlike blast and gives Jesse powers rivaling those of God. The Lord himself, it turns out, quits Heaven the instant this happens and goes into hiding on earth, leaving two sets of angels, the administrator Adephi (feckless males in blue thermal underwear) and Seraphi (scary warrior angels) in charge. They immediately send a hit man to destroy Genesis because "it holds a power like unto that of God almighty. It seeks to join with the spirit of mortal man: if it succeeds, the two together will know the secret of paradise as no other mortal has done." And, adding the obligatory apocalyptic note: "TOGETHER they could END US ALL."[54]

Genesis, Jesse tells his girlfriend Tulip, was "something never happened before—a mix of demon and angel, a *NEW IDEA*." When she questions the possibility of "good and evil together," Custer answers, "Because Genesis was a new idea, it was as powerful as either of the old ones [good and evil]. . . . I think it's as strong as God almighty." This new idea now incarnated in him is "just as strong as [God's] old black-and-white bullshit."

In a plot twist that clearly reveals Ennis's familiarity with Dan Brown's muse *Holy Blood, Holy Grail* (which came out in England before its U.S. publication), a secret organization called the Grail, located in a heavily fortified location in southern France known as Masada, is also interested in finding Genesis (and Jesse). Why? Because for 2,000 years they have been protecting the familial line of Jesus—who, as it happens, paid off the officials, survived crucifixion in a drugged coma, and had three children with his wife, Mary, before being run over by an offal cart at the age of forty-eight. (When he hears this, Jesse comments only, "If God can go missing from heaven, why can't his son fake the crucifixion?")[55] Meanwhile,

Jesus' children were taken to the desert, where they were allowed to mate only with each other. When the Grail moved to Europe in the sixth century, Jesus' descendants came, too.

The last of Jesus' line, however, shows the unfortunate effects of two millennia of inbreeding: he's an idiot boy who pisses on the roses and mutters, "Suffer the little children! Humperdumperdoo! . . . Fisher of men! Humperdom!" and has to be stopped from chugging a gallon of pesticide while chanting "Changed it into wine! Humperdido!" Or as Jesse succinctly puts it, "Son of God or son of man. . . . You can't fuck your sister and expect much good to come of it."[56]

Since God has quit (there's no mention of Satan here) and Jesus' idiot heir is accidentally squashed in a coup to depose the Pope-like Allfather, Jesse by default becomes the new godhead, a man-god entity combining the old Christian opposites of good and evil, as the warrior seraph who was the father of Genesis explains: "The being in your mind joined with your soul: it knows all that ever came to pass in heaven. Every action. Every reason . . . It is more than power. It is sentience and instinct and memory. All it lacks is will." The last quality, will, is what Jesse, its human host, provides, along with the resonant name of Jesus' forefather.[57]

What does Jesse do in the glory of his ascension? Following his only mentor and spiritual counselor, John Wayne (who once gave Jesse's human father a "Fuck Communism" cigarette lighter), in the best American cowboy/superhero tradition he breaks free of society's constraints and rides off into the sunset (for the time being, naturally) with his girl in a stolen car.

The saturation of mainstream popular culture by radical Gothick demonologies has had an impact on devout Christians who consume Gothick works of fiction alongside the Bible, as chapter 11 will explore in greater detail. Though there is no shortage of Christian comic books (notably those of the prolific fundamentalist author-publisher Jack T. Chick) proselytizing orthodox doctrine, the ubiquity of decidedly heterodox spins on Christianity was bound to create some theological confusion. In posts dated 2002 and 2004 on the Baptist Theology and Bible Study forum, a message board limited to Baptists only, Ben W. asks on the thread titled "Does Satan have a son called Mammon?":

> I watched that film by Keanu Reeves—*Constantine* which loos[e]ly
> follows a story about how Mammon the son of Satan leads a rebellion

and the demons that follow him attempt to enter from the Spiritual Realm into the earth. In researching the term Mammon, is it [*sic*] either a Syrian term for money, or it is suggested that the way it is rendered in the Bible means that Mammon is a deity who uses lust for money to ensnare people. Interested in your thoughts. . . .

The poster Soulman answers:

IF Mammon were the son of Satan he certainly would not be d[ei]ty. Satan is an angel and it is NEVER mentioned in scripture that he had a son. The movie *Constantine* is just that. A movie. Entertainment. No scriptural accuracy or real basis. Garbage. Ben, [i]sn't it amazing what folks can come up with?

Sound information, but one wonders if the recipient will be able to erase from his mind the vivid impression the movie demons left on him. And another poster, Old Regular, only adds to the problem when he demands to know, "Just where in Scripture does it say Satan was is an angel?"[58]

The more interesting social and theological implications, such as they are, lie in the selective translation of *Preacher* and stories like it to the big screen. Starting as early as the late 1980s with *Superman* and *Batman*, growing exponentially and building to a dizzying peak in the first decade of the twenty-first century, all these characters—Constantine, Hellboy, Spawn, Preacher, and virtually every other comic and graphic novel superhero and antihero ever invented—vaulted out of their narrow Gothick niche into global pop culture via the medium of blockbuster film. What does the spectacle of these twenty-foot-high men-gods suggest? First off, in the historical context of the war-consumed opening decade of this century, the exaggerated muscles and armature of superheroes such as Iron Man on the big screen suggest nothing more than suited-up American combat soldiers in the Iraq and Afghanistan conflicts. (It may be no coincidence that the original Iron Man was co-created by Don Heck, the Leonardo of World War II and Korean War comic book covers.)[59]

But this big-screen saturation also suggests, in the metaphysics of American sub-Zeitgeist popular culture, that the Christian God and Satan have both left the building, leaving their half-human, half-supernatural offspring poised to take over. The universe, fate, or man-made warping of nature in the form of nuclear radiation or environmental pollution has granted all these human demigods powers equal to or surpassing divine and demonic ones. Since the new divine humans mostly trace their Gothick lineage to Satan, not God, and thus partake of his dark nature, good and evil are no longer discrete opposing categories. Good seems to spring not from a divine source—since most of the angels in these stories are as blasé and corrupt as the demons (and they're *all* muscle-bound warrior-killers)—but rather from the human, nonsupernatural side of their nature.

In the global setting, finally, the elaborate Gothick cosmologies of comic books have been added to, hybridized, and transformed by graphic novelists, animators, and filmmakers of other cultures, notably Asia, to produce an even more wildly syncretic universe of imaginary beings. After 1990, the pendulum swung from imperial Disney-centric America to Japan, where writers, animators, and game designers were busy erecting elaborate new fantasy universes on the foundational narratives of U.S. pop culture. As we have already seen, Japanese manga and anime have enthusiastically embraced the faux Catholic in spite of the latter's cultural incongruence, so it comes as no surprise that the Christian Satan was present in Japanese manga as early as the 1950s.[60] One commentator notes that the prevalence of the Christian Devil and many other seemingly indigestible elements of the Western Gothick in Japanese manga stems from the circumstance that "Shinto . . . is polytheistic, which means that gods from other religions can be accepted and assimilated."[61] Reverse Asian influence on the Anglo-American Gothick through comics and film will be further explored in chapter 9.

The paradox remains that even as belief in Satan seems to be on the increase in the United States, his presence in the Gothick imaginary here and abroad has become less prominent. In shifting story lines over the last three decades, Satan looks to be stepping down in favor of half-breed, morally ambiguous action heroes who ultimately opt for the light. The Devil has signed over his territory to others besides his children, however. We must also take into account the two other dark supernatural figures whose roles in the Gothick often overlap with his: Death and Dracula. Together, all three figures—Satan, the vampire, and the zombie—make up the Gothick black Trinity. By the year 2000, however, the vampire had almost completely supplanted Satan as the primary Gothick antagonist, only to brighten curiously into protagonist or heroic lover in the following decade (as chapter 6 will explore). Then came Death in the form of zombies, now vying with vampires for the Gothick World Cup of the Undead (see chapter 7). Both figure prominently in the new postapocalyptic subgenre of Gothick novels, graphic novels, and movies, where Satan no longer merits even a walk-on part.

What's been missing so far in all this Thanatos, however, is its opposite number, Eros. Before there was a Gothick, way back in the Old Goth Middle Ages and stretching beyond that into time immemorial, the mythic role of wooer, of the fatal lover who cannot be resisted, was perversely reserved for the original guy himself.

Let the Devil's son make way for the bride of Death.

Death takes the bride. From *Danse macabre des femmes*, ms. 995, Bibliothèque Nationale.
Bibliothèque nationale de France.

FIVE

GOTHICK ROMANCE

The Danse Macabre of Women

Death: Take my hand, pretty Bride.

Let's go take off our clothes;

There's no more work for you

You will come to bed in another place.

—From *Le danse macabre des femmes*

"The Age of Romance," Thomas Carlyle said a long time ago, "has not ceased; it never ceases; it does not, if we will think of it, so much as very sensibly decline."[1]

I first read *Jane Eyre* at the age of twelve, in a Signet paperback edition with a fake sepia cover drawing of a young woman considerably more beautiful than Charlotte Brontë's heroine claims to be. It was summer in Encinitas, north San Diego County, California; I'd already burned through the paperbacks on the single rack at the town's Rexall drugstore, so I mail-ordered it (along with *Ivanhoe*, which I never got around to reading) from the publisher in New York for 35 cents plus postage scotch-taped to a piece of cardboard cut to fit the envelope. Like the twelve-year-old girls today who gobble up the *Twilight* series, I devoured *Jane Eyre* the minute I got it in my hands. Poleaxed by Romance, I read it again, and again, and again. Treasured it, kept it. Today the ancient paperback's fragile yellowed pages disengage from the binding as I turn them, calling up a memory of the tattered Gothick novels in the Hammond Collection.

Brontë's tale of an unglamorous, independent-minded young woman who captures the heart of her arrogant, sexually dangerous older employer not only drew a huge and still-growing readership, it also established— in the year 1847—another major subgenre of the Gothick: the sentimental romance that is still coming-of-age reading for young women everywhere. There were sentimental romances before the Gothick, but they were mostly not written by women. By the same token, the female writers of the classic Gothick, including Clara Reeve, Charlotte Dacre, Sarah Wilkinson, and many others besides Radcliffe, exerted an enormous influence on Brontë and her successors, but their novels do not belong to the Gothick subgenre we now know as women's romance.

First, a quick look at that slippery term *romance* and its kissing cousins *Romance, Romantic, romantic,* and *roman.* All of them, and their historically linked meanings, derive from the ancient cultural matrix of Rome. Modern European Romance languages (Italian, French, Spanish, Catalan, Portuguese, Romanian) are the end products of regionally mutated Latin after the fall of the Roman empire. In the Middle Ages, *romance* was the term for a tale translated from Latin into one of these tongues. Gradually the category came to include a wide-ranging group of vernacular poetic and prose narratives glorifying either combat or love, from earlier chivalric epics such as *The Song of Roland* to the great French thirteenth-century flowering of literature in dream vision poetry, including *The Romance of the Rose* and the legends of King Arthur in the lais of Chrétien de Troyes and Marie de France. The nostalgia these stories of love and adventure expressed for an already vanished feudal past—a fond look backward that would surface again in the later English metrical romances—made the medieval romances themselves, arguably, the first examples of "medievalism."

In the early nineteenth century, Gothick and Romantic writers alike wrote self-styled prose and poetry "romances" of knights and ladies in Old Goth times, but it was the sensationalistic Gothick writers who fixed that term for a wide readership as a prose fiction recounting extraordinary events set in far-off times. Horace Walpole, as we have seen, described *The Castle of Otranto* as "an attempt to blend the two kinds of romance, the ancient and the modern"—that is, a way of combining the fantastic and supernatural elements of the medieval form with his own age's growing taste for realistically drawn characters.[2] Sir Walter Scott's "historical romances," starting with *Waverley* in 1814, added fact-based regional and historical detail to the by then familiar Gothick convention of stories set in the medieval past.

Such tales stood in sharp contrast to the new (hence "novel") long-form prose fiction that focused on everyday life.[3] Since then, the term *novel* has replaced *romance* in the English-speaking world for every kind of long prose narrative save one: today's literary genre of romance (a love story geared to women readers), along with the adjective *romantic* in its narrower meaning of "amorous." (To add to the confusion, *roman* in its simple sense of "fiction" remains the generic word for "novel" in French, German, and some other modern European languages.)

In his famous apology for the genre in its oldest and broadest sense, the critic Northrop Frye declared romance to be an extremely stable literary form over thousands of years, from the so-called Greek novels of the Hellenistic world through the kind of prose tale that he saw as constituting the "bulk of popular literature" in the second half of the twentieth century. For Frye, the "improbable, desiring, erotic, and violent world of romance" is not inferior to the more realism-oriented world of the mainstream bourgeois novel; in fact, he argued, most new literary conventions emerge directly from popular literature, "with romance at its center." Tellingly, his defining example is the Gothick novel, which, he noted, had appeared "just as the eighteenth-century English literary neoclassicism of Pope and Swift was beginning to ossify."[4] With this assertion Frye implied that Romantic and Gothick should not be thought of as two separate literary movements, one high and one low, drawing from the same sources; rather, the Gothick should be regarded as the foundation of the Romantic. Given the primacy of the Gothick in the fading sunset of the modernist-postmodernist twentieth century, Frye might find cause for reflection about what is coming next in "high" literature if he were alive today.

The road from the classic Gothick to today's romance genre is not a perfectly straight one, however. Because of its particular heritage, the women's romance took a particular direction in the English-speaking world, and once again there are eighteenth-century Gothick and medieval Old Goth sources to contend with.

First, the Gothick: Walpole and his male successors liked to pit a helpless young woman against a devilish villain whom she is going to be forced to marry *(The Castle of Otranto)* or who forcibly ravishes her *(The Monk)*. This role of imperiled young female, furthermore, is often doubled (or even tripled, in the case of *The Monk*): one female dies at the hands of an older man in a position of power, another lives to marry the devoted young man her own age. In the female-authored Gothicks that followed Walpole, in contrast, the single heroine (whose point of view we usually inhabit) escapes the villain's clutches and marries the young man. Where the early male Gothick writers, drawing directly from the medieval romance tradition, used a faux medieval aristocratic cast of characters, the women Gothick writers frequently introduced a bourgeois female protagonist into the mix.[5] Where male authors favored supernatural elements, female authors—most famously Radcliffe herself—liked to titillate their readers with ghostly, chill-inducing phenomena before revealing the human agency behind them.

Using alternating third-person points of view that shifted rapidly between male and female characters, Walpole and his male heirs cast the fervent emotion of the Gothick in conventionally stylized terms ("How cutting was the anguish the good man felt, when he perceived this turn in the wily prince!" etc.).[6] In foregrounding a single female protagonist and telling the story chiefly from her point of view, Ann Radcliffe and the other women writers who made this genre their own typically displayed a more nuanced attention to the inner world of their main characters, as in this exchange from Anna MacKenzie's *Mysteries Elucidated* (1795):

> "You are melancholy, my beloved Ella," said Adela, who had remarked the changes of her ingenuous countenance. She started—it was a welcome interruption, and broke the clue of her ideas, which she was happy to follow no further.[7]

Radcliffe herself remains the queen of intensely felt subjectivity. Emily, the heroine of *The Mysteries of Udolpho*, is sensitive, *too* sensitive; she interrupts her father's last words with so much fainting and sobbing that he is obliged to leave off dying to warn her about her excess of "sensibility."[8]

It is just this emphasis on feeling that marks the Gothick female writers' championing of what would soon be the hallmark of the Romantic movement: internalization and subjectivity. Terry Castle has argued that Radcliffe, like the English Romantic poets, shifted the locus of transcendent from an external, extradimensional realm to the inner world of human consciousness, creating a "supernaturalism of mental space" in the intense love yearnings the more sensitive characters feel for each other. Pointing out that the word *mystery* in the title of Radcliffe's most famous novel represents that era's secularization of the word (from the Latin *mysterium*, "secret rite," or its Christian sense as the sacred redemptive events in the life of Jesus), Castle says that for Radcliffe, as for the Romantics to come, "the new mysteries are those of the imagination."[9] The female Gothick writers, in short, preferred to see their ghostly mysteries elucidated in the human heart. This displacement of the numinous into consciousness stands at the beginning of an arc that culminates in the twentieth century's extreme high-art psychologizing of the supernatural, best represented in Virginia Woolf's claim that "it is at the ghosts within that we shudder, and not at the decaying bodies of barons or the subterranean activities of ghouls."[10]

The obvious gender differences in works by Gothick novelists of the classic period led the critic Ellen Moers to coin the useful term "Female Gothic" to refer to all works in this genre written by women.[11] Many critics after her, including Castle, Julia Kristeva, and Eve Kosofsky Sedgwick, have examined the gendering of Gothic in different ways.[12] Anne Williams believes that the male Gothick, culminating in its overreaching hero's death, is tragic, whereas female Gothick—like the original medieval romance, like folktales, and like Shakespearean comedy—"demands a happy ending." The heroine "experiences a rebirth" through marriage, with the "imagined threat dispelled." Such gendered patterns still operate in, for example, Bella's happy reincarnation as a vampire married to her vampire love in Stephenie Meyers's *Twilight* series and the fiery death of the camerlengo, "an isolated overreacher punished for his hubris" if ever there were one, in Dan Brown's *Angels and Demons*, respectively.[13]

Looking further back to Old Goth times, the roots of these gender differences are visible in the historical period the Gothick drew inspiration from: for the male Gothick, in what Erich Auerbach called the *avanture* narratives of chivalric romance ("trial by adventure," a form that would be deliberately imitated by medieval scholar Tolkien in his mid-twentieth-century Gothick *Lord of the Rings* trilogy); for the female Gothick, in the twelfth-century *fin amor* or courtly love traditions unique to European culture that were absorbed into the allegorical dream vision poetry and romances as well as folktale motifs.[14] With few exceptions that we know of (Marie de France being the most notable), authorship of the mostly anonymous romances of medieval times was presumably male and so were their fictive protagonists. This was also mostly true of the Romantic movement that revived the form, which makes it an interesting fact that Mary Shelley, whose husband Percy Shelley and close friend George Gordon, Lord Byron, made up between them the great second generation of English Romanticism, popped up on the Gothick side of the fence to write a quintessentially male Gothick romance—for both the protagonist of *Frankenstein* and his monster are male, and the ending is tragic.

If male protagonists and tragic outcomes are the criteria, Anne Rice's Vampire Chronicles 150 years later is also male Gothick. Joseph Sheridan Le Fanu's late Victorian erotic vampire story "Carmilla" (1872), however, told from the point of view of its female protagonist, is an interesting hybrid: the heroine escapes death from the female vampire bent on possessing her, but her narrative is interspersed with bits of factual "official" testimony that break the subjective mood. And notwithstanding its frame of a fireside tale told by a wellborn male, Henry James's *The Turn of the Screw* (1898)—with its hapless governess heroine operating in the vacuum of a hoped-for romance with her aristocrat employer that never happens—is pure female Gothick. The fastest-growing subgenre of women's romance today, finally, is "paranormal" romance, which overwhelmingly foregrounds the supernatural, formerly the provenance of the male Gothick, in a bewildering array of forms. Given these and many more anomalies, the category of female Gothick might be modified simply to include any work of Gothick fiction, by either a male or female writer, with a woman as protagonist and a plot that conforms to Anne Williams's useful synthesis.

Female Gothick is most certainly the category to which *Jane Eyre* belongs. Published two generations after Radcliffe, Lewis, and their contemporaries, only one generation removed both from the great Romantic poets Byron and Percy Shelley and from the last of the classic-period Gothick novelists, Charles Maturin and Mary Shelley, Brontë's work gave the female Gothick a radical twist, setting a template for the small-*r* romance genre that still obtains today.

Jane Eyre has all the classic Gothick elements—a cynical, womanizing, Byronically wicked nobleman, an impoverished heroine who is at his economic and erotic mercy, and an ancient family mansion haunted by a malignant being that is revealed, in the best Radcliffean manner, as no specter at all but the master's flesh-and-blood psychotic wife.[15] Though Brontë gives Jane moments of paranormal clairsentience when she "hears" Rochester calling her from many miles away in a moment of crisis, Radcliffe's explained supernatural becomes synonymous, in this foundational narrative of the sentimental romance, with explained wickedness.[16] And in the best manner of both male and female Gothick, the cursed ancestral mansion ultimately burns to the ground.

So far, so good. But meanwhile Brontë has been busy transforming the most crucial Gothick convention of all: the flawed, power-mad male principal/antagonist who declines into evil and ultimately dies. In her refashioning, the despot villain of the late eighteenth-century Gothick, though still arrogant and domineering, is revealed to be an innocent man victimized by his mad wife; Edward Rochester sincerely seeks true love and finds it in the arms of his dear "mouse," the governess. Through separation, suffering, and expiation—he is left blinded by the fire set by his wife that consumes the mansion, a physical injury and psychological humbling that, along with a convenient inheritance for Jane, helps dismantle the social and economic barriers between them—the lovers are happily united in holy matrimony.

This is the classic happy ending of medieval romance oddly grafted onto the shell of a horror story and thus, we might say, ultimately more Romantic than Gothick in sensibility. It's as if Isabella in *The Castle of Otranto* found herself against all reason attracted to the tyrant Manfred, learned he had not done any bad things after all but was merely the victim of jealous gossip, and dropped the insipid Theodore/Frederic as her dreaded arranged marriage to Manfred is revealed to be the hoped-for happy ending. Or that Emily in *The Mysteries of Udolpho* discards her own blandly upright Valancourt in favor of the charismatic Montoni. Just this set of plot twists became, in fact, a favorite stratagem of twentieth-century Regency romances: a penniless but respectable heroine is forced into marriage with a cold, insolent aristocrat only to find perfect happiness with him after their clashing wills find romantic resolution. The darkly attractive character is always suspected of all sorts of crimes and sexual profligacies (the structural echo of his former role as villain), but in the end he is proven innocent (explained wickedness) and pledges lifelong domestic fealty to the heroine.

The deep character on whom this Gothick transformation is enacted is, of course, the familiar Old Goth figure of Satan. The Devil, as we have seen, stayed front and center stage in the male Gothick from *The Monk* through late twentieth-century graphic novels. He figures in the female Gothick in a more shadowy but intriguing way. Mario Praz was the first to point out the strong resemblance of Montoni in Radcliffe's *Udolpho* and the priest Schedoni in her *The Italian* to Milton's brooding fallen angel Lucifer in *Paradise Lost*, on whose face "Deep scars of Thunder had entrencht . . . under Browes / Of dauntless courage, and considerable Pride."[17] Lucifer was the template, Praz argued, for the Gothick's flawed, hubristic male aristocrat, whom he dubs the *homme fatal* or fatal man. As identifying traits of the *homme fatal*, Praz lists "mysterious (but conjectured to be exalted) origin, suspicion of a ghastly guilt, melancholy habits, pale face, unforgettable eyes."[18] His less frequent female counterpart, the Gothick *femme fatale* or fatal woman, is embodied in Matilda, the demon temptress of *The Monk*.

In the Romantic generation that followed Radcliffe, Lord Byron (famously styled by his lover Lady Caroline Lamb in her diaries as "mad, bad, and dangerous to know") self-consciously adopted the *homme fatal* persona in his life as well as in his work, even jesting that he had "lifted his scowl" from Ann Radcliffe's villains.[19] Both Lamb in her Gothick roman à clef *Glenarvon* (1816) and Byron's disillusioned young physician John Polidori in *The Vampyre* (1819) used the poet as their model for the villain/fatal lover who is irresistible to women and brings about their destruction. The outline of this hybrid Milton-Byron-Polidori human Lucifer is clearly visible in Edward Rochester, as Jane Eyre describes him: "He had a dark face, with stern features and a heavy brow; his eyes and gathered eyebrows looked ireful and thwarted. . . . [H]e searched my face with eyes that I saw were dark, irate, and piercing."[20]

Brontë's sister Emily also flips villain into lover in *Wuthering Heights*. This unique and brilliant novel, published the same year as *Jane Eyre*, belongs squarely in the category of male Gothick, not sentimental romance. As irresistible as he may have been to Cathy, Heathcliff remains an unreconstructed demonic figure, a destructive and untamed force of nature. Compared to this male fury, Charlotte's misunderstood Edward Rochester looks puny indeed, especially in his final state of humbled incapacitation. Emily Brontë, of course, draws even more heavily than her sister on both the literary Satan and folkloric demon figures in her ever-raging "dark-skinned gypsy" Heathcliff, as this barely secularized demon is seen through the eyes of the housekeeper Nelly Dean on his deathbed:

> Those deep black eyes! That smile, and ghastly paleness! It appeared to me, not Mr. Heathcliff, but a goblin. . . . "Is he a ghoul or a vampire?" I mused. I had read of such hideous incarnate demons. And then I set myself to reflect how I had tended him in infancy, and watched him grow to youth, and followed him almost through his whole course; and what absurd nonsense it was to yield to that sense of horror. "But where did he come from, the little dark thing, harboured by a good man to his bane?" muttered Superstition, as I dozed into unconsciousness.[21]

Whereas in *Wuthering Heights* the fatal man retains his wild, death-dealing nature to the end, in *Jane Eyre* this figure is redeemed by the woman who loves him. (Let it be noted that no equivalent literary transformation of a *femme fatale* into a loving, faithful helpmate springs immediately to mind.)

Paradoxically, *Jane Eyre* loses its erotic charge in exact proportion to Rochester's transformation from bad to good. Rochester ends up a maimed and chastened shadow of his former self; Heathcliff's demonic rage, in contrast, never diminishes, nor does his perverse charisma. The aura of danger and evil surrounding the *homme fatal* is precisely what constitutes his sexual attraction, and it is a problem romance writers have struggled with ever since. What is it, exactly, about the lover who promises destruction, the demon lover who offers the "kiss of death," that makes him so irresistible?

The erotic link between sex and death taps into mythic constructs that stretch much further back in time than medieval Christian demonology and its secularized echoes in the Gothick. Behind Heathcliff, Rochester, and Edward Cullen, behind even Satan, stands the older, mightier figure of Death, Lord of the Underworld. Behind the persecuted woman stands the bride of Death, Queen of the Underworld, the virgin sacrifice—the young person whose untouched sexual energy will nourish the god beyond the grave. These mythico-religious figures were personified as Hades and Persephone in the ancient Western world; European Old Goth Christianity gives us an immediate forebear in the form of Death personified as the Lord of the Dance.

The visual emblem of Death leading people from all walks of life in a circle dance was introduced by a school of painting in Paris during the plague years of the late 1400s, and the emblem of the danse macabre spread rapidly across the Continent and to England. Philippe Ariès comments that for fifteenth-century Europeans the figure of Death was "less an allegorical character than a supernatural agent that has taken the place of the angels and devils to execute the decrees of God. . . . He is not altogether on the side of God, whose decrees he executes, nor of Satan, whose realm he fills. He communicates with a hidden world which, in the fifteenth and sixteenth centuries, he helped reveal: a world that emerges from the depths of the earth and from the interior of the body, inhabited by worms, toads, snakes, hideous monsters."[22]

During the plague years, the image of the danse macabre changed from communal dance to intimate pas-de-deux between Death and individual men and women from all walks of life. In the celebrated late fifteenth-century illustrated poem *Danse macabre des femmes*, Death calls to his dance not just the bride depicted in the frontispiece to this chapter but thirty-five other women, including a wet nurse, a bathhouse attendant, a theologian, a prostitute, a saleswoman, a shepherdess, a duchess, and a queen. In this shift we see that, in Ariès's words, "the former master of ceremonies [in the dance of death] has become a hunter of humans."[23]

Explicit eroticism, however, does not surface until the next century, when Death taking the bride (along with the nun, the baker, and everyone else) becomes Death taking *a* bride. Shakespeare has Romeo exclaim in disbelief:

> Shall I believe
> That unsubstantial Death is amorous,
> And that the lean abhorred monster keeps
> Thee here in dark to be his paramour?[24]

but by the end of the sixteenth century "Death and the Maiden" had become a familiar visual arts convention throughout western Europe. Made popular by painters such as Niklaus Manuel and Hans Baldung Grien, these images of a half-corpse figure or a skeleton embracing or kissing a beautiful young woman as he drags her off to his tomb would be enthusiastically revived two centuries later by Romantic poets, painters, and composers. Sometimes Death is even shown biting the young woman's neck, an indigenous western European trope that would later transfer seamlessly to the Gothick vampire romance.[25] By this time, the "lean abhorred monster" was also arguably more attractive than his worm-eaten fifteenth-century predecessor. As a consequence of the new scientific study of anatomy, Death was reimagined as a bare, spotlessly clean skeleton stripped of all rotting, maggot-infested flesh, a sanitized icon that would reign supreme for 400 years until the mainstreaming of the zombie in global pop culture around the year 2000.[26]

In the sentimental romance as shaped by Charlotte Brontë and her heirs, the motif of the bride of Death or Satan serves as titillating bait for readers, but it is not the overarching blueprint. Even as the outlines of the painted-over devil are still faintly visible under the gilded angel's wings, the apparent villain transforms himself into the true hero. Death is cheated of his victory and the descent to the underworld is averted. The female Gothick, Anne Williams argues, is a positive quest genre that involves Psyche's search for Eros, not Hades or the Devil. In contrast to the male Gothick's "individuation through violence, conquest, and the establishment of a hierarchy with the conquering hero at the top," the female hero's journey is one of emotional development in order to enter into relationship. Marriage is the "goal of the quest, the establishment of the self that can exist only in relation to others." This establishment of self is possible only at the story's "blue-sky happy ending," when the male villain/hero, thanks in large part to the transformative powers of the love he feels for the heroine, is revealed as a good man and loyal mate, not (as is always first feared) a devil.[27] The story structure of women's romance, contemporary romance writers Linda Barlow and Jayne Ann Krentz further insist, propels the heroines on their own very active knightly *avanture* "quests to encounter and transform these masculine creatures of darkness."[28] Transformation happens to the heroine as well because her lover is able in turn to deliver her to her true self. The integration of the masculine and feminine that heterosexual marriage represents is also by this account the "integration of the internal self" both in the heroine and in the female reader.[29]

Throughout its history, the women's romance has always embodied a Gothick-Romantic mix of dark medievalisms transmuting to fairy-tale brightness. As Williams has pointed out, the genre is very much in the spirit of Keats's faux Catholic "Eve of St. Agnes," which the poet admitted was itself influenced by the writings of Ann Radcliffe.[30] In this narrative poem packed with images drawn straight from the Gothick novels—moldering castle, aged friars, cold winter wind blowing the dead autumn leaves, et cetera—the *homme fatal* baron and his guests toss and turn under the pressure of their standard-issue nightmares of witches, demons, and coffin worms as Porphyro and Madeline flee the charged Gothick space, heading straight for that blue sky. At heart the women's romance is not really about death, even though that is its Gothick departure point. It's about love as liberation and rebirth.

Literary critics have not been kind to Gothick romance. Fred Botting has dubbed contemporary women's romance "girly-girly Gothic" after Mark Twain's label "girly-girly romance" for the identical literature of the nineteenth century.[31] Traditionally, Gothick scholars and literary critics alike have delivered scathing and condescending critiques, and commentators have noted the continued low status of the women's romance in mainstream culture despite being statistically the most popular literary genre. (In the year 2010 romances constituted about 21 percent of U.S. retail book trade, and the figures are comparable elsewhere.)[32] Increasingly, however, younger scholars and its reader-based champions have raised their voices in protest. "To attack this very old genre, so stable in its form, so joyful in its celebration of freedom," complains Pamela Regis, "is to discount, and perhaps even to deny, the most personal hopes of millions of women around the world."[33]

Forever impervious to bad press in all its subgenres, in this case the Gothick had mutated Romantic *and* romantic to produce a hybrid formula that has proven just as durable as the classic dark Gothick. From *Jane Eyre* through the late twentieth century, the formulaic cover illustration of any 1970s Gothick historical romance paperback—a distraught young woman in a long gown with the dark outline of a castle or ancestral mansion looming behind her in the moonlight—made a perfect palimpsest for Jane and Thornfield Manor. Edward Rochester was the prototype for 150 years of romance novel "devil-heroes" as the secularized demon aristocrat lover was housebroken over and over again in a ritual mating dance in which male eyebrows were cocked, arched, and lifted (always ironically) and female chins were tilted, tipped, and cupped.

All that changed somewhere around the year 1990.

As part of an unparalleled hybridization of Gothick subgenres during that decade, women's romance underwent an explosive growth process, producing a range of new variants that grafted the female Gothick onto other previously separate genre categories. In place of the two rigid mid-century categories "historical" and "contemporary," new romance story types borrowed the frames of hard-boiled detective, time travel, science fiction, and fantasy.[34] The traditional single first-person voice of the female protagonist was replaced by multiple points of view, particularly that of the male lead, thereby allowing the reader, in Wendell and Tan's words, "to experience the process of falling in love from both [lovers'] perspectives."[35] Most striking of all was the intrusion of two elements formerly associated only with male Gothick: sex and the supernatural.

The introduction of explicit sex into what had formerly been a virginally discreet genre was in part a reflection of the major shift in women's social roles in the late twentieth century. The shift was foreshadowed during the 1970s and 1980s by a queasy new romance convention licensed by, though not quite in the spirit of, the sexually liberated 1960s: this was the almost obligatory rape of the heroine early on in the story by the man she will eventually fall in love with and marry. Most often featured in historical romances that allowed a reader to suspend the mores of the times she lived in (hence the nickname "bodice rippers"), rape became the extreme but ubiquitous version of the classic romance story arc in which the domineering male attempts to force his will upon the heroine, only to be conquered in turn by the depth of love and passion she inspires in him.[36]

In the pivotal 1990s, however, this dubious trope gave way to sexuality of all shapes and sizes in the woman's romance. Not surprisingly, the first venue devoted solely to erotic romance, Ellora's Cave, was fan based. It began as a rogue website in 2000 and grew to become a major online publishing player. The 2009 Ellora's Cave website listed its erotic romance categories as "capture/bondage," "contemporary," "historical," "paranormal," "romantic suspense," "time travel," "western," "vampire," "werewolf/shape-shifter," and "futuristic/sci-fi"; by 2011, themes and imprints had multiplied exponentially.[37] The new subgenre officially went mainstream in 2005, when the classic romance publishers Harlequin, Avon, and Penguin created their own erotica imprints.[38] Gone now (except in a handful of subgenres, such as the very popular Amish romances, nicknamed "bonnet books") is the single kiss or passionate embrace between the heroine and her lover as the sole marker for the consummation of their love.[39] In its place are detailed erotic scenes that can happen almost from the first meeting. These erotic romances carry perhaps a faint echo of the more libertinish male Gothick novels of the late eighteenth century, but in the long history of the women's romance they are unprecedented.

Even with all the new flavors, however, the structural conventions of the classic sentimental romance remain so strong that they tend to trump those of the genres they have blended with: soft-core pornography is essentially framed within a heterosexual relationship that is monogamous after the first encounter.

In outer space or contemporary Manhattan, in the year 3000 or in Regency London, a charismatic Byronic hero and a strong-willed heroine will meet, hate, fall in love with, and ultimately pledge eternal loyalty to each other. Even in highly erotic stories, the spine of the story remains mostly, and somewhat incongruously, the same: a fiery initial clash between two indomitable wills violently attracted to each other, a subplot in which the apparently dubious character or activities of the male lover are gradually revealed to be good, their reconciliation and his pledge of absolute monogamy at the end. He dominates, she challenges; he conquers sexually but in the end is bound by sexual fidelity.

What prompts this unlikely about-face in sexual habits? The conventions of the new Gothick romance demand that the male lover's (and far less frequently the heroine's) promiscuity is permanently quenched by what the "Smart Bitches," romance critics Sarah Wendell and Candy Tan, have wittily dubbed the "Magic Hoo Hoo," or best sex ever, dispensed by his new mate.[40] It's like nothing he's ever experienced before, ever, and very quickly brings him to his knees, so to speak. It is also a convenient device for guaranteeing the time-honored status quo of middle-class heterosexual marriage in the face of the potential disruptions of unbridled sexuality.

Stephanie Laurens's 1998 Regency historical, *Devil's Bride*, offers a good example of a traditional romance writer juggling these old and new erotic conventions within a hybrid mystery-romance. The heroine—in a mild twist, an aristocrat of independent means who hires herself out as a governess only to exercise her skills as a teacher—meets her future mate in a familiar, if more heated, version of Jane Eyre's first encounter with Rochester on horseback: "A massive black stallion screamed and reared over her, iron-tipped hooves flailing within inches of her head. On the beast's back sat a man to match the horse, black-clad shoulders blocking out the twilight, dark mane wild, features harsh—satanic."[41]

The rider's nickname, appropriately, is "Devil" (his male relatives are Scandal, Demon, Gabriel, and Lucifer), and the novel's back cover sums up the classic romance conundrum the story presents: "Was he the husband of her dreams . . . or a devil in disguise?" When Honoria's reputation is compromised by spending the night with Devil as they guard the body of a murder victim in a storm, he insists they marry, mainly because he desires her so intensely. Honoria refuses, on the surface because she wants her freedom and wishes to travel to Africa, but in reality because she has been profoundly traumatized by the deaths of a younger brother and sister.

As the murder mystery subplot works its way through the story, Devil's lust is transmuted into love and his mother tells Honoria he is a "good man" under all the wild behavior. When Honoria's own sexual desires are awakened, he refuses to satisfy her until she has pledged to become his wife with her full heart. This she is able to do after Devil's own life has been put in jeopardy and she realizes the depth of her feelings for him. Their marriage, which takes place after they have several episodes of perfect initiatory sex that relieve Honoria of her virginity, occurs two-thirds of the way through the story instead of at the end, where the old conventions would have it. This displacement of the traditional romance climax and resolution allows the unveiling of the murderer to provide the final plot point and resolution in this mixed-genre romance-suspense tale.

In other romance subgenres, however, fault lines were rapidly appearing in the foundational tenet that the story must close in a traditional monogamous relationship between a man and a woman. In the 1990s Laurell K. Hamilton and Poppy Z. Brite introduced heroines who were not tied sexually to a single partner; in the latter case the sexual partners were not necessarily male. Multiple partners, nonconventional "couple units," and same-sex romance erotica (with male on male being especially popular with female readers, a preference that fan slash fiction also demonstrates) represented a small but growing component of women's romance as it moved into the twenty-first century.

The second big change of the 1990s was the ditching, in many of the new hybrid subgenres, of the Radcliffe "explained supernatural" model.

As part of the larger post-1960s mainstreaming of supernaturalism out of its pulp and B movie ghetto, werewolves, vampires, supernatural creatures, and otherworldly phenomena of all sorts have completely overrun the traditional world of romance. Gone forever are the teasing hints of ghosts but in the end no ghosts at all, only a very human lover. The dominant subgenre of women's romance is now the paranormal romance. (*Paranormal*, of course, is one of those great twentieth-century euphemisms, like *extradimensional*, that gives the old-fashioned supernatural a quasi-scientific spin.) Editors express surprise at the current ubiquity of the paranormal romance, vaguely hypothesizing that it taps into "age-old longings" as they genuflect to a bona fide commercial behemoth.[42]

As this new trend developed over two decades, the heroine herself, taking on the male warrior role for the first time, was initially represented as a foe of the traditional dark-side supernatural. Inevitably, however, this character began literally and figuratively sleeping with the enemy, and pretty soon she wound up "Changed" into a new member of the other side, which suddenly started looking not so dark after all. In the post-2000 paranormal romances, as Sarah Wendell and Candy Tan have pointed out, the old rape theme plays out on a different level when the heroine, following the possession trope of demonology, is Changed against her will into a supernatural creature. After losing her humanity/virginity, she must adjust to the consequences of her forever altered, but also weirdly empowered, existence.[43] This is the arc traversed, for example, over the numerous volumes in Hamilton's Anita Blake, Vampire Hunter series (1993–), but it can also be traced as an overall pattern in new Gothick fictions of all descriptions. (The vampire subcategory of the paranormal romance will be the subject of the next chapter.)

A precursor of this trend by a literary writer working outside the romance genre, Hillary Mantel's *Fludd* is a late twentieth-century bridge novel that throws some light on the direction these stories would take. The Gothick women's romance always had its high literary satirists, starting with Jane Austen and *Northanger Abbey*, and many twentieth-century Anglo-American women writers in the psychological-realist tradition (including Iris Murdoch, Muriel Spark, Margaret Atwood, and Joyce Carol Oates) have also tried their hand, seriously as well as satirically, in this genre. Mantel's novel *Fludd* (1989) is something different, however. A hybrid Gothick supernaturalist satire, it still falls more in the classic romance category than this author's other arguably literary Gothick novels *The Giant, O'Brien* (1998), and *Beyond Black* (2005). Featuring a dangerous stranger and an imperiled woman who are erotically attracted to each other, *Fludd* launches an insider's (not Protestant) faux Catholic attack against (among other targets) shallow attempts to drag a superstitious flock into the modern era. Mantel replaces the stock figure of Satan as *homme fatal* with a shadowy transgressive supernatural figure, based on the sixteenth-century natural philosopher Robert Fludd, who brings the story to its pre–Vatican II (and pre-Enlightenment) alchemical resolution.

The charged Gothick locus of Mantel's black supernatural comedy is St. Thomas Aquinas, a decrepit Gothic Revival Catholic church in the hinterlands of 1950s provincial England. The church's "music-hall medievalism" of mongrel architecture and cheap stained glass still harbors within it, mysteriously, "aggregations of darkness, with channels of thicker darkness between." In that haunted space stands a bevy of plaster saints that the benighted parishioners (who, as their long-suffering priest declares, are not Christians but "Catholics and heathens") worship in a haze of tribal confusion about the magical properties each possesses. The saints' statues have attracted the ire of the parish's ambitious bishop, who brands them as "idolatry" and—in an eerie echo of the stripping of the altars during the English Reformation—orders the priest, Father Angewin, to remove these superstitious relics of the old image-based religion from his church.[44] At the critical moment when the bishop helpfully suggests that Angewin may need an assistant to help him, footsteps sound in the empty room above them and the priest feels an invisible hand brush his arm. The very atmosphere itself is materializing to produce what is needed to effect supernatural Change.

After the priest has the statues buried in shallow graves behind the church, a Gothick knock on his door late one stormy night reveals "a tall, dim shape, a man wrapped in a dark cloak, holes for mouth and eyes." This shape resolves into "the figure of a young man" in clerical costume who remains, for the rest of the story, very hard for the other characters to perceive as a physical body. The moment this entity introduces himself as Fludd and announces he's come to stay, however, the alchemical process officially gets under way.

Alchemy, that amalgam of Old Goth medieval Aristotelian science and heterodox religiosity, is all about "releasing spirit from matter," as the newcomer Fludd puts it. It is both a material and an immaterial process, a "transformation . . . of body, soul and spirit" all at the same time.[45] According to its vitalist principles, an adept can transmute materials in the world outside him—turn lead to gold, find the lapis or philosopher's stone—only if he is working a similar moral transmutation inside himself.[46] The sham curate Fludd, an alchemist who has transferred his work from metals to human beings, rightly declares, "I think I can only help myself," adding significantly, "And make, perhaps, one or two little adjustments in the parish."[47]

Make adjustments is exactly what Fludd proceeds to do in all the principals, but most especially in Sister Philomena, a young sister from Ireland who belongs not in the nunnery but in the world. In a slow seduction as delicately titillating as one any old-style romance writer could create, Fludd liberates Philly to her true self, aka Roisin O'Halloran, via sexual initiation. But it is a very unusual seduction, since the rules of alchemy demand that the instigator must be Philly herself and not this mysterious newcomer. Fludd knows he "can't light the furnace" for her; furthermore, "the spark must be set" not by Philly herself but rather, in a blasphemous echo of Mary's impregnation by the Holy Spirit, "by a shaft of celestial light" paradoxically experienced from within.

When they first meet secretly in a chilly outdoor shed, then, it is to have an earnest theological discussion. In the course of their conversation, Philly feels warmth that builds slowly to a "Mediterranean frenzy of heat." Fludd, startled, wonders if the transformative process, the heating of the vessel, has begun in her. It has, and Fludd in turn feels himself having human, fleshly desires for the first time as he lays out for Philly a very Hermetic interpretation of Christian doctrine. The thing they must both murder, he tells her, is the past, not the flesh. "I think we must accommodate our bodies, you know. I think we must find some good in them. . . . [G]race perfects nature. It doesn't destroy it."[48] Later that night, back at the nunnery, he takes off her cap and the pins in her hair, kisses her, tells her she knows what she must do.

Like the lovers fleeing the baron's castle in "The Eve of St. Agnes," Fludd and Roisin escape from St. Thomas Aquinas and the nunnery straight to the clean sheets of a good hotel in Manchester. In a total upending of romance convention, however, Fludd doesn't stick around to pledge lifetime fealty after taking her virginity. By giving her "Heaven instead of Hell," he has indeed delivered Roisin into the journey of her true life, but as an embodied principle of change, he "cannot travel the route on [her] behalf."[49] This is in fact the covenant of the "Alchymical Wedding," the internal union of opposites within the self, that takes the place of real-life marriage for Roisin, *née* Philomena.

What Fludd also gives her—in a nod to the lead-to-gold prosperity quest that is equally important in the alchemical process—is a hefty wad of money to start this new life with. Reflecting on the fact that he has left her this instead of a love note, Roisin correctly concludes: "This money is like love. . . . Once you have some, once it has come into being, it can go on multiplying, each part dividing itself, doubling and doubling like the cells of an embryo. . . . And they say it's the root of all evil. Well, Protestants say that. Catholics know better."[50]

Roisin gets her own blue sky happy ending when she walks out of the hotel alone to find that the leaden city of Manchester has also turned to gold:

A ground-frost forms a gilded haze over the pavements, and great buildings, the temples of commerce, shimmer as if their walls were made of stone. . . . [E]verything about her . . . seemed to her to have been freshly created—made overnight, manufactured by some new and ingenious process that left them clean and hard-edged and resplendent, faces immaculate, pavements without a stain.[51]

In this newly transformed world she can go anywhere, do anything—and she will. The former bride of God is reborn not as the bride of Death but as a human woman with her life before her.

Back at St. Thomas Aquinas, Fludd's catalyzing presence has triggered the digging up of the buried saints and their restoration in the church, the turning of alcoholic Father Angewin's whiskey into healthful water, and the transfer of a disfiguring wart from the person of his housekeeper to the dreadful Mother Perpetua, the abbess with "tombstone teeth" who mysteriously bursts into flames (in place of the church building) before she can prevent Philly from making her escape. Even the saints themselves have been not been spared the alchemical fires; when the statue of Agatha is unearthed, as a result of her temporary *mortificatio* (the alchemical process of decomposition prerequisite to rebirth), the formerly saintly expression on her face has turned "sly."

Though various characters in the story debate this point, Fludd is not to be confused with the Devil. He is not the "great rough thing" Sister Philomena thought she heard breathing outside her door when she was seven, nor even the one Mantel herself claims to have seen at the same age in the family garden.[52] The Devil in this story, as Father Angewin understands better than Fludd himself, is an obsequious tobacconist named Judd McEvoy, a dangerously ordinary, morally ambiguous fellow who pops up everywhere and declares himself only an "onlooker" to life's events. Fludd, on the other hand, proves an *homme fatal* only to hidebound orthodoxy, hypocrites, and fuzzy revisionism. Along with all the chemistry set paraphernalia, his Art demands "knowledge and faith, gentle speech and good works." These are not the Devil's tools.

Mantel's brief epilogue to the story is a curious set piece, a description of an Italian master's painting of the Virgin and Child. In the background outside her chamber a small white dog resonates in the reader's mind with the white dog that the children of the benighted village St. Thomas Aquinas serves touch for good luck, not to mention St. Dominic's stalwart companion. The Virgin is reading the First Psalm "with its message of utter reassurance: 'For the Lord knoweth the ways of the just; and the ways of the wicked shall perish.'" Though she looks sad, closer inspection reveals a "near-smirk" on her face. These two sly, smirking virgins, Mary and Agatha, suggest that in Mantel's Gothick, very heterodox faux Catholic universe, the categories "good" and "evil" alike are subsumed within the deeper life principle that expresses itself as transformation into fullness.

Even romance heroines more conventional than Roisin find their true identity by passing through spiritual death and rebirth in the alchemical refiner's fire. As the next chapter will show, the vampire romance writers of the twenty-first century reinvent this rite of passage when they turn the vampire *homme fatal*, portrayed for two hundred years as a ruthless, unredeemed killer, into the ethical, committed lover of a heroine whose fate is to find her true identity by dying and triumphantly joining him on a transformed dark side. In this radical reinvention of the Gothick, not only is the

Lord of the Underworld tamed to enter the domestic world of marriage, but the young girl enters his world as an equal, assuming his otherworldly powers and more.

Or as Fludd the alchemist put it, "It is no more surprising to be born twice than to be born once." 115

The vampire Edward displays his diamond Tantric body. From the movie *The Twilight Saga: New Moon* (2009). © Summit Entertainment.

SIX

THE BRIGHT GOD BECKONS

The New Vampire Romance

Think of it Lover! I and Thee
Permitted—face to face to be—
After a Life—A Death—We'll say—
For Death was that—
And this—is Thee—

   —Emily Dickinson

Hard though it may be to imagine, vampires at one point were considered hideous, terrifying creatures.

   — Sarah Wendell and Candy Tan

I.

Before they were invited in the open window of Gothick and Romantic literature slightly more than two centuries ago, vampires barely figured in the Western European record. Unlike the indigenous werewolf, whose legendary paw prints lead from Greek and Roman antiquity through twelfth-century French lais and English histories, vampires are exotic transplants.[1] Their story is native not to Hungary or Transylvania, as is almost universally believed, but rather to a different well-defined eastern territory that includes Silesia, Bohemia, the southern Slavic regions, and Greece. Vampires were unknown in Western Europe by either name or bloodsucking habits until the late sixteenth century, when accounts of revenants climbing out of their graves to attack their own families began to trickle in from southeast Europe.

Though French newspapers were reporting cases in Poland and Russia in the 1690s, it was early eighteenth-century accounts of vampire "epidemics" in south and southeast Europe, particularly Serbia, that captivated the imaginations of French and English newspaper readers, so much so that vampires quickly became "the Enlightenment's favorite undead."[2] The object of western European fascination was quickly converted into a handy political metaphor as well as the subject of moralizing tales and medical speculations.[3] Possibly the most notorious journalistic report of this period was about a soldier in the Austro-Hungarian army, one Arnold Paule, who complained of being attacked by a Turkish vampire and then, after death, became one himself and menaced his own family until his body and those of his victims were exhumed. When no signs of decay were visible, villagers pierced the corpses' hearts with stakes, burned the bodies, and threw the ashes back into the graves.[4]

This widely circulated report of the 1720s came from a Serbian town near Belgrade, an outlying territory of the Austro-Hungarian empire that had formerly been part of the Turkish empire. Because that incident, and others like it, happened in Serbia, and because Serbia lay within the borders of the greater Hungarian kingdom, Hungary became forever linked to vampires in the western European imagination even though the Hungarian word *vampir*, borrowed from Polish and Russian *upyr* (meaning "rush of wind" and suggesting swiftness) did not appear in that country until more than a century after it had spread through the major European languages.[5]

The link to Austria-Hungary would be permanently cemented at the end of the next century by Bram Stoker, who located his vampire aristocrat in another outpost of the Holy Roman Empire, Transylvania. Count Dracula's fictional lineage, of course, was nominally Romanian, not Hungarian or Transylvanian, but that distinction was dissolved when a Hungarian actor, Bela Lugosi, took the count's role in the 1936 movie version. Now, thanks to its global circulation in Gothick pop culture, a Hungarian loanword became the generic label for reanimated corpses of varying sorts in folklore the world over.

The historian Gábor Klaniczay links western Europe's sudden love affair with the vampire with the simultaneous decline of the belief in witches in the early eighteenth century. In England the last execution for witchcraft took place in 1682, the last trial in 1717. In 1735, the last of a series of Witchcraft Acts was radically altered to make the "pretence" of sorcery, rather than sorcery itself, illegal—a real-world move that helped open wide the door of the imaginary for vampires.[6] Though witches were still being burned across central and eastern Europe during this time, the handful of vampire reports from the southeast regions excited much greater interest in England, France, and Germany, where the great shift in worldview during the seventeenth century had led, as we have seen, to much ambivalence around the matter of supernatural agency.[7] As God's heaven and the natural world were increasingly seen to operate from very separate rules, it became less and less defensible to use the "witchcraft explanatory grid" (in Stuart Clark's words) for inexplicable or catastrophic events in one's neighborhood.[8] Because witchcraft couldn't be proven using the materialist rubric of the new sciences, the idea of witches as a real phenomenon began to fade in mainstream intellectual thinking even as a nostalgic attraction to supernaturalism lingered in the popular mind.

In the vacuum left by witches, vampires presented a convenient vehicle for metaphysical fudging. On one hand, they could be handed over to medical experts who could expound physical theories about the phenomenon.[9] On the other, the ghastly parody of the Christian blood sacrament that vampires seemed to enact made a seamless replacement for the witches' Sabbath and its blasphemous reversals of Christian ritual.[10] The figure of the vampire would be denounced by Christian doctrinalists of all denominations even as it rang a loud, clear bell in the sub-Zeitgeist of the popular imagination—a bell that would keep on ringing, louder if not more clearly, for the next three centuries. And on the third hand, vampires as an infection imported from the exotic east were so very conveniently "not our kind," allowing for an easy form of not-so-subliminal ethnic scapegoating. By the time Bram Stoker wrote *Dracula*, the real-life tidal wave of immigrants from eastern Europe dovetailed all too neatly in the English public's imagination with the sinister Russian death schooner *Demeter* embarking from Varna, Bulgaria, loaded with the count's sinister coffin.[11]

Enlightenment Europe's appropriation of vampire stories was also made possible by the lingering presence at home of Old Goth folk beliefs, formerly held as true but by this time mostly consigned to the wastebin of superstition. Vampirelike creatures of early medieval Germanic lore included witches who could suck out a man's insides, the Icelandic corpse demons known as *draugrs*, and other forms of the undead. Across northern Europe the bodies of these revenants traditionally required burning to destroy their power.[12] In England pounding a stake through the heart of a corpse was already a well-known custom; according to Keith Thomas, it remained the "legally required method of burial" for suicides until 1823, presumably to keep the unquiet soul from wandering among the living.[13]

As medical interest in the phenomenon waned, poetry and stories about vampires or vampirelike fairy queens began appearing in Germany (e.g., Goethe's "The Bride of Corinth") and elsewhere on the Continent around the turn of the nineteenth century. In the Gothick crucible the vampire quickly shed the coarse behavior of Serbian peasants who simply threw themselves upon family and neighbors for a convenient feed and reinvented himself as a suave, sophisticated *homme fatal* aristocrat. In what Christopher Frayling wittily dubbed the "haemosexual" erotic motif, these transformed vampire characters were not just villains, they were sexual predators administering the kiss of death to their victims as they stole their blood.[14]

The seminal story establishing this new Gothick subgenre was John William Polidori's *The Vampyre: A Tale* (1819), a work that grew indirectly out of that infamous summer of 1816 when Lord Byron, the poet Percy Shelley and his wife, Mary, and other guests gathered at the Villa Diodati near Geneva. Byron had just received a copy of Coleridge's Gothick poem "Christabel" and repeated some verses about the malicious fairy Geraldine's breast to Shelley, who (in the words of Polidori, who was Byron's youthful attending physician), "suddenly shrieking and putting his hands to his head, ran out of the room."[15] The group thereupon began a Gothick conversation about sex and horror that led, later that night, to the famous storytelling wager proposed by Byron that produced Mary Shelley's *Frankenstein*, a fragment of a vampire story from Byron (later incorporated into "The Giaour"), and a long novel, *Ernestus Berchtold, or the Modern Oedipus*, by Polidori that history has long forgotten.

What history does remember is the novella Polidori produced shortly afterward that borrowed shamelessly from Byron's fragment even as it slandered its author, whom Polidori had formerly hero-worshipped, in the unflattering portrait of the charismatic Lord Ruthven, a revenant aristocrat who woos young women and feasts on their blood to give himself eternal life. Showing greater (if possibly accidental) historical accuracy than vampire chroniclers before or after, Polidori has his dissolute lordling undergo his Change in Greece, which was not coincidentally Byron's own stomping ground.[16]

Polidori's achievement in *The Vampyre* was to fuse the exotic folklore of the vampire seamlessly with the figure of the Romantic/Satanic *homme fatal* in a setup made much more acceptable to western European popular imagination because the main character contracts the supernatural contagion not at home but in a remote corner of Catholic Europe. Lord Ruthven the vampire, vile seducer and murderer of maidens, was eagerly appropriated by a generation of playwrights working in the new Gothick-linked genre of melodrama. In the rowdy London theaters a large component of the audience was thirteen-year-old fanboys, not coincidentally also Hollywood's current target demographic for horror films.[17] Theater productions that were either direct borrowings from Polidori or later adaptations of James Malcolm Rymer's serialized potboiler *Varney the Vampire: or, the Feast of Blood* (1845–1847), and other vampire fiction were wildly popular on the stages of Paris, London, and cities across the United States from the 1820s through the mid-nineteenth century.[18]

By this time a new Gothick subgenre, the Victorian ghost story, had also emerged, foregrounding mostly malevolent spirits of the dead that were often tied to the classic Gothick castles or mansions dating to the Old Goth Catholic past. Vampires quickly found a place in these tales, helping to create a new supernatural imaginary that claimed a territory outside a specifically Christian context while reinforcing the Protestant Gothick ambience of malignant evil. Joseph Sheridan Le Fanu's daring "Carmilla" (1872) is the story of a homoerotic female vampire whose exquisitely slow seduction and attempted murder of a young girl is set in the vampire-associated region of Styria.[19] Writers famous and obscure, including Poe, Hawthorne, Baudelaire, Maupassant, Gogol, and even Tolstoy, tried their hand at tales of vampires or closely related supernatural entities over the course of the nineteenth century.[20]

Polidori's work remained the Gothick vampire standard in England and America until the publication of Bram Stoker's *Dracula* (1897), which in turn established a new template that would last another hundred years.[21] A Dubliner who became the actor Henry Irving's longtime stage manager and confidante, Stoker spent six years researching and writing his novel.

Originally setting the tale in Styria, the venue of Le Fanu's "Carmilla," he switched to Transylvania mainly after reading an article by an Englishwoman, Emily Gerard,[22] which described the Transylvanian folklore tradition of *strigoi*, reanimated corpses, using the vocabulary of the already familiar vampire trope.[23] Stoker's notes show that in his reading of histories of Romania, his eye was caught by the word *dracul*, meaning "devil" or "dragon," and the fact that one voivode named Dracula waged war against the Turks and was defeated by them.[24] Not until twentieth-century commentators got to work on Vlad the Impaler and his son Vlad Dracul, however, did these historical figures (along with the conflation of impalement as the Turkish-influenced method of executing soldiers with the preferred way of destroying vampires) become inextricably fused with the fictional character of Dracula, who Stoker has Van Helsing declare was a "most wonderful" man while he was still alive.[25] There is no evidence that Stoker knew anything as much about the two Vlads as we do now or ever based his character on either of them. As with the evolution of the word *vampire* itself, several centuries' worth of mythologizing of individual authors' creations has effectively erased the line between fiction and folklore.

Just as the regions native to the *upyr* tradition gladly embraced the post-Polidori sexualized aristocratic vampire as their own, regions with no such indigenous tradition whatever began experiencing vampire outbreaks in the wake of the European reports followed by Polidori, *Varney the Vampire*, and endless productions of vampire melodrama. Most famous of the so-called New England vampires was Mercy Brown, a young Exeter, Rhode Island, woman whose body was exhumed and her heart removed in 1892 after rumors of vampirism.[26] Found among Stoker's paper was an American newspaper clipping from 1896 detailing the digging up of numerous graves in the vicinity of Newport, Rhode Island, for the purpose of burning the corpses' hearts. An ethnologist declared the belief in vampires to be "rampant" in isolated regions of the state.[27]

The novel *Dracula* introduced many new elements to the Gothick vampire story, most notably the term *undead* and the use of the crucifix as a faux Catholic charm for warding off vampires. (Stoker's character Jonathan Harker dismisses this as a "superstition" of the Transylvanian peasantry until he discovers that it actually seems to work.) Other soon-to-be conventions that Stoker created include the vampire's aversion to garlic (from actual Romanian folk beliefs about the *strigoi*), the coffin filled with native soil, the vampire's inability to cast a reflection in the mirror, and its requirement of an invitation to enter a human household.[28] Count Dracula can, however, walk in the daylight; the sun as destroyer of vampires was a twist added in twentieth-century movie versions. Dracula is, finally, more powerful than previous fictional vampires: he possesses a demigod's power to change the weather according to his needs and to shape-shift into a bat, a dog, or a cloud of mist.

Like the male Gothick writers Walpole and Monk before him, Stoker splits his imperiled female character in two: Mina Harker, who survives the vampire attack, and Lucy Westenra, who does not. Lucy is the first fictional vampire to be shown before and after her Change, uniting in one character the innocence and monstrousness previously expressed in such dualities as Laura and Carmilla in Le Fanu's story and Jane Eyre and mad Bertha Rochester before them. In the vampire subgenre Lucy would serve as a provocative model for many two-in-one hybrids to come.

The charismatic Henry Irving has often been cited as a probable model for Dracula; what's intriguing is how much Stoker's decades-long role as faithful employee and factotum recalls John Polidori's much briefer subservient relationship to Byron. Though the count is an aristocrat who goes after young women (as well as Jonathan Harker himself) in the best *homme fatal* manner, he displays a great deal more Thanatos than Eros. Stoker's Dracula is a pale, ugly old man unless he's recently been feeding, a rejuvenating activity that improves his complexion and darkens his hair. He has foul breath and a thick white mustache; unlike Polidori's Byron-modeled Lord Ruthven, he's neither handsome nor inherently attractive to young women. He works his will on Lucy and Mina not by seduction but rather by the old Satanic template of involuntary possession: they simply lose their power to resist in his presence.

Dracula enjoyed considerable success as a novel, but the story did not become a broad popular culture phenomenon until it made the journey into film: first by the German filmmaker Friedrich Murnau (*Nosferatu, eine Symphonie des Grauens*, 1922), then most famously in Tod Browning's 1931 *Dracula*, adapted from a hit Broadway stage version of the novel and starring the Hungarian actor Bela Lugosi, who became completely identified with the role.[29] This was followed in Europe by Carl Theodor Dreyer's *Vampyr—Der Traum des Allan Grey* (1932). For the next few decades the Hollywood version produced a deluge of Dracula-inspired vampire films, sequels, and parodies as the opera-cloak-clad Transylvanian vampire became an iconic image in the sub-Zeitgeist.[30] The midcentury comic parodies especially, starting with movies such as *Abbott and Costello Meet Frankenstein* (1948), in which Lugosi appears as a buffoon Dracula, right through to *Love at First Bite* (1979) and others, served to soften the sinister Gothick figure and lay the foundations for the appearance of the first halfway sympathetic media vampire, the tortured but lovable Barnabas of the soap opera *Dark Shadows* (1966–1971).[31]

The next great tectonic shift in the mythos flipped the vampire from antagonist to protagonist, villain to antihero. Anne Rice's novel *Interview with the Vampire* (1976) was a radical innovation in this subgenre because it was the first to tell the story from the vampire's point of view, foregrounding him not exactly as a good person but certainly as far more dimensional and ethical than any vampire character before him. There is no dearth of the traditional dark Gothick in Rice's vampire world, which is full of sadomasochism and scenes of brutal butchery, but Louis, the vampire who tells his story to a human witness, has moral qualms about murdering humans, and his involuntary metamorphosis into a killer is rendered with sympathetic understanding.

Polidori framed his vampire's murderous need to suck blood in a bogus courtship and marriage with a young female; whether Lord Ruthven has intercourse with his doomed brides is left an open question since he seems to marry and kill them virtually at the same moment, and offstage to boot. Rice's vampires do not have intercourse with each other or with humans, and Louis's thwarted love for Claudia, whom he has made an eternal six-year-old, becomes the object of her frustrated scorn. For Rice as for Stoker, the fatal bite takes the place of sex, creating an atmosphere that is perversely erotic by virtue of this displacement. Though they freely kill men, women, and children, Rice's male vampires prefer turning their male victims, a preference that creates a strong homoerotic undercurrent.

Representing vampires as subjects, not objects, was the first of three new late twentieth-century elements introduced by Rice and others that would prove crucial in shifting some portions of the vampire subgenre away from the dark side of traditional Gothick. The second new element was a more explicit disassociation of vampires from a Christian matrix. Bram Stoker had repositioned his undead creatures within the classic faux

Catholic Gothick when he made them vulnerable to crucifixes and holy water (throwing in a black dog, traditionally the Devil's familiar, for good measure). Rice's vampires, in contrast, are not frightened by crucifixes unless they were devout Catholics in their lifetimes, and her sophisticated European vampire Armand emphatically tells the newbie Louis that they are not the "children of Satan." Vampires have no "discourse" with either God or the Devil, Armand says; if God doesn't exist, then vampires have the "highest consciousness" of any being in the world because they have the perspective to understand the passage of time and the value of human life.[32]

This leads us to the third important element Rice adds to the legend, the upgrading of vampires from "undead" to "immortals," with the strongest vampires becoming gods over the centuries. As she develops her story in subsequent volumes, Rice establishes a sacred genealogy of vampires that stretches back from the "Mother and Father," Egyptian gods Isis and Osiris, to the human queen Akasha, who becomes Mother of the vampires; Stoker's Transylvanian vampires figure here only as a shambling subspecies in a walk-on part.[33] In this new representation, the process of becoming a vampire is one of expansion of consciousness leading to divinization: vampires as transfigured humans, gods incarnated on earth—a theme that will be taken up again and again in the twenty-first-century versions of the mythos.

The shadow of the old, bad vampires still falls heavily over the first novels in Rice's series, however. For Louis, who can't stomach the acts of extreme violence he and the other vampires commit, evil remains an "all-consuming subject . . . obliterating all other concerns," a focus that may reflect Rice's own position as an ex-Catholic as well as a foreshadowing of her own later shift in spirituality.[34] Lestat, who becomes the central character in the series, passes through a rock star period (around the same time, the eighties and early nineties, that Satan is being drawn as David Bowie and John Constantine as Sting in the graphic novel world). The later novels wax grandiose: in *Memnoch the Devil* (1995), a kind of latter-day apocryphal gospel written twenty years into the series, Lestat meets Satan in the figure of "the Ordinary Man," who then takes Lestat on a Dantesque tour of hell and heaven (with a *very* brief glimpse of God). By the end of *Memnoch*, Lestat has foresworn blood drinking, a key step in the ongoing transfiguration of the vampire; in *Blood Canticle* (2004) he allies himself with the Church.[35] Shortly thereafter, in a change of heart very much in sync with the larger Gothick millennial shift, Rice renounced her Vampire Chronicles, returned to Catholic Christianity, and began writing novels about the life of Jesus. (Rice's subsequent fiction and later repudiation of Catholicism will be discussed in chapter 11.)

The vampire tale underwent the same intense cross-fertilization and hybridization in the 1980s and 1990s as women's romance and Gothick fiction in general did. Chelsea Quinn Yarbro was one of many who grafted the new story of a partially rehabilitated, non-Satanic vampire onto the trunk of the traditional historical romance. Yarbro's series featuring the elegant, ethical 800-year-old vampire Saint-Germain, Sieur Ragoczy—aristocrat, protector of impoverished women, progressive agriculturalist, publisher, and patron of the arts, who feeds without killing—began in 1978 with *Hotel Transylvania* and still continues. The count's lengthy life span allows him to leapfrog through European history, alighting in the midst of famous hot spots such as the Black Plague, the aftermath of Napoleon's conquest and defeat, Venice during the Reformation, and so on.

Like Lestat, Saint-Germain (based on a real-life figure, an eighteenth-century Frenchman and alchemist around whom many esoteric legends have clustered) has taken advantage of his centuries-long existence to invest wisely and accumulate untold wealth.[36] The character of the Wandering Jew popular with classic Gothick writers such as Monk, Maturin, and Sue—a man who suffers the angst and depredations of immortality while reaping the benefits of compound interest—made an easy leap into the vampire subgenre and shows no signs of dying there, either. An important new twist was that Saint-Germain feeds on his female victims without killing them and thus is able to engage in actual sex with them, a significant marker in the growing humanization of these characters.

With his *Space Vampires*, published the same year as *Interview with the Vampire*, Colin Wilson created the first of what would become an avalanche of hybrid vampire horror/sci-fi stories. His extraterrestrial sexual predators kill humans for their energy, not their blood, and their fifty-mile-wide derelict spacecraft, whose interior is "vast as a cathedral," becomes the new Gothick mansion in a trope that will carry through to *Alien* and beyond.[37] Whitley Strieber's *The Hunger* (1981) introduces a sympathetic female vampire, an androgynous creature formed by "parallel evolution" with humans and the last of her alien-seeded species, who shows deep loyalty and love for the humans she has turned even when they inevitably die before her.[38] The character of the ethical extraterrestrial female vampire would be taken up by Octavia Butler in her 2005 novel *Fledgling*, which explores themes in power and enslavement in the context of a benevolent vampire's deep moral obligation to her human dependents.[39]

During the 1990s the hybridizing of genres and folkloric borrowings accelerated into a dizzying array of new forms. Because of the stronger structural DNA of the sentimental romance, most of the women vampire novelists who began building on Rice's mythos and adding elements of their own characteristically folded their stories into a framework of romance, not horror, to create the new subgenre of vampire romance. Where Yarbro, like Rice, created a male protagonist, others reverted to the female main character of the women's romance, though sometimes in a radically altered form.

Tanya Huff's Blood series, begun in 1991 and variously labeled as "vampire detective stories" or "urban fantasies," features Henry Fitzroy, vampire and bastard son of Henry VIII, as a love interest of the female protagonist, a wisecracking heroine drawn from the groundbreaking feminist detective stories of the 1980s. In a bold switch from the classic romance tradition, the main character is a hard-fighting, hard-loving, aggressive female, but she enjoys a notably more old-fashioned and extended period of courtship and foreplay with the vampire Henry than she does with her human partner, a fellow detective with whom she has a contentious, nonexclusive relationship. When they're finally going to have sex and Henry tries to "scoop her up in his arms" in classic Harlequin fashion, however, Huff's heroine insists on being the aggressor, pulling the vampire down and kissing him hard.[40]

Huff, like Yarbro before her, allows her vampires to feed without killing their human lovers. Her imaginary world also includes demons and a Demon Lord, but as in all Gothick entertainments from *Otranto* through late twentieth-century horror fiction, no balancing figure of a Bright Lord is present. Of an Easter service the narrator comments: "Just for that moment the faith in life everlasting as promised by the Christian God was enough to raise a shining wall between the world and the forces of darkness. Too bad it wouldn't last."[41] Nonetheless, learning that there are vampires in the world moves Vicki to visit a Catholic Church she attended as a child. While she is sitting in a pew looking at a statue of the Madonna, she sees a historical vision of Henry Fitzroy, who is wearing the "colors of the Madonna," saving the image from destruction by a Puritan Round-head as he proudly declares, "The Blessed Virgin is under my pro-tection."[42] Far from being a foe of the Church, the vampire Henry has been its protector.

In an increasingly popular trope, Huff mixes vampires and werewolves in the same story. Warm, emotional, impulsive, and social, ruled by an al-pha male *and* an alpha female, Huff's "wer" clan in rural Canada make a nice contrast to the cold, solitary vampire Henry. We will see this Apollonian/Dionysian, hot/cold pairing resurface in Stephenie Meyer's *Twilight* series, along with the recurring problem of what to do about your underwear once you change into a wolf and what to do about your nakedness when you flip back into human form—a dilemma Marie de France's twelfth-century ly-canthrope also faced, along with the added disadvantage that anyone taking possession of his cast-off clothes would keep him from turning back into a human.[43]

The next big turn of the vampire screw came from its comedy sub-subgenre. The 1992 movie *Buffy the Vampire Slayer*, written by Joss Whedon, laid the foundational myth for Whedon's enormously popular television series, which began in 1997 and ended in 2003. The story follows an arche-typal Valley girl cheerleader as she moves with her mother from Los An-geles to a new town, Sunnydale, that just happens to be situated on the lip of Hellmouth. As a Chosen One, a special hero selected in each generation to be a "Slayer" of evil spirits, Buffy battles the menacing creatures, mostly vampires, who pour out of this metaphysical San Andreas fault. In the film and the early episodes of the TV series, the vampires are very much old-fashioned pre-*Interview* antagonists: evil entities with demonic, distorted mask-faces to complement their fangs. The traditional identification of vampires with the Devil is also underscored with echoes of Satanic ritual in the character of a ruling underworld vampire called the Master whose ascension to our world is an imminent threat.

Then the series added a new character, a "bridge" vampire much like Henry Fitzroy of Huff's series: the significantly named Angel, a vampire who gets his human soul back as a result of a gypsy curse and becomes Buffy's great unattainable love. When he and Buffy try to consummate their love and experience "perfect happiness," Angel is fated to lose his soul again and returns to evil vampire mode, forcing him into a self-imposed exile. This thwarted outcome belongs not just to the Gothick vampire tradition but also (as we will see in the *Twilight* series) to a much older trope in which sex between humans and supernatural creatures (whether vampires, fairies, or gods) is likely to be fatal to the human. The Angel character got a series spinoff of his own (*Angel*, 1999–2004) in which his hybrid half-human, half-demon sidekick receives visions from unspecified "powers that be" directing Angel to save people trapped in bad situations. Like the assorted sons of Satan in the graphic novels of this decade, vampires such as Henry and Angel who strive to do good in spite of their inherently evil nature are markers for the growing shift from the traditional dark supernatural into a wider and more flexible vocabulary of good and evil.

The most striking new element in the Buffy story, however, was the transformation of the passive Gothick heroine assaulted by vampires into an indomitable female warrior who prevails by equal parts force of character and athletic prowess. Two influences came to bear in creating this new figure: first, the sexually liberated characters that Yarbro, Huff, Laurell K. Hamilton, Poppy Z. Brite, and other postfeminist romance and horror writers were already incorporating in their work; second and very different, the sexy-babe, martial-arts-proficient female action characters created during those same decades in Japanese anime and transferred to America mainly via videogame adaptations. (The anime babes, however, were probably also inspired in turn by the busty female superheroes of American Silver Age comics.) The female videogame characters and story lines (created by and aimed at male gamers exclusively) were translated in turn into post-2000 blockbuster movies such as *Lara Croft: Tomb Raider* (2001), *Resident Evil* (2002), and their sequels. The kick-ass heroine figure was picked up in other television and movie franchises such as *Xena: Warrior Princess* (1995–2001), the vampire-werewolf saga *Underworld* (2003) and its sequels, and many others.[44]

The main character of Laurell K. Hamilton's long-running Anita Blake: Vampire Hunter series (1993–) inhabits a world where vampires, zombies, werewolves, and other supernatural creatures are integrated into ordinary life. Lycanthropy has been officially labeled a disease; federal laws have been passed protecting vampires' rights; breath-mint-ingesting vampires and humans mingle (albeit uneasily) on the evening streets. Anita takes a master vampire and a werewolf as her lovers and develops telepathic links with both of them. As the series progresses, Anita herself makes the post-2000 Gothick shift and slowly begins to Change into the creatures she has been hunting.

The conceit of mainstreaming vampires out of the underworld of horror and into "real life" was taken up by Charlaine Harris in her Southern Vampire novels (2001–), which reached a global audience when they were adapted to Alan Ball's *True Blood* HBO television series starting in 2008. About his guiding vision for the series, Ball articulates the quintessential post-2000 Gothick position: "Instead of the supernatural being something that exists outside of nature, I wanted it to be something that was almost like a deeper manifestation of nature. Deeper and more primeval. Something that maybe humans, with our brain structures that we've created as a way to filter reality, can't comprehend or sometimes even pierce."[45] By its fourth season, *True Blood* had added werewolves, fairies, witches, and other supernatural creatures, all of whom, in a mad display of Gothick hybridity, engage in sex with humans and each other.

By the turn of the twenty-first century, the vampire story had expanded its territory exponentially across media platforms into any number of odd pockets of popular culture.[46] In the madness of proliferating and crossbreeding story lines, the characters themselves also became *babewyn* hybrids: half vampire and half human, half werewolf and half human, half devil and half human—part of an escalating trend to graft the special powers of these creatures onto human characters in the same way that comic book writers had previously created superheroes who were ordinary humans possessing a second hidden supernatural identity and graphic novelists were fusing their human characters with gods or devils. The end result in all cases was a hero or heroine possessing something not of this world in his or her deepest biological nature.

At the same time, inevitably, the vampire mythos began to generate its own fictional theology and cosmology. White Wolf's role-playing game *Vampire: The Masquerade* (1991) and its innumerable offshoots sets up a Gnostic universe in which vampires are the evil demiurges who rule the world. Its guiding premise is that all major events in human history are caused by the manipulations of vampires (known as the Kindred) descended from the father of vampires, Cain.[47] In an interesting blend of the Gnostic Gospels and the Wandering Jew legend, the movie *Dracula 2000* (2000) reveals the count's true identity as Judas Iscariot, sentenced to the hell of eternal life in an undead body for his betrayal of his Lord.[48] In *Blade*, originally a comic book, then a series of graphic novels and movies boasting the now-familiar main character who is half human and half vampire, the vampires are shown as having their own religion, sacred texts, and Blood God.[49] Adding fuel to the fire was a tidal wave of pseudoscholarly compendia, encyclopedias, and annotated editions of all things vampire; much like Wikipedia entries, their lack of factual accuracy is irrelevant in the long run, as they stoke the flames of legend creation by further blurring the boundary between fiction and reality.

In the first novel of her series, Anne Rice had replaced Stoker's figure of the aggressive vampire hunter, Professor Abraham Van Helsing, with a nameless "interviewer," an initially neutral but gradually fascinated and ultimately seduced observer who decides by the end of the story that he wants to be a vampire, too. Readers of the Vampire Chronicles shared his reaction. Reporting excitedly that "these were beautiful people and they got such intense passion and feelings for life," fans flocked to Rice's national reading tours and annual New Orleans Halloween extravaganzas. Closer identification among fans with the vampire figure led to a growing lifestyle subculture that adopted the new vampire worldview as its own. Many Rice fans were inspired to adopt a vampire persona, forming their own substantial brigade in the ranks of the Goth and heavy metal music movements of the 1980s.[50] Father Sebastian and his "Endless Nights" were a fixture of the New York club scene, and similar vampire scenes flourished in big-city subcultures across Europe and North America through the next decade.

The vast vampire subculture, composed of much larger, more flamboyant, and heterogeneous populations than the plain-Jane Lovecraft fans and covens, now ranges from fashion (those elegant Goth Lolis of Tokyo pop) to the pancake makeup and black nail polish of Goth clubbers and serious costumers; the extremes of tattooing, piercing, and vampire orthodontics (a flourishing industry in the United States); the lifestyle practices of "psychic vampires" exerting dominance (expressed as "feeding on the energy" of others) in personal relationships; and, finally, those who actually do take blood, typically with razor cuts or hypodermic needles. Because of the emphasis on strength, power, and dominance, the vampire lifestyle culture has strong ties to the sadomasochistic sex scene. On the endless self-posted and quasi-documentary videos available online, these Secondary

Believers, dressed flamboyantly and fanged for the many vampire conventions held in this country and abroad, usually hedge their bets on the question of whether vampires are real. "What is reality?" is a common response, based on the underlying assumption of personal gnosis that the individual creates his or her own metaphysical/imaginary world. On many of these sites, one also finds the plaintive recurring question: "What does it say about vampires in the Bible?" (Answer: nothing.)

Carrying practice into worship are unknown numbers of Primary Believers, fan-based practitioners of religions founded on the vampire mythos of Rice and her successors. The Vampire Bible of the Temple of the Vampire, officially registered as a religion in 1989, states that "we worship the ancient Sumerian vampire dragon goddess Tiamit, and trace our priesthood to the ancient city of Ur." Its creed runs as follows:

> I am a Vampire.
>
> I worship my ego and I worship my life, for I am the only God that is.
>
> I am proud that I am a predatory animal and I honor my animal instincts.
>
> I exalt my rational mind and hold no belief that is in defiance of reason.
>
> I recognize the difference between the worlds of truth and fantasy.
>
> I acknowledge the fact that survival is the highest law.
>
> I acknowledge the Powers of Darkness to be hidden natural laws through which I work my magic.
>
> I know that my beliefs in Ritual are fantasy but the magic is real, and I respect and acknowledge the results of my magic.
>
> I realize that there is no heaven as there is no hell, and I view death as the destroyer of life.
>
> Therefore I will make the most of life here and now.
>
> I am a Vampire.
>
> Bow down before me.[51]

There is no mention of the undead, and here human divinity ("I am the only God that is") is simply a metaphor for self-hegemony within a materialist worldview (there is no heaven or hell, and death is "the destroyer of life"). The statements "I recognize the difference between the worlds of truth and fantasy" and "I know my beliefs in Ritual are fantasy but the magic is real" have built-in caveats. "The magic is real" is a pragmatic Chaos magick creed holding only the barest hint of supernaturalism.

In contrast, the Order of the Vampire, yet another branch of Michael Aquino's Temple of Set that began in the 1990s, "embraces the concepts of Vampyric Presence as a means to personal power and potential immortality." The Order asserts that "Vampyric powers" including "invisibility, manipulation, [and] the power of sound and breath" are real and can be accessed by adepts who master such skills as the Posture of Effortless Power. Acknowledging the "glamour" of vampires, it also promises instruction in use of cosmetics and techniques of voice and gaze to gain control over others.[52]

Why so many, many forms of vampire performativity? Noting that the earlier Dracula mythos had never given rise to such a phenomenon in the way the Anne Rice novels did, Katherine Ramsland expressed the changing sensibility of the 1990s when she wrote: "You might say that the collective cultural subconscious was building toward the day when many of us would identify with the monster, who in earlier vampire tales had to be annihilated as the Evil Other. We were beginning to understand that to take out the vampire with a stake through the heart was to kill a part of ourselves—a part that might yield some real treasures."[53]

What does it mean to become the monster? In part it means identifying with the dark and rejected aspects of the self that exist in every person, including the taboo primal energy around violence and sex. That is the classic Gothick, and by extension Goth, connection. But it also means desiring to experience a reality beyond the material world, even if the need itself is not consciously acknowledged and even if the only vehicles available are the uniformly dark imaginary supernatural characters that pop culture presents outside organized religion. Getting to *that* treasure ultimately requires balancing the scales more evenly between good and evil supernaturalism and is a prime reason the nature of Gothick monsters, including vampires, began to change after the turn of the century.

Meanwhile, vampires in their myriad fictive forms keep on serving as vivid social metaphors much as they did in the eighteenth century. Where an 1819 American knockoff of Polidori titled *The Black Vampyre* served up an uneasy moral about slavery,[54] almost two hundred years later vampires are stand-ins for AIDS, racial bigotry, sexual orientation, and "the terrors of intimacy";[55] for the transition from adolescence to adulthood;[56]

for menstruation;[57] for power relationships between masters and servants;[58] for addiction and abstinence;[59] and on and on. Most broadly, vampirism in the new Gothick seems to function as an emblem of a kind of original sin; it represents the irresistible impulse to evil the now thoroughly humanized supernatural character must struggle against to stay a moral person. These characters retain their generic identity (demon, vampire, werewolf) along with the innate dark desires connected with that identity (killing humans) but are able to rise above their instincts by an act of will that must be tested again and again.

By the time Stephenie Meyer began publishing her *Twilight* series in 2005, the big question, not surprisingly, was whether the vampire mythos had anywhere left to go.

2.

The answer was that it did.

Like all the most successful Gothick novelists, Stephenie Meyer was able to combine a number of familiar elements in unfamiliar ways that moved the subgenre in a strikingly new direction. Where most of her predecessor-contemporaries made (and continue to make) typical late twentieth-century choices in constructing their evil vampire narratives, Meyer directly taps into the new Gothick sensibility of the twenty-first century that blends the monstrous with the divine. And the wild success of her series, which she conceived in the best Gothick manner from a dream, ramped up the vampire craze even further.[60] Over four novels Meyer tells the story of sixteen-year-old Bella, a self-described klutz who in the time-honored tradition of Jane Eyre and her "drab merino pelisse" favors sweats over designer fashions, as she moves back to a small town on Washington's Olympic Peninsula when her childlike mother remarries and relocates to Florida.[61] Like Buffy, Bella is a mother to her own divorced, feckless Muggle-like parents, whom she calls by their first names. Despite her low opinion of herself, Bella attracts boys at her new high school, particularly the wealthy, devastatingly handsome Edward Cullen, of whom she says, "It was hard to believe someone so beautiful could be real."[62]

As it turns out, he isn't, at least not a real human. Edward is a vampire, frozen in his seventeen-year-old human body for almost a century since his death during the 1918 influenza epidemic. Edward's "family" is in fact a coven run by patriarch Carlisle, an ethical vampire who has foresworn feeding on humans for the less tasty blood of animals, which he and his cohorts discreetly seek out at regular intervals in national parks.

Following the old-time women's romance setup of a bourgeois young woman of humble means encountering a family of wealthy, mysterious aristocrats, the Cullen family is much higher up on the social ladder than Bella's. The "parents" Carlisle and Esme, however, are not only more mature, sophisticated, and attractive, they are also far more emotionally supportive of Bella than her own human mother and father.[63] Family dynamics in the Cullen coven are civilized and positive. Their light, airy McMansion located on an estate outside of town is the striking reverse of Dracula's decrepit castle or Rochester's gloomy Thornfield, though it is not unlike the ancient vampire Miriam Blaylock's "fresh and light" Manhattan townhouse in Whitley Strieber's *The Hunger.* A huge wooden cross, carved by Carlisle in his pre-vampire days when he was a minister in seventeenth-century England, hangs in the living room. As is the case with all Gothick vampires except the wretched Transylvanian throwbacks in *Interview with the Vampire,* compound interest keeps the Cullens staggeringly wealthy.

Edward's first reaction to Bella is fury because he fixates on her blood: it's his heroin, the exact smell he craves most, a fateful circumstance that forces him to struggle even harder with his vow not to feed on human blood. Bella the outsider is likewise instinctively drawn to him, and after Edward uses his vampire's superhuman speed to save her from being killed by a runaway truck, their love affair begins.[64] To Bella's suggestion that he is like Bruce Wayne or Peter Parker, the human alter egos of comic book superheroes, Edward responds heatedly, "What if I'm not a superhero? What if I'm the bad guy?" After Bella figures out he's a vampire, he's incredulous when she tells him that "it doesn't matter."[65]

This is an unusual affair on a number of counts. Most obviously, Edward must keep his bloodlust for her constantly in check, for when his coven brother Emmett fixated this same way, it's implied that he killed the women. "'You . . . have to risk your life every second you spend with me," Edward warns Bella. "You . . . have to turn your back on nature, on humanity." Calling himself "the world's best predator," Edward demonstrates his preternatural strength, ripping thick branches off trees, snorting derisively, "As if you could fight me off," as he zooms up to her in an eyeblink. "He'd never been less human . . . or more beautiful," Bella observes. "I sat like a bird locked in the eyes of a snake." Even so, somewhat counterintuitively, she always feels "secure" and "completely safe" in his company.[66]

What this also means, in terms of a romantic vampire-human relationship, is that Edward is physically so strong they can't have sex because he might accidentally hurt her or, worse, give into his vampire instincts in the height of passion and begin feeding. "I can never, never afford to lose any kind of control when I'm with you," he concludes.[67] As a result, Bella and Edward enjoy endless foreplay, a situation that goes a long way toward explaining this series' enormous popularity among young adolescent girls. That their emotional relationship is foregrounded over sex may also explain why the mothers of Meyer's "fanpires" are great enthusiasts of the books, too. As Laura Miller notes, the vampire romance offers its readers "the opportunity to enjoy an 18th- or 19th-century courtship while remaining a 21st-century woman."[68] Postponement of sex in favor of an elaborate wooing staged as a battle of wills was and remains a time-honored convention of many subcategories of women's romance, and here it plays out over the issue of Bella's determination to become a vampire and Edward's resistance to her wish.

Another primal current Meyer taps is the adolescent's inner world of emotional extremes, bipolar ups and downs, and black-and-white thinking fueled by the feverish dream of absolute, eternal love that is the essence of *Romeo and Juliet* (one of the classics, along with *Wuthering Heights*, she repeatedly references in the series). The same age group that gravitates to horror is also drawn, moth to flame, to the idea of perfect love. As Bella expresses this dream of first love: "The bond forged between us was not one that could be broken by absence, distance, or time. . . . As I would always belong to him, so he would always be mine."[69] The heart of these books is the romantic interaction between Bella and Edward (and, for a time, between Bella and the werewolf Jacob). School life is represented in the most perfunctory way, and other characters are scarcely more than names; the only reality is the love that Bella and Edward have for each other. Significantly, both are virgins, physically and emotionally: Edward died too young ever to have had a human love relationship, so Bella (who has never had one, either) must show him how.

Miller also notes that the *Twilight* series hews to the classic Gothick romance "feminine fantasy," first laid down in *Jane Eyre*, "of being delivered from obscurity by a dazzling, powerful man, of needing to do no more to prove or find yourself than win his devotion, of being guarded from all life's vicissitudes by his boundless strength and wealth." This, she says, is itself a kind of vampire sapping women's strength, exerting a seductive, irresistible pull as it sucks them back into outmoded attitudes about female behavior.[70]

Meyer is guilty as charged. She presents Edward as the archetypal Harlequin romance male love object: the well-to-do, sophisticated, dangerous male lover as dominating father who is forever uttering "low oaths," who treats his woman "like a misbehaving child," tilting Bella's chin up with his finger and engaging in other acts of parental control: "He pulled me around to face him, cradling me in his arms like a small child," "reached out with his long arms to pick me up, gripping the tops of my arms like I was a toddler."[71] As Claire Kahane has shown, the underlying hint of father-daughter romantic love predicated on an absent mother is a central subtext of the Gothick women's romance, and (for the first three books, anyway) Bella the emotional orphan clearly craves this kind of masterful paternal attention.[72] The fact that Edward has been to Harvard *twice* and drives a brand-new Ferrari does nothing to detract from his charms. She gives up on the idea of going to college herself because this affair has become her whole life. Continuing the theme of the old-fashioned Cinderella-style makeover of the ugly duckling, Edward's fashionable "sister" Alice gives dowdy Bella beautiful clothes to wear in spite of Bella's fervent desire to stay a wallflower.

Miller is not the only critic to find Bella "deplorably passive," but it's important to remember that her flaws are self-described: when Bella keeps insisting that she's "ordinary," Edward replies, "You don't see yourself very clearly, you know."[73] In her determination to sacrifice her own life to save her parents, Bella shows enormous bravery and forbearance. In fact, she is mighty like the Victorian victim heroine identified by Nina Auerbach who "consecrates herself into a queen." "Behind the victim's silence," Auerbach says, "lurk mystic powers of control."[74] Bella also resembles the very impressionable Emily in *The Mysteries of Udolpho*: what seems on the surface her greatest liability, extreme emotional sensitivity, is in fact her greatest strength—the ability to *feel* (as opposed to understand) a situation as it really is.

It would be a mistake, I think, to dismiss the power exchange of the classic Gothick female romance as one-sided, because the underlying dynamic of male sexual and social dominance in these stories is offset, as we saw in chapter 5, by the woman's counterassertion of her own values. Bella rights the lopsided balance of power with Edward by means of a startling decision: against his violent objections, she wants to become a vampire. Why? Because it will give her the same status Jane Eyre insists on having with Rochester: parity in the relationship. "A man and woman have to be somewhat equal," Bella tells Edward,

> as in, one of them can't always be swooping in and saving the other one. They have to save each other *equally* . . . I can't always be Lois Lane . . . I want to be Superman, too.[75]

With this declaration she effectively lays down the conditions for their relationship.

By the end of the third novel, however, the internal contradictions have mounted to the point where the story seems destined to hit a dead end. For many hundreds of pages Bella and the statuelike Edward have been frozen in their standoff and seem caught in a shadow play of projected desire whose creepy but inexorable logic is pointing to the next big step in the story: Bella's death and transformation into a kind of monster-god in exchange for sexual consummation and eternal love. Though Bella is fiercely looking forward to it, readers can't help feeling a tad apprehensive about this choice for a young girl. But then Bella herself stops being a real girl in *Breaking Dawn*, the last volume in the series, and this is where both the terms and the feeling tone of the story change drastically. Not only does she get her wish to be a vampire, she also becomes a demigoddess who engages in marathon sex and possesses superpowers exceeding even Edward's.

To bring this transformation about, Meyer pulls various bright threads from a tapestry of story traditions originating in the folktales, religious apocrypha, and legends of premodern Western culture, some via the Gothick and some not. The first of these threads is one we have already seen: Bella is the bride of Death. She's in love, after all, with a being whose deepest instinct is to kill her. In the classic vampire story, the woman who is seduced by a vampire dies horribly, only to become one of the undead herself. By the 1990s, the new convention of "feeding without killing" allowed a female protagonist to have a vampire lover without having to die and become a vampire herself; she could now be the girlfriend of Death, not the bride, and suffer no fatal consequences. Bella follows Lucy Westenra's path through death and out the other side without becoming either a victim or a monster.

The presence of another ancient trope in the *Twilight* series helps subliminally underscore Bella's overdetermined role as the bride of Death. It appears in the two striking physical qualities Meyer's vampires possess. First, in daylight they don't turn to dust; rather, they sparkle beautifully, "like thousands of tiny diamonds were embedded in the surface."[76] The sparkling body has immediate associations with the diamond or rainbow body of Tibetan Buddhism, the normally invisible sheath surrounding the physical body that connects consciousness to the transcendent realm.[77] After death, the diamond body, like the Christian resurrection body or the Gnostic "radiant" astral body, promises immortality.[78] The fact that the vampires' diamond bodies are visible to the naked eye in daylight strongly suggests they belong to some category of the divine, not the demonic. In accordance with a number of esoteric religious traditions, they have reached the highest state of human development on earth, in which, in the words of a contemporary Theosophist, "enlightenment becomes a literal fact through the transubstantiation of flesh and blood into an immortal body of light."[79]

Second, building on a convention established by Rice, Meyer's vampires look and feel like statues.[80] Edward's chiseled beauty does not recall the sinister figures of Dracula or Lestat but rather the classic outlines of a Renaissance statue, "carved in some unknown stone, smooth like marble, glittering like crystal"; his body is "hard and cold—and perfect—as an ice sculpture." The words *marble*, *statue*, and *perfect* repeat over and over, creating the sense of a bright and beautiful moving idol (and statues, recall, are the material doubles of divinities, thought to draw down and possess their special powers). Bella says cuddling with him feels like "snuggling with Michelangelo's *David*, except that this perfect marble creature wrapped his arms around me to pull me closer."[81]

The motif of loving a statue has been around since Ovid's story of Pygmalion and his stone bride, picked up in the Old Goth French dream-vision poem *The Romance of the Rose* and circulated in other medieval works along with myriad popular tales of loving an image of either Venus or Mary, the result being the taking of holy vows (if the statue was of Mary) or death (if it was Venus).[82] The nineteenth-century French writer Prosper Mérimée gave the story a typically Gothick twist in his "Venus d'Ille" (1837), about a thoughtless bridegroom who puts his wedding ring on the finger of a blackened, recently excavated Roman statue as a joke, only to find the unamused Goddess of Love crushing him to death (just as Edward fears he will do to Bella) in the course of demanding her erotic due. As Kenneth Gross puts it, in these stories "certain qualities of the statue begin to catch hold of those around it. . . . The living statue turns living persons to stone or brings about their death."[83]

A Western storytelling tradition of more than 2,000 years, then, dictates that loving a statue, getting sucked into its frozen stasis, means you are going to die. But even as Bella praises Edward's "stone chest," his "glass-smooth lip," his "sweet breath . . . cold and delicious," the *Twilight* scenario has a major erotic disconnect: in plain human terms, sex with a creature whose skin is a cold, hard surface is not very sensually enticing, and the descriptions of their endless foreplay fall understandably flat.[84] This is why readers turn in relief to Bella's almost–love affair with Jacob, the Native American who is obliged to become a werewolf when the Cullen vampire family invades his ancestral turf. Jacob is as hot-blooded and emotional as Edward is cool and distant.

The third link between love and death in Meyer's story is the ancient notion of love too passionate and perfect to be experienced in mortal life. "Fatal passion" is more than simply a function of teenage mood swings; it was the basis of the Old Goth *fin amor* or courtly love tradition that began in the south of France and has deeply impacted Western ideas of romantic love ever since.[85] Provençal *trouvères* such as William of Poitiers expressed their undying love, either unrequited or never consummated, for a high-born lady married to another man: in feudal and religious terms, he is her obedient vassal, her worshipful supplicant. With its code of secrecy, correct behavior, and nuanced chastity, *fin amor* was, as Michael Camille and many other scholars have described, a form of "pseudo-sacred worship" of the love object as quasi-divinity.[86]

By some Old Goth accounts, however, a powerful desire left unfinished on earth builds up energies that can ascend to the upper realm to be released and consummated. This idea was advanced by the Albigensians, also known as the Cathars, a powerful sect that flourished alongside the troubadours in the south of France during the twelfth century. A ubiquitous fictional presence in the new Gothick from Dan Brown to scores of other novels and a cartload of folkloric "nonfiction," the Cathars were admired for their renunciation of material goods by no less than St. Dominic himself but were ultimately ruthlessly exterminated by Pope Innocent III's crusade of 1209. Their elite group of elect, whom the Inquisition called the *perfecti* or Pure Ones, practiced sexual abstinence on the grounds that unconsummated earthly love ensures that the worshipper will be granted a divine union after death. (Saints, of course, are the orthodox Church's own *perfecti*, divinized virgin humans whose special access to the celestial world gives them superpowers.)

In his *Love in the Western World* Denis de Rougemont famously argued that the troubadours' unique take on romantic love was based on the heretical notions of the Cathars. As an extraordinary time of cultural expansion in France, the twelfth century witnessed, in de Rougemont's words, the relaxation of the "patriarchal bond," the splitting up of the Father deity into various gods (including, for the Cathars, Lucifer and an unincarnated Jesus) and the introduction of a feminine principle—both the cult of the Virgin in the Church itself and Maria, an "immaterial" (not incarnated) female principle and mother of Jesus who exists outside of our world, for the Cathars.[87] This Manichaean legacy of passionate love that cannot be fulfilled in a mortal lifetime on a flawed earth ruled by Lucifer, de Rougemont insisted, lived on to exert through the troubadours' poetry a massive influence on Western love mores and literature. "The passion which novels and films have now popularized," he concludes, writing in the 1930s, "is nothing less than *a lawless invasion and flowing back* [his italics] into our lives of a spiritual heresy the key to which we have lost."[88]

Many strong echoes of Cathar dualism are present in the *Twilight* series, from the notion of the perfect realization of love after death—the medieval Arab poet Al Hallaj's cry, "In killing me you shall make me live, because for me to die is to love and to live is but to die," is something Bella could easily have uttered—to the imagery of the novel titles as Bella moves closer to her heart's desire: the Pure Ones' opposition of "terrestrial Night and transcendent Day" is reflected in the sequence *Twilight, New Moon, Eclipse*, and the last book, *Breaking Dawn*, chronicling Bella's rebirth and ascension.[89] In the *Twilight* series, however, the *fin amor* roles are reversed: the human supplicant is female, not male, and when Bella dies, she becomes a perfect immortal being.

Bella's elect status after death connects her to another set of ancient and pancultural story traditions: those around a human loving a god and thereby gaining some form of divinity herself. In the Christian matrix of Western culture, that same great period of cultural flowering during the twelfth century also saw, along with Mariolatry, *fin amor*, and assorted heresies, the rise of many popular stories about Christ, Krishna-like, choosing an earthly bride who must (in the manner of a nun's vow) stay a virgin until her death, at which time the union will be consummated.[90] This, of course, is a distant echo of the widespread practice in older religions of sacrificing a virgin of either sex to a god to become the god's lover after death. In the Western tradition before Christianity there are innumerable stories of the gods of the Greek and Roman pantheon choosing human lovers. These stories often feature a competing claim between an earthly betrothed and the divine one (in Bella's case, between Jacob and Edward); sometimes one wins, sometimes the other.[91]

Various rules and prohibitions are attached to human-god love, one of which is never to look directly at the god. The mortal Psyche, for example, is forbidden to look at Cupid, the god of love, and so they meet only in darkness; when she breaks the rule and sees him in all his shining (one wants to say "sparkling") glory, Psyche is sent into miserable exile until she completes various acts of contrition imposed by his mother, Venus.[92] In the *Twilight* series the vampires do their best never to show their sparkly essence to humans; Bella, like Psyche, must keep her god-lover's true identity secret, and she endures an equivalent exile in the second volume, *New Moon*, when Edward leaves her in order to ensure her safety.

When a human takes an immortal as a lover in these pre-Christian stories of antiquity, such a union results in the human's translation into another plane of existence entirely. If statues infect their human lovers with their own static natures, gods do this in spades, sucking their mortal consorts into their own extradimensional vortex like an ant down a drain. In the old stories this fate often amounts to a punishment: the human either cannot get back (vanishes and is never seen again); can come back, but only for limited periods (Persephone after she marries Hades, god of the underworld); or comes back but discovers that three days in that extradimensional place are a hundred years in earthly time and all family and friends are gone (Celtic folklore). When Bella marries her god, however, she doesn't leave the planet; she is translated into a different level of existence right here on earth after she dies.

This unexpected outcome taps into still another esoteric religious current of Western culture, if an even more radical one, that appears over and over again in the new Gothick: that of becoming a god, or at least accessing godlike powers, while still on earth and in one's own body. Just like the man-gods from Hell of the graphic novels, Bella has taken the dark path to divinity. Unlike them, she finds transcendent beauty and peace on the other side.

To see how Meyer plays out this motif, let us return to the story: Bella gets that she has to die if she wants to unite as an equal with her immortal lover. Not yet realizing that sex in her immortal state will be far more wonderful but knowing that she can only get pregnant as a human, she elects to have sex with Edward (only when they are married, at his proper insistence) while she's still human. So after much negotiation Bella and Edward agree to marry first, after which Edward will make her a vampire. Following a trope that encompasses both sex with the Devil and sex with fairies in Old Goth times and UFO abductees' reports of sex with aliens today, Bella's body is heavily bruised during their violent lovemaking.[93] She does become pregnant during their honeymoon and, following another folk and popular culture trope about the Devil's spawn, the baby grows in her womb with alarming and unnatural speed.[94] Edward barely has time to inject Bella with the venom that will make her a vampire when she starts to die giving birth to their hybrid vampire-human daughter, Renesmee.

Bella's transition from life to death to immortality is an epic passage. In effect, she becomes Mary and Christ rolled into one, first birthing her half-human and half-immortal child, then undergoing a three-day harrowing of Hell—an unbearable sensation of endless, excruciatingly painful burning of her flesh—before she emerges in her new identity (which might equally be read, Old Goth Catholic style, as the assumption of Mary to heaven in her intact body). And this is where everything really does change and the tone of the story radically alters.

When Bella comes to, she finds herself not in Pluto's Hades nor in the dank subterranean burial vaults holding the coffins of the undead, nor even in a dangerously pretty otherworld run by malevolent fairies. Instead, she resurfaces in the ordinary world, which now stands revealed as an earthly paradise thanks to her incredibly heightened vampire senses, which allow her to penetrate deep into the life energies of the planet: "I could see the dust motes in the air, the sides the light touched, and the dark sides, distinct and separate. They spun like little planets, moving around each other in a celestial dance." Rice's Louis reports a similar experience after he Changes: "It was as if I had only just been able to see colors and shapes for the first time," and when Lestat starts laughing at this, he says, "It was confusing, each sound running into the next sound, and then they overlapped, each soft but distinct, increasing but discrete, peals of laughter."[95]

The language of religious transfiguration continues when Bella tries calling up the forms of her former "cloudy" human world, "dim human memories, seen through weak eyes and heard through weak ears," but it feels like "trying to squint through muddy water"—another way of saying, in the language of 1 Corinthians, "For now we see through a glass, darkly; but then face to face: now I know in part; but then shall I know even as also I am known." When she observes herself telepathically in her daughter Renesmee's thought images, she sees "both of my faces, hideous human and glorious immortal."[96]

In the same way, Bella's own image in the mirror is "flawless," her body is "smooth and strong, glistening subtly, luminous as a pearl," her face "perfectly composed, a carving of a goddess." Edward's beauty is just as overwhelming: "For the first time, with the dimming shadows and limiting weakness of humanity taken off my eyes," Bella says, she sees its flawless perfection. His voice is "the most perfect symphony, a symphony in one instrument, an instrument more profound than any created by man." Looking at Edward's "father," Carlisle, is like "staring at the sun."[97]

These exquisitely beautiful demigods not only sparkle in the sunlight, they smell like "cinnamon, hyacinth, pear, seawater, rising bread, vanilla, leather, apple, moss, lavender, chocolate." In a trope that echoes the *X-Men* graphic novels and movies, each has his own special paranormal gift completely unrelated to traditional vampire traits: Alice can see the future, Edward can read people's thoughts, Benjamin can "influence the elements—earth, wind, water, and fire," and Zafrina "can make people see what she wants them to see."[98] But Bella's own two superpowers, which no vampire has ever possessed before, surpass them all: she can control the overwhelming thirst for human blood a newly turned vampire experiences, and she can build protective auric shields around her loved ones. In addition, this former klutz is now stronger than Edward; she runs faster than him, leaps over rivers, kills a mountain lion. She and the other vampires possess the miraculous physical powers of saints or siddhis, but (in the terms of what is present in the novels) they are outside the governing framework of a God or controlling Oneness.[99] The vampires answer to no one's law, human or divine, but their own.

Furthermore, in a significant departure from twentieth-century tropes of hybrid offspring (recall "Alia the abomination," the spice-infused mutant child in Frank Herbert's *Dune*), Bella's half-human and half-vampire daughter Renesmee, who possesses even greater superpowers than her mother, is not represented as a horror of nature, even though she, like Rice's Akasha, is a kind of female monster-god.

Stephenie Meyer's Mormon faith has often been noted by reviewers, usually in a faintly scolding reference to conservative social politics vis-à-vis the story line in which Bella and Edward are sexually abstinent for three books out of four. Deeper currents of Mormon theology inform her fictional universe, however, most particularly the doctrine of exaltation, the belief that humans can achieve physical resurrection and godhead in the afterlife.[100] Like the American Spiritualists who came after him, Joseph Smith took from Emanuel Swedenborg the notion that angels were humans who evolved into semidivine beings after death, where they keep their earthly male or female gender and continue having sex ("heavenly marriage") with angels of the same level and communities.[101] But Mormon exaltation means that those who lived righteously in life will live eternally as gods and goddesses, keeping "celestial marriage" with the mate they had on earth and capable of having spirit children. They will also share the full "power, glory, dominion, and knowledge" possessed by God the Father and Jesus Christ.[102] In the much quoted words of Latter-day Saints church president Lorenzo Snow, "As man is, God once was—and as God is, man may become."[103]

Bella's vampire Change is an apotheosis. Having been granted physical superpowers, an "infallible vampire mind" with total recall, and above all immortality, she has become a perfected being. A divine human now, she walks the earth not with the murderous spawn of Cain or Satan but with the angels, her vampire peers.[104] She has entered the bright shining company of the immortals, her "true place in the world, the place I fit in, the place I shined."[105] Her heightened senses and perfect sexuality match the conditions both of pre-Fall Paradise and of Swedenborgian-Spiritualist heaven, where celestial sexuality is an exalted alchemical wedding that re-unites the world and the two sexes.[106]

And how does this happy consummation of their love play out in the afterlife, which, for these divine humans Edward and Bella, is right here on earth? Rather prosaically, Bella tells us what eternal sex means for her and Edward: "I was never going to get tired, and neither was he. We didn't have to catch our breath or eat or even use the bathroom; we had no more mundane human needs." And in this manner, she says, they "continued blissfully into this small but perfect piece of our forever."[107]

By giving the vampire story the blue sky happy ending of the Romantic-slanted folktale coupled with various new-old mythic elements about im-mortality, Meyer has injected a strand of esoteric religious thinking—and in a much more organic way than Dan Brown's expository riffs on the Cathars, the divine feminine, and so on in *The Da Vinci Code*—into a pop-ular culture genre that reaches a very wide audience of readers around the world. It is part of the normalization of the supernatural happening across many Gothick subgenres: after Bella has undergone her transfiguration, her supernatural powers now seem completely "natural" to her. "Maybe now that I was a part of the supernatural myself," she tells us, "I would never be a skeptic again."[108]

Dubbing the vampire a being in a state of "suspended transcendence," Beth McDonald has noted the intense focus on vampires at the turn of the last three centuries in terms of a century's-end wrestling with the numi-nous.[109] The quietly subversive shift that Meyer and a few other twenty-first-century Gothick practitioners have accomplished within the tra-ditionally dark mold of their genre is a backward version—in effect, a reversal—of the transition Alexandra Walsham and others have described taking place in late sixteenth- and early seventeenth-century English rural congregations as they made the slow adjustment from image-based late medieval Catholicism to ascetic, idea-based Protestantism.[110]

Today Anglo-American popular culture is in the midst of a shift in the other direction, toward an image-based, heterodox, supernaturalism-embracing religious consciousness that is as gradual but ultimately pro-found as the one our cultural ancestors underwent 400 years ago. This time, the theological debate is raging not in a seventeenth-century church shorn of its trappings (a sacred place where the Catholic royal vampire Henry Fitzroy or the Protestant minister vampire Carlisle Cullen might have felt equally at home) but in a ruined Gothick castle undergoing serious renovation. The blood-spattered walls have been scrubbed down and receive a fresh coat of white paint as a greasy black bat born of the Reformation morphs into a shining heterodox angel.

Meanwhile, much of the Gothick remains very Gothick. In the online world of Second Life, traditional vampires fiercely debate the merits and legitimacy of their lifestyle with the softer Meyer vampires. Gothick horror got a boost at the turn of the millennium with a savage new "torture porn" subgenre. Fans post pornographic *Twilight*-inspired fiction on the website Twilighted. In the newest *Dracula* videogame, a faux Catholic priest gets sent to Transylvania to investigate claims of sainthood for a female physician, only to discover she's a reborn undead in league with the dastardly count.[111]

"We live now in an apocalyptic culture, ripe for revelation about ourselves," McDonald says, adding presciently, "Who can truly say where these vampires will take us in the course of the twenty-first century?"[112] To this question, let Bella have the last word: "Edward had always thought that he belonged to the world of horror stories. Of course, I'd known he was dead wrong. It was obvious that he belonged *here*. In a fairy tale."[113]

Gwen Dylan, zombie gravedigger and part-time girl detective. From *I, Zombie: Dead to the World* (2011). Artist: Michael Allred; Writer: Chris Roberson. © DC Comics. Used with permission.

POSTAPOCALYPTIC GOTHICK

That Means Zombies

(and the Occasional Zampire)

Zombie remains a devastating word, unrivaled in its power to conjure up so
many memories of emotions.

　—*World War Z: An Oral History of the Zombie War*

I mean, isn't "zombie" a silly name we come up with for a state we don't
understand?

　—Julie in *Warm Bodies*

Plakanek Valley, Bohemia, sometime in the near future: Under a tree an
Englishman sketches the fourteenth-century Kost Castle as an American
writer interviews him about the crucial role this imposing Old Goth fortress, and many others across Europe and the British Isles, played during
the great Zombie War of the early twenty-first century. The global epidemic, which followed directly on the heels of the Iraq War, has been over
for more than a decade, and the artist is compiling several volumes' worth
of drawings to commemorate the service these localized fortifications
performed in helping save humanity.

Castles, the Englishman says, as products of more than a thousand
years of "institutional anarchy since the fall of Rome," proved invaluable
sites of refuge after governments and social organization collapsed. North
America, in contrast, handicapped by its tradition of "standing national

governments," offered relatively few fortified hilltop eyries to retreat to.[1] When the ammunition ran out, the more fortunate Old World folks had maces, halberds, claymores, flaming moats, and Molotov cocktails to fall back on—close-range killing devices that proved far better at staving off the zombie hordes than cumbersome high-tech military weaponry. Not that the castles were always impregnable: within their battlements disease, human frailty, and the occasional zombie outbreak were often enough to finish off the inhabitants with no outside assistance. Queen Elizabeth elected to stay at Windsor, and it is implied, by her countryman's silent emotion, that she did not survive.

Charged Gothick spaces in which the internal mayhem mirrors that of the larger dysfunctional societies they belong to: Max Brooks's *World War Z: An Oral History of the Zombie War* brings us full circle to the foundational tenets of the eighteenth-century Gothick as Walpole's ur-castle Otranto gets co-opted in service of the zombie apocalypse. As the second decade of the new millennium begins, the living dead vie with the undead as the dominant Gothick monster even though their historical journey in the genre, if not their gait, has been a little swifter and narrower than the vampire's. But as we will see, they traverse a very similar arc from colonial Object to postcolonial Other to the new Gothick's rehabilitated Subject.

An African import, the concept of the zombie first surfaced in western European consciousness through stories told by slaves in the colonized islands of the Caribbean. Originally designating an African god, the word *zombi* mutated in the West Indies to refer to a puppet-corpse animated by a sorcerer.[2] Marina Warner has dubbed the zombie the quintessential product of the "Imperial Gothic," illustrating a classic colonial exchange of "words and images . . . borrowed from the host cultures by the incomers" and co-opted into a primitive, exotic, evil Other.[3] Unlike the vampire, however, the zombie did not make the transition from folkloric import to homegrown fictional Gothick character in the First World imagination right away; over the course of the nineteenth century, no reanimated corpse hopped a cargo ship out of the Caribbean to terrorize the populace of England or America.

After a lurid best seller of the 1920s had laid the groundwork, zombies shambled onto the broader stage of American pop culture in the twentieth century via the movie *White Zombie* (1932), set in Haiti.[4] Starring Bela Lugosi fresh from his success as Dracula the year before, this screen story of a bride turned into a zombie (rationalized here as a drug-induced soul-less coma) to satisfy the lust of a white plantation owner and his facilitator, the evil Murder Legendre (Lugosi, as a Svengali-style mesmerist), put the twin ideas of zombie and voodoo permanently on the Gothick map.[5]

Besides linking the zombie with the figure of the enslaved artificial human worker (a character already floating in the 1920s sub-Zeitgeist) in scenes showing black zombies robotically grinding sugarcane at night, *White Zombie* helped lift this creature out of regionalized Afro-Caribbean folklore into the Western Gothick imaginary by depicting people of European origin Changed into zombies.[6] It also followed the classic Old Goth/Gothick trope of devilish possession by making its main white zombie female, with her vulnerability in this soulless state leaving her equally open to sexual possession.[7] The trope of the possessed female was carried through in Jacques Torneur's more ethnographically nuanced (and *Jane Eyre*–influenced) *I Walked with a Zombie* (1943).[8] The zombie-Caribbean–*Jane Eyre* connection was developed more extensively in Jean Rhys's 1966 novel *Wide Sargasso Sea*, a revisionist prequel that beautifully imagines mad Bertha Rochester as a haunted young woman in Dominica (where Rhys herself was born) who dabbles in voodoo to make her new husband Edward love her. As Warner has pointed out, Antoinette (rechristened "Bertha" by her husband, who married her only for her money) in effect winds up a zombie herself.[9]

The Gothick territory of zombies, however, remained exoticized in this and the scattering of other B movie zombie films that followed; white or black, these puppets of a sorcerer or mad doctor were still ghettoized in the West Indies,[10] a Louisiana plantation,[11] and even Cambodia.[12] During World War II, the new white zombies swapped gender to become male pawns of the Nazis, assuming the same role of worker automata that the black millworker zombies had played in *White Zombie*.[13] Still in place, courtesy of the Third Reich, was the role of the evil sorcerer controlling them. Once they had been represented on Hollywood's big screen as white characters, however, zombies were destined to shed their colonial trappings and further assimilate with European folklore of the dead risen to haunt the living.

The animated dead were abundantly and gruesomely present in 1950s pre-Code horror comics, often in the form of old-fashioned ghouls come back to exact retribution on those who sinned against them in life: a man who killed pedestrians driving drunk, a fake doctor who did in his patients, a judge who sentenced prisoners to die. Ghouls of a different sort, now relabeled "zombies," also began to appear in comics of this decade whose mythos was set in World War II, and this time—arguably following the twentieth-century arc of the "revolt of the robots"—the new zombies were showing more, if not quite total, autonomy. The comics scholar Jim Trombetta's point cited earlier, about war trauma as a motivator of 1950s horror, is clearly evident in such stories as "The Living Dead" (1954), in which concentration camp ghouls exact revenge on a Nazi doctor.[14]

The link between war and zombies is made even more dramatically in "Corpses Coast to Coast" (1954), the story of an undertaker who dreams that gravediggers go on strike and corpses come back to life.[15] In this dream he is a high-ranking member of a secret global organization called the United World Zombies; in a clear echo of the Nazi death camp trains, the UWZ dispatches the newly risen corpse soldiers by train and truck across the country. In this early Cold War version of the zombie apocalypse, different factions of the organization take over all the countries of the world, which then proceed to go to war with each other because zombies make "perfect soldiers"; the U.S. and Russian zombie militaries use atomic bombs to wipe out each other's countries, since zombie flesh "doesn't stand up well under radiation." The undertaker wakes up to discover this was all a dream, and—surprise—he turns out to be a zombie himself.

But zombies were still awaiting their Bram Stoker. This turned out to be the filmmaker George Romero, who reimagined them in the 1960s as man-eating corpses possibly animated by radiation from a NASA satellite or a meteor. In *Night of the Living Dead* (1968) and its sequels, Romero laid down the foundational conventions for a new Gothick subgenre, conventions that are still in place fifty years later.[16] In this framework, zombies are no longer animated by a sorcerer; typically, they are the accidental result of a scientific mistake. Once created, significantly, they cannot be commanded and stand entirely outside human control. No longer automata with intact bodies, these creatures who only minutes ago were everyday folks (your brother, your wife, your local cop) are now the rotting corpses of the Old Goth plague years.[17] Taking a page from vampire stories, Romero had his killer corpses feed on their prey and infect whomever they killed with their bite, thereby creating the potential of a zombie population explosion whose Malthusian proportions the vampire Lestat and his descendants could never hope to match.

In the wake of Romero's films, the new subgenre was carried on by such Italian gore masters as Lucio Fulci (*City of the Living Dead*, 1980; *The House by the Cemetery*, 1981) but stayed mostly overshadowed by the vampire subgenre until its revival in Japanese videogames of the 1990s. The first big zombie videogame was a vast franchise created by Mikami Shinji in 1996 called *Biohazard* that became, in its U.S. and global version, the more Gothickly resonant *Resident Evil* and spawned innumerable game sequels as well as four post-2000 U.S. movie spinoffs.[18] Using Western characters, the game positions players as members of a military unit fighting against dead scientists who have turned flesh-eaters after a laboratory accident with hazardous chemicals. The Gothick space is an underground facility known as the Hive whose controlling artificial intelligence, known as the Red Queen, has killed all the workers to prevent a deadly "T-virus" from escaping. The virus, however, resurrects them as zombies, and the contagion quickly spreads to the neighboring city—and the world.

An unexpected phenomenon of the videogaming subgenre, however, one that mirrors (and may well have influenced) the turn from villain to hero in the Gothick, was the fact, quickly noted by videogame developers and marketers, that players chose to be the bad guys (orcs, vampires, zombies) as often as they chose to be the good guys. Wildly popular games such as *Warcraft* and *Diablo*, accordingly, were redesigned so that a range of roles was available on both sides of the moral divide. This effect was magnified when gamers began forming their own online communities, such as Zombie Nation; videogame companies quickly adapted to these new communities, making the evolving story lines of their games a complex trade-off between developers' marketing needs and gamers' preferences.[19] More recent zombie videogames such as the *Left 4 Dead* series (2008–) pit postapocalyptic survivors more conventionally against zombie hordes; the *Dead Space* series (2008–) moves the action, *Alien* style, to an abandoned spaceship infested with zombies.

The man-devil heroes of the graphic novels of the 1990s and earlier typically had to fight Satanic forces within themselves as well as in their adversaries to avert an imminent apocalypse (or Armageddon, or Second Coming). As the century and the millennium turned, these apocalyptic visions gave way, appropriately, to an equally dark postapocalyptic one: Armageddon has come and gone, and it was man-made, in the form of nuclear or viral destruction. With a nonsupernatural base narrative established back in the 1970s by Stephen King in *The Stand* (to be discussed in chapter 11), which was preceded in turn by many postapocalyptic sci-fi novels including George Stewart's great *Earth Abides* (1949) and Walter J. Miller's *A Canticle for Leibowitz* (1960), this scenario did not move into mainstream consciousness until after 2000, when it played out widely in Anglo-American literary novels such as Cormac McCarthy's *The Road* (2006), Jim Crace's *The Pesthouse* (2006), and other gritty, naturalistic depictions of ravaged countrysides where evil manifests on the strictly material level as marauding and occasionally cannibal humans.

The supernatural vacuum in this new subgenre was not left empty for long, however, as the two prime monsters of twentieth-century Gothick moved in to fill the void: the zombie first, followed by the ubiquitous vampire. In scenarios where a virus and not a bomb has wiped out most of humankind, the piles of human dead make the easy transition from zombies to vampires in works such as *The Strain* novels (2009–) by Chuck Hogan and Guillermo del Toro, Justin Cronin's *The Passage* series (2010–), and Jim Mickle's Depression-flavored movie *Stake Land* (2011).[20] Building on the escaped-government-virus-that-wipes-out-most-of-humanity template of King and his predecessors, these works imagine a postapocalyptic Gothick America overrun by zombiefied, flesh-seeking vampires who are far more relentless than their garrulous, dandified, seductive forebears. Neck biters and brain feeders alike are completely powered by the blind instinct to feed on (and thereby kill) their human prey. Though they retain their frightening speed (in contrast to typical zombie shuffling), the postapocalyptic vampires, like zombies, have also been stripped of personality, speech, and individual consciousness (the "virals" of *The Passage* have telepathic communication with their hive masters), making up a whole new subcategory that might be called *zampires* (or *vombies?*). With antecedents that include the urban ravishers of Richard Matheson's seminal *I Am Legend* (1954), these new hybrids have triggered endless debates in the online fan base about, for example, the virtues of fast zombies over slow zombies or the fighting skills of vampires versus those of zombies.[21]

So far zombies easily win the head count over vampires and zampires in the new postapocalyptic subgenre, both in the number of films and novels they appear in and simply in the sheer number of zombies per story. Zombies, indeed, are all about numbers; until very recently, there was no such thing as *a* zombie character, only the shuffling masses. In these survivalist adventures that pit isolated groups of humans against massive populations of the hostile undead, the postapocalyptic zombies remain mostly faithful to the conventions laid down by Romero: usually brought back to living death by whatever disaster produced the end of civilization, they are irresistibly drawn to feed on living humans. Zombies typically constitute a collective Gothick monster that lone individuals must fight and conquer; further, the zombies quickly become a global menace that can only be combated locally, because social institutions have collapsed.

Like other creatures real and imaginary, Gothick monsters must eat to stay alive, but the specific part of the human organism they crave varies from species to species. The zombie has been given a different, if no less implacable, lust than the vampire's: it is for brains, not blood. What is the ontological difference? The brain itself has taken on greater importance with late twentieth-century advances in neurology; we are constantly told in the popular press that all human agency rises either from genetic patterning or from neurological connections in the cerebral cortex. Brains also have a cooler, more rational (one wants to say "cerebral") sub-Zeitgeist vibe than primal red blood.

The paradox is that most twenty-first-century cannibal zombies (the exceptions will be taken up later) have no consciousness whatever, save for their overriding drive to find and feed on humans, whether brain matter or flesh generally (the other hybrid variant). Max Brooks's zombies have "no conscious thought, just pure biological instinct," but the brain is their only living organ; unlike the human brain, his characters tell us, the zombie brain doesn't need the support system of the rest of its body to survive.[22] But if they possess a live brain *and* consume brains to stay alive, why can't zombies think? The answer, as we will see later, lies in the link between loss of consciousness and large numbers of formerly human individuals: mobs don't think.

As the century ended, then, a generic scenario of the "zombie apocalypse" emerged in a range of novels, graphic novels, videogames, and films. And despite best-selling novelty items such as *Pride and Prejudice and Zombies* (2009), a mash-up interspersing Austen's original with a Regency zombie narrative in which the Bennet sisters display their martial arts skills against the living dead, the post-2000 sub-Zeitgeist's fascination with zombies is all about this apocalypse. In the early part of the decade, movies such as *28 Days Later* (2002) focused on the immediate onset of the zombie epidemic that has been triggered, in the Gothick bioconvention set in the 1990s, by a mysterious virus.[23] This scenario quickly shifted into postapocalyptic gear in dozens of new novels, graphic novels, and movies as the zombiefied Gothick world, now stripped of government and all the amenities of civilization, becomes the site of an entrenched, never-ending struggle between a handful of humans and the hordes of living dead that massively outnumber them. The film's sequel, *28 Weeks Later* (2007), assumes just this as the contagion spreads from England to the Continent (and hence the world) at story's end.[24]

On the surface, Robert Kirkman's postapocalyptic graphic novel series *The Walking Dead* (2006–), also a popular cable television series, seems to illustrate the back-to-basics appeal of this subgenre for Generation Y and the Millennials, forced to imagine the horror of living without cell phones, Facebook, or the Internet. In a world of almost medieval simplicity that is "ruled by the dead," with "no government, no grocery stores, no mail delivery, no cable TV," as the back cover blurb on one volume puts it, "we are forced to finally start living."[25] The irony, of course, is that this pioneer landscape, stripped of all technology, is displayed and consumed on the most sophisticated 3-D big screens replete with 12,000-watt Dolby sound, not to mention all the Xbox consoles, iPads, and iPhones that a still-robust late capitalist economy can provide.

The obvious metaphor here, and one also laid down by Romero in his first sequel, the shopping mall allegory *Dawn of the Dead* (1978), is that the zombies are the doubles of the survivors' preapocalyptic selves, all those shambling human hordes who enjoyed the consumer abundance of bygone days. Zombies work effectively as alter egos, caricatures of the living, to the point where, as Kim Paffenroth puts it, "humans and monsters become very hard to distinguish."[26]

On a deeper level, however, Kirkman's story, rendered in jagged, violent black-and-white visuals, carries the same current of generalized war trauma as the horror comics of the 1950s. Kirkman has cited the attack on the World Trade Center as a "big part" of his inspiration in this ongoing tale of a handful of humans at war with each other as well as the zombies as one potential safe harbor after another (a gated community, the abandoned offices of the Centers for Disease Control in Atlanta, a maximum-security prison) turns into the charged Gothick space where all things bad congregate.[27] In the end, as ever, it's no safer inside the castle than outside.

The post-2000 zombie apocalypse, in short, carries with it the same subliminal links with armies, warfare, and mindless (literally) mob instinct that were attached to its twentieth-century incarnation. Even though the Afghan and Iraq conflicts directly affected far less of the U.S. population than the Vietnam War did, together they make up both the longest extended period of warfare this country has ever known *and* the entire political memory of most members of the Millennial generation. The zombie apocalypse and its catastrophic aftermath mark, among other things, the sub-Zeitgeist's cathartic working through, in the realm of the imaginary, of 9/11 and its consequences. Representing, in the words of a scholar of this generation, "the collapse of a society without a government capable of keeping its promises," it also foregrounds the dilemma of a small group of people pitted against an overwhelming majority who have experienced a collective loss of identity, consciousness, and soul.[28]

Nonetheless, humor and social satire remain strong undercurrents in the post-2000 zombie stories. Taking up the subtext of *Dawn of the Dead*, movies such as *Shaun of the Dead* (2004) and *Zombieland* (2009) are hybrid horror-comedies with happy endings.[29] The lackluster hero of *Shaun of the Dead* becomes a heroic zombie fighter only to return to his own zombielike mundane life when the horde has been defeated. The characters in *Zombieland* call each other by the destroyed cities they hail from (Wichita, Columbus, Tallahassee), nicely allegorizing the nation's bereft status. The hero is a neurotic college kid whose obsessive-compulsive disorder, in the form of strict adherence to a lengthy numbered list of behavioral rules around zombies (cast-iron skillets as weapons, Bounty paper towels to soak up unwanted fluids, etc.), has guaranteed his survival. The list itself is an obvious play on the avalanche of mock zombie survival guides and tongue-in-cheek scientific reports over the last decade.[30]

What is the effect of all this faux vérité documentation around imaginary creatures? Like the *Paranormal Activity* series and *Blair Witch Project* before them, they tease—not always playfully—the boundaries between imagination and belief, spawning new conventions of Gothick performance on one hand and Secondary/Primary Belief in the notion of impending global disaster on the other. In a tradition that started at the beginning of the decade and grew exponentially after the mid-2000s, annual Zombie Walks now take place in major cities across North America, including Toronto, Seattle, Denver, and Pittsburgh (the last is where Romero's *Night of the Living Dead* was shot, thereby making it the Whitby of the zombie subgenre).[31] Wearing disheveled dress and ghoul makeup, participants move en masse to squares and town centers using the distinctive "slow death walk" of Romero's films. Meanwhile, young Secondary Believers dutifully stock up on canned goods in anticipation of the apocalypse, weirdly echoing both the Lovecraft fans who mimic their hero's frugal diet and the bomb shelter enthusiasts of the 1950s.

Foremost among these groups is the Zombie Squad, "a zombie suppression task force" (motto: "We make dead things deader") dedicated to "educat[ing] the public about the importance of personal preparedness and self reliance, to increase its readiness to respond to disaster such as Earthquakes, Floods, Terrorism or Zombie Outbreaks."[32] This sizeable community holds its own annual convention and lists twenty-four chapters across the country, one in Canada, and one in the United Kingdom. Chapters are required to sponsor at least two disaster-oriented charities (such as blood, canned food, or clothing drives) and, summoning the dire prospect of zombie police officers or untrained vigilantes, offer zombie survival seminars to fill in the gaps that official agencies won't be able to provide. The U.S. Centers for Disease Control climbed aboard the Zombie Squad bandwagon when Dr. Ali Khan, a rear admiral and assistant surgeon general, posted a notice under "Emergency Preparedness and Response" that playfully merges preparing for a zombie apocalypse with preparing for other disasters such as hurricanes and pandemics that might require people to have an emergency kit in the house and a plan for proceeding to an evacuation center.[33] Cities in various countries have issued similar mock advisories.[34]

The spirit of the Zombie Squad, as much as one can determine, wavers somewhere between Secondary and Primary Belief: as one Millennial member told his older brother about stockpiling canned goods, "You never know."[35] But these Secondary and Primary Believers alike pride themselves on being survivalists, not worshippers. With their distinctive documentarian component, most zombie apocalypse narratives are unique among twenty-first-century Gothick subgenres in actively discounting the supernatural and any kind of spiritual framework. "The inevitable onslaught has, of course, nothing to do with the supernatural," Max Brooks's mock survival manual sternly counsels. "Satan's soldiers are not out to invade God's house. Ultimate evil is not doing battle with ultimate good. The walking dead attack churches for one good reason: It's where the food is."[36] Regarding "religious institutions," the Zombie Squad site asks pointedly: "Your soul may be in good hands but wouldn't you like the training to stick around a little longer in this world when the dead invade your neighborhood?"[37]

This position, however, begs the question that man-eating corpses do not walk in the actual world we live in. What lies behind it, one suspects, is the desire to remove what is technically "supernatural"—the concept of the resurrected dead—from a Christian, magical, or even moral framework. No cross, no Druidic spell, and no pure hero will be able to defeat these uncanny creatures. Neither will advanced technology, since in the universe of the zombie apocalypse it has completely evaporated. In the end, only naked human persistence stands a chance against this Gothick monster.

Some of the authors of the faux manuals went on to write fully developed serious book-length zombie narratives. Following on the heels of his *Zombie Survival Guide*, Max Brooks's *World War Z: An Oral History of the Zombie War* (2006) is an impressive novel hiding under the cloak of faux documentary.[38] Much more than a "mockumentary," it brings an epic spirit to the late twentieth-century horror movie trope of blurring the line between the imaginary and the real world. Purporting to be transcripts of the author's recorded interviews of survivors of a global zombie war that ended twelve years previously, the novel features the almost obligatory blurb from a real-life functionary of the National Center for Disaster Preparedness on its book jacket. But its admirable sweep and convincing realistic detail, unspooling in the words of characters from every country and walk of life, puts this story on a different level than most Gothick narratives. (The gatekeepers of literature have de-Gothicized, but not elevated, this novel with the Library of Congress subject heading "War–Humor.")

Brooks's zombies eat any kind of human flesh, not just brains, though their blood, following zombie convention, has coagulated to a thick black fluid. The virus producing them originated in China but nonetheless quickly gains the label "African rabies." Meanwhile, China has started a war with Taiwan to distract attention from its zombie problem. The United States also drops the ball, but for a different reason: in democracies "public support must be husbanded as a finite national resource," and the country, burned out from the length and cost of the needless Iraq War, fails to back the massive mobilization that defeating the zombie threat requires.[39] In detailed, historically convincing scenarios of how each country (mis) handles the zombie apocalypse, civilian and military leaders alike are displayed almost universally as incompetent, but in different, culture-specific ways. In the catastrophic Battle of Yonkers, for example, American soldiers are sent infantry-style against the zombies in body armor and bulky suits intended for biowarfare, and their missile explosives don't stop the zombies the way a simple shot to the head does. Result: they are slaughtered and turn into zombies themselves. Eventually North America will be overrun with more than 200 million hostile undead.

Ultimately humans win the Zombie War thanks to a cold-blooded tactic called the Redeker Plan, originally developed by a South African Boer to support apartheid, that mandates abandoning large segments of the population to the zombies in order to save a small minority. In the wake of this calculated strategy, adopted in one country after another, a more thoughtful survivor reflects: "I've heard it said that the Holocaust has no survivors, that even those who managed to remain technically alive were so irreparably damaged, that their spirit, their soul, the person that they were supposed to be, was gone forever. I'd like to think that's not true. But if it is, then no one on Earth survived this war."[40] Waging the Zombie War, various characters conclude, has turned the human race itself into zombies of another kind. This sentiment, one of the major themes of the zombie apocalypse subgenre, is echoed at the end of one installment of Kirkman's series when the hero, a former cop, surveys the carnage he and the others have wrought against each other and declares, "We are the walking dead."[41]

As relative latecomers—and no doubt also because of the seemingly insurmountable fact of their repulsive physical appearance—zombies stayed locked in a nonerotic, antagonist role long after other Gothick monsters had begun their reverse Change to lovers and heroes. As a substitute for natural propagation, these celibate zombies were forced to convert others to their status in the manner of "a cult of cannibalistic Shakers," in Kim Paffenroth's words.[42] They were also mute. According to the conventions set by old-school zombie narratives and faithfully observed in the Zombie Walks and other areas of zombie fan performativity, the only sound a zombie could legitimately make was "Graah."

Even so, surveying the field in the early 2000s, one could safely predict it was only a matter of time before a novel, graphic novel, movie, or videogame surfaced about a sensitive, conflicted undead cannibal fighting his or her primal instincts—or better, the offspring of the hybrid mating of a zombie and a live human pledging (like any number of Gothick hybrids) to save humans from his or her own monstrous kind. (The fact that the "cute" subculture derived from J-Pop has taken up zombies with merchandise such as baseball caps with half-eaten brain matter embossed in felt was a clear harbinger of this emerging trend.)[43] As we have seen in other Gothick subgenres, there is also an irresistible pull in contemporary Gothick to have the monster tell the story, to let the subjectivizing force of the first-person voice transform the formerly loathsome collective antagonist into a sympathetic individual protagonist. (The special interiorizing intimacy of the first-person voice, it is worth remembering, is possible only in prose and graphic novel text, not dramatic representation.)

By the end of the decade, in fact, the humanizing and divinizing of the zombie was well under way. The arc of transfiguration we have already seen traversed by vampires is neatly embodied in a series and two subsequent novels by Stacey Jay. In 2009 she began a series based on a character called Megan Berry, Zombie Settler, about a Buffy-type human girl who (since this is the 2000s and not the 1990s) "settles disputes" arising around zombies rather than slaying them.[44] The first in the series, *You Are So Undead to Me*, a junior high romance novel aimed at tweener girls, is the first-person account of a perky tweener who has powers to lay the Unsettled (the risen dead) but must also fight their more dangerous kin, the magic-raised, flesh-eating kind of zombie. As in some strands of the vampire subgenre (notably, *True Blood*), zombies are represented here as a visible, troublesome minority in a functioning human society with an intact government.[45]

In Jay's *My So-Called Death* (2010), however, the breezy first-person narrator is now a former cheerleader who falls from the top of her fancy pyramid formation to biological death, only to discover she carries a genetic anomaly from a Cuban ancestor (the persistent exoticizing factor, like a Transylvanian ancestor in a vampire story) that converts her to Undead, subcategory Death Challenged (as opposed, following the convention of the Megan Berry series, to those raised from the dead by a sorcerer's spell). This obliges her to be enrolled in a *Harry Potter*–style special school for the Undead, who are technically immortal like vampires but considerably more fragile in their body parts. Like the *Twilight* vampires, they have sublimated their feeding lust from human to animal brains, served up three times a day in healthful combinations. By story's end the heroine, Karen, has solved a murder with her handsome zombie classmate Gavin and looks forward, in the author's tongue-in-cheek riff on Bella's prediction about herself and Edward in *Breaking Dawn*, to "hundreds of years of blissful yet argument-filled coupledom."[46]

Scott Kenemore's *Zombie, Ohio* (2011) is a hybrid mystery-horror story of a college professor turned zombie in a car accident (in fact, his own suicide), a first-person character who can talk and think, unlike other zombies, but nonetheless loves to kill humans and eat their brains.[47] Over the course of this funny and sophisticated story, the hybrid human-zombie hero discovers hard truths about his human life, realizes he has been braver as a zombie, and lies down peacefully at story's end to die for real. Similarly, the graphic novel *I, Zombie* introduces a sentient female zombie who resourcefully becomes a gravedigger so that she can satisfy her need to eat human brains without killing live people.[48] This zombie girl detective, Gwen Dylan, is represented as beautiful but with "weird colored skin." Because she accesses the thoughts of those whose brains she eats, she's able to solve, Nancy Drew style, the mysteries of their deaths.

Isaac Marion's *Warm Bodies* (2010) moves zombies much further along the post-2000 pan-Gothick track from evil dead to sympathetic hero to transcendent immortal. The first-person account of a nameless young male zombie "still in the early stages of decay" seamlessly transfers this unpromising creature to the next stage of the process of subjectivizing, humanizing, and ultimately divinizing.

The narrator lives with a population of his fellow undead in an abandoned airport where they enact feeble parodies of human ceremonies ("marriage," "praying") orchestrated by the sinister Boneys, skeletons with no flesh remaining who seem to act as shadow rulers of the community. When he and a cohort hunting pack discover a pod of humans in a hospital, our zombie kills a young man named Perry and is rewarded with telepathic flashbacks from Perry's life as he feeds off his brain. This allows him to voyeuristically experience Perry's love for his girlfriend, Julie, who's about to be devoured herself. Struck by atavistic feelings of love and protection, the narrator saves Julie from his pack and takes her back to his own lair, an abandoned 747 fuselage at the airport. There, listening to vinyl records of Frank Sinatra he has scavenged, the two form a tentative bond that is the bridge to this zombie's burgeoning rehumanization. Meanwhile, he has saved Perry's brain in order to eat it slowly, calling up Perry's memories of Julie so that he can relive their relationship through Perry's eyes as human love.

Before long the narrator, whose mind and heart are stirred by the growing love he feels for Julie, realizes he must take her back to the human enclave in a heavily fortified stadium nearby. Only the oldest guard of the zombies, the Boneys (who the author hints are of a different level of reality altogether), try to prevent them from leaving; the other zombies seem to feel the stirrings of sympathy or longing and refrain from attacking Julie. When Julie abandons R (the most he now remembers of his human name), he returns to the airport and begins regressing back to his zombie existence. But the miracle that has happened between him and Julie has caused a mysterious "movement" across the entire zombie population back at the airport. They begin to have dreams and recall memories of their human life, and a few leave with R when he decides to head for the stadium regardless.

Slipping into the human compound by passing as live, R finds the living as hidebound and locked in their own shuffling hypersecurity routines as the dead. He is reunited with Julie, and the two grow closer. Even the revelation that he killed her boyfriend and ate his brain is no longer a deterrent to their love. Rather, the big question in this Beauty and the Beast fable is whether kissing a zombie will cause Julie to die.

Meanwhile, as he becomes increasingly human, R realizes that his killer instinct is actually a choice he can manage in consciousness: he can *choose* not to feed, and so he does. Reverting to classic Romantic fairy-tale mode, the story reveals that when he and Julie do kiss, not Julie but R is infected (the post-2000 Gothick word for "cursed" or "enchanted"), but in a good way. Unlike Bella, who Changes from human to vampire, R Changes from zombie back to human: "I feel the death in me stirring, the anti-life surging toward her glowing cells to darken them. But as it reaches the threshold, I *halt* it. I hold it back and hammer it down, and I feel Julie doing the same. We hold this thrashing monster between us in a relentless grip . . . and something happens. It changes. . . . It becomes something altogether different."[49] This is the Dan Brown moment of intentional personal gnosis: accessing his own supernormal, quasi-divine aspect, R *chooses* to be human, and becomes so.

Afterward, in a Christlike moment, R begins to bleed freely from his wounds, demonstrating his full return to humanity. At the same time, he sees the irises of Julie's eyes change color to a "brilliant shade of solar yellow that I have never seen before on any human being," and he smells "something similar to the life energy of the Living but also vastly different," a smell that, significantly, is coming from him and Julie alike.[50] With their exchange of love, Marion suggests, both R and Julie have become something more than human, and that something is good, not evil. Following the familiar trope, the story suggests that there's not much to choose from between humans and zombies. (When R asks Julie if things will ever return to the way they were, she says, "I hope not.") Hope resides instead, as in so many other post-2000 Gothick fantasies, in the divine humans themselves. Not yet a man-god but with a suggestion of superhuman hybridity, R has claimed mastery over his own physical essence and transformed it, affirming, "We will *be* the cure because we *want* it."[51]

In *The Passage*, similarly, Justin Cronin's zampire heroine Amy, the Chosen One by virtue of being the thirteenth supervampire "viral" created by the government, is a godlike monster who, like Bella in the *Twilight* series, has conquered her need to kill humans. The near-immortal Amy, this first volume predicts, will live a thousand years and lead humankind out of their bondage to the virals. (Her destiny, like that of so many new Gothick heroes, was anticipated in the character of Neo in Larry and Andy Wachowski's *Matrix* series: a godlike human also bearing the title of Chosen One and predestined to lead humankind out of their bondage to a race of machines who feed, vampirelike, off the heat their bodies generate.)

In the sequels to the American movie versions of *Resident Evil*, the human heroine Alice undergoes a similar mutation: like Amy, she is able to bond with the virus without being zombiefied, and as a bonus, she gets superhuman powers. Both these story lines quote *Alien 3* (1992), in which the heroine, Ripley, becomes impregnated with the embryo of the monstrous creature she is sworn to destroy.[52] At story's end Ripley kills herself by leaping into a vat of molten metal, but in *Alien Resurrection* (1997) she has been cloned into a being endowed with mixed human and Alien DNA, enhanced powers, and telepathic communication with the Alien creatures.[53] Hybrid, transfigured Ripley has made the classic late twentieth-century Gothick hero's journey: half human, half monster or demon, she must fight the forces of evil both out in the world and within herself, and she must win—which of course she does, while also giving birth to a hybrid human-Alien girl child who joins Ripley on the side of the good by helping her destroy the Alien Queen. Following the twenty-first-century Gothick hero's path forged by Stephenie Meyer's Bella, however, Cronin's Amy and Marion's ex-zombie R have been moved up to the next Change after monstrous-to-superhuman: apotheosis.

But how, exactly, does a zombie negotiate ascension when technically it does not possess a soul? As we have seen, the most salient trait of this Gothick creature is loss of soul or consciousness. The first step away from this condition is thus toward becoming human again, as Isaac Marion's R does. This restored consciousness and humanity are precisely what allow him to take the next step up to the "something more" level, though paradoxically (as with the comic book superheroes) he would not have been able to do this if he had not first been made a monster.

Even more directly than vampires, zombies are about resurrection, rising from the grave. Whereas other religions maintain that the soul rises, leaving the body behind, Christian teaching states that the dead will rise from their graves with their bodies intact when Christ's second coming heralds Armageddon, as laid down in 1 Corinthians 15:

> Behold, I shew you a mystery; we shall not all sleep, but we shall all be changed, In a moment, in the twinkling of an eye, at the last trump: for the trumpet shall sound, and the dead shall be raised incorruptible, and we shall be changed. For this corruptible must put on incorruption, and this mortal must put on immortality.

In this framework, the zombie represents a spiritual problem, not a social one. In the zombie apocalypse of the Gothick imaginary, the body rises without its soul as raw, disintegrating matter fueled by the ghost of its biological imperative.

Many in the zombie fan subculture riff on the similarity between Christ rising from the dead and zombie resurrection (witness a favorite Zombie Walk tag: "He died for your sins. Now he's back for your brains"). Like the drinking of human blood, the eating of human flesh reverberates with the sacrament of communion: "Whoso eateth my flesh, and drinketh my blood, hath eternal life; and I will raise him up at the last day" (John 6:54). Accordingly, a probably not-so-serious online Church of the Resurrection, founded in 2008, posts some still-shocking images of, for example, a zombie Last Supper and a "Sweet Zombie Jesus."[54] All this, of course, must be subsumed under a now widespread sub-Zeitgeist confusion about the actual precepts of Christianity, as reflected in the widespread tendency to mistake the tagline to *Dawn of the Dead*—"When hell is full, the dead will walk the earth"—as a line from the Bible.[55]

So what exactly, at the level of spiritual problem, does a zombie apocalypse signify? Like the vampire, the zombie has engendered any number of social metaphors—soldiering, consumerism, herd instinct, and so on—but ultimately the grotesquely disfigured corpse with a relentless killer instinct powerfully revives the Old Goth images of what Death really looks and acts like, up close and personal. An apocalypse is first of all a revelation, a great discovery as well as a great disaster. The revelation zombies carry to a culture divorced from many of its ancient life rituals—a revelation about the ultimate state of loss of consciousness, death, and the dreadful creature with decaying flesh (not the post-1600 anatomically bared skeleton)—still carries this ancient and visceral personification. It is no coincidence that the lurid images of animated rotting corpses the 1950s comics delighted in presenting are dead ringers for late medieval engravings.[56] (The sheer rawness of these comics, coincidentally, makes one feel a certain sympathy for the now ridiculed Dr. Fredric Wertham's desire to censor them.)

Big-screen images of zombie corpses staggering through ruined cities in quest of human prey have helped further reify the figure, long dormant in Protestant Anglo-American consciousness, of Death the hunter. We have seen how this figure evolved from Old Goth into Gothick and its long-running presence in the twentieth-century sub-Zeitgeist even as Death was gradually banished from mainstream Protestant culture. When the hordes of zombies burst out of their comic book and B-movie ghetto after 2000, it's as if those quaint etchings of weeping willows on eighteenth-century tombstones in old New England graveyards had suddenly been switched for the grinning skulls gracing the headstones of the century before.

Mr. Death is back. And so, as the next chapter will show, is his Missus. 167

Everywoman kneels before Lady Death. From *Skin & Bones/Flesh & Blood*. Image courtesy Antenna Theater.

EIGHT

THE GOTHICK THEATER
OF HALLOWEEN

Performing Allegory

Goth is Death.

—J. Gordon Melton

Such a beautiful, respectful Lady. . . . There is nobody as beautiful as she.

—Man's voice in *Skin & Bones/Flesh & Blood*

Until 2006, when street violence by outsiders finally closed it down, the night of October 31 in San Francisco's Castro district was a bacchanal of several hundred thousand revelers, gay and straight, cavorting in outrageous and lascivious costumes more reminiscent of Brazilian Carnival than Halloween. The street celebration still goes on in other urban U.S. centers, notably Greenwich Village in New York. There is also the Halloween Ball in New Orleans (originally an Anne Rice vampire fandom event), other large costume balls, and millions of private parties across the Americas, Europe, and many parts of the rest of the world.

Halloween, in fact, is such a big deal these days that it is easy to forget that before the late twentieth century it was not the Dionysian adult costume party that has spilled over into every corner of North American society but rather a low-key trick-or-treat event strictly for kids and conducted on the streets of one's immediate neighborhood. In the current ubiquitous observance of this strange holiday, ghouls, corpses, vampires, and hookers serve you in broad daylight at the dentist's office, grocery store, government offices, and other public venues.

The reinvention of Halloween has its immediate origins in the Goth subculture of the last thirty years, itself self-consciously camp, role-playing, and performative. The only part of the Goth lifestyle to have crossed over wholesale into mainstream culture, Halloween has become an ecumenical Carnival, the closest thing to a Gothick religious holy day we have. With their white makeup, black nails, black hair, and heavy black eyeliner, often wearing ankhs, crosses, or other religious amulets, classic Goths embody a stylized, eroticized vision of Death. For most of its non-Goth celebrants, the growth of Halloween into the largest group party in North America and western Europe has become an equally intuitive and enthusiastic embrace of this figure banished to the margins of the secularized twentieth century. Along with costuming and concealed identity comes the freedom to let go of inhibitions, dress seductively, and act with abandon.

The absence of any equivalently exuberant Protestant Christian celebration in the service of the light—in terms of observance, Christmas and Easter come nowhere near it—mirrors that same odd overemphasis on the dark in the Gothick literary tradition. (Some devout Protestants have reacted to this lack of proportion by substituting "harvest celebrations" for Halloween, but these demure observances are all but drowned out by the raucous din of ghouls and goblins surrounding them.) Since 2000, however, the sub-Zeitgeist has also registered that there's more to recognizing death than just Halloween. Most religions balance the scary bones-and-ghouls side with some sort of ritual honoring of the dead that also affirms the existence of a realm beyond the material world where dead souls go. Within Christianity, at the stroke of midnight on October 31, Protestant Gothick Halloween (or All Hallows' Eve) turns into the Old Goth Catholic All Saints' Day on November 1, followed by All Souls' Day November 2.

All three holy days stem most directly from the late medieval Catholic cult of the dead in western Europe, but their roots are now conventionally traced to the Irish pre-Christian celebration of Samhain, the first day of Celtic winter, when the doors of the underworld open and the souls of all who died that year gather to enter just as demons gather on the other side to pour out. Bearing in mind that the reconstruction of this pagan event may itself be a nineteenth-century act of nostalgic Gothicizing, trick-or-treating by this explanation is a performative reenactment of dead souls

GOTHICKA

collecting food and other gifts on their way to the underworld.[1] What does seem likely is that the very large immigration of the Irish to America in the nineteenth century accounts for the fact that Halloween became a major American folk custom.[2]

The Mexican Day of the Dead, a religious celebration that includes the first two days of November, is not much observed by non-Catholics in our culture (though we will come across some ecumenical adherents later in the chapter). One Catholic image-based custom of honoring the dead, however, has been widely adopted in recent years. This is the practice of roadside memorials to victims of car accidents, utterly unknown in Protestant societies until the 1980s (the same decade that saw the rise of the Goth subculture and the carnivalization of Halloween). Festooned with baseball caps, photos, handwritten letters and cards, teddy bears (if the deceased was a child), and other talismanic objects commemorating the person's life, these impromptu *retablos* represent a deeper and more respectful mode of acknowledging death than the wound makeup, skulls that change color, and "sexatary" outfits at your local Halloween superstore. Possibly reflecting the sharp spike in immigration from Catholic Mexico and Central America to the United States, the observance quickly widened to include public memorials to any person struck down in an untimely way, from murder victims to celebrities such as John Kennedy Jr. and Princess Diana. It's now ubiquitous in North America, the United Kingdom, and Europe, with offerings left by total strangers as well as family and friends.

Through Halloween and public memorials alike, the idea of death is now present front and center in the Anglo-American sub-Zeitgeist in a way it never was fifty years ago—as rotting zombie bodies and pale cold vampires, but most of all as performance, scary Gothick performance. The primal purpose of modern secularized Halloween, after all, has been mainly to provoke fright for purposes of entertainment. Back when it was still a kid event, an energetic mother would round up all the neighborhood kids in the den, turn out the lights, and pass around bowls of grapes ("eyes"), spaghetti ("intestines"), and calf's liver ("heart") to a group of small, squealing ghouls. Now Halloween haunted houses featuring the same scares in more sophisticated versions are a multimillion-dollar national business in the United States that ranges from Halloween theme parks to blockbuster stage shows. Many of these productions are interactive participatory environments choreographed by skilled theater directors. All aim for maximum shock effect—monsters jumping out of closets, et cetera—with the exception of a few relatively high-toned urban productions, which lean toward the quieter Radcliffean ambience of unseen but anticipated horror.[3]

This chapter explores two examples of Gothick Halloween performance. The conservative Christian *Hell House* productions held in many locations around the United States every October draw deeply both from the Gothick tradition and from Old Goth sources, chiefly the mystery and morality plays; so does a contemporary California theater company's Day of the Dead performance. On one hand, Antenna Theater reinvents the late medieval morality play in a site-based performance that follows a suburban matron Everywoman in her journey through life and death. On the other, the equally site-based and experiential *Hell House* graphically stages archetypal situations in life that will catapult a person into the infernal afterlife. In a feature that immediately sets them apart from the Gothick literary tradition, both performances, the avant-garde and the Christian, are didactic in the time-honored manner of Old Goth morality plays. Both seek to reinvent the Gothick macabre by infusing popular entertainment with moral edification. Both use allegory and a premodern supernaturalist worldview to draw very different moral conclusions.

Samuel Johnson once remarked that he would rather see the portrait of a dog he knew "than all the allegorical paintings they can show me in the world."[4] In this comment the good doctor captured the preference for representations of the real and tangible that would govern his own century's audience and those of the next two centuries to come. To understand this Old Goth mode properly, however, some serious backstory on allegory—that is, the aesthetic device of representing ideas, emotions, or personal qualities as people—is necessary.

Though it endured straight through the nineteenth century as a mainstay of public monuments, epic painting, political cartoons, and popular religious instruction (via such perennial texts as John Bunyan's *Pilgrim's Progress*), allegory was dead in the water in art and literature by the beginning of the modern era. We still recognize, of course, if only ironically, such stereotypical figures as Mother Nature, Father Time, Justice as a blindfolded goddess holding a scale, and the Seven Deadly Sins. Some striking if rather less familiar examples include Opportunity, from Edmund Spenser's *Faerie Queene*, who is a beautiful maiden in flowing garments when she is coming toward you, but a hideous bald and naked hag from the back after she's passed you by. Or the figures of the King and Queen as a form of scientific notation for gold and silver, respectively, in the Old Goth science of alchemy. Or the Money Critic, robed in a garment patterned with financial symbols and nibbling various denominations of world currency to assess their bouquet, in Will Self's 1993 novel *My Idea of Fun*. Or Death as a cute, caring bisexual Goth girl with a philosophical streak in Neil Gaiman's graphic novel *Sandman*.[5]

With the exception of Self's Money Critic and Gaiman's Death, these allegories all date from well before the Enlightenment. To the secular twentieth-century sensibility most of us still inhabit, allegory seems the hollowest of aesthetic shells because the worldview behind it—based on the gut conviction, as Peter Kingsley puts it, that "what isn't there, in front of our eyes, is usually more real than what is"—isn't just one we no longer subscribe to, it is so remote from contemporary ways of perceiving that our minds resist even trying to imagine it.[6] Examining on its own terms the metaphysical engine that powered this formerly omnipresent rhetorical device can help us understand the tremendous influence allegory— what Angus Fletcher calls "the authoritarian mode of literature and art and discourse"—once exerted as a conceptual tool in our culture and is now beginning to exert again in various popular culture genres.[7]

Though personification was already a deeply entrenched feature of the Greco-Roman imagination, the beginnings of allegory in Western art are usually traced to Rome around the first century C.E., when the custom of erecting statuary personifying human qualities such as Fidelity (with a capital *F*), Honor, Virtue, and the like flowered during the Augustan age. The worldview of the Western ancients was refined and modified in Christianity's Neoplatonic matrix, which recognized at least two realities: the greater cosmos or macrocosm (for Christians this would become the living body of God) and the smaller cosmos or microcosm, the physical world around us that mimicked the forms of the divine world that ruled it.

This belief in a dual reality, filtered through a Christian matrix, dominated Western philosophy up to the seventeenth century. Within its framework of visible/material and invisible/transcendental, an allegory was no fanciful conceit or even an abstraction from the material world. The exact reverse of our present-day humancentric formulations, allegory was a way of giving substance and form, for the benefit of our mortal senses, to the world we cannot see or hear or touch or taste—the realm of Ideal Forms inhabited by gods, ideas, intellect, conditions of life, even emotions. For medieval Christian Europeans, contemplating an allegory in art or in literature amounted to considerably more than an edifying aesthetic experience. The allegorical image, visual or verbal, did not "symbolize" forces in the superior world; it embodied them almost in the way a graven image does, as a kind of direct manifestation of the holy realm beyond the senses. As an expression of divine reality, an allegory carried the added theurgic charge of that world and thus was most correctly experienced as a *presence*, the immanence of the transcendent in this world, not just a symbol of it.

The ubiquity of allegory in philosophical argumentation and science as well as religion, art, and literature during the thousand years between late antiquity and the Renaissance also greatly influenced the ways in which both human emotions and the boundaries of personhood were viewed in Western culture before the Enlightenment. What we now think of as subjective feelings originating within a person, such as anger and pity with a small *a* and *p*, were viewed in the frame of allegory as impersonal or transpersonal forces acting from outside upon the individual. In his portion of *The Romance of the Rose*, Jean de Meun presents a familiar allegorical character, Reason, who expounds, after Cicero: "Youth impels all men and maids to deeds / That jeopardize their bodies and their souls."[8] Neither Youth nor Reason are qualities that can be ascribed to a specific person; they are absolute conditions invading and animating persons under their dominion. Possession by the goddess Venus—in allegorical terms, being pierced by Cupid's arrows—is likewise a very different experience, ontologically, than the contemporary interpersonal event we call "falling in love."

The act of turning abstract qualities into walking, talking characters with names as identity markers—a fat man named Greed, a dandy called Vanity—makes the stage allegory's most effective vehicle. The Corpus Christi cycles put on by the English town guilds of the late medieval period did not use allegory, but the layering of simultaneous realities, earthly and heavenly, that allegory suggests did shape the underlying assumptions of these Old Goth pageant plays that drew their stories from the Old and New Testaments. When a cart full of amateur guild players paused in the town square to act out scenes from the Passion, the players—in that doubling of identity so characteristic of allegory—fully inhabited their biblical characters in the same way that the towns of York, Chester, Towneley, and Wakefield became, in the moment, Jerusalem. This convergence of past and present also joined the particular and mortal with the holy and universal, a sensation citizens could savor the rest of the year while they walked these temporarily transformed streets, rubbing shoulders with those who had briefly been the mortal simulacra of Joseph, Mary, and Abraham. As Jody Enders puts it, the late medieval mystery play was a genre that "did something *in* real life as well as *to* real life."[9] These Primary Believers were, in effect, the first reenactors.

Allegory found its supreme expression in the secular morality plays of the fifteenth century. Staged, like the miracle plays before them, in outdoor sites in England and on the continent but performed by traveling professional players, these dramas typically presented a spiritual biography of the average person and the war waged between good and evil for his soul. Their narratives exteriorize this lone man's inner spiritual struggles as a series of picaresque encounters with personified qualities or forces in the course of a journey or pilgrimage. In *Everyman*, the most famous of the morality plays and known all across Europe, the character Death, on God's instruction, tells Everyman it is time to take his last pilgrimage (itself an allegorical construct), and Everyman, completely unready, tries to find companions for the journey.

In this strange abstract landscape where absolutes masquerade as human characters, the play presents Fellowship and Kindred, external qualities of social intercourse, side by side with (to our modern way of thinking) interior qualities of character such as Discretion and Five-Wits. In a complex winding up that remains completely faithful to the dynamics of human nature, all these qualities desert Everyman—though Knowledge doesn't depart until Everyman knows whether or not he is going to Heaven. After that moment of revelation Knowledge vanishes, and only Good Deeds remains to keep Everyman company as he climbs into the grave.

Rather surprisingly, from our perspective, the resolution of this calculated schematic produces a strong and satisfying emotional effect in its audiences.[10] We realize that what allegory loses in nuances of characterization—the distinguishing marks that separate individuals from each other—it makes up for in deep identification. Where naturalism emphasizes empirical particularities ("the portrait of the dog that I know"), allegory shows people everything they have in common. Moreover, for their original audiences the allegorical characters that seem so cartoonishly undeveloped by the standards of naturalism served another important function: as magical talismans. In the Old Goth two-world universe that allegory inhabits, the memorized lines that players uttered functioned as a kind of incantation that activated their characters' theurgic powers as animated emblems capable of drawing down the energies of the divine realm.[11]

Eventually allegory succumbed to "the same great process of Internalization," as C. S. Lewis once put it, "which has turned *Genius* from an attendant *Daemon* into a quality of the mind," in which "century after century, item after item is transferred from the object's side of the account to the subject's."[12] Against the twentieth century's extremes of subjectivity and internalization, however, our new century is witnessing a complex aesthetic move back to objectivity and externalization, a move that includes a revival of traditional allegory in certain areas of Gothick entertainments and even computer media. A whole generation has grown up enacting *Pilgrim's Progress*–style allegorical life adventures in role-playing and videogames. Games routinely include allegorical characters; the popular *Dead Space* features Witch (the most powerful), Hunter (a Gen X flake who skateboards and puts others at risk), and Boomer (a fat, greedy no-hoper who keeps throwing up on you, the hapless gamer). Internal qualities externalized as characters is a much more familiar device to the generation born in the 1990s than it is to their parents or grandparents.

For cybertheorists, too—many of whom are naive Neoplatonists with little awareness of their perspective's ancient roots—what began as metaphor has been transmuted effortlessly into allegory. Thus the reflexive premise that cyberspace is a "real" territory underlies not just the imaginary of popular film and literature but much theoretical discussion as well. Typical fictional products of this mind-set are the personified computer programs in Andy and Larry Wachowski's futuristic Gothick *Matrix* trilogy (1999–2003): the Oracle, an aboriginal wise woman the hero consults, is in reality "an intuitive program who complements" the Architect, a male character embodying the original program that created the Matrix. (There is even the suggestion that the hero, Neo, has been "planned" by the Architect, making us wonder if Neo is human or a program that is "humanizing," in the classic narrative arc of the simulacrum who becomes human.)

Along with *Everyman* and the passion play staged once a decade in Oberammergau, Bavaria, many of the Old Goth mystery and morality plays are produced today in revival in the English provincial towns where they were originally held. In the 1990s, Grant Morrison produced a marvelously layered graphic novel, *Mystery Play*, about one of these revivals.[13] It's a subtle Moebius strip of a story that evokes the contradictions between the all too human players and their exalted roles within the classic Gothick story frame of an escaped asylum inmate and murderer who ends up crucified in place of the actor playing Jesus. Typical for Morrison, it is not at all clear that the moral order has been restored by this act.

How exactly do the conventions of medieval Catholic mystery and morality plays get retranslated in twenty-first-century Protestant evangelical productions of *Hell House*? The long shadows of Milton and John Bunyan, of course, helped allegory remain a vehicle for Protestant religious instruction through the nineteenth century generally, going dormant during much of the twentieth century only to reemerge in this new kind of Christian didactic theater. *Hell House* in its various permutations has played to literally hundreds of thousands of people in the decades since it began, making it closer in impact to that of the original mystery and morality plays than Oberammergau and the other scattered revivals of the Catholic mystery plays across England and Europe.[14]

Hell House offers its players and audience something akin to the participatory experience of the mystery cycles and the didacticism of the morality plays—but minus, in good Gothick fashion, the bright, joyous parts. Combining the tenets of Protestant fundamentalism with Halloween traditions in a new/old medium, *Hell House* draws almost exclusively from dark-side conventions of the late twentieth-century Gothick. Two cross-fertilizing trends are evident here: the rise of the Devil in twentieth-century conservative Protestant theology and the fact that the Anglo-American Gothick itself is deeply rooted in Christian theology.

By various reports, *Hell House* was first conceived in the 1960s at a Pentecostal church, the Trinity Assembly of God, in Cedar Hill, Texas. (A "respectfully presented" production was restaged by an avant-garde theater group in New York using the "Official *Hell House* Outreach Kit" sold by a pastor in Colorado.) In 2001 a documentary was made of the tenth annual performance of a newer *Hell House* production in this same church, but in the decades since it first began the concept has spread to hundreds of evangelical and fundamentalist churches across the United States.[15]

Hell House's creators, of course, had the option of presenting lives of struggle that end in the Light, the experience Bunyan's pilgrim Christian has when he reaches the Celestial City. Grasping the Gothick's vast popular appeal as well as its implicit religious subtext, however, these conservative Christians correctly understood that their potential recruits, craving the extreme scares of horror movies, would "come to see *Hell House* when they'd never walk inside a church," as one *Hell House* organizer put it.[16] Underlining the connection with the "haunted house" entertainments of secular Halloween celebrations, *Hell House* productions are held in the month of October through Halloween night. Hell itself is rendered as a Gothick space straight out of Dante via horror movies and comic books: monster-masked demons torture the damned in a simulated burning pit. In the best Protestant tradition, only the demonic is visible, in excruciating detail, and not the divine: Heaven is rendered simply as a doorway filled with light that we can't see into. As the presenters themselves stress, the purpose of *Hell House* is to awaken a single emotion—fear of the consequences of sin—as a motivator for becoming a saved Christian.

This is not conventional theater presented on a stage with a seated audience. Instead, "tour groups" of fifteen to twenty people are led from room to room in a specially constructed *Hell House* edifice to watch emblematic scenes of damnation and salvation: A boy mocked by his classmates commits suicide. A young woman dying a bloody death from an abortion accepts God and is saved. A homosexual dying of AIDS spurns God and goes to Hell. A girl gets interested in the "other side" by reading the Harry Potter books, graduates to Gothick role-playing games like *Magic: The Gathering* in high school, and then converts to Satanism, only to find she's the one who gets to be the blood sacrifice to the Devil.

The goal of this experiential melodrama, all its participants stress, is Christian edification, just as it was for the morality plays. Here, though, the more specifically focused goal is that of saving lost souls. Whereas Everyman at his death is escorted by an angel with "great joy and melody" into heaven, in the penultimate scene of the Trinity *Hell House* a church member exhorts audience members—under threat of damnation to the Hell full of suffering sinners they have just shared a room with—to make a choice: they can enter the last chamber, a prayer room with church counselors ready to help them be saved, or they can walk off alone into the Halloween night. (This is doing something *in* real life and *to* real life with a vengeance.) Quintessentially late twentieth century in its Gothick feeling tone, *Hell House* evokes Anne Rice's Vampire Chronicles and the *Left Behind* Christian Rapture saga more than it does the brighter twenty-first-century Christian allegory *The Shack* that chapter 11 will explore.

In contrast, the performance piece *Skin & Bones/Flesh & Blood* moves us directly out of the spiritual territory of Halloween into that of the Day of the Dead. Allegory, puppets, and medieval mystery cycles all find a home in the works of Antenna Theater, a site-based company located in Marin County, California, just north of San Francisco. Founded by its artistic director Chris Hardman in 1980, Antenna produces "experiential art forms" in which audiences walk from site to site (often outdoors) to witness silent performances mimed sometimes by puppets, sometimes by human actors wearing large puppet heads, while listening to interviews with real people broadcast on individual headsets. During the months of October and November 1996, Antenna staged a Day of the Dead celebration in the form of a Gothick morality play that ingeniously reinvented the genre in its staging and conception while remaining faithful to the aesthetics and deeper precepts of the original form.

The late twentieth century and early twenty-first century have seen a flowering of international high-art puppetry and the widespread incorporation of puppets in both mainstream and avant-garde theater, a trend that started in the early twentieth century when the Expressionists elevated puppet theater from a low-end mass entertainment to a high art form.[17] Because they are simulacra animated by a human creator, puppets have a universalizing quality that carries them easily into allegory's territory of personification and the animation of objects, pulling us automatically back into the Old Goth matrix of macrocosm and microcosm, greater and smaller, invisible and visible worlds.[18] Almost a hundred years ago, E. Gordon Craig expounded on the "religiosity" of puppets and the unconscious connection they still possess in our very secular imaginations to the graven idols of olden days.[19] Since then, the sense of the uncanny that Freud identified with automata fashioned in the likeness of humans has leaked out into a generic aura of strangeness, with supernatural overtones, that once gathered around holy objects and saint's statues.[20]

The female main character of Antenna's *Skin & Bones/ Flesh & Blood*—the reversal of the common expression in this title already tilts us away from the living and toward the macabre—is a Marin County matron we know only as "the Mrs." but whom we gradually come to perceive as a multi-voiced Everywoman carrying all our own readily identifiable human flaws. Her ruling sins, not directly personified, are clearly Vanity and Greed (with a helping of Lust and Gluttony); her quest is for Beauty, whom she does find personified, but not in the form she expects.

Stereotyped in real life as the ultimate affluent California New Age sub-urb, Marin County easily served as the topos for this allegorical journey. The physical site, the county's central recycling center, offered a similarly charged symbolic space whose double meaning for human life and death was as perfectly accessible to every member of its present-day audience as the use of a live lamb for the Christ Child in the Second Shepherd's Play would have been for audiences in Wakefield, and the pungent odor wafting from the center's adjacent state-of-the-art pig and goat farm underlined the Old Goth atmosphere of this production.

Hardman has acknowledged the original *Everyman*, along with medi-eval roving pageants and cart shows generally, as an inspiration for *Skin & Bones/Flesh & Blood*. A second source was Mexican folk culture, in partic-ular the rich collection of Catholic Christian customs clustered around the Day of the Dead. With his original group, Snake Theater, Hardman did an ur-version of *Skin & Bones*, in conjunction with the Galeria de la Raza and other Latino organizations, as a Day of the Dead celebration in the Mission district of San Francisco; he also began the first Day of the Dead parade in that city, driving an old pickup truck with a fake skeleton in the back. Over the years this parade has become a huge celebration that the Latino community itself now organizes. When Hardman moved to Marin, he started another Day of the Dead parade in that county's biggest city, San Rafael. He and his family privately observe the day with a home-made altar containing the names of everyone they know who died the previous year. All these observances, he believes, are a way of revitalizing the meaning of the autumn season, returning the ritual from its juvenil-ized Halloween version back to a celebration of death that fulfills a deep need in the adult human psyche. Other influences Hardman cites include the Belgian Expressionist painter James Ensor, in particular his painting *The Entry of Christ into Brussels in 1889*, and the Mexican artist José Posada, whose work, particularly his etchings of the *calaveras*, the skeletons who cavort and dance on All Souls' Day, is permeated with Day of the Dead imagery.[21]

A typical Antenna Theater production demands physical participation from its audience, who must walk from one location to another like the actors did in the old mystery plays, but also in the same way as videogamers traverse a series of simulated landscapes and *Hell House* participants explore their Gothick space. Hardman usually serves as master of ceremonies and guide, leading his flock from site to site. Antenna's "Walkmanology" aesthetic—still operative in the twenty-first century, though the technology has upgraded—calls for each "audient" to function as the silent double of the play's main character, "experiencing the drama first hand while listening to their own soundtrack filled with musings about who they are and what they're doing."[22]

Voices—inside the head, banal, oracular, and hallucinatory—dominate the Antenna Theater experience. But the voices come only from headsets, making this a very different playgoing experience than either traditional theater or the medieval pageants. Listening through a headset is a special kind of auditory experience located somewhere "between autism and autonomy," as one commentator has noted.[23] Surrounded by other audience members, one has only the "portable intimacy" of the audio commentary as a companion; the shared, and often audible, emotional reaction that is part of theater experience across cultures since time began—fear, laughter, all of it—is gone. The fact that each person makes the lonely pilgrimage in the sole company of disembodied voices recorded at another time and place creates a further distortion in perceptions of space and temporality. Compared to the shared group experience of the *Hell House* productions, it's an exercise in isolation.

The solipsism of this experience, the uncanny feeling of aloneness that it engenders, is enhanced by the fact that the taped voices played through the headset are not interactive dialogues but snippets of overlapping monologues skillfully edited with cutting, fading, panning, echo, and other sophisticated audio techniques. Never formally identified, the repetitive, incantatory fragments—words, phrases, full sentences—are typically presented out of context, often for comic effect. The speakers are not actors speechifying from a script but real people in the community talking about their lives and jobs.

Typically, a single actor (usually the Mrs. herself) serves as a mute medium channeling this often comically mundane babble while pantomiming the stories these voices tell. "My voice is not something that I merely have, or something that I, if only in part, am," Steven Connor reminds us. "Rather, it is something that I do. A voice is not a condition, nor yet an attribute, but an event."[24] As a series of mimed voice events detached from individual speakers, the continuous oral commentary has the interesting effect of turning the performance even farther away from the interactive conflict of conventional drama and toward the picaresque journey of allegory.

So let the performance begin. Imagine you are standing outside the recycling center on a dark October night, plugged into your Walkman and waiting with a group of fellow audients for the journey to begin. After some anticipatory static, your ears are filled with the sound of crickets and gentle snoring. The corrugated iron door of the recycling center lifts to reveal a sleeping woman, the play's nameless heroine, played by a human actor wearing a giant puppet head. As she tosses and turns, you deduce from the speech fragments in your Walkman that she's in the grip of a nightmare about growing old. A man's voice (it belongs to the owner of a modeling agency, though we don't know this yet) intones the phrases "Over the hill," "Going into the older period," "She's full under the chin . . . a double chin," followed by a child's voice gleefully pronouncing: "A long nose . . . a green face . . . a big wart . . . a big hat . . . a *witch!*"

The Mrs. wakes up to the sound of a shrill alarm and the loud ticking of a clock, an important audio motif in the play. To the noise of cars, a radio traffic report, and a woman saying "I'm late . . . I'm late . . . I really hate it when I'm running late," she rushes off to a busy day. Tagging along after the Mrs., you walk upstairs with your silent headset-wearing group to scenes set in a modeling agency (where women try to get hired as affirmation of their beauty), an aerobics class (figured as dancing silhouettes behind a curtain), a beauty salon (to color ugly gray hair, various voices suggest), and finally a plastic surgeon's office, where the central line of this play is delivered for the first time: "Every single person in this world is concerned about their appearance." This statement is pronounced by the cool, self-satisfied voice of a female plastic surgeon given to deadpan asides about the necessity of "keeping up with the twenty-year-olds." She is mimed by an extraordinarily tall puppet-woman, bobbing and simpering, whose face has movable parts that rotate into various combinations judged to be more or less pleasing. As another voice says, "The eye region of the face is the first thing we look at," a puppet-headed surgeon sharpens his knives.

Our Everywoman disappears offstage for her procedure (voiced, scarily, as a whining buzz saw), then reemerges minus two of her three chin folds and straight-nosed, prancing and preening in front of a mirror: "My face . . . my beautiful face," a woman's voice says happily, and the female surgeon declares, "Plastic surgery just makes you feel so good about yourself, it really does." Excitement builds on the soundtrack about the Black and White Ball, a formerly exclusive San Francisco social event now converted to a fund-raiser open to anyone with the price of a ticket. As your group walks downstairs, many voices, male and female, chatter: "It is wild, it is crazy, it is exciting," "The event of the year," "Always done really pretty," "Everyone gets all dressed up in their best," "Dance all night and party and have fun." And here comes the Mrs., crooning to herself on her way to the ball: "My beautiful face . . . my skin . . . my hair . . . my eyes."

Suddenly, to the plaintive refrain of a Mexican folk song and the modeling agency owner's comment "They're all trying to get in," two fearsome twelve-foot-tall apparitions made of shredded newspaper glide out of the darkness. Your initial terror turns to pity when you hear the poignant voice of a homeless child describing (in an obvious allusion to Joseph and Mary) how he and his family were turned away from various houses and finally had to sleep under some stairs. Miming the angry words of a xenophobic activist, the Mrs. rants against these aliens who "illegally cross our borders," "displace white American citizens out of their jobs," and "devalue real estate values" in San Rafael. "You would not know you were in America," she concludes, and calls the police.

Another change of scene and rooms and now at last you're at the Black and White Ball, where the Mrs. makes her grand entrance. To the butcher's itemization of sirloin cuts ("this part is more tender—this is the round, this is a loin"), the Mrs. poses and preens, then proceeds with other guests to devour an Expressionist carcass with bestial gusto and loud smacking of lips. But without warning, her bright, superficial life takes a downward turn: her precious reconstructed face gets injured, and the Mrs. is rushed on a stretcher to the hospital, where she's on the operating table suddenly facing the prospect of death. You hear a clock loudly ticking; its hand is an arrow pointing at Everywoman's pulsing, glowing heart. A male voice saying "I haven't finished what I came here to do" overlaps with the female activist's "Illegal," "Crossing the border," and "When they say they will overwhelm, they mean it."

As the spectral homeless *gigantonas* restlessly circle the operating table, your ears absorb the layered meanings in the soundtrack. The broken-record, fetishistic repetition and juxtaposition of key phrases and themes, disorienting at first, has taken on an almost symphonic logic that becomes emotionally easy to follow. There is the merging of models and "model citizens," or (in a good Shakespearean conflation) the body and the body politic; there is crossing the boundary from Mexico to the United States, invading the boundary of the body with surgical knives, and crossing the border from life to death; there is the conflation of cosmetic surgery, butchery, and embalming; and finally there is the Black and White Ball as a social event (a dance of life), an ethnic and class separator, and, in the ultimate conjunction of opposites, a dance of death.

Now Death makes his first entrance, the familiar Old Goth/Gothick erotic male predator who's caught a whiff of his prey. A human actor wearing a huge puppet skull head, a top hat, and a black suit of Mexican folkloric tradition, he swoops and hovers around the Mrs. After an interlude about the "terminal restlessness" of some dying people, Death reappears and embraces her, and they do a stately tango as a hospice worker describes the dying person's state of mind: "It's okay. You're going to be okay." As the Mrs. moves into deeper acceptance, Death gives her one last gallant tango swoop—and takes her.

A bell tolls ominously; the "Lord is my shepherd" prayer is recited. Accompanied by Gothick sounds of thunder and lightning, rain, the creaking open of a large gate, and low chanting voices, you descend a stairway into the bowels of the recycling center. It's dank and cold down here in the land of the dead. Surrounded by mountainous bales of newspaper, crushed plastic, and glass, you watch the danse macabre of the *calaveras*—full-body puppet skeletons manipulated by humans standing behind them—to sprightly vibraphone music in our Walkmans. As the voices on the audio track take up the refrain of "crossing the border" once again, the Mrs. is rolled in, lying in her coffin. Cackling ghouls help her out and dance her off to yet another operating table, where they chop off her flesh and behead her. Here voices of the butcher, the plastic surgeon, and the modeling agency owner intertwine ("We trim the flank," "Saddlebags, droopy chin," "Maybe a double chin or a nose that is hulking," "We use this for ground meat"), only to be drowned out finally by the ghouls' maniacal laughter.

Stripped of her flesh as well as her earthly possessions, the Mrs. has no personal identity left. A man says in your ears: "That's a fear of people—that they're going to lose what they have when they go to the other side." The hospice worker says, "Suddenly they're going to find they're no different than everyone else." At this lowest point, another voice (presumably that of a man who survived a near-death experience) breaks in with a soothing, extended (and, significantly, uninterrupted) monologue:

> There was a conscious choice made that it was no longer useful to have this body/mind. Spontaneously there was a great relaxation that was felt through the universe and release and a sense of joy, and spontaneously at that moment I found myself with no awareness of any tragedy or any problem in life. I was actually looking up into a night sky. . . . There was this grand imagination, this open consciousness that seemed to go out into infinity. . . . I was this point of consciousness, radiating, and the whole mood was absolute bliss and joy.

A woman's voice adds, "Most beautiful place . . . don't bring me back." The music swells, and our heroine's head, now reattached to her skeleton, elevates high overhead in blue light.

The skeletons return, performing their danse macabre, and you understand that this is the ultimate Black and White Ball, the place, many disjointed voices tell us, where you "don't have to worry about fashion, taxes," where "there are people hugging and kissing," "having fun all day long"—in short, a rather dubious Paradise. With Hardman's music soundtrack providing a good medieval subtext, you understand that Hell is the cacophonous many, Heaven the harmonious one. As the wild dance ends, Death reappears for the last time bathed in blue light—but this time as a she, not a he, a towering puppet with a female's head and a long dress.

As the Mrs. kneels before transfigured Death, the multitude of voices gives way to one, that of a Latino man: "Such a beautiful, respectful Lady," he tells us, "like the faithful bride" ("Bone structure is very important," the plastic surgeon interrupts). "The one who doesn't have any rivals," the man continues. "Death represents this ideal bride, this perfect lover . . . there is nobody as beautiful as she." As choral singing voices rise, Lady Death lifts up the Mrs. and cradles her like a baby, the formerly male lover now a bride-mother reunited with her child. The Mrs.'s quest for physical beauty has reached its only possible conclusion, and with it comes peace and completion. In the allegory of Beauty, Death is the perfect Form and the Mrs.—you, me, all of us—are her pale imitators.

Skin & Bones is over. As the lights go on, you don't remember the puppet-headed, formerly triple-chinned lead character's insufferable vanity or her xenophobic hatred of immigrants. You've walked with the Mrs. through the various chambers of the House of Life into the underworld and seen her stripped to her essence, which is your essence. Because she has lost the last trace of her individuality and is "no different than everyone else," you've experienced her death as if it were your own.

What is the nature of the animating force ensouling the Mrs. that makes her seem an extension of ourselves, some kind of externalized soul carrier? Absent a metaphysics that allows us, among other things, the consolation of a heavenly city resonant with San Rafael, California, it's our own shared experience of life as evoked by a Babel of voices channeled into this half-human, half-papier-mâché entity. Because allegory embodies the intrahuman experience, not the subjective life of the individual, identifying with the performing object allows us, her ambient doubles, the experience of many lives at the same time. Even though critical wisdom decrees that such deindividualizing is psychologically distancing, something curious happens as we listen to the voices of real people in our headsets and watch the grotesque main character before us mime their chatty stream of consciousness. Instead of fragmenting our sense of the Mrs., this acting out of diverse stories perversely solidifies our sense of her, and our own, living wholeness. Against the whole postmodern agenda that hybrid technologies dissolve the unitary boundaries of self, here all the disparate pieces come together into a satisfying, if most unfashionable, resolution.[25]

In *Skin & Bones/Flesh & Blood*, multimedia theater techniques conventionally regarded as destabilizing have helped invest the Gothick with the spirit (if not the dogma) of Old Goth Catholic folk religion to produce a powerful unitary effect that is also a defining feature of the New Expressionist supernatural melodramas I will discuss in the next chapter. Like one of those nameless pageant masters of the Towneley or York cycles, Chris Hardman offers his local community an aesthetic experience deeply rooted in the details of its everyday reality. It's also, thanks to the universalizing powers of allegory, an experience capable of moving the rest of us as well.

The female revenant Sadako crawls out of a video into the real world. From *Ringu* (1998), directed by Takashi Hideo.

NINE

THE TEN RULES OF SITGES

Global Gothick Horror and Beyond

"[*L'Age D'or*] looks like an American movie," Dalí told me, which was his idea
of a compliment.

—Luis Buñuel

Fifty miles south of Barcelona in the almost autonomous state of Catalu-
nya, Spain, lies the pretty, slightly overpolished resort town of Sitges. In
this former fishing village full of date palms and red tile roofs that is now
completely given over to the tourist trade, you find yourself walking down,
down, *down* winding narrow cobblestone streets toward that magic patch
of blue framed in an archway—the Mediterranean.

Sitges is home every year to the largest festival devoted to fantasy cinema
in Europe. Besides the kind of film the word *fantasy* suggests, the festival
features a wide range of formerly B-movie, now big-budget mainstream
genres: thriller, horror, science fiction, noir, martial arts, and animation.
There is also what might be called the metaphysical avant-garde. Most of
these genres belong to, or draw from, the Gothick tradition.

Europeans generally take horror cinema (as opposed to mere movies) a
bit more seriously than American critics do, just as a century and a half
ago they embraced Edgar Allan Poe more enthusiastically than his own
compatriots did. Yet Sitges, with its scaled-down Croisette (the Platje de la

Ribera) and truncated carpet from the parking lot of the Sitges Meliá to its hotel-basic front entrance, is still distinctly a step down from Cannes. Press and fans (including a substantial geek element) come mostly from Barcelona and other parts of Spain, with a smattering from France, the United Kingdom, and other parts of Europe.

The movies come from all over.

Over ten days midway through the first decade of the twenty-first century, I viewed eighteen films from Spain, Korea, France, Denmark, the United Kingdom, and the United States, emerging from each morning's screening at the hotel's cavernous Auditori to greet again and again that pale flat sea winking in the sunlight. The Mediterranean's lack of surf, always surprising to a Californian, brought up an ancient cinematic memory: a Honolulu audience erupting in heartless laughter during the Woody Allen movie *Interiors* as a lead character drowns herself in a one-foot Hamptons shorebreak. As all present in that Waikiki theater knew, you would practically have to hold yourself down by the neck to make this happen.

Strolling along the promenade between films, I found myself ruminating on what the Gothick has become as it traveled around the world in mostly American films, only to return alchemically transformed in the crucible of other cultures but still indisputably itself. Out of these random reflections, and in the spirit of the Dogme doctrine, a plethora of strictures around "authenticity" irreverently proposed a decade ago by the Danish director Lars von Trier and his cronies (and officially dissolved in 2005 after being taken all too reverently by disciples around the world), I would like to propose the Ten Rules of Sitges. I take as my guiding muse for this manifesto the distinguished son of Spain, great filmmaker, and lover of the Gothick Luis Buñuel, who—moving as he did from the Surrealist avant-garde to grinding out B movies in Mexico to a felicitous late blossoming that lay somewhere between these two extremes—constitutes a little Sitges all by himself.

Rule 1. *In the popular culture of commercial genre movies, including the Gothick, the United States rules like late Rome—that is, shaky but still dominant.*

This parallel is a vivid one at Sitges, where first-century Roman sarcophagi are still being dug out of the ground. In the same way that the makers of these artifacts succeeded in imposing their language and culture on indigenous peoples of the Mediterranean and much of western Europe,

Hollywood imposed its storytelling conventions around the world, creating a distinct brand of popular film in its own image. For much of the twentieth century we colonized the rest of the globe with our blockbuster movies dubbed into their languages, and from time to time they gave us back pale imitations of our crowd-pleasing commercial fare along with unsurpassed treasure troves of art film.

Hollywood has also discovered the lucrative side business of bankrolling "local-language" movies that are produced, shot, and released in their own countries: Walt Disney has begun making its first Chinese-language films, and Sony has produced no fewer than twenty-seven such local-language films since 1995.[1] More significant, the Asian martial arts movies produced since the 1970s and plentifully represented at Sitges demonstrate not only that the tide is reversing—the colonies often making better product than the mother country—but also that these new genres and styles have reentered the American-dominated matrix and transformed it in turn.

Even now, many Americans still naively believe that U.S. hegemony in pop culture products during the twentieth century was a result of something inherently superior in the essence of the home product, not simple market domination. But as Buñuel once astutely remarked of this country's dominance in world literature in his day: "Without the enormous influence of the canon of American culture, Steinbeck would be unknown, as would Dos Passos and Hemingway. If they'd been born in Paraguay or Turkey, no one would ever have read them, which suggests the alarming fact that the greatness of a writer is in direct proportion to the power of his country."[2]

The same holds for commercial cinema. Despite the many significant inroads to be discussed under rule 2, our pop culture entertainment empire still wields a mighty clout, and most of its international market remains very much colonized. America still rules in the realm of "tent pole" blockbuster movies, action-adventure films whose very high-tech special effects and 3-D capabilities can so far only be bankrolled by U.S. studios.[3] At Sitges, big-budget American movies (*Serenity* and *Flight Plan* the year I attended) drew the largest audiences and press conferences, and arrivals of U.S. stars such as Jodie Foster and Quentin Tarantino were prominent in the press and on Spanish television almost to the exclusion of film personalities from other countries. In contrast, many of the more sophisticated non-U.S. Sitges entries that year, such as *Allegro, Antarctic Journal,* and *Lemming,* never found a North American distributor.

Trailing in Hollywood's exhaust much as Britain's Hammer Films did in the 1950s and 1960s, the Barcelona studio Filmax has become a prolific producer of low-budget English-language horror films since the 1990s. These faux American features are aimed at the international market and usually boast an American star with a recognizable name. During his press conference, Filmax's president, Julio Fernández, took heat from the mostly Spanish journalists present about making English-language movies in Spain. His impassioned response—essentially, that his movies were always 100 percent Spanish no matter if the language spoken were English, Spanish, or Chinese—seemed disingenuous in view of a line uttered by a character from one of Filmax's more ambitious horror entries, *The Nun*, directed by Juan de la Madrid: "Is this supposed to be 'I-Know-What-You-Did-18-Summers-Ago'?"

To the rule of ongoing U.S. dominance, my Sitges viewing experience suggested the following:

Corollary a: *Even with the growing importance of global over strictly North American box office returns, the international Gothick smorgasbord still tastes like burgers and fries.*

Those productions with any hope of international distribution must ideally be in the English language and feature well-known American stars. Shoehorning the obligatory American lead actor into a story set and shot outside the United States can lead to some awkward cinematic moments, however. Take *Fragile* (2005), the ghost story from Filmax's best and most visible director, Jaume Balagueró. It's set on the Isle of Wight (great tax breaks) and stars Calista Flockhart (recognizable American star) as a beleaguered hospital's high-strung replacement for a nurse who has mysteriously died. The audience's unspoken question—what's an American doing working temp in the United Kingdom?—is tersely addressed by Flockhart's character as follows: "It's a long story." The presence of Elena Anaya (a readily identifiable star for the home audience in Spain) is similarly dealt with by having her character declare, during a tough turn of events, "I wish I were back in Madrid!"

In *The Nun* (part of a Gothick sub-subgenre Douglas Cowan has dubbed "nunsploitation"), a very Spanish Gothick Catholic girls' school setting is converted into a most unlikely "international boarding school" in order to accommodate characters who are nominally American.[4] The culture gap between Catholic-majority and Protestant-majority countries (to say nothing

of the rest of the world) widens when the ghost of the crazed, sexually repressed mother superior, murdered in impulsive retaliation by the six school-
girls she tormented, proceeds to finish them off one by one according to the
gruesome death met by the martyred female saint each is named after. To
audiences in the American heartland, this ingenious idea (conceived by
Jaume Balagueró) is likely to seem more exotic than the faux Catholic secret-
department-in-the-bowels-of-the-Vatican movies routinely churned out
in the United States.[5] Balagueró's later zombie movie *Rec* (2007), about an
apartment building whose inhabitants are turning into zombies one by one
and staged as TV breaking-news reportage, had breakthrough international
distribution and garnered (the ultimate compliment of a U.S.-centric industry) its own American remake (as *Quarantine*) the next year.[6]

Rule 2. *Still, most of the new Rome's colonies are well on their way to pop culture
autonomy and ultimate hegemony.*

Out of the indigenous dialects of Latin spoken around the Roman Empire came the rich harvest of modern Romance languages. Two millennia
later, Latin is dead and three of its colonial offshoots, Spanish, Portuguese,
and French, have had their own run as imperial languages imposed in turn
on new colonial populations.

Today the world of Gothick horror film is still in the early stages of postcolonial transformation. After the imitations came the hybrids (such as
the Filmax products); after the hybrids came a variety of lively indigenous
progeny using the imperial film language as a point of departure but making it ineffably their own. All that began to change as early as the 1950s,
when the United Kingdom's Hammer Films brought out its famous line
of Gothick period horror films (*The Masque of the Red Death*, spinoffs of
Dracula and *Frankenstein*) whose lurid Technicolor was especially effective
in showcasing gouts of bright crimson blood. In the 1970s, Italian movie-
makers such as Dario Argento and Mario Bava crafted distinctive horror
movies that upped the gore quotient even higher. In the same decade,
Asian martial arts movies basically killed off and replaced the Hollywood
western, and the Japanese conquest of American children's imaginations
inserted new cultural elements that would radically modify the traditionally dark Anglo-American Gothick over the next forty years. The hybrid
conventions of the Asian live-action adult horror films that flowered in the
1990s affected the U.S. horror genre profoundly both in their original

forms and in the flood of Hollywood remakes that followed in the new century.

Corollary a: *The new Rome of Gothick film is Japan, closely followed by Korea, with Thailand bringing up the rear.*

More than any other of these former cultural colonies, Japan has emerged as the front-runner in the new tide of world pop culture domination. Japan had its own supernatural high literary tradition independent from the Anglo-American Gothick, but the works of twentieth-century writers such as Izumi Kyoka, rooted in indigenous folklore, were given that convenient label when they were translated into Western languages. Japanese ghost stories retold by the Irish-Greek-American expat Lafcadio Hearn in his hybrid collection *Kwaidan* (1903), much better known in the West and also labeled Gothick, were made into the 1964 Japanese movie of the same name that gained a worldwide following.[7] Further down the road, however, Japanese folklore mutated with Gothick imports from America to form the brand-new hybrid known as J-Horror.

Japan had begun its first tentative inroads into U.S. popular culture during the country's post–World War II recovery by making toys for the American market, the first being, appropriately, toy U.S. Army jeeps made from tin cans.[8] Over the decades Japanese animators went on to break Walt Disney's stranglehold on children's fantasy culture with everything from Power Rangers to Pokémon to Yu-Gi-Oh and most of the cartoons American children watch today on cable TV. The subtle switch in the balance of cultural hegemony is reflected in the move from total Americanization of the remade product (for example, converting the Japanese hit anime/TV show about boy and girl teenage superheroes, *Mighty Morphin Power Rangers*, to an all-American cast and setting in the 1990s) to the Japanese-language signs, rice consumption, and other flagrantly unassimilated artifacts of current anime shown on U.S. TV. Today, tellingly, Japanese manga in English translation are published to be read back to front, as in the original Japanese.[9]

Fan culture is a far more intense phenomenon in Japan than it is in the United States, recognized by government and populace alike as an industry, a lifestyle, and a distinct kind of social existence. Costuming as a daily practice is common, particularly such iconic and fetishistic looks as the national schoolgirl uniform and, in our neck of the woods, the Gothic vampire Loli costume. Growing out of university hobby clubs in the 1980s, the fan scene now dominates Akihabara, a whole suburb of Tokyo taken over by otaku (extreme fan) merchandising that operates as a kind of fan theme park.[10]

A major subcurrent in otaku culture involves refashioning Gothick gore into something appealing and childlike. Out of this come "cute" (the word *kawaii*, which can also mean "deformed") Cthulhus, zombies, and other blood-spattered toys rendered in bright colors and a cuddly Hello Kitty–like style meant to evoke fantasy, fun, and childhood.[11] The following description of a forthcoming anime on an English-language otaku site is typical:

> *Haiyoru! Nyaruani: Remember My Mr. Lovecraft:* A Cthulhu deity has taken the form of a seemingly harmless silver haired girl. While wandering around, she comes across a high school boy, Mahiro Yasaka, being attacked by aliens and saves him. For those unaware, that's never just the end of it when it comes to Cthulhu.[12]

The concept of cute monsters has traveled the Pacific to capture the sensibility of young American tweeners in much the way the not-so-cute Japanese radiation-engendered monsters captured the Western imagination a half century before. From Godzilla, Rodan, and Mothra, Japanese *kaiju* (translation: "strange beasts") morphed into today's kaleidoscopic menagerie of misunderstood creatures, everything from animistic water faucets and other household objects to alien monsters such as the Dimensional Bug Mother, a creature who sucks the life force out of humans with her tongue.[13]

Blending Eastern elements with the Western Gothick for a hybrid result is well illustrated in the work of Japanese anime giant Miyazaki Hayao. *Spirited Away* (2001), Miyazaki's best-known film outside Japan, has a cast of solidly indigenous supernatural characters, as does the earlier *Princess Mononake* (1997). His faithful adaptation of a British fantasy novel by Diane Wynne Jones, *Howl's Moving Castle* (2004), is a direct homage, like the novel itself, to Gothick-Romantic Victorian children's fantasy. (Miyazaki changed the generic fantasy kingdom setting of the original into Regency England, making Howl a libertine English lord rather than merely a wizard.) Of the heroine of his anime film *Nausicaä of the Valley of the Wind* (1984), a postapocalyptic eco-tale that also became a graphic novel series, Miyazaki has said that he was fascinated by a description of the "Phoenician princess" in a dictionary of Greek myths but was disappointed by the brief mention she gets in *The Odyssey*. Remembering a Japanese folk-tale heroine who loved insects, he blended the two.[14] In the giant mutant Ohmu insects of this story, however, American readers can also see the influence of Frank Herbert's science fiction epic *Dune*. Through many of Miyazaki's works runs a thread of metamorphosis from young girl into ugly crone, a transition that is also found in western Europe's Old Goth "loathly lady" tradition. Widely adopted by the first Gothick and Romantic writers (e.g., Keats's "Lamia"), the loathly lady figure is far less common in twentieth-century Anglo-American horror, which has been highly male-centric.

A series of J-Horror films based loosely on indigenous folk belief but featuring striking technological twists began to make an impression on the international market starting in the late 1990s. The best known was *Ringu* ("The Ring" [i.e., of the telephone], 1998), which uniquely combined the traditional Japanese theme of a vengeful female ghost with the high-tech world of video and telephones: assorted people receive a mysterious video in the mail, receive a phone call from a silent caller immediately after screening it, and die within days. The video turns out to be cursed by the spirit of a murdered girl who crawls out of the television set to kill anyone who watches it.[15] In *Kairo* ("Pulse," 2001), ghosts invade the Internet to lure the living to their website and join them in death.[16] *Ju-on* ("The Grudge," 2000) is the story of a curse passed on from a murdered wife to living victims who are possessed by her rage, commit murder, and die in turn.[17]

South Korea has produced its own distinctive Gothick brand, K-Horror, with notable proponents including Park Chan-wook *(Thirst, Oldboy, Sympathy for Mr. Vengeance)*, Bong Joon-ho *(The Host)*, and Kim Ji-wan *(A Tale of Two Sisters)*.[18] Park Chan-wook's faux Catholic vampire tale *Thirst* (2009), written by Park and Jeong Seo-geong and based rather unexpectedly on Emile Zola's novel *Thérèse Raquin* (which contains the core story of a love triangle, minus the vampires), is a classic piece of contemporary Asian hybrid Gothick filmmaking. In Park's version, a Korean Catholic priest working as a missionary in Africa (an unlikely figure to start with, given that South Korea's large Christian minority is mostly evangelical Protestant) falls victim to a virus (a now well-entrenched quasi-scientific agency for Gothick vampirism) that turns him into a bloodsucker.[19] Back home, the disease transforms the priest from a selfless ascetic into a reckless sensualist who converts the wife of his cousin to lover and fellow vampire. When her bloodlust proves even more out of control than his, he elects to lock her in a car with him at dawn, waiting for the rays of the rising sun to vaporize them both.

In a vestige of the old colonialism that is long gone from children's entertainment, the new wave of Japanese and Korean horror films have been widely remade by Hollywood with American actors and settings, often resulting—with a great deal of poetic justice—in a poor and culturally indigestible imitation of the original. *Ringu*'s rich cultural matrix was diluted in its American remake into a pallid pastiche unconvincingly relocated to the Pacific Northwest, and its gripping plot was rendered incoherent by overediting.[20] The trend has continued with every other international horror movie of any worth being remade (more than a dozen Japanese horror movies as well as Balagueró's *Rec*, the 2007 Spanish horror film *The Orphanage*, the 2008 Danish vampire movie *Let the Right One In*, and many others).

It is an interesting circumstance that so far Hollywood has been far more deeply influenced by filmmakers from other countries at the genre level, especially horror and martial arts, than in its middlebrow mainstream, which remains steadfastly parochial and ethnocentric. This circumstance is partly due to the dramatically lower cost of the genre movies; the United States still hogs the market in blockbusters, whose budgets as yet can't be matched in other countries. Meanwhile, in what one critic has called "a yearly reminder of the American film establishment's systematic marginalization and misapprehension of much of world cinema," the Academy of Motion Picture Arts and Sciences allows exactly five foreign movies out of hundreds, and only one per country, to be nominated for its annual Oscar awards.[21]

Rule 3. *As a result of horror movie imports, the supernaturalism of other cultures has begun to reshape the classic Anglo-American Protestant Gothick.*

Not just Asian folk and religious tradition but also the popular beliefs of non-Protestant-majority countries from Russia to Spain inform the new Gothick.

Corollary a: *Among the many reverse imports from the former colonies, perhaps the most notable is the supernatural female hero or antagonist who is immortal, undead, or monstrous.*

In one of those imponderable marks of cultural difference, the Protestant Gothick literary tradition rarely represented women as menacing

THE TEN RULES OF SITGES

natural or supernatural figures. Up to the last decade of the twentieth century the Anglo-American horror film has drawn from a strong tradition of evil male supernatural creatures (vampires, werewolves, man-made golems of various sorts) who actively menace a passive imperiled heroine. When women did make a supernatural appearance, it was usually as benign, often victimized ghosts, the proverbial woman in white wafting down the corridor of the ancient mansion; female monsters on the order of Sheridan Le Fanu's predatory female vampire Carmilla are the exceptions to the rule. (Not coincidentally, a touchstone of twentieth-century U.S. scholarly and popular tradition alike was that the witches of Salem were innocent scapegoats of social bigotry.)

U.S. horror and sci-fi films have featured a handful of female monsters, but most have been artificial humans fashioned by the crucial Gothick figure of the mad scientist, Mary Shelley's post-Enlightenment update of the sorcerer/alchemist who makes a pact with the Devil. Shelley's own Victor Frankenstein, significantly, forswore making a female bride for his monster. From the spinoff movie *Bride of Frankenstein* (1935) to *Attack of the 50-Foot Woman* (1958) to *Species* (1995) to *Splice* (2009), the scant handful of American female monsters have usually been Adam's rib–type golems fashioned by men and animated by electricity, nuclear radiation, extraterrestrial DNA, or animal DNA, a progression that nicely mirrors scientific advances over the last century.

This kind of gender typing is not as pronounced in Asian and some European Catholic/Orthodox folk traditions, all of which feature some sort of female divinities and thus allow more imaginative space for the representation of female supernatural power.[22] A common thread uniting those countries whose horror films feature female monsters is that their predominant religion is not Protestant Christian. Japanese movies have always foregrounded the folk traditions of female spirits of the dead whose unnatural deaths keep them restlessly searching the material world for vengeance. From *Kwaidan* to *Ringu* and beyond, they are mostly revenants. These spirits aren't the namby-pamby ladies in white of Anglo-American tradition; a new and scary addition to the Gothick, they are malign, fiercely aggressive, and out to get you. The long black hair of the silent killer girl-child ghost of *Ringu* that completely covers her face, to give only one example, is an image that takes up residence in your imagination in a most unpleasant way. With the globalization of the Gothick, the evil female entities of these other cultures have been steadily crawling off the screen much like the *Ringu* entity to lodge themselves permanently in international cinematic consciousness.

Japanese manga and anime have traditionally favored female main characters as well as evil ghosts. The sexy, big-breasted female martial arts fighters of early games such as *Aeon Flux* and *Resident Evil* migrated to American videogames; from there, as we have seen, they moved into American TV shows such as *Buffy the Vampire Slayer* in the 1990s. *Blood: The Last Vampire* (2000), an anime feature film that was remade in English as a 2009 live-action film of the same name, presents a hero and villain who are both female and both supernatural: they are also mother and daughter.[23] Though this might be labeled the "Matilda" strand of the male Gothick (from the female demon in *The Monk*, who may in fact be only a demon inhabiting a female body), examples are few and far between in the Anglo-American Gothick.[24]

Blood also grafts the bloodsucking habits of the Western vampire onto a traditional Japanese demon figure. The hybrid half-human and half-vampire sword-fighting heroine Saya, conscripted by the U.S. Army on a military base in Japan right before the Vietnam War, must finally make the decision to kill her own mother, Onigen, billed as the most ancient, most evil demon ever. Vampirism here becomes a marker for original sin as Saya in effect faces the same moral challenge as the men-gods of the Anglo-American graphic novel: to conquer her most basic instincts in order to live a moral life. Onigen's dying taunt to her daughter is that by using violence Saya is now no different, and no better, than she is.

A very human female monster dominates the Korean-made *Thirst*. In Park's reimagining of the Zola story, the termagant mother-in-law silenced by a stroke proves a more powerful force of nature than even the vampires. Forced to watch the lovers incinerate themselves from the backseat of their car, she turns out to be (in Carol Clover's immortal term) the Final Girl, the archetypal last survivor in late twentieth-century horror film.[25] Her mute, contorted face, bulging with apoplectic rage, is the image we leave the theater with.

The middle-class, middle-aged (and decidedly nonsupernatural) matriarch as monster is a familiar character in the literature and film of Catholic Europe (besides Zola's mother-in-law, think of the title character of Benito Peréz Galdós's 1876 novel *Doña Perfecta*) as well as Asia. Her opposite number in mainstream American movies, in contrast, is more likely to be an ineffectual people pleaser either dominated by her husband or desperately seeking a boyfriend (vide *Buffy* and the *Twilight* series). Yet the character of Buffy herself and the vampires Victoria and Jane (not to mention Bella herself) in the *Twilight* series demonstrate that the long-term reverse influence of other cultures on the Anglo-American colonial-imperial Gothick has undeniably contributed in equal measure as social progress since the 1990s to a new generation of powerful female heroes and villains where few were present before.

The female spirits of my season at Sitges were Spanish and French. Disappointed or thwarted in love, seeking total possession or revenge, they are negative vortices of repressed emotion.[26] The ghost of the evil mother superior haunts *The Nun;* in a French entry, Dominik Moll's *Lemming* (2005), a dead woman's pervasive influence possesses the other characters, possibly even inhabiting the bodies of the living as she seeks revenge on her hated husband. In *Fragile* (now being remade in an English-language version) director Jaume Balagueró and his cowriter Jordi Galceran created a truly frightening apparition who haunts the handful of children remaining in the pediatric ward of a remote, partially evacuated hospital. Seemingly the ghost of a girl who died forty years earlier of a rare bone disorder, the demonic spirit turns out to belong to her obsessed nurse, who secretly injured the girl, fitted her own legs with braces in morbid identification, then hurled herself down an elevator shaft. The visiting temp must pull herself together in time to vanquish the nurse's spirit, who is determined to keep the remaining children with her in the hospital.

Far-fetched, yes, and it got a terrible review from the hard-nosed *Variety* critic, but the rest of the audience and I were squirming in terror every time we were transported to the hospital's abandoned second floor for brief glimpses of the "mechanical girl's" prosthetic legs.

Rule 4. *The Gothick horror film is structured like a folktale.*

Writers of the original Gothick-Romantic nexus drew heavily from Old Goth medieval folktales and romances for their stories. Regardless of their country of origin, the stories that power the new global Gothick also contain such universal folktale motifs as the demon lover, the house that takes on the features of its dead owners, and the unquiet dead, especially victims of murder, who return to haunt the living.

But Gothick horror movies draw from folktale in form as well as content. After analyzing a hundred Russian fairy tales, the Russian formalist Vladimir Propp derived a single narrative structure composed of irreducible units he called "functions." Every fairy tale, he asserted in his classic *Morphology of the Folktale* (1928), has a total of thirty-one such functions, always in the same sequence. Each tale begins with a misfortune or lack that forces the hero to leave home, struggle with a villain, return home, and experience transfiguration in the form of a new physical appearance, a wedding, material gain, or other life change.[27]

The same is true of genre movies, whose form is governed partly by rules of folklore, partly by rules of corporate marketing. As we have seen with many subgenres, what seems like copying in the Gothick is actually a kind of folkloric repetition, and what seems like commercial formula is, at a deeper level, folkloric form.[28] "All folklore distinguishes itself by a mixture of repetition and innovation," as the French historian Lucien Febvre once said.[29] Contemporary mass entertainments, of course, do not operate by the same rules as folklore of preindustrial times; a complex interplay of market forces with individual authorship is involved. Nonetheless, some of the same elements are visible at times, especially the elaboration of familiar themes with individual variations, typical of genre building in popular entertainments across all media.

As we saw in the case of *The Da Vinci Code*, popular novels and films borrow plot and character elements openly from past works in a way contemporary high art with its strong modernist heritage frowns on. Form is the engine that powers the story as themes, subthemes, and motifs travel from film to film in a way that seems like blatant plagiarism to the high literary mind (which judges by rules of authorial originality) but is actually a kind of fractal replication that is deeply satisfying to audiences steeped in this tradition. Genre fans expect the familiar tropes to show up again and again, to be either reinforced, extended, or reversed.[30]

In the United States, folklorist and Jungian Joseph Campbell carried on the structuralist tradition of the Russian formalists in his *Hero with a Thousand Faces*, which influenced a whole generation of filmmakers and writers on film craft.[31] A very Proppian theory of storytelling is widely disseminated today through the popular "Story Structure" screenplay writing classes of Robert McKee, a latter-day Russian formalist disguised in Ralph Lauren sportswear who made a notorious cameo appearance in the movie

Adaptation.[32] In *Story: Substance, Structure, Style and the Principles of Screenwriting*, a distillation of McKee's workshop lectures, Propp's lack or misfortune becomes the "inciting incident," otherwise known as the "Quest":

> For better or for worse, an event throws a character's life out of balance, arousing in him the conscious and/or unconscious desire for that which he feels will restore balance, launching him on a Quest for his Object of Desire against forces of antagonism (inner, personal, extrapersonal). He may or may not achieve it. This is story in a nutshell.[33]

McKee punctuates his dense but lively discourse with highly complicated flowcharts of plot development that underline his formalist emphasis on structure above all other elements. It is, of course, the structure of Auerbach's *avanture*, the quest of medieval epic, and the basis of the male Gothick as well, but now it applies to female heroes, too.

The old Hollywood movies were pure, unadulterated Propp because studio bosses knew Americans craved the simple Story of fairy tale. In one of the great anecdotes of *My Last Breath*, his memoir as told to Jean-Claude Carrière, Buñuel exposes the formalist rules of Hollywood morality, deeply encoded in character and story arc. In his "frequent moments of idleness while under contract in Los Angeles," Buñuel recalls, he constructed "a bizarre document—a synoptic table of the American cinema" consisting of several movable columns set up on a large piece of pasteboard; the first one for "ambience" (Parisian, western, gangster, war, tropical, comic, medieval, etc.), the second for "epochs," the third for "main characters," and so on. Altogether, there were four or five categories, each with a tab for easy maneuverability. The purpose of the table, according to Buñuel, was to show "that the American cinema was composed along such precise and standardized lines that, thanks to my system, anyone could predict the basic plot of a film simply by lining up a given setting with a particular era, ambience, and character. It also gave particularly exact information about the fates of heroines."[34]

The table became such an obsession with Buñuel and his friends that his screenwriter friend Eduardo Ugarte, who lived upstairs, had committed it to memory. When the producer of Josef Sternberg's *Dishonored*, a vehicle for Marlene Dietrich, boasted of the movie's daring originality—the star, Dietrich, actually dies at the end—Buñuel retorted that he knew in the first five minutes that this would happen. To prove his point, he woke up Ugarte and briefly rattled off the details: ambience–Viennese; epoch–World War I. After Buñuel mentioned that the movie opens with a whore (Dietrich) rolling an officer, the sleepy Ugarte "stood up, yawned, waved his hand in the air, and started back upstairs to bed. 'Don't bother with any more,' he mumbled. 'They shoot her at the end.'"[35]

Rule 5. *For fervent consumers of Gothick horror (films, books, or comics), folkloric repetition becomes repetition compulsion.*

Following the end of each screening at the Meliá's cavernous auditorium, I found myself in a deep depression. Was it merely a consequence of watching too many movies in the morning, as real film critics routinely do? Or did it come from encountering too many buckets of fake blood slopped over the unacknowledged trauma underlying such films? The in-your-face cruelty and sadism of the horror genre have always been one of its most troubling features.

Elsewhere I've discussed the psychological dynamic of repetition compulsion as the engine driving the near-addictive attraction fans feel toward genres such as romance and murder mysteries as well as horror.[36] My argument, briefly, is that the teasing, indirect effect of formulaic storytelling is to create an endless cycle of desire provoked by lack of gratification. Much like the symbolic games traumatized children typically like to play, for the true aficionado reading or watching horror on a regular basis amounts to a ritual displacement of trauma experienced but never resolved. The very rigidity of the genre's structure tends to shield its true addicts from the deeper experience of identification with suffering. Instead, it shepherds them safely through a fake reenactment of violent and terrifying events as stylized as a gavotte, a reenactment that retriggers the feelings of terror and helplessness without ever actually engaging with the trauma itself. Seeing the first *Saw* movie does not engender catharsis; instead, it triggers the craving to see *Saw II* and *Saw III*—to feel the scary feelings over and over again without having to engage with what lies beneath them.

For that reason it is not surprising that for more than 200 years male adolescents have remained Gothick horror's largest single demographic. The lifelong appeal that the Gothick holds for some still incites the same chaotic feelings—free-floating panic, anxiety around sexuality and bodily transformation, extremes of love and hate and rage—that beset young people of both sexes at that difficult age. Noel Carroll believes that teenage boys use horror movies as a rite of passage for achieving mastery of fear and overall emotional management; Carol Clover believes these same boys find pleasure in vicariously identifying with the lone female survivor of many of these films.[37] My own feeling is that the deeper compulsion powering the desire to consume horror is by definition never fully addressed, and for that reason—given the very large number of adult horror fanboys and fangirls—it does not represent a true rite of passage.

Bearing all this in mind, and given numerous exceptions within both camps, I propose two broad categories of contemporary horror film roughly corresponding to the classic male and female Gothick: those that appeal to thirteen-year-old boys and those that appeal to fifteen-year-old girls. Each category, naturally, has its own rule.

Rule 6. *The thirteen-year-old boy's Gothick rule of horror* = torture, blood and guts, despair, and destruction.

Until recently, American boys enjoyed being scared to death by such relatively innocuous gorefests as *Tales from the Crypt* and the *Halloween* series. Since the year 2000, however, the stakes of violence in mainstream American horror films have been substantially raised, thanks in no small part to the influence of the colonies, where the gore quotient first began to climb.

The groundbreaking Italian horror movies of the 1960s and 1970s were quickly one-upped by the Asia Extreme movement that started in the 1990s—including works by Tsukamoto Shinya (whose *Tetsuo* series features a "metals fetishist," played by Tsukamoto himself, who pushes increasingly larger shards of iron into his body) and Koreans Takashi Miike (especially *Audition*, 1999) and Park Chan-wook. Inevitably, elements of the Extreme movements in various countries began finding their way into Hollywood. *Hostel* (2005), screened at Sitges by the film's writer/director Eli Roth and executive producer Quentin Tarantino, was one of the first of a new wave of American horror movies that sought to equal their Asian and Italian counterparts in bloodthirstiness. (The equally violent *Saw* series and *Wolf Creek* have Australian roots, though the *Saw* movies are American made.) The critic David Edelstein, himself a fan of violent horror, was the first to dub this new subgenre "Torture Porn."[38]

Hostel is the story of two callow American lads and their Icelandic acquaintance who are lured to a remote corner of Slovakia by the prospect of unlimited sex with beautiful girls, only to become grist for the torture mill of a mad Dutchman. The sole survivor manages to wreak equivalent vengeance on the Dutchman, whom he tortures and murders in a train station toilet before resuming his journey home. In the final shot, the former fun-loving frat boy now bears the stern features of a hardened combat veteran, a character arc if ever there was one. But the delicacy (if that is the right word) of this effect stands in striking contrast to the virtually unbearable violence perpetrated during the story and is perhaps not sufficient to counteract it, given the fact that the main character is now no better than his tormenter.

One might, of course, simply read *Hostel* as a larger, Jamesian metaphor for the whole reverse-import phenomenon of naive American directors falling under the spell of their worldlier, more decadent counterparts in other parts of the globe, including but not limited to Europe, where more recent horror auteurs such as the Dutchman Tom Six (*The Human Centipede* series, about a mad doctor who sews living human beings together), the Frenchman Pascal Laugier (whose *Martyrs* sends a young woman and her friend on a quest for vengeance against her childhood tormentors), and Norwegian Tommy Wirkola (*Dead Snow*, about reanimated Nazi zombies wreaking havoc on the world) are reviving the extreme horror tradition of their Italian predecessors Argento and Bava.[39] Back home, *Hostel* also launched an "antiglobalization" subgenre about young, privileged First World travelers getting their comeuppance from the natives or the locals—such as *Turistas* (2006) and *The Ruins* (2008)—with a rich colonial subtext of exoticized evil that has shown little change since Bram Stoker's day.[40]

Another U.S. entry in this sweepstakes, *The Devil's Rejects*, director/writer/rock musician Rob Zombie's sequel to his 2003 *House of 1,000 Corpses*, has the forces of law and order, in the name of justice, commit equivalent out-of-control sadistic violence on the perps, a family of depraved serial killers who (I think) are supposed to come across as humorous rednecks. I skipped this film at Sitges and turned off the DVD after some quick sampling and thus I didn't get to see, among other moments, the scene where the family leaves a woman hanging from a motel doorway wearing the cut-off face of her husband. "Stephen King has written that horror 'feeds the alligators of the mind,'" Edelstein comments, "yet it remains an open question whether those alligators have a little nap after they're fed or get busy making more alligators."[41] Making more alligators is a perfect metaphor for the repetition compulsion phenomenon of addictive horror, a beast whose appetite gets doubled, not quenched, when it is fed. The more realistically that the details of intense scenes of violence are rendered within the narrow, stylized boundaries of the horror genre, the less real the product becomes.

Real horror, of the kind attempted by the Austrian director/writer Michael Haneke, is another animal entirely. *Funny Games* (1997), his tale of two young serial killers who eliminate the members of a young family one by one (remade in an English-language version in 2007), comes much closer to the anarchic, authentically hideous spirit of real-life murder for pleasure than any of the formulaic melodramas that Zombie and most other horror auteurs are capable of cranking out. What the savage level of faux violence tends to shield from our awareness is the deeply false sentimentality underlying these stories. Torture porn, like the Gothick in general, usually demands some kind of nod to an ersatz moral order even when the vanquished villain returns for a last-minute shock epilogue that also guarantees a sequel, such as the hand bursting through the grave dirt in the film version of King's *Carrie*. In Wes Craven's *The Hills Have Eyes* (1977, remade in 2006), mutant rednecks slay the mother, sister, and father of one family along with one dog—but another dog, and a baby, survive. The *Devil's Rejects* victims, similarly, are granted eye-for-an-eye revenge in the form of a right-wing sheriff who administers horrendous retribution to the killers.

The cheerful young murderer of *Funny Games*, in contrast, offhandedly kills the couple's eight-year-old son first. He's equally lighthearted when, after a breezy kiss on the cheek, he unexpectedly tips the last survivor, the bound and hooded mother, over the side of a sailboat on the way to his next set of victims. Though the actual deaths take place mostly offscreen, the net result is a deep experience of horror that is far, far more unbearable than any close-up of fake skinned faces can ever be. Declaring its subject to be Hollywood's attitude to violence, Haneke has called his film "anti-genre" and admits to attempting to "rape the viewer into independence," converting the imperiled-heroine passivity of the spectator into a state of active horrified awareness.[42] For that reason a film like *Funny Games* does not trigger the old genre-fueled compulsion to see *Funny Games II*. Because it has given you something much closer to a real-life experience of sense-less murder with no cavalry on the horizon, you never want to see it, or anything like it, again.

That is what real horror looks like.

Rule 7. *The fifteen-year-old girl's Gothick rule of horror* = romance, terror, some (but not as much) gore, occasional redemption.

I'm not saying girls are nicer than boys, just that there is a bit of a gender divide in the level of mayhem considered palatable in a horror movie. As a result, these kinds of movies often garner the softer label "supernatural thriller."

An example from Sitges: *The Dark*, a British film with beautiful production values shot in Wales and directed by the talented Canadian John Fawcett (whose debut feature, *Ginger Snaps*, cleverly paired lycanthropy with menstruation and teenage alienation).[43] As unsettling in its own way as *Hostel* even though it is a female Gothick story entirely lacking in gore, *The Dark* chooses the ending of permanent imprisonment inside supernatural evil. When her daughter dies by drowning, the neglectful mother, Adele, learns that she can restore her daughter to life if she travels to the under-water realm and sacrifices herself, which she does. By the iron logic of folk-tale, since Adele has paid with her own life, her daughter should be allowed to return to the world of the living. Instead, an evil young girl revenant comes back in the daughter's body, fooling the unwitting father, who is the only survivor of this family.

From the fifteen-year-old girl's point of view, something fundamental to the folktale genre has not been respected here even though the film stays well within the bounds of conventional taste: namely, the natural order has not been restored. The traditional female Gothick horror movie, though it is just as much a sentimental melodrama as this one, shows more of a fairy-tale concern for the meting out of justice—real justice, not the blood-soaked vengeance of *Hostel* and *The Devil's Rejects*—followed by a return to normal life.

We find this balance of forces in two supernatural Spanish horror films that both debuted at Sitges in 2001: Spanish director/writer Alejandro Amenábar's *The Others* and Mexican director/writer Guillermo del Toro's *The Devil's Backbone*. Even as *The Others* relies on the same gimmicks as the Filmax movies—American star (Nicole Kidman), English-language production, and an English setting (the Channel Islands, maybe another tax break?)—Amenábar's deeply original story of a Gothick mansion in which subjects and objects, haunters and haunted, are reversed surpasses in every way its equivalents in Hollywood as well as in his own country. Similarly, del Toro's Buñuelian ghost story, set in an orphanage during the Spanish Civil War, exposes in its many layered subtexts the roots of violence in personal and cultural hauntings. (Del Toro's work will be explored in more detail in the next chapter.)

Rule 8. *The hero of a supernatural horror film, male or female, must take a trip to the underworld that corresponds to an inner character arc and results in an expanded or diminished fate.*

"The finest writing," Robert McKee declares, "not only reveals true character, but arcs or changes in that inner nature, for better or for worse, over the course of the telling."[44] Mainstream American movies of all kinds demand that their principal characters undergo this kind of Proppian development, preferably in a positive direction. Despite the traditional folktale's turn toward a happy ending, however, the modern Gothick horror narrative, both literary and cinematic, presents a forked path of possibility at the end of the story: (1) after being very bad, things turn out OK, or (2) after being very bad, things get even worse (i.e., *The Dark*).

More specifically, the folkloric dimension of the supernatural horror film, like that of a Scottish ballad, requires its hero or heroine to risk his or her life in a perilous journey to an underworld or an otherworldly realm (or at the least, a fight to the death with otherworldly entities)—and in the best-case scenario come back again. In the most basic sort of horror movie it's usually enough just to get out of the underworld alive. The person breaks free from the spell or the murderous maniac and moves out of the cobwebs of the dark Gothick space into the sunlight—an exteriorized character arc, if you will. In the more sophisticated redactions, those who get out alive are different on the inside, too. But for better or for worse? Herewith two psychologically nuanced European examples from my time in Sitges.

The expanded fate: In *Allegro* (2005), Danish director Christoffer Boe's tightly wound concert pianist Zetterstrom (rough translation: "jerky stream," perhaps an allegorical marker of his compromised creativity) has jettisoned his emotional life on the road to fame and artistic perfection.

When he finds himself suddenly unable to play, he is forced to journey to an underworld uniquely conceived as "the Zone," an urban territory that springs up spontaneously in Copenhagen and cannot be penetrated (intruders simply bounce off its image) except by special dispensation. Zetterstrom has lost first his memory of all but the last ten years (from the crucial moment when he withdrew from his great love) and then his musical ability. His psychopomp, a matter-of-fact old bourgeois in a wheelchair named Tom, tells Zetterstrom he left his talent in a small jar in the kitchen, back in the Zone. To retrieve it, he must wholeheartedly relive the memory of his lost love, chase her down, and unequivocally acknowledge his love for her. All these acts Zetterstrom performs, and though it's too late to win back his lover, when he finally leaves the Zone he is able to deliver the most heartfelt performance of his career. Viewers of this film were probably not aware they were watching an allegory and might not have enjoyed it as much if they had.

The diminished fate: Though well represented in *The Dark*, this outcome also dominates Dominik Moll's *Lemming*, about a woman who shoots herself dead yet seemingly continues to control subsequent events from beyond the grave. Played to tortured neurotic perfection by Charlotte Rampling, this character leads the hero even deeper into her web of corruption and murder after her death midway through the film. Hallucination and reality merge as he becomes the unwitting means of carrying out her urgent last wish: to watch her husband die. Though her scheme succeeds, an ironic if precarious balance is maintained between the forces of good and evil as the main character resumes his mundane suburban existence in a state of complete moral ambiguity. Here the transformation of a man's inner life from naive happiness to compromised, corrupt sophistication while everything stays unchanged on the surface has been beautifully and convincingly represented.

Both expanded and diminished fates unspool in a trio of films about feckless young heroes romantically bound to a living/dead woman: the Quay brothers' *Piano Tuner of Earthquakes*, Tim Burton's *Corpse Bride*, and Terry Gilliam's *Brothers Grimm*.[45] These three works (two of which premiered at Sitges during my stay) redefine, each in its own way, the classic folktale life task facing their protagonists, all high-strung, sensitive young fellows (their collective sensibility is perfectly expressed by the German word *Luftmensch*, literally "man aloft") who must use brute force to get out from under the queen of the underworld (allegorized during the twentieth century as the "mother complex"). They must come back to earth and set their feet firmly on the ground before they can win a flesh-and-blood woman, and gain their manhood, in the real world.

It's fair to say that Burton, Gilliam (who was the executive producer of *Piano Tuner*), and the Quays all feel a bit ambivalent about this triumphalist story line. The title character of the playful *Corpse Bride* (based, by Burton's account, on a Russian folktale but with a great deal of Mexican Day of the Dead lore mixed in) is a much more sympathetic female revenant than her equivalents in *Ringu* and *Lemming*. A spurned bride murdered by her lover, she latches onto the hero, a young man who is engaged to a nice girl but is perhaps not quite ready to get married, and carries him off with her to the land of the dead. It is one of the better conceits of this film that whereas the land of the living—a generic mid-nineteenth-century Victorian Gothick town—is uniformly drab and sterile, the underworld is a kaleidoscope of brilliant color, music, and gaiety. In what is actually a subtle and psychologically acute rendering of a fluttery young intellectual's rite of passage into adulthood, as the bridegroom of Death young Victor slowly learns how to forge a differentiated emotional relationship with a woman, albeit a dead one. Ultimately the corpse bride releases Victor from his accidental vows so that he may marry his human fiancée. Then she dissolves into a flock of butterflies spiraling into the light, an image that neatly cues, and is the transformative end product of, Victor's own distanced scrutiny of a butterfly under glass at the beginning of the story. Fate: expanded.

In *The Brothers Grimm*, the 500-year-old hag queen (a classic Old Goth loathly-beautiful lady) is defeated, the abducted village girls are restored to life, and an earthly woman, the woodsman's daughter, is attached first to one brother and then to the other—but they abandon her to carry on their bachelor adventures even as a fragment of mirror holding the queen's glaring eye continues to hover over the proceedings, suggesting that her power is far from broken. (If you recall *Brazil* and its hero's attempts to escape from his ever more surgically enhanced mother, this ambiguity of outcome, vis-à-vis the mother complex, is pure Gilliam.) The brothers' fate must be rated, provisionally, as diminished.

Another pair of brothers, London-based American avant-garde filmmakers Timothy and Stephen Quay, take Gilliam's regressive move a step further. *The Piano Tuner of Earthquakes* unfolds as a series of overlapping tableaux vivants out of which a story, sad and gentle, gradually surfaces. On the eve of her wedding to her accompanist Alfonso, the opera singer Malvina is murdered by a mysterious admirer, Professor Droz. The evil doctor spirits away her body and revives it into a sort of half-alive zombie state at his secluded island villa, managed by the seductive housekeeper Assumpta. Wandering around the wonderfully stylized island set (think Max Ernst meets *The Island of Dr. Moreau*) are the doctor's seemingly lobotomized male patients, the "gardeners," performing sundry synchronized tasks.[46] When the piano tuner Felisberto (played by the same actor who plays Alfonso, in a referencing of the Quays' real-life identical twinship) is brought to the island to tune up the professor's seven hydraulically operated automata cum musical instruments, he falls in love with the somnambulant Malvina and the interrupted romance seems about to begin anew.

Deliberately thwarting our expectations, however, the Quays' Felisberto doesn't succeed in freeing either Malvina or himself from the underworld. The lovers end up trapped in a jerky, repeating film clip inside the sixth automaton, a miniature stage behind glass (best described as a cross between a fish tank and an eighteenth-century large-screen television set) that is a microcosm of the island. Defying the laws of fairy-tale logic but holding true to the deeply solipsistic ethos of the German Romantic tradition they belong to, the Quays keep their hero hermetically imprisoned—along with his true love—inside the imagination of his human creators. As in *The Dark*, no one gets out of the underworld here. Fate: diminished.

Rule 9. *In the new international vernacular of the Gothick supernatural, the underworld is located in some surprising places.*

Many of the Sitges movies I saw shared a fascination with what is called in Spanish the *más allá*, in Catalan the *més enlà*—the beyond, the other world, the underworld, the place that is not here and now, the place inside and outside the mind where, as Tom tells Zetterstrom in *Allegro*, "infinity doesn't reach into the universe, but into the self." Now Hollywood has absorbed this concept; the *más allá* has literally become "the Further," a dark realm where evil spirits trap a child's spirit in the U.S. horror film *Insidious* (2011), which, like *The Dark*, also features the theme of a parent whose own spirit gets taken in exchange for the return of his child.[47]

The films I viewed locate this realm in some very unorthodox spaces.

Besides *Allegro*'s cordoned-off urban Zone, there is underwater. *The Dark* puts the underworld in a spot common to many cultures—under the ocean directly offshore from a high promontory. In *The Nun*, the presence of the ghost of the drowned mother superior is announced by sudden floods of water from nearby appliances (a toilet that erupts like Yellowstone's Old Faithful moved the Sitges audience to inappropriate laughter).

The underworld can also be found at the earth's poles. In Korean director Yim Pil-sung's *Antarctic Journal*, shown at Sitges, a group of explorers and their driven leader seek a mythic location known as the "Pole of Inaccessibility." The confection they eat while celebrating Christmas at the hopeful beginning of their journey contains ice that is far older than any member of the eager party. As they gleefully consume this ancient frozen water, we know they have entered the magical territory of the South Pole romance, in which the journey to the pole down under is also the journey to the inmost regions of the self—and beyond. We also sense, by the rules of this subgenre from Coleridge to Poe to Lovecraft, that they are unlikely to return from this underworld grotto, which is also the Gothick supernatural realm. Always beneath them lie treacherous chasms that drop into nothingness. As the camera peers up at them out of the cavernous ice holes gaping at their feet, it allows us to inhabit, as it were, the underworld's "point of view"—the frighteningly impersonal perspective of the void, a vortex of nothingness that makes these humans look like tiny brightly colored insects, and equally short lived.

More familiarly, the underworld can be entered through dreams. Always a prominent feature of the traditional Gothick (usually in the form of warnings of impending doom), dreams have also been claimed as muses by Gothick writers from Walpole and Shelley to Stephenie Meyer.[48] The classic Gothick dark dream was maintained in such late twentieth-century horror films as the *Nightmare on Elm Street* series (the bogeyman erupts out of the nightmare into real life) but also showed an interesting move toward the topography of medieval allegory in faux scientific Gothick movies such as *Dreamscape* (1984), in which researcher-dreamers enter other people's dreams and explore entire interior landscapes replete with monsters and helpful figures.[49] At Sitges the film *Somne* (directed by Isidro Ortiz) confusingly mixed bad dreams with a device for changing DNA that produces a malady translated in the subtitles as "Husband O'Brien's syndrome"; *Oculto* (written and directed by Antonio Hernández) seemed to be leading its audience into a dark underworld of precognitive dreams but reversed itself to become a complex, well-wrought revenge story.

The "dream researcher" story line gets its most elaborate treatment in British director/writer Christopher Nolan's megabudget *Inception* (2010), an intricately layered story-puzzle about "dream thieves" in search of corporate secrets who invade others' dreams only to become trapped in the intricate palimpsests of dream limbos and realities they have constructed. The most interesting new development in this Gothick subgenre, however, comes from *Inception*'s immediate predecessor, the Japanese anime *Paprika* (2006), directed by Satoshi Kon from a serialized novel by Yasutaka Tsutsui.[50] In a gender and moral reversal of the Dr. Jekyll/Mr. Hyde doppelgänger of Gothick/Romantic horror, a female psychiatrist and dream researcher uses a new piece of technology that allows her to invade the dreams of others in the form of a sprightly, shape-shifting dream avatar named Paprika.

Soon Paprika takes on an exuberant independent existence of her own as she tracks down a rogue intruder who is prowling the researchers' own dreams and pulling them into other people's waking reality. Just as a corporate male patriarch's dark mechanical dream is about to consume all of Tokyo in the story's climax, little Paprika swells into a gigantic mature woman overshadowing the city. The menacing body of her antagonist shrinks to fit her mouth and Paprika swallows him, morphing the pervading darkness he has created into the blues and whites of the sky and her own extended macrocosmic body. *Paprika*'s apocalyptic resolution epitomizes the Gothick's millennial turn away from the demonic to the ancient landscape shared by medieval Western dream vision and the folkloric traditions of the world's other cultures.

Rule 10. *The territory beyond Gothick has no formula rules. It asks of its audience only a willingness to surrender to the unknown.*

Buñuel himself once said, "A film is like an involuntary imitation of a dream," but added that the cinema is almost never used as a medium to express the "mysterious and fantastic," the poetry of the subconscious that emerges in real dreams.[51] Instead, he complained, even sophisticated filmmakers latch onto the clichéd plots of sentimental novels that they then attempt to dress up with fancy visuals. That charge can be leveled against the horror genre and the Gothick generally, whether the story is rendered as a prose narrative or as a movie. Genre has strict rules of formal composition; what is called art, though it builds on genre's form and shares its themes, is a more elusive territory. Finally, the question must be asked: Are there any instances where the Gothick throws off the armor of its formulas, the solace of pure Story, and enters the territory of art?

Even though they produce work that looks Gothick, the Brothers Quay, to take one example, aren't really Goths, old or new. Their work doesn't aim to inspire shock or horror. Nor is it Surrealism, though it is often labeled so and draws considerable inspiration from that school (most notably, in *Piano Tuner*, from the mad inventor Canterel's allegorical machines in the Surrealist writer Raymond Roussel's *Locus Solus*). It's not postmodern, either. The Quay sensibility is, rather, deeply immersed in Gothick-Romantic-Symbolist imagery, most notably the still lake waters of Arnold Böcklin's painting *Island of the Dead*, an image that dominates *Piano Tuner*'s last scenes. Spurned as kitsch by most contemporary high art painters, Böcklin, Caspar David Friedrich, and others of this school are quoted in the works of a handful of film directors, including Burton, Guillermo del Toro, and Lech Majewski.

To take another example: David Lynch's *Mulholland Drive* (2001) and Thai director Apichatpong Weerasethakul's *Tropical Malady* (2004) both employ the device of the twice-told story: one version as dream or personal fantasy, the other as "real." Lynch uses familiar Gothick characters and situations (the imperiled woman pursued by bad guys); Weerasethakul draws on shamanic folklore to intercut the mundane "real" story of two men who experience a growing attraction to each other with a mythic substory of a shape-shifting creature in the jungle. Lynch's "fantasy" story, in contrast—an aspiring young actress's hopeful arrival in Hollywood and her encounters with an array of feel-good eccentric characters—is innocuous and sentimental, whereas the "real" story underlying it—this young woman, with a different name and identity, is a failed actress who has her female lover/rival killed by a hit man and then kills herself—is supremely dark. In both of Lynch's story lines a black-faced wild-haired wolfman-looking creature lurks behind the same diner's dumpster, skewing these parallel illusions toward the supernatural, as the emcee of the spectral "Club Silencio" makes some motions toward explaining.

At first glance, the many Gothick conventions of Lynch's Janus-faced, over-the-top melodrama would seem on the surface to bar it from the "art" category. But Lynch, Weerasethakul, and the Quays belong to the motley assortment of international filmmakers, theater directors, and writers I call New Expressionists, artists who build on the formulaic elements of genre to produce something a little stranger and not so immediately accessible.[52] They make intricate, nuanced, sophisticated works you must watch a number of times to savor completely, a repetition fueled not by compulsion but by an equally visceral aesthetic desire for expanded meaning.

An umbrella sensibility rather than a school or movement, what I call New Expressionism in the performing arts and literature began in the 1990s, at the tail end of Expressionism's colorful trawl through the twentieth century.[53] New Expressionist writers and filmmakers employ the formula themes of pop culture at the same time as they explore metaphysical issues. They characteristically collapse the boundary between the internal and external (thereby "objectifying" internal forces and feelings as characters and objects in the landscape); depict supernaturalism as a positive, beneficent force; combine melodrama with characters that are often explicitly or implicitly allegorical; and employ kitsch, camp, and cliché for non-ironic effect. This post-postmodern trend in film, theater, and (to a more limited extent) literature can be linked in the visual arts to a phenomenon variously identified as "post-ironic" and, in one region of the United States, as "LA PostCool"– a sensibility, in one curator's words, that "deals openly with such art world taboos as spirituality, commitment, celebratory decoration and psychological confession."[54]

Independently of each other, these New Expressionists have produced a bevy of what might be called supernatural melodramas. This sensibility abounds in international theater (including works by groups such as Mabou Mines and Gardzienice; the American novelist Denis Johnson's less well-known plays, such as *Hellhound* and *Shoppers Carried by Escalators into the Flames*; and even mainstream productions such as Tony Kushner's *Angels in America*). Born in the early nineteenth century as the Gothick novel was peaking as a popular literary mode, melodrama shares many features with the Gothick, as Peter Brooks has pointed out: both genres, which ended up cross-fertilizing each other extensively, are "preoccupied with nightmare states, with claustration and thwarted escape, with innocence buried alive and unable to voice its claim to recognition . . . with evil as a real, irreducible force in the world."[55]

In film, we find supernatural melodrama in the work of such diverse film directors as Guy Maddin and Lars von Trier as well as Weerasethakul and Lynch. Of melodrama, conventionally regarded as a low form, Maddin has said that it is "not exaggerated feeling but the uninhibited primal feeling of dreams—the truest feeling."[56] And melodrama is, as Brooks has noted, "an expressionistic form."[57]

In Maddin's self-styled "oneiric portraiture" *(The Saddest Music in the World, Cowards Bend the Knee, Heart of the World, My Winnipeg, Keyhole)*, his main characters are anguished fraternal alter egos locked in primal battle with their fathers and each other for the love of the same woman, who is also in some way their exteriorized soul or animating spirit. In his New Expressionistically autobiographical *My Winnipeg*, the character of Citizen Girl is the allegorical figure who will restore the "heart of the heart," the forks beneath the Forks, the symbolically charged site in downtown Winnipeg where the Red and the Assiniboine rivers meet.

Allegorical drama must always be melodrama because the feeling mode of allegory, as we saw in chapter 8, is identification, not empathy. In the context of melodrama, allegory exaggerates those qualities of the human condition we all share, not the qualities that set us apart as individuals. Like the Antenna Theater production, and echoing the Gothick move to female heroes, Lars von Trier's works *(Breaking the Waves, Dancer in the Dark,* and the allegorical *Melancholia)* typically center on a woman character who is both an Everywoman and a Christ figure sacrificed for the sins of humans. The Polish writer/director Lech Majewski has produced a series of Hermetic New Expressionist films ranging from *The Roe's Room* (1997), based on his opera of the same name, to *Angelus* (2000) and *The Garden of Earthly Delights* (2004). *Northfork* (2008), directed by Michael Polish and written by Michael and Mark Polish, creates an equally phantasmagoric upper midwestern Gothick space in which angels, possibly dreamed by a young boy, participate in the evacuation of a town before the area is flooded for a dam.

With *Antarctic Journal,* Yim Pil-sung also reveals himself as a budding New Expressionist master in his powerful rendering of humans overwhelmed by a natural landscape of transcendent mystery and power. Like *Moby Dick, Antarctic Journey* tells a story of a dangerous expedition led by a madman from which only one person returns to tell the tale. Beyond this simple frame, however, there is no formula; the film simply reverberates meaning on many levels. Even as they seem to be following a familiar genre path as they retrace the footsteps of a lost 1922 British expedition (and come upon such Gothick tokens as a tattered journal buried under a flag and a withered corpse), Yim's group of explorers are treading virgin territory artistically. *Antarctic Journey*'s solemn, assured pace and world-class cinematography recall the sensibilities of works by two great Russian directors of the Soviet era—the layered metaphysics of Andrei Tarkovsky's 1972 *Solaris* (based on the novel by Stanislaw Lem) and the romantic naturalism of Mikhail Kalatozov's 1959 Siberian epic *The Letter That Was Never Sent*.

At Sitges or anywhere else, enjoying films like these requires neither great effort nor a sharp intellect. All it takes is the willingness to release the craving for familiar structure—in this case the coffin of the Gothick—and make a real emotional surrender to the particularities of the film's imagined world. "The darkness that settles over a movie theater is equivalent to the act of closing the eyes," Buñuel said simply of this act of surrender. "Then, on screen, as within the human being, the nocturnal voyage into the unconscious begins." Genre in general, and the Gothick in particular, takes you on a quick trip to the familiar, wished for but frequently untrue. If you can relax your defenses and reset your aesthetic register to the early nineteenth and early twenty-first centuries instead of the modernist-postmodern prairieland of the century just past, the Gothick's younger sibling New Expressionism (which could just as easily be called New Romanticism) will carry you more slowly to that less familiar but deeply interesting place, the true.

Notebook sketch of the character Cathedral Head for *Hellboy II: The Golden Army* (2008) by Guillermo del Toro. © Universal Pictures.

TEN

CATHEDRAL HEAD

The Gothick Cosmos of Guillermo del Toro

"The entire world we live in is fabricated."

—Guillermo del Toro

Among the dizzying array of grotesque entities crowding our vision in the Troll's Market scene in *Hellboy II*, a creature in a fur-trimmed red velvet robe flashes briefly across the screen. Over its simian eyes and muzzle where a forehead should be, sits a miniature cathedral complete with double towers and decorated archivolts. "Originally the idea was to have little humans running around the ramparts," this creature's only begetter, the movie's writer/director Guillermo del Toro, cheerfully reported, "but the budget wouldn't allow it."[1]

One of about thirty "throwaway" creatures del Toro created for a bravura tableau clearly intended to trump the space cantina scene of George Lucas's first *Star Wars* film, the monster called Cathedral Head is a Gothick emblem of its creator in much the same way the Troll's Market (described in the script as a "steamy, medieval nightmare") sums up the manic whirlwind of a story it is embedded in. *Hellboy II*, cowritten, like the first *Hellboy*, with Mike Mignola from the latter's graphic novel series and aptly dubbed "*Pan's Labyrinth* on speed" by one of its producers, lacks the emotional coherence of del Toro's previous work but expands his distinctive vocabulary of images in a baroque explosion of forms.[2] It's emblematic of the larger world of this director's work, which uniquely infuses Old Goth elements into the Gothick in a weird and very heterodox re-Catholicizing of the faux Catholic.

Born and raised in Guadalajara, Mexico, del Toro has often described his childhood infatuation with monsters and the scandalized reaction of his devout grandmother, who twice attempted to perform exorcisms on him. "It's a spiritual reality as strong as when people say, 'I accept Jesus in my heart.' Well, at a certain age, I accepted monsters into my heart.'"[3] In his articulate commentary track on the special edition DVD of an earlier film, *The Devil's Backbone*, del Toro defines the Gothick as a way of seeing that discovers beauty in the monstrous. Because it "celebrates, embraces, and cherishes the darkness" we've been raised to reject, he asserts, the Gothick is the "only genre that teaches us to understand otherness."[4] Of *Hellboy II* he has said: "I find monstrous things incredibly beautiful, in the way that the most beautiful carvings in Gothic cathedrals are the grotesque carvings. If I were a mason, I would be carving gargoyles."[5]

Del Toro's insistence that the monstrous is sacred is closer to the spirit of premodern Catholic Europe than his grandmother may have realized. Especially at the level of popular belief, Christians of the Middle Ages worshipped a more inclusive pantheon of entities than post-Reformation and Counter-Reformation Protestants or Catholics do. "There are monsters side by side with angels in cathedrals for a reason," del Toro explained to an interviewer. "They occupy the same parcel in the imagination of mankind that angels occupy."[6] Or as David Williams explains in his fine study of the medieval monstrous and its relation to the sacred: "All monsters are negations whose apophatic function is to raise the mind to a higher level of reality."[7] By its very denial of the laws of nature, the monster forces us to consider the existence of other realities besides our own. As a phenomenon that is above nature, not contrary to it, the monster's purpose in sacred art is "to declare truths that do not have their origin in phenomenal nature." In this way the grotesque and monstrous

become a sacred language used to reveal a reality in which . . . virile maiden, serpent angel, or three in one express phenomena that language itself cannot. . . . This is the description of the world as symbol, an allegory to be read and interpreted toward the understanding of something beyond the words and signs . . . it is only through [a] monstrous combination of contrarieties that the supralogical truths about divinity and humanity can be communicated.[8]

One thinks, for instance, of the dog-headed St. Christopher (still depicted this way in the Eastern Orthodox Church) or the virgin martyr St. Wilgefortis, who miraculously grew a beard to protest her marriage to a pagan king and was promptly crucified by her father. Depicted as a gowned and bearded being on a cross—in effect, a seditious image of a female or hermaphroditic Christ—Wilgefortis was a special object of God's favor and the very popular patron saint of unhappy wives and happy widows in the fifteenth century.

Williams, however, has no doubts we are seeing "the representation of the Godhead as monster" in figures such as Wilgefortis and in Julian of Norwich's description of the Trinity as "the property of Fatherhood, and the property of Motherhood, and the property of Lordship—in one God!"[9] Medieval alchemy also used the figure of the hermaphrodite to stand for the quintessence, and by extension the ineffable, that which cannot be expressed.[10] Late medieval manuscript illustrations not only gave Jesus a bird's head, they also gave him three human heads (sometimes Satan got three heads, too) and a nursing mother's flowing breasts.[11]

These deformed entities are of a different order than the gargoyles, demons, and assorted hybrids the word *monster* (which derives from Latin *monstrare*, "to show or display") usually suggests. God as a hybrid freak, *babewyn*, hermaphrodite, jars the mind sufficiently loose from its moorings, this thinking goes, to allow us an authentic experience of the sacred. The later Christian reluctance to link a hybrid or malformed shape with the divine is our cultural inheritance not just of the Protestant Reformation but of the humancentric Renaissance and the subsequent transfer of the agency of deformity from God to the material world.[12]

The ineffability of the monster whose very essence lies beyond our dimensional comprehension, an effect oddly echoed in eighteenth-century notions of the secular "sublime," was well grasped by one of del Toro's principal muses, H. P. Lovecraft. Lovecraft was the first modern to restore the monster, in the "hideously" deformed shapes of his Great Old Ones, to a quasi-transcendent status by virtue of just those adjectives he characteristically used to describe them—*unspeakable, unnameable, indescribable*—along with the permanently mind-altering terror the sight of them engenders in the human unfortunate enough to behold them.

The first fictional monster of the Gothick-Romantic nexus—a hybrid resurrected being halfway between the older golem and the later zombie—was the famous one fashioned by Mary Shelley. And what a tragic, poetical monster the Creature (as Victor calls him) was, a sympathetic character now completely obliterated by a grunting, mute Boris Karloff and his successors on the big screen. (Richard Holmes has shown how the novel *Frankenstein*, like the later *Dracula*, first gained notoriety through dramatic adaptations, in this case five different stage productions through the 1820s, all of which muted Shelley's Creature.)[13] In his original incarnation the Creature grows quickly out of a tabula rasa mental infancy into an articulate being who is able to give eloquent voice to his grief and bitterness about the disgust his appearance inspires and his deep desire for a wife and companion. He becomes the doctor's antagonist only when Victor, reneging on his promise, destroys the female Creature he has half completed.

For the rest of the nineteenth century monsters were mostly shelved, only to be gloriously reborn in twentieth-century comics and movies. These later monster-antagonists had no interior lives to speak of. John Gardner's *Grendel* (1971) was a literary writer's retelling of *Beowulf*, an epic Old English creature feature sanctified by twelve-odd centuries of high art transmission, but the novel notably—in a manner that would become fashionable during the 1980s—retold the story from the point of view of a minor character, in this case a monster. Anne Rice would apply the same monster POV technique to her vampire Louis. Though mutant monsters had become heroes in the comics as early as the 1950s, Mike Mignola's post-1990 Hellboy, as we saw in chapter 4, is an archetypal graphic novel monster hero born of darkness but striving for the good. *Shrek* (2001), a book-turned-film with many sequels, presents the twenty-first-century twist to the traditional fairy-tale universe by presenting a good monster protagonist whose love, in the story's happy ending, is revealed to be a green-skinned ogre just like him and only temporarily disfigured by the shape of an ordinary human.[14]

Del Toro, who has his own version of *Frankenstein* in development, draws his aesthetics from a mélange of sources, historical and contemporary, including Old Goth architecture and the eighteenth-century engraver Giovanni Piranesi. Like his fellow New Expressionists, he's a fan of the late nineteenth-century Symbolist painters Arnold Böcklin, Caspar David Friedrich, and Odilon Redon as well as the twentieth-century Surrealists. (The Troll's Market conceit, of course, is a nod to Christina Rossetti.) His monsters, however, follow the conventions laid down in graphic novels, videogame creature design, and the Lovecraft-influenced Hollywood horror movie canon. *Hellboy II*, whose Irish gnome serves as a Charon-like guide to the underworld, references Greek and Celtic mythology; its Angel of Death as an androgynous female with sphincters for eyes and eyeballs embedded in her wings turns Death female in the twenty-first century Gothick manner even as it echoes Old Goth Catholic iconography, which frequently featured angels with eyes in their wings. Much like the way multimedia effects operate in an Antenna Theater production, these "unified beings" are the paradoxical result of combining digital and animatronic technologies.[15]

As a child, del Toro reports in many interviews, he gave his heart equally to comic books and art books. In this lack of discrimination between "high" and "low" he shows the same all-embracing sensibility of medieval illuminated devotional texts, whose margins display, for example—among other images the modern reader finds shocking in conjunction with the sacred—tiny nuns carrying bowls of turds or picking penises from a phallus tree, men defecating eggs or pierced in the anus by arrows.[16] Also referencing the Mexican folk tradition of *alejibres*, made-up creatures drawn from the individual artisan's own imagination, del Toro describes his movies as "my personal bestiaries of fanciful creatures."[17] The compilations of fantastic creatures found in medieval bestiaries, he stresses, were important for their "cosmological, symbolic and spiritual meanings," and it is this deeper significance that he wants his creatures to carry.[18]

To understand what these deeper meanings were, we must return once again to the larger worldview shared by western Europeans up to the pivotal seventeenth century. These denizens of the premodern era saw themselves nested inside concentric dimensions of reality within which they, their dwellings, their villages and cities, and all the plants, animals, and natural landscape around them were little worlds that imperfectly mirrored the attributes of the larger immortal world and also drew down its wrath or blessings. This top-down relationship between the macrocosm of the eternal realm and the microcosm of our finite material world is summed up in the dictum of medieval alchemy, "As above, so below." In the Old

Goth/medieval way of seeing things, our natures down here, our little worlds, resonate with all the other little worlds around us and the world above because they are all, large and small, composed of the same elements. Because the ripples of an unnatural act extend through all of nature, a person's failings or evil acts can show up in withered crops and lightning from the heavens.

Robert Bly echoes this animistic spirit in his poem "My Father's Wedding":

> If a man, cautious,
> Hides his limp,
> Somebody has to limp it! Things
> Do it; the surroundings limp.
> House walls get scars,
> The car breaks down; matter, in drudgery, takes it up.[19]

The difference between Bly's human-centric Jungian psychological perspective and that of a person of the European Middle Ages is that for an Old Goth, a limp down here on earth is not necessarily always the causal agent that produces all the other limps. Rather, everything limps by virtue of an acausal principle emanating from a higher level of reality ruled by harmony and the higher good. C. G. Jung and the many new religious movements under the New Age label call this effect synchronicity; our cultural ancestors called it the law of correspondences.[20]

Distinctly hierarchical, the Old Goth version of this scheme has it that all things in the physical world are bound up in an invisible web of influences ruled by forces in that other dimension outside time and space; the higher world holds the moral and spiritual template that our material world must conform to. When we mortals do wrong, it throws nature out of whack and invites retribution from above to restore the template. This is a conundrum that Shakespeare presented over and over again in his works (cf. Lear's invocation of "all the plagues that in the pendulous air / Hang fated over men's faults"). An eighteenth-century Gothick revivalist such as Walpole presents the same effect decoratively, nostalgically, and apologetically when he destroys his castle of Otranto with an earthquake for the sins of its inhabitants. A Gothick New Expressionist such as del

Toro uses the law of correspondence in his works both as a convention and as an expression of his own metaphysics.

Just as it was going out of fashion as a way of explaining phenomena in the material world during the seventeenth century, the law of correspondence was briefly reinvented as a scientific principle by the Swedish engineer and mystic Emanuel Swedenborg, then reified as a religious concept by Jakob Boehme and the early Theosophists. It and other elements of the scientifically obsolete Old Goth worldview traveled to the New World via the Radical Reformation and today—as chapter 1 explored in relation to Dan Brown's *The Lost Symbol*—they appear in New Age alternative religious movements and popular self-help psychology works such as *The Secret* (based on the "law of attraction," that thinking positive thoughts attracts positive outcomes in the outer world).

The old worldview is also preserved in some sectors of conservative Christianity, for it is precisely a belief in the law of correspondence that moves preachers such as Pat Robertson to declare that Hurricane Katrina's devastation of New Orleans and the earthquake in Haiti were manifestations of God's wrath triggered by the sinful acts of the inhabitants. The law of correspondence, finally, has also found a new life of sorts in the mathematical notion of the fractal, as chapter 11 will examine, though fractals lack both the hierarchy of degree and the moral framework that informed the Old Goth worldview.

The twenty-first-century Gothick terrain of del Toro's films suggests the top-down moral universe of Shakespeare. *The Devil's Backbone* (2001; written by del Toro and Antonio Trashorras), a ghost story set in a remote orphanage during the Spanish Civil War, has the look of a classic architecturally obsessed Gothick romance, which, as del Toro reminds us in his director's commentary on the DVD edition, focuses on the Gothick house, the domicile, as an emblem and warped container of the human self. This symbolically charged structure, he says, always conceals a "dark secret," linked to a treasure and deep passions, "that is buried in the past and affects the people living in it." At the center of the darkness stands "a very pure hero—a new set of eyes to explore the secret and through the purity of his heart unravel the mystery."[21]

Looming over a desert wasteland much like the palace of the dead in Herk Harvey's 1962 B-movie horror classic *Carnival of Souls*, the orphanage does conceal a secret (the murder of one of its young charges), along with thwarted love and a hidden treasure in gold ingots. The opening scene frames the imposing structure's empty entrance: an unknown voice (belonging, we later learn, to its dead physician) asks, *"Qué es una fantasma?"* (What is a ghost?) as the newly orphaned Carlos, the pure soul of *The Devil's Backbone*, arrives at its gates by car. As the story unfolds, the deceased doctor's rhetorical question frames our sense that all the characters, living and dead, are imprisoned in this edifice—"frozen in time" like "insects in amber," a recurring del Toro image.

But when an enormous bomb lands in the orphanage courtyard immediately after a child's death, our minds connect these two events not by the genre conventions of post-Enlightenment Gothick storytelling but rather by the folkloric logic of the old worldview. The two acts have no immediate cause-and-effect connection. What they do is resonate with each other's violence. The war is an evil, unnatural world of violence that is mirrored in the smaller world of the orphanage. "Like the best fairytales of my childhood," del Toro says, "what's inside the castle reflects what's outside." The bomb—a nod, the director tells us, to the enigmatic giant's helmet that drops out of the sky to land in the castle courtyard at the beginning of *The Castle of Otranto*—never does explode, but "all the characters will reenact the savage nature of the war within the [orphanage's] walls" and the murdered child's ghost will penetrate the material realm to exact vengeance.[22]

In the awards-laden 2006 *Pan's Labyrinth* (more precisely, *El laberinto del fauno*, "The Faun's Labyrinth"), set in the aftermath of the Spanish Civil War during World War II, the pure hero is the young girl Ofelia—a name resonant with doomed maidens who return to the elements—and the orphanage is replaced by a rural mill deep in a forest in northern Spain where Ofelia's evil stepfather, one Captain Vidal of Franco's army, has established his headquarters to fight the last-ditch post–Civil War Republican guerrillas. Del Toro has described this film—and it was interpreted by critics and received by international audiences—as a political parable about the Spanish Civil War. From this perspective, its fantastic elements (a faun, fairies, other denizens of a supernatural underworld to which the main character seems to return upon her death) are either figments of the young heroine's imagination or simply a secondary set of metaphors for the violent events that unfold in the story's "real" world.

The essence of *Pan's Labyrinth*, however, lies in more in Old Goth metaphysics than modern politics. In this movie the good people are all good and the bad people are all bad. This was a deliberate decision, according to del Toro, who declared in a Writers Guild interview that "if you're going to deconstruct [a fairy tale], you can't be crazy enough to deconstruct the structure *and* characters. Little Red Riding Hood has to be Little Red Riding Hood. The Big Bad Wolf has to be the Big Bad Wolf. So, up to a point, function determines these characters to be not as shaded as in *The Devil's Backbone*."[23]

Judged by the standards of psychological realism, Captain Vidal as an embodiment of Fascism is far less dimensional than Jacinto, the troubled young villain of *The Devil's Backbone*, whose escalating murderous violence clearly derives from the great lacks and fears of his displaced childhood. But this absence of shading also means that political-historical shadings are lost, too, a lack that renders the film's politics (much like those of Herbert Biberman's 1953 cheer-the-hero, boo-the-villain trade union epic, *Salt of the Earth*) secondary rather than essential. No matter how righteous the cause, rendering political messages as fairy-tale good versus evil can easily devolve into the us-or-them thinking that autocrats find so useful in molding public opinion. *The Devil's Backbone* mostly walks this tightrope successfully; the strengths of *Pan's Labyrinth* lie more in its dynamic reinvention of the Gothick. Because del Toro devised the story himself, it's the most comprehensive statement to date of his Old Goth/Gothick personal mythos.

Pan's Labyrinth begins literally in darkness with the labored breathing of the dying Ofelia. She is lying inside the old stone labyrinth behind the mill, at the edge of a hole in the earth that, we will learn, is the last open portal to the underworld. As in *The Devil's Backbone*, an unknown supernatural voice (in this case, the Faun's) speaks first, this time the familiar words that open a fairy tale: once upon a time, he says, the great Princess Moanna came to live among humans and forgot she was an immortal being. As the camera closes on Ofelia's open eye, the blood running from her nose reverses its flow, a startling antirealist signal that the story is moving into a flashback.

After this quick opening frame, incomprehensible until the movie's end, the story begins with Ofelia's own journey by car with her pregnant mother to join Captain Vidal in the country. Ofelia discovers a carved stone eye by the wooded roadside and reinserts it into the crudely carved trailside stele of a faunlike creature, an act that seems to animate two magical flying stick bugs who follow the entourage to the mill, which will serve as the dysfunctional Gothick house of self for this story. The mill reminds us that in the old fairy tales millers are tricky characters who sell their daughters to the Devil—and that in myth and folklore generally, the demonic is often represented by mechanical, endlessly repeating movement that never reaches completion (think Tantalus and Sisyphus).[24]

The mill's ancient cog-and-wheel innards, visible in the room where Captain Vidal is camped, are coequal with the mechanism of the watch he obsessively repairs, cleans, and rewinds, endlessly resuscitating it from mechanical death. The watch's cracked face in turn is not only coequal with the captain's fractured personality—the Old Goth medieval worldview does not recognize "metaphors," only equivalents operating at different levels of reality that mirror or "correspond" to each other—but serves as a kind of tombstone for his father, a general who deliberately smashed it as he fell in battle in Morocco so that his son would know the exact moment of his death.

Like all things mechanical in a del Toro movie, the captain's watch exerts an irresistible fascination even as it also carries the negative charge of unredeemed repetition compulsion that is the dark side of the underworld. The centerpiece of del Toro's first movie, *Cronos* (1993), was a micro cog-and-wheel clockwork device made of gold that houses a magical insect whose bite inoculates victims with its own blood, bestowing eternal life and a vampiric need to drink the blood of others; the centerpieces of *Hellboy* and *Hellboy II* are macro versions of the same device, grinding away in the underworld realm. As an overarching influence on his obsession, del Toro cites the grinding mill wheels that kill the evil village doctor in Carl Theodor Dreyer's *Vampyr*. "I have myself tried to reproduce the beauty of those gears, incessantly and not very fruitfully," he says.[25]

As del Toro reminds us in his commentary to *The Devil's Backbone*, the dark secret of the classic Gothick story is often found underground, in the basement or crypt of the edifice (castle, mansion, house) that is coequal with the human body and psyche. In his universe, however, the region below ground always opens onto another dimension, the Old Goth/ Gothick supernatural reality of the underworld. In *The Devil's Backbone*, this is the vaulted cellar of the orphanage (a former monastery) haunted by the ghost of Santi, the murdered child. The underworld of *Pan's Labyrinth* is located beneath the old stone maze behind the mill, a site Ofelia is immediately drawn to. At the center of this ancient labyrinth, itself an emblem of immortality, she finds a dried-up stone well containing a winding staircase that she follows to the bottom. Here Ofelia encounters a fantastical man-goat, Faun, who eagerly welcomes her home as "Princess Moanna" and instructs her in three tasks she must complete to regain her status as an immortal.

Beyond the Faun's antechamber, the underworld of *Pan's Labyrinth* unfolds as a series of vaulted old Gothic corridors and chambers suffused in a womblike red-gold aura.[26] This warmly lit space is a sharp departure from the Gothick urban grottos and crypts that served as del Toro's underworlds in his earlier movies *Mimic* (1997), *Blade 2* (2002), and *Hellboy* (2004). In *Mimic*, giant man-eating mutated insects and humans mirror each other in manifold ways in abandoned tunnels of the New York subway, where the dripping stalactites that are the insects' enormous turds hang from rusted-out subway machinery, making this subterranean grotto as anal as the *Pan's Labyrinth* underworld is uterine.[27] The portal to the underworld in the first *Hellboy* is located in a Gothick staple, a ruined abbey in Scotland, but del Toro's trademark juxtaposition of uncanny organic and uncanny inorganic plays out more fully in the underworld beneath Rasputin's tomb, a Piranesian nightmare where the formidable death-dealing, perpetually wheeling mechanical devices are paired with giant pulpy, tentacled Lovecraftian entities who seek domination of our world through the reanimated Russian priest.

More than any other element of the Old Goth worldview, however, the imagery of alchemy permeates del Toro's films.[28] The frame story of *Cronos* concerns a sixteenth-century alchemist (probably modeled on Nicholas Flamel) who turns into a vampire to sustain his eternal life. The fetus in a glass jar—an image that references alchemy's famous homunculus, a microcosmic "little man," transformed within the alchemical retort into a bringer of new life and possibilities—is the iconic opening image of *The Devil's Backbone*. As in *Cronos*, here the crucible imprisons rather than transforms: the impotent Dr. Casares pickles embryos deformed by spina bifida (the "devil's backbone" of the title) in liquid that he bottles and peddles in town as an aphrodisiac. Far from carrying hope of a new life, in the universe of this story the dead babies are equivalent to (again, as distinct from meta-phors for) the lost souls, adults as well as children, trapped in the orphan-age. These broken characters are the product of a human development process that del Toro has vividly compared to the deformed beggars of Victor Hugo's *The Man Who Laughs*, grown inside jars as babies by human traffickers. "I think that's what the world does to kids," he said to an Austra-lian interviewer. "You are born into your family jar and you grow into the shape of it, and the rest of your life you are limping like a motherfucker."[29]

Pan's Labyrinth leavens this classic Gothick darkness with the brighter atmosphere of fairy tales that is closer to both Romantic and Old Goth sensibilities. As we saw in Hilary Mantel's *Fludd*, the alchemist, following the law of correspondence, seeks moral and physical transformation both within himself and in the outside world. The prime alchemist in *Pan's Labyrinth* is none other than Ofelia, and most of the transformations in both worlds, material and supernatural, mirror her own moral develop-ment toward goodness. When she first encounters the stick bugs, the en-chanted world is in as much disarray as the human one; it is, in del Toro's words, "a magical universe that's been left out in the rain too long."[30] This tattered realm perks up as soon as the former immortal enters the picture, however, thanks to the higher resonating force her presence provides. The stick bugs obligingly morph into Victorian sprites after Ofelia asks them if they are fairies like the pictures in her storybook. Though mainstream audiences are quick to interpret this transformation as Ofelia's own make-believe fantasy, it also indicates that she has already gained the magical ability to change objects in her surroundings simply by focusing her awareness on them.

Performing the three tasks brings more of the same kind of benefits. When Ofelia retrieves the golden key from an enormous toad who vomits up his whole body inside out, she is following two essential principles of alchemy. The first, *unio oppositorum* (the attraction and inevitable joining of opposites), brings her together with the hideous toad. The second, *in stercore invenitur* (literally, "it is discovered in the excrement"), involves finding physical and spiritual treasure in the least likely place. And as Ofelia completes each task, says del Toro, "the magical universe around her start[s] healing itself." Under her powerful gaze, "the fairies become more and more human and the faun becomes more and more elegant and beautiful."[31] After Ofelia's sacrificial death, even the resistance fighters, as downtrodden in the beginning as the fairies, revive to enjoy a limited victory: they kill the captain and take the newborn prince with them into the future.

The lines between inside and outside, subjectivity and objectivity, ordinary life and the supernatural, blur as the two realms of *Pan's Labyrinth*, the "real" world and the underworld, begin to mirror and alchemically transform each other. The Faun gives Ofelia a mandrake root homunculus that comes to life as a plant-baby when Ofelia bathes it in milk. The mandrake root baby's exuberant health calms its human coequal, the unquiet baby in Ofelia's mother's womb. But when the captain discovers the root and it gets burned in the fireplace, the healing link between the two congruent life-forms is broken and Ofelia's baby brother bursts out in a murderous rush, killing his mother.

Roger Ebert has noted how del Toro transitions between these two dimensions of reality in *Pan's Labyrinth* with a "moving foreground wipe," that is, presenting "an area of darkness, or a wall or a tree that wipes out the military and wipes in the labyrinth, or vice versa. This technique insists that his two worlds are not intercut, but live in edges of the same frame."[32] Swapped back and forth between the two realms is the vexing issue of unquestioning obedience to untrustworthy authority figures: the captain shoots the village doctor for euthanizing a tortured rebel against his orders; the Faun, an obsequious, morally ambiguous trickster, bars Ofelia's return to the underworld when she refuses his command to give him her baby brother as the blood sacrifice of the final task. Just as the captain's soldiers riding horseback up the hill start to look more like centaurs than men, the captain's dinner table where he entertains corrupt local functionaries is the aboveground equivalent of the ghastly cannibal's table in the underground lair of the Pale Man.

An archetypal negative father figure and the captain's underworld coequal, the Pale Man is also the Saturnian king who devours his children in the alchemical process of mortification (melting or "killing") of metals; del Toro references the Goya painting of this god swallowing his son as his inspiration.[33] When Ofelia breaks a taboo and eats grapes from the Pale Man's table, she brings this hibernating cannibal back to life. Popping his disarticulated eyes into slits in the palms of his hands (further elaborating this film's eye motif, to grotesque and sinister effect), he staggers after her, devouring one of the unfortunate stick bug fairies on the way. This violent act sends an alchemical ripple back into the upper world, where his alter ego the captain in effect murders his wife by ordering the paramedic to save the baby over the mother. When he shoots Ofelia in the film's climax, her death becomes the paradoxically "blessed" act that fulfills her third task (shedding the blood of an innocent) and frees her to return to the land of immortals.

Pan's Labyrinth ends much like Ingmar Bergman's medieval-folktale-inspired *The Virgin Spring*, along with that film's hint of local legend: just as a spring erupts on the spot where Bergman's maiden was raped and murdered, after Ofelia's death the dead fig tree in the forest sprouts an incongruous flower. The striking difference between the stories is that the double worlds of *Pan's Labyrinth* are presexual. Though the figures of Ofelia and the Faun trigger echoes of Cocteau's *Beauty and the Beast*, the Faun does not woo Ofelia. In del Toro's vision, this lascivious mythological figure has no genitals; neither do the Pale Man or the fairies. Even though the captain is almost exaggeratedly "Vidal"—full of life, sexual energy, violence—he sleeps downstairs, apart from his pregnant wife, to protect his unborn heir. When Ofelia crawls out of the hollow under the fig tree after retrieving the golden key (which is also the key to the storehouse that the servant Mercedes gives to the rebels), she's distraught and smeared with dark mud, suggesting rape.

In the alchemical container of del Toro's story, however, these markers of violation indicate that she's gone through a chthonic initiation in the underworld that does not include sex. Recalling the toad's regurgitation, however, let it be noted that in the Middle Ages one emblem for a woman's vagina was a toadskin turned inside out—and that traditionally a votive toad hung beneath the cross St. Wilgefortis was suspended on.[34]

After her stepfather shoots her in the maze, Ofelia emerges in the underworld inside a magnificent faux Gothic cathedral decorated with Celtic symbols (the screenplay says "vast hall," but the vaulted interior boasts a spectacular rose window). Here her transformed mother and father sit on golden thrones perched on spindly, impossibly high Gaudí-esque columns. To complete this heretical Sagrada Familia, a third empty throne between the royal pair awaits the newly restored Princess Moanna.[35] In this ritual reunion, as distant emotionally as it is physically, the princess's parents are way too far above her for a hug, but of course none of these three immortals is human anymore.

We return to the dying Ofelia as we saw her at the beginning. The extended flashback that lasted the entire movie has taken up only a second in the "real" timeline of this story—a neat demonstration of the collapse of space and time in the supernatural reality that del Toro has situated below, not above, the material world. Now the blood is running its natural course from Ofelia's nose. At the moment of her death the camera closes once again on the staring eye, signaling either the end of Ofelia's fantasy or the ancient Egyptian belief that the eye is the portal through which a dead person's soul escapes into the afterlife. The Faun tells us that the princess ruled wisely in her realm for many years. And some of her goodness, he says as the discreet white flower blossoms on the dead fig tree in the forest, even had a small manifestation in the world above.

So far, the absence of sex in *Pan's Labyrinth* is faithful to the tradition of children's stories—and their deep roots in medieval folklore and romance—even as it avoids the racy Gothick eroticism we moderns are used to. Where del Toro departs even from fairy-tale convention, however, is in denying his princess a mate. *Pan's Labyrinth* ends regressively as Ofelia/Moanna's prince turns out to be her baby brother, just as Mercedes's beloved partisan is no lover but likewise her own brother. Instead of marrying a prince in the underworld, Ofelia is reunited with a fairy-tale "father" (a wise old king with a white beard) and her aboveground mother, both now revealed as the rulers of the underworld, and ultimately she makes her baby brother a prince, too—a chaste if vaguely incestuous family constellation echoed in *Hellboy II* by the characters of Nuala and Nuada, the twin fairies (evil brother, good sister) who rule the autumnal underworld of this film when their father dies.

Ofelia is a virgin sacrifice, but she is not the bride of Death; instead, she becomes ruler of the underworld herself, an ascension (or reascension) to the status of immortal. Judged by Sitges rule 5, Ofelia has it both ways: she never returns from her journey to the underworld (diminished fate), but when she stays there, she becomes a god (expanded fate).

It's tempting to insist, because it's so psychologically authentic, that the true frame of this story is that of a suffering girl in flight from unbearable reality who is desperately imagining a happy ending in the last seconds of her life. Tellingly, when the commentator Terry Gross interviewed del Toro on National Public Radio, she described Ofelia's "fantasy life" in just these terms, passing over the director's rather astounding statement that although the story is set up to allow either of these two positions, he believes the reverse: that the other world Ofelia sees is "a fully blown reality—spiritual reality."[36] Gross for her part was expressing the psychologically oriented assumptions of most older mainstream viewers in the United States, England, and western Europe—namely, the materialist side of the "Is this real or am I crazy?" conundrum so ubiquitous in genre horror film. In this equation, when something uncanny happens the main character experiences it as a supernatural occurrence, but everyone else thinks that person is crazy for believing so.

The original model for this archetypal setup, Henry James's *The Turn of the Screw*, left the question open (are the ghosts of the former governess and her lover real, or is the present governess crazy?), and Radcliffe's "explained supernatural" remained a staple of Hollywood B movies well past midcentury. As yet another marker of the gulf in underlying worldview separating high and popular culture, however, the typical late twentieth-century horror film landed squarely on the side of the beleaguered main character, providing many independent proofs that the supernatural *is* real, and he or she (usually she) is not crazy.[37]

From the origins of the Gothick in the eighteenth century through the present day, the fact that the supernatural has been acceptable only rarely in "serious" art may offer one reason, finally, for *Pan's Labyrinth*'s favorable reception by older art house film audiences as well as by horror and fantasy fans. Because this film allowed *The Turn of the Screw*'s double possibility—the underworld is real, or Ofelia is crazy—it could safely be labeled a political parable rather than that far more troubling and transgressive animal, a story that positions the supernatural as a more powerful dimension of reality than ours. As Michael Chabon has so astutely pointed out, "parable" is the label that mainstream critics like to apply to a lowly genre work to justify their favorable attention.[38] It also serves to sanitize the supernatural as part of the parable's strictly metaphorical universe.

Meanwhile, younger audiences, more comfortable (in movie theaters, anyway) with accepting the premise of the supernatural as objective reality rather than subjective delusion, were more likely to share del Toro's perception—that on her throne in the alternate-world cathedral Ofelia has become an immortal entity in a realm apart from ours. Like the *Twilight* series, *Pan's Labyrinth* moves its dark Gothick story to a bright fairy-tale ending in the afterlife; for both heroines, death brings transfiguration and demigoddess status.

If Bella more closely resembles Persephone by marrying the equivalent of the male prince of the underworld, Ofelia eventually becomes its ruler in her own right. While Bella and her *perfecti* vampires preside over a heaven on earth periodically menaced by the dark energy of less evolved vampires, Ofelia, like Persephone, more conventionally sends flowers to the earth in the spring as a token of her presence. Within his underworld cathedral (where grinding cogwheels are notably absent) del Toro, like the twelfth-century Cathars of Toulouse, has installed an entire parallel divine hierarchy, one in which the feminine principle is given equal power. *Pan's Labyrinth* reimagines the universe of the Old Goth Middle Ages by presenting a spiritual universe balanced between the forces of light and darkness, masculine and feminine, and accessed via the monstrous through the morally ambivalent figure of the Faun.

As a dedicated Lovecraftian, del Toro has also extensively developed the Providence author's novella *At the Mountains of Madness* with a script cowritten with his *Mimic* collaborator Matthew Robbins.[39] This story belongs to the venerable Gothick subgenre of South Pole romance, whose literary proponents range from Coleridge and Poe through the Surrealist Leonora Carrington *(The Hearing Trumpet).*[40] Besides Yim's Sitges entry *Antarctic Journey,* other filmmakers who have reveled in sending their characters on a dual journey to the ends of the earth and their own psyches include John Carpenter *(The Thing,* from a story by John W. Campbell), Ridley Scott *(Alien,* script and story by Dan O'Bannon), and Larry Fessenden *(The Last Winter).*

At the Mountains of Madness offers one of the most extravagant examples of the haunted Gothick space in both its architectural and wilderness versions, embracing edifices, the natural environment, and even the cosmos. In Lovecraft's Antarctic, the human explorers are dwarfed by the deserted "Cyclopean" city they discover hidden in a titanic, Nicholas Roerich–inspired mountain range, with its "vast aggregations of night-black masonry embodying monstrous perversions of geometrical laws" and subterranean labyrinth of creature-made tunnels deep beneath the polar ice.

For Lovecraft, geological stratigraphy and the human psyche are coequivalent. Boring into the earth, the upheaval of ancient Precambrian rocks, means that something ancient, monstrous, and catastrophic will soon erupt, inside and out. The bottom of our souls, the center of the earth, and outer space are all the same place, the transcendent underworld where the monsters live and where Lovecraft finds the ultimate horror, the *horror vacui*, of the Gothick sublime. Del Toro shares Lovecraft's "Pascalian horror, the horror of the empty spaces," which he also finds in Piranesi's architectural fantasias.[41] How this American master's Mexican heir apparent will translate his grandiose Gothick landscape onto the screen—and whether del Toro's new audience of older art house aficionados will follow him into pop culture Ultima Thule—is a Gothick tale still in the making.

Which brings me back to Cathedral Head. The idea behind it, the director has said, was of "somebody that, instead of talking about his home city, carried it around." I don't know how closely this creature's forehead resembles the main cathedral of Guadalajara, but it's fair to say the edifice del Toro carries around in his own head has been permanently molded, baby-in-a-jar style, by the Catholic Church—and inside its sacred space I like to imagine there is a tiny chapel dedicated to Wilgefortis. Where his hero the twentieth-century master Luis Buñuel could proudly proclaim, "I am an atheist and a Catholic, thank God!" Guillermo del Toro can say, "I am a heretic and a Catholic, thank God!"—and mean it.[42]

"The house you build out of your own pain." Cover illustration for William P. Young's *The Shack*. Used with permission of Hachette Book Group, Inc.

ELEVEN

THE NEW CHRISTIAN
GOTHICK

The Shack *and Other Cathedrals*

The shack once again stood old and ugly, doors and windows rusted and broken. . . . He was back in the real world. Then he smiled to himself. It was more likely he was back in the un-real world.

—William P. Young, *The Shack*

For a devout Christian of the twelfth century entering Abbot Suger's cathedral of St. Denis, the procession from the porch into the luminous nave was a journey out of darkness into light. The essence of divine radiance is captured in the tinted glass of the rose window, embodying the soul's ascent to heaven and reflecting back, as all living things on earth do according to their capacity, the absolute light of God the Creator.[1]

We have seen how this upward movement to the light was reversed, in the post-Enlightenment literary Gothick, into a downward plummet to darkness and destruction, as the Old Goth sacred spaces of the medieval church were converted into the Gothick chamber of horrors: the nunnery crypt in *The Monk* where murder and rape are enacted by monks and nuns, the mausoleum under the church at Castle Dracula where vampires nest, and so on and so on.

The twenty-first-century Gothick, however, is reinscribing brightness on its dark base in the same alchemical way as Maurice Lévy describes the process the painter William Turner used to make the engravings in his

Liber Studiorum, creating "subtle gradations and fine variations of light" from a ground of utter blackness.[2] The first shift up was to relocate the charged Gothick space out of the crypt and into more comfortable contemporary venues. Side by side with the Cullens' airy and immaculate house in the *Twilight* series is the compound of spacious California country houses with plenty of built-in bookcases and a fireplace in every room that the vampire Ina and her utopian coven enjoy in Octavia Butler's *Fledgling*. In spite of the big cross in the Cullens' living room, however, neither of these vampire residences could quite be considered a sacred space. It was left to William P. Young's Christian Gothick novel of 2007 to transform a rundown shack where a child has been brutally murdered into the heavenly mansion in the form of a cheerful, quintessentially American log cabin. The new Gothick is all about framing horror within a larger, sunnier transcendental framework, highly heterodox but Christian at its roots.

This post-2000 shift in a few corners of the Gothick sensibility is nicely embodied in the career turn taken by Anne Rice. In 1998, after decades of writing about vampire demigods, she returned to the Catholic Church; in 2004, she abandoned tales of vampires and witches to write two novels retelling the life of Jesus Christ.[3] In a statement posted on her website in 2007 justifying the earlier vampire novels as part of her spiritual journey, Rice wrote: "The one thing that unites [the Christian and the vampire novels] is the theme of the moral and spiritual quest," with a second common thread being "the quest of the outcast for a context of meaning." Louis, the main character of *Interview with the Vampire*, is miserable "because he cannot find redemption and does not have the strength to end the evil of which he knows himself to be a part. . . . It is an expression of grief for a lost religious heritage that seemed at that time beyond recovery." She concludes: "For me, the entire body of my earlier work, reflects a movement towards Jesus Christ."[4]

As we have seen, one of Rice's innovations in the vampire Gothick was to tell the story in first person from the vampire's point of view, a significant late twentieth-century move toward changing the formerly antagonist-villain-monster-Other into a protagonist who becomes sympathetic by virtue of the primacy of his structural position in the narrative: a subjective "I" to identify with instead of a repellent "he," "she," or "it" to be vanquished (or not) by the hero. Rice's early twenty-first-century move, telling the story of Jesus from this same first-person perspective, has the further effect of subliminally linking Jesus with Louis and Lestat. The seven-year-old Jesus' early exploits in *Out of Egypt* include turning clay sparrows into real birds and killing a schoolyard bully, then bringing him back to life. Rice proceeds to recast these stories from the Apocrypha, which also circulated widely in medieval European folklore, in the terms of the contemporary Gothick subgenre made familiar by Stephen King (cf. *Carrie* and *Firestarter*) and extended by J. K. Rowling in her Harry Potter series: the bildungsroman of the special child with paranormal powers.

The changes in the paranormal bildungsroman over the last forty years parallel those in the Gothick generally. In King's fictive world of the 1970s these children traveled an arc of doom. Put in desperate situations where their talents were either reviled or exploited, his outcast child superheroes use their powers as raw, unconscious instruments of their fear and rage, bringing death and destruction to themselves and others. Some twenty years later, Rowling situated Harry Potter and his adolescent cohorts in a much more positive fantasy world where their abilities are carefully nurtured and disciplined within the beneficent matrix of a magical fellowship.

Rice's young Jesus, similarly, learns to stop using his paranormal powers for personal revenge and harness them instead for the well-being of others as a demonstration of God's goodness. His death will not occur as collateral damage to his own vengeful reaction to a series of personal humiliations like those King's Carrie endured; it will be instead a conscious choice to redeem mankind and he will become an immortal of a rather different order than the vampire Lestat. Still, something in the act of giving a god incarnate the "I" voice suggests, ultimately, a merging of the personal and human with the divine in the same way that giving that voice to an evil supernatural creature suggests an analogous merging, one that also carries over to the reader's own congruence with both these entities. The intimacy of first-person narrative marries both these transcendental extremes to our own human identity.

Yet the fact remains that at this moment in cultural history Rice's Jesus is a fictional character whose story (excepting its climax, of course) is less familiar to most of her readers, at home as well as around the world, than those of Harry Potter and Frodo Baggins. Decades ago Northrop Frye made the useful point that in the Middle Ages the Bible expanded to become "a vast mythological universe" generating hundreds of what might be called Christian literary romances, including saints' lives, the story of the harrowing of Hell, legends of the Virgin, and the like.[5] These days the material of the Hebrew and Christian scriptures (not to mention the apocryphal gospels, which are proving a bountiful resource for the new Gothick) has now become what Greek and Roman mythology was for Western culture through the eighteenth century: a compelling imaginal system of the distant past to be refashioned to the mythic needs of the present day.

Or, simply put, more great superhero story lines to riff on.

After completing her Jesus novels, Anne Rice began a new series, Songs of the Seraphim, that reengaged with Gothick elements within a Christian framework. The first, *Angel Time* (2009), has a hybrid plot (crime, historical, supernatural) that allows its author to have her Gothick cake and eat it, too. After a suitable amount of blood has been shed in luxury hotel settings (a staple of Rice's later novels), a suicidal hit man's guardian angel, Malchiah, presents him with an opportunity to save his soul. Taking a page from Chelsea Quinn Yarbro's St. Germain novels, Rice has her hit man given the dispensation to time-travel to various periods of Old Goth Europe to perform good deeds. In this case, it's to thirteenth-century England to save Jews from persecution. Though Toby isn't totally successful in his mission, by story's end he has become a Christian again, performing acts of contrition.

Angel Time's Gothick/Gothic reconsecrated sacred space is the ruin of the San Juan Capistrano mission church in California, destroyed in real life by an earthquake in 1812, only a few years before John Polidori wrote *The Vampyre*. The hit man, Toby, likes to attend mass in the restored chapel next to the ruin; it is his favorite place in the world. "It gave me special pleasure at Capistrano," he says, "that the layout of the Mission was an ancient monastic design to be found in monasteries all over the world. . . . Through history monks had laid out this plan again and again as if the very bricks and mortar could somehow stave off an evil world, and keep them and the books they wrote safe forever."[6] In the second book of this series, *Of Love and Evil* (2010), Toby continues his vow to the angel Malchiah to expiate his past sins and do good instead of evil, time-traveling to Renaissance Florence and once again rescuing Jews from their Christian persecutors. Though the San Juan Capistrano church also figures here, when his mission in the past is completed Toby finds solace instead in

Manhattan's St. Patrick's Cathedral, "this vast beautiful space . . . with its soaring arches and unapologetic grandeur."[7]

Rice's return to Catholic sacred spaces irresistibly recalls the similar turn taken by J. K. Huysmans, the French Decadent writer of the fin de siècle directly preceding hers. Huysmans did not have to grind his fiction-making transmission gears quite as hard as Rice did when she shifted from the vampire Lestat to Jesus, however. Durtal, the protagonist and authorial stand-in both of *A Rebours* (1884) and Huysmans's influential 1890 Gothick novel of decadence and Satanism, *Là-Bas*, is the same character who embarks five years later on a retreat in a Trappist monastery in *En Route* (the "white book" he wrote to counteract his "black book" *Là-Bas*), and devotes himself, appropriately, to a study of the architecture of the great Gothic cathedral of Chartres in *La Cathédral* (1898).[8] In his journey from the Gothick back to the original Gothic, Huysmans himself became a lay member of the Benedictine order. In 2010, however, Rice withdrew from the Church in protest of its policies on abortion, homosexuality, and science research and announced a new religious position. She "quit being a Christian," Rice said, while remaining "committed to Christ"—a move to personal gnosis and an individual relationship to Jesus very much in tune with twenty-first-century alternative spirituality and the new Gothick.[9]

We saw in the case of *The Da Vinci Code* how mainstream Christian believers are subliminally imbibing nonstandard doctrine directly from popular Gothick fiction, but this trend is also present in novels by Christian writers targeted specifically at Christian readers. The unintended result has been that the powerful Gothick matrix is now shaping contemporary Christian religious doctrine. Fundamentalist Christian fiction in particular has drawn deeply from the well of the Gothick, a notable example being the twelve-volume apocalyptic *Left Behind* series (1995–2007) by Tim LaHaye and his cowriter Jerry B. Jenkins.

Far from being a literalist version of the Rapture (itself a rather Gothick creation of nineteenth-century American evangelism), the theology of these novels, written in the style of male action-conspiracy thrillers, bears the stamp of the Gothick at every turn. Especially interesting is the authors' depiction of the Antichrist in the figure of Nicolae Carpathia (his surname referencing the mountainous territory in Transylvania that Bram Stoker made Count Dracula's home). This evil Romanian becomes head of the

United Nations and preaches a seditious message of religious ecumenism and global community while secretly plotting the destruction of humankind. Nicolae dies but, "resurrected and indwelt by the Devil himself," returns to rule the world briefly before the Second Coming and the thousand years of peace on earth take place.[10]

The Antichrist as a vampire? Given the seditious parody of the Christian blood sacrament that the vampire subgenre promotes, wrapping the Antichrist in Dracula's cloak rather than the other way around—and making this character a political cipher as well—might well be the doctrinal equivalent of letting the fox into the chicken coop. The tremendous sales of these books (more than 65 million, another 10 million in children's and graphic novel versions) suggest that the Gothick formula, and specifically the ubiquitous figure of the vampire, is so powerful that it tends to override the conventions of any other genre it mates with, even those of a 2,000-year-old religion.[11]

The reflexive anti-Catholicism of this story lies in the circumstance that Nicolae's principal henchman is the ex-Pope, now styled "Pontifex Maximus Peter Mathews, Supreme Pontiff of Enigma Babylon One World Faith," who has become head of all other religions in the world collapsed together in one blasphemous ecumenical mess.[12] In a wonderful Gothick about-face, however, the website for the official *Left Behind* videogames shows an image of three cowled figures peering into the mouth of a lighted cave with the caption "Life is a grand mystery waiting to be discovered."[13] They may be Essenes, granted, but those monkish hoods are awfully redolent of *The Secret*. Even in an appeal to connect to God and not be left behind at the Rapture, a hint of the faux Catholic still makes for spicier bait.

Rather unexpectedly, we find an equivalent end-times Gothick battle between good and evil in Stephen King's seminal *The Stand* (1978), a fat (more than 1,000 pages) novel about a lethal flu bug that escapes a secret government facility and within weeks kills most of the U.S. population. Setting a template for much postapocalyptic fiction to come, *The Stand* was made into a television miniseries and a graphic novel and is now being developed as a feature film. One of this novel's noteworthy qualities is its overt Christian morality with supernatural overtones. With the notable exception of the graphic novels, most Gothick supernatural fiction and film of the late twentieth century assiduously avoided any explicit links to Christianity apart from the usual ornamental faux Catholic trappings, a token Gothick Satan, and an often humorously depicted Hell. One odd-ball exception was the movie *The Rapture* (1991), directed and written by Michael Tolkin, a highly original take on the spiritual journey of a sexual adventuress who becomes a devout born-again Christian, only to discover that the sacrifice she makes to impending Armageddon—killing her daughter—leaves her stranded in tragic mortality.

King, however, has explicitly described the spiritual orientation of *The Stand* as one of "dark Christianity" in his introduction to the 1991 expanded edition.[14] In an interview he elaborated on the difficulty of representing religion in other than cartoon terms within the Gothick, summing up his own personal gnosis in this way:

> Too often, in novels that are speculative, God is a kind of kryptonite, and that's about all that it is, and it goes back to Dracula, where someone dumps a crucifix in Count Dracula's face, and he pulls away and runs back into his house. That's not religion. That's some kind of juju, like a talisman. I wanted to do more than that. I wanted to explore what that means to be able to rise above adversity by faith, because it's something most of us do every day. We may not call it Christianity. I wanted to do that. I wanted [*The Stand*] to be a God trip.[15]

In the story survivors of the superflu congregate around one of two accidental spiritual leaders: either the cowboy "dark man" Randall Flagg, embodiment of evil, who gathers his followers around him in that metonym of sin, Las Vegas, or "the oldest woman in America," a 108-year-old African American woman named Mother Abagail, who is the embodiment of good.

When one of the characters asks whether Satan isn't just the "scared, bad part of all of us,"

> Abagail recognized this thinking as that of the "new preachers." There wasn't really any Satan, that was their gospel. There was evil, and it probably came from original sin, but it was in all of us and getting it out was as impossible as getting an egg out of its shell without cracking it. According to the way these new preachers had it, Satan was like a jigsaw puzzle—and every man, woman, and child on earth added his or her little piece to make up the whole. Yes, all that had a good modern sound to it; the trouble with it was that it wasn't true.

And if Nick was allowed to go on thinking that, the dark man would eat him for dinner.[16]

This dark man, Randall Flagg, has paranormal powers: he can levitate, send his eye out into the wilderness, and control the movements of wolves and other Gothick dark animals. On occasion, like Stoker's Dracula and the Devil in European folklore before him, he can shape-shift into them. "He ain't Satan," Mother Abagail says, "but he and Satan know of each other and have kept their councils together of old."[17]

Flagg's paranormal powers derive, as we have seen again and again, from the still-operative post-Reformation legacy of the Gothick that likes to bestow more supernatural powers on the bad guys than the good guys. In contrast, Mother Abagail's special strengths (apart from her not inconsiderable ability to survive for weeks in the wilderness without food and water) are limited to spiritually directive visions that lead her and her followers to Boulder and guide their moral and ethical choices. Trashcan Man, the pyromaniac who ultimately destroys Las Vegas with a nuclear bomb, is able to intuit the metaphysical essences of these two Manichaean opponents:

> He knew this dark man all right, his was the face you could never quite see, his the hands which dealt all spades from a dead deck, his the eyes beyond the flames, his the grin from beyond the grave of the world.

Mother Abagail appears to him in a terrifying dream,

> as if it wasn't an old woman at all he was peeking at but at some secret, some barely concealed light that seemed ready to break out all around her, to play over her with a fiery brilliance that would make the flaming oil tanks of Gary seem like so many candles in the wind—a light so bright it would chalk his eyes to cinders.[18]

During an interlude when Mother Abagail has mysteriously disappeared, another character wonders if the dark man is

> just the last magician of rational thought, gathering the tools of technology against us. And maybe there's something more, something

much darker. I only know that he *is*, and I no longer think that sociology or psychology or any other *ology* will put an end to him. I think only white magic will do that . . . and our white magician [Mother Abagail] is out there someplace, wandering and alone.[19]

This is the battle between good and evil framed not in Christian terms but rather in the Gothick fantasy conventions of Tolkien's *Lord of the Rings* trilogy and all the innumerable videogames that borrow the same conceit.[20] It is also, of course, the much older ubiquitous frame of folktale and myth: a duel between sorcerers resulting in the victory of light over darkness. King seems to have rejected a direct confrontation between the two mythic opponents as a resolution for his story, however. Instead, Flagg and his followers are vaporized in Trashcan Man's finest pyrotechnic moment: setting off the nuclear warheads Flagg has assembled as weapons against the other side. In this logic, evil destroys itself through its own tactics and not through any final Armageddon with the forces of good. (Flagg returns as a character in King's *The Dark Tower* series.)

Whereas King's Trashcan Man sets off a "holy fire" in which, significantly, "the righteous and unrighteous alike were consumed," LaHaye and Jenkins opt for the traditional, more selective immolation in which Armageddon does involve a literal physical battle between the forces of good and evil. In the penultimate volume of their series, *Glorious Appearing: End of Days* (2004), Christ vanquishes the armies of the Antichrist when he returns to earth. Inaugurating the thousand years of his reign, he sends the unrighteous screeching into the chasm and brings to life all his martyrs. These include the two previous wives of one of the characters, Rayford, who worries about how he is supposed to behave toward them. He's reassured by another character, who quotes Matthew 22:30 about the resurrection: "For when they rise from the dead, they neither marry nor are given in marriage." Unlike the domestic arrangements in the realm of Mormon exaltation conjured in Stephenie Meyer's *Twilight* series, the spiritual beings of LaHaye and Jenkins's imaginary world retain their mortal personalities but do not enjoy physical relationships after death.

The bellicose *Left Behind* series was also representative of a particular late twentieth-century religio-political perspective that found metaphorical fulfillment in the early twenty-first-century Iraq War. The videogame version of *Left Behind: Eternal Forces* was shipped to U.S. forces in Iraq in "Freedom Packets" with U.S. Defense Department approval. The fact that players were set in violent combat against a United Nations force led by the Antichrist and given the cry "Praise the Lord!" each time a UN soldier was killed led to a mild uproar that resulted in some hasty repackaging emphasizing that prayer, not killing, won the most playing points.[21] But even in this context the trickster factor always present in the Gothick trumped any moral edification the game might provide in the one incontrovertible fact of gaming: that players could have just as much fun fighting for the Antichrist as they could for Christ. Since then LaHaye, in partnership with a new collaborator, Craig Parshall, has kicked off a new series with the novel *Edge of Apocalypse* (2010), whose main character has invented a missile defense system that will defend against a North Korean strike on New York City as the prophesied apocalypse begins.

In the meantime, *Left Behind* was to have an unlikely successor in Christian best-sellerdom: William P. Young's quietly powerful Gothick allegory *The Shack*, the story of a man who loses his daughter to a serial killer and spends a weekend years later in the wilderness shack where she lost her life. Here, in a magical moment outside time and space, he finds resolution for his grief, guilt, and rage in the company of no less than the Trinity itself personified as a middle-aged African American woman (there are echoes of King's Mother Abagail here), an ethereal Asian woman, and a not particularly good-looking Middle Eastern carpenter.

As we saw in chapter 8, allegory hasn't been much on view in high literature since the end of the eighteenth century (the same time that the Gothick began), but it has lived on in popular Protestant religious homily. John Bunyan's *Pilgrim's Progress*, first published in 1678, was still widely read across America well into the twentieth century. Young's novel, which has elicited admiring comparisons to Bunyan's work, had been on the *New York Times*'s best-seller list for 126 weeks by December 2010, and according to the publisher has 10 million copies in print.[22] An assured, sophisticated storyteller, Young ably revives this venerable Christian didactic tool with its suggestions of congruence and interpenetration between the material and spiritual world. The shack itself, Young has said, is an allegory for the soul of a human being, "where you hide your shame and addictions with a ¼-inch façade"; it is "the house you build out of your own pain."[23]

On a brilliant winter morning, three and a half years after his daughter was abducted and murdered on a camping trip, Mack, a survivor of childhood abuse whose comfort level in church is low, finds a note in his mailbox from "Papa" (his wife's private nickname for God) inviting him to spend a weekend at the "place of his nightmares," the shack in the Oregon wilderness where Missy's bloody clothing was found. Since that horrific event he has been caught up in what he calls a "Great Sadness" toward life and a God who let his daughter suffer a terrible death. Mack wonders to himself about the heretical possibility of actually meeting God:

> In seminary he had been taught that God had completely stopped any overt communication with moderns, preferring to have them only listen and follow sacred Scripture, properly interpreted, of course. . . . It seemed that direct communication with God was something exclusively for the ancients and uncivilized, while educated Westerners' access to God was mediated and controlled by the intelligentsia.[24]

But he decides on impulse to make the trip.

The shack itself, when he first arrives, is a traditional dark Gothick space: it "looked dead and empty, but as he stared it seemed to transform into an evil face, twisted in some demonic grimace, looking straight back at him and daring him to approach." Once he is inside, all his rage and grief explodes at the sight of the faded stain on the floor where Missy's bloody dress was found. After contemplating and rejecting suicide, he slumps to the floor and, in the best Old Goth dream vision convention of losing consciousness because of a troubled mind, falls asleep. Minutes later, when he wakes up (he thinks), Mack tears up the note and makes for his car, deciding he will never go looking for God again; God, he decides, will have to come find him. Just as Mack has this thought, the ice on the trail melts, wildflowers bloom, birds and small animals emerge, and Mack smells not just local flowers but "the richness of roses and orchids and other exotic fragrances" in a "postcard perfect" landscape. In place of the shack he just left is "a sturdy and beautifully constructed log cabin" with smoke curling from the chimney and a white picket fence.[25]

Growing understandably apprehensive about a one-on-one with God, Mack returns and knocks on the door. Instead of "a really big grandpa with a long flowing white beard, sort of like Gandalf in Tolkien's *Lord of the Rings*"—a description reflecting Young's astute understanding of the Gothick pop culture overlay that shapes so many people's perceptions of their deity—Mack is confronted with "a large beaming African-American woman" smelling of his mother's perfume who "crossed the distance between them and engulfed him in her arms, lifting him off his feet and spinning him around like a little child. And all the while she was shouting his name—'Mackenzie Allen Phillips'—with the ardor of someone seeing a long-lost and deeply loved relative." This is Papa, aka Elousia, the "Creator God who is truly real and the ground of all being."[26]

As Mack starts to cry in realization, a small Asian woman enters with a brush and bottle to collect his tears. Elusive and hard to perceive, given to humming Gaelic tunes, this is Sarayu or Wind, who is also "Holy Spirit, Creativity, Action, Breathing of Life, God's Spirit." Last but not least enters a Middle Eastern man in jeans and a plaid shirt covered with sawdust. This is Jesus, Yeshua, Joshua, or Jesse, who, like the women, we discover, enjoys cooking and gardening.

Faced with this Trinity of "two women and a man and none of them white," Mack asks which of them is God. "I am," they all answer. Papa explains further: "I am neither male nor female, even though both genders are derived from my nature." The form in which God has chosen to appear to Mack, he is told, is meant to break down paternalistic as well as popular culture religious stereotypes. Papa in her own way, however, is another kind of stereotype (at one point she utters the exclamation "Sho 'nuff!"); though Young's invocation of an Aunt Jemima–type character was probably deliberate, it leaves the reader uneasy nonetheless. Mack finds Papa easier to accept as a personification, we learn, because his own father was so violent.[27]

Later that evening, after a multicultural meal seasoned with exotic spices, Mack and Jesus lie out on the dock looking up at the stars. Faced with this ordinary-looking Middle Eastern guy, Mack realizes he doesn't really know Jesus at all; up to now, he has held in his mind an ideal or icon or image. Jesus tells Mack about the importance of relationship, how Mack can be "indwelt" by spiritual life in a dynamic relationship with God. But even though the Trinity operates as a "circle of relationship, not a chain of command," Jesus tells him, humans are irresistibly drawn to power hierarchies that make it hard for them to experience this kind of true relationship. Later Jesus says, "I don't want slaves to my will. I want brothers and sisters who will share life with me." The Church, Jesus' bride, is a living community, not a man-made institution. "I don't create institutions," Jesus tells him.

Just as marriage is a relationship, not an institution, Jesus has come to Mack and everyone else to offer life in relationship. The world is broken because in Eden humans abandoned relationship with God to take the "ravaged path of independence." Paradoxically, the illusion of freedom granted by independence has forced people into unequal power relationships in which men sought their identity in work and women in men, with the result that men took "power" over women. "We will come and live our life inside you," he tells Mack, "if you can kill your independence."[28]

Mack, however, is still fighting to suppress his rage toward a God who allowed his daughter to be brutally murdered. Next morning Papa, in an African robe and multicolored headdress, tells Mack that God doesn't punish people for sin. Mack must learn to believe in the reality of good that is absolute. If Mack gives up the need to judge good and evil, he will begin to know the wonder and adventure of living in God. "Just because I work incredible good out of unspeakable tragedies," Papa tells Mack, "doesn't mean I orchestrate the tragedies. Don't ever assume that my using something means I caused it or that I need it to accomplish my purposes."[29]

This is a radically different theodicy from that of Stephen King or Tim LaHaye. In the *Left Behind* series, Lucifer appears as a golden man-shaped apparition when he is briefly separated from his human vessel Nicolae. At the Last Judgment, as per Revelation, Lucifer morphs from lion to dragon to serpent as Jesus tells him he is responsible for everything evil in the world, then has Michael fly him, bound in chains, into the bottomless pit for another thousand years. And sinners here are most definitely punished by "the wrath of the Lamb": they are hurled into the bottomless pit.

The Shack, in contrast, presents no Satan, either as himself or in allegorical human form. Papa even goes one step further: "Evil is the chaos of this age that you brought to me," she tells Mack, concluding, "What you see as chaos, I see as a fractal." With this pronouncement she sends him outside to the kitchen garden, which she dubs "chaos in color," to help Sarayu uproot one section. Together Mack and Sarayu cut down a whole section of plants, and Mack's task is to dig up all the roots. Later he will learn that this messy garden is his heart and what he has laboriously uprooted is the bitterness that has taken hold there. Sarayu tells Mack the garden itself is a fractal: "something simple and orderly that is actually composed of repeated patterns, no matter how magnified. . . . I love fractals, so I put them everywhere."[30]

Fractal is the operative word in Young's allegorical universe, and his use of the concept recalls the Swedish mystic Emanuel Swedenborg's post-Enlightenment version of the Old Goth law of correspondences, in which man contains God as an infinite whole within him just as much as God contains man.[31] A fractal, in mathematics, is a fragmented, infinitely divisible shape whose parts mirror each other structurally (or show "self-similarity," as mathematicians say) at every level. In fractals, every whole is composed of similars. (The New Age concept of the "holographic universe" also resembles this ancient belief, minus the top-down hierarchy of divine to mortal and recast in scientific metaphor.)[32] A fractal organization of equivalent levels has recently been identified in the original Gothic cathedrals, and one can assume from this that the medieval masons and architects were consciously investing these sacred buildings with the pre-fractal notion of harmonious correspondence between great and small.[33]

Mack's heart, this garden, is thus an infinite whole that contains God. And if evil is chaos, and chaos is also a fractal, then chaos also has the power to replicate itself big and small, within people and in the environment around them. But Young does not pursue this line of reasoning. Satan is not an agent in this story; in Young's theodicy, evil is the absence of good. Evil is manifest in the brutal act that took Missy's life, but it does not surface in any other characters' actions.

Back at the cabin, Jesus is making a small casket. He asks Mack to travel with him to the other side of the lake, where Mack finds to his astonishment that, just like the medieval saint Christina Mirabilis we met in chapter 6, in the company of Jesus he is able to cross the lake on the surface of the water. Unlike Bella, who gains her superpowers by virtue of becoming an immortal after death, Mack is able to do miraculous things while still in his body on earth because the power of God is working through him while he is in full relationship to Jesus. Probably to avoid the charge of heresy, Young has placed this event, along with everything else that happens at the cabin, within the framework of a dream; technically Mack doesn't "really" walk on water because he is outside of space-time in this allegorical realm.

Readers, however, do not register this fine point as much as they recall the spectacle of Mack as a man-god, a human briefly accessing divine powers as he strolls across the surface of the water.

Following a trail on the other side of the lake, Mack reaches a solid rock wall, pushes through it as if it were nothing, and enters a deep tunnel where he encounters "a tall, beautiful, olive-skinned woman with chiseled Hispanic features" sitting behind an ebony desk. This is Sophia, "a personification of God's wisdom," who tells Mack: "You have judged the actions and even the motivations of others as if you somehow knew what those were in truth." She has him sit down in her chair, where his feet barely reach the ground, and tells him that "judgment is not about destruction but about setting things right."[34]

Young presents Sophia as an embodied divine feminine principle like Papa and Sarayu, and in doing so he has tapped into a venerable tradition. Worshipped by the Gnostics as a goddess in late antiquity, she was the muse of the sixth-century Roman writer Boethius, whose *Consolation of Philosophy* (*philosophy*, of course, signifying "love of wisdom"), vastly influential in the Old Goth European Middle Ages, detailed his dream vision dialogue with this allegorical figure while in his prison cell.

Historically, Sophianic mysticism has been a powerful strand in American alternative religions, especially in Protestant Theosophy, a seventeenth-century turn to direct spiritual experience and personal gnosis initiated by Jakob Boehme, the Silesian shoemaker and mystic whose youthful vision of sunlight glittering on a pewter bowl triggered a vast opus of theological writings. Like Boehme, Emanuel Swedenborg also spoke of the "conjugal love" that takes place when the human soul marries Sophia or Divine Wisdom.[35] Boehme's English disciple John Pordage wrote a treatise called *Sophia* that declared the existence of a Holy Virgin Sophia, a female divinity who is "co-essential" and "co-eternal" (but not "co-equal") with the Trinity.[36]

Sophianic teachings were disseminated in America by, among others, an eighteenth-century Theosophical community in colonial Pennsylvania called the Ephrata that practiced astronomy, astrology, alchemy, and magic.[37] Long after science and mainstream intellectual culture abandoned it, this image-based tributary of Protestant esotericism retained, as Arthur Versluis puts it, the "hierarchical medieval Christian cosmology as reflected in, say, Dante's *Divine Comedy*, which is marked throughout by astrological symbolism and correspondences."[38]

As the nineteenth century began, these beliefs in a female God and in an animistic universe of living interconnections were still being affirmed by the United Society of Believers, commonly known as the Shakers, who held that their founder, Ann Lee, embodied the second appearance of Christ, and later by Mary Baker Eddy, whose Christian Science scripture *Science and Health with Key to the Scriptures* (1875–1910) declared equally that "the mortal body is only an erroneous mortal belief of mind in matter" and that "in divine Science, we have not as much authority for considering God Masculine, as we have for considering Him feminine, for Love imparts the clearest idea of Deity."[39]

Theosophy itself was taken up more prominently in the late nineteenth century by figures such as Helena Blavatsky and Rudolf Steiner, and it fed into any number of alternative New Age spiritual practices in the following century. Echoes of Theosophical doctrine are present in the "time dimensional coupling" that Sophia grants to Mack, allowing him to enter a kind of heaven on earth where he and Missy and his other children are together— even though Sophia tells him, paradoxically, that among them only Missy is real.

What Sophia means is that Mack is now in a transcendental dimension of reality that trumps material existence. "All of this is very much real, far more real than life as you've known it," she says. Later Jesus tells Mack that heaven is not a place with "pearly gates and streets of gold"; rather, it will look very much like this ideal version of earth that Mack has just experienced, because heaven represents "a new cleansing of this universe."[40] Heaven as a transformed earth is a Theosophical doctrine as well as a Swedenborgian one: it is the belief that "heaven is all around us" if we only permit ourselves to be loved by God, an act of grace that enables us to move mystically into an experience of that other dimension.

With Sophia's help Mack is finally able to let go of his "Great Sadness." When he returns to the cabin, the Holy Ghost Sarayu touches his eyes to heal them, which causes Mack to experience blinding light followed by preternatural awareness. Like Bella in the *Twilight series* when she becomes a vampire, Mack finds that his heightened senses transport him into a state of pre-Fall perfection. The cabin has vanished, replaced by a night hillside under a sky full of stars:

Even in the darkness of the night everything had clarity and shone with halos of light in various hues and shades of color. The forest was itself afire with light and color, yet each tree was distinctly visible, each branch, each leaf. Birds and bats created a trail of colored fire as they flew or chased each other. He could even see that in the distance an army of Creation was in attendance: deer, bear, mountain sheep, and majestic elk near the edges of the forest, and otter and beaver in the lake, each shining in its own colors and blaze. Myriads of little creatures scampered and darted everywhere, each alive with in its own glory.[41]

Out of the forest comes an army of children who surround him, followed by a circle of adults that includes his own violent father, who embraces Mack. As part of this process, Mack forgives his father and then extends his ultimate act of forgiveness to Missy's murderer.

When he wakes up in the cabin from this dream within a dream, Mack discovers that the sharing of mutual love and forgiveness with his biological father means that the father image has finally lost its fraught associations for him. As a result, he finds that Papa has changed from a woman into a silver-haired goateed man. Young finesses the issue of whether God has stayed African American (we are only told he "looked a bit like Papa; dignified, older, and wiry and taller than Mack"), but on the page, at any rate, in the best Boehmian, Swedenborgian, and even Wilgefortean manner, God has become an alternating male-female divinity.[42]

In the meantime, Jesus the carpenter has made a most un-Protestant-looking coffin for Missy that he has ornately inscribed with scenes from her life. They bury this Roman-style sarcophagus in the garden of his heart in the exact place where Mack dug up the bitter roots. On the grave Sarayu scatters all Mack's tears that she has carefully been collecting. Very much in the spirit of Catholic Old Goth religious folklore and miracle stories, flowers bloom where the tears fall. From one special teardrop the tree of life grows, "young and luxurious and stunning, growing and maturing until it burst into blossom and bloom."[43]

After this ceremony Mack falls asleep once again in the living room only to wake up, again following medieval dream vision convention, in the "unreal real world." In this case he is back in the original squalid shack with Missy's bloodstain still visible on the floor. Events unfold rapidly and not as satisfyingly after this awakening. Broadsided by a car as he is driving home, Mack ends up in a coma in the hospital for four days, an authorial device that fudges any suggestion of the immanence of the supernatural in this world and immediately inserts Mack's experience at the shack into the old-fashioned "Is this real or am I crazy?" default mode of the twentieth-century Gothick that rationalizes a character's presumed supernatural experience as his own subjective delusion.[44] When he does regain consciousness, Mack finds that his memories of Papa and the others are fractals no more, but merely "shards from a broken mirror."[45] In a too-neat windup that is the only false note in a powerfully executed story, Missy's body, the killer, and the bodies of the killer's other victims are all located and earthly justice is served.

In the *Left Behind* series, people from various faiths convert to Christianity in order to be saved by Christ. Young's position on salvation, however, is Theosophist: a person does not have to be Christian to be saved by Jesus, though it must be Jesus who saves him. "Those who love me," Jesus tells Mack,

> come from every system that exists. They were Buddhists or Mormons, Baptists or Muslims, Democrats, Republicans and many who don't vote or are not part of any Sunday morning or religious institutions. . . . I have no desire to make them Christian, but I do want to join them in their transformation into sons and daughters of my Papa, into my brothers and sisters, into my Beloved.[46]

Mack reflects on his church friends who "were also sold out to religious activity and patriotism."[47] Sarayu replies that religion "is about having the right answers, and some of their answers are right. But I am about the process that takes you to the *living answer* and once you get to him, he will change you from the inside." Again and again the three gods in one tell Mack, "Don't look for rules and principles; look for relationship—a way of coming to be with us."[48]

Young has been severely criticized by some conservative Christians for the strands of alternative Christianity he has woven through his narrative. One writer, listing thirteen points of heresy in the novel, concludes, "For those not trained in orthodox Christian doctrine, this book is very dangerous." "Wrongful" concepts include the rejection of traditional

Christianity, the notion that "experience trumps revelation," the rejection of scriptural authority, a depiction of the Trinity as three separate bodies, a view that the Father suffered Christ's wounds (Papa shows Mack her crucifixion scars), denial of hierarchy in the godhead and in human relationships (including Young's assertion that women should not submit to men), ignoring the role of the church, a "wrongful inclusive notion of those who will be saved, and others."[49] Interestingly, this list does not include Mack's assumption of godlike powers as he walks over the lake. But *The Shack*'s wild popularity among all kinds of Christians suggests that, like many of William Blake's quietly radical poems, this new Gothick story "win[s] the assent of the heart before their doctrinal implications become apparent."[50]

Young's emphasis on a personal relationship with Jesus fits Harold Bloom's template for the "American Religion" all too neatly. This collection of ostensibly Christian beliefs that foregrounds "a very solitary and personal American Jesus," Bloom has argued, "masks itself as Protestant Christianity yet has ceased to be Christian"; "walking alone with Jesus," he flatly declares, is heresy. As personal gnosis, it is also very much of a piece with Anne Rice's declaration of leaving Christianity while remaining committed to Christ. "The American finds God in herself or himself," Bloom says:

> What makes it possible for the self and God to commune so freely is that the self already is of God. . . . The American self is not the Adam of Genesis but is a more primordial Adam. . . . Higher and earlier than the angels, this Adam is as old as God, older than the Bible, and is free of time, unstained by mortality.[51]

We are back in the territory of the divine human. Papa has already told Mack that God embraced human limitations to embody as Jesus, and thus Jesus was "fully human" and able to perform miracles "as a dependent, limited human being . . . only as he rested in his relationship with me, and in our communion. . . . [W]hat you are actually seeing [embodied as Jesus] is me; my life in him. That's how he lives and acts as a true human, how every human is designed to live—out of my life."[52]

"Dependent, limited" human beings such as Jesus—and Mack, by implication—can perform supernatural miracles if they are in full communion with God, and the last words of *The Shack*'s narrator, Willie, hold out a teasing possibility. Mack, he's convinced, still goes back to the shack, "walks out to that old dock, takes off his shoes and socks, and, you know, puts his feet in the water just to see if . . . well, you know. . . ."[53]

Out on the lake Bella Swan and Jesse Custer stand on the water, waiting for him.

Daimon Hellstrom debates his dual nature in *Son of Satan*. Artist: Jim Mooney. Writer: Steve Gerber. Son of Satan, TM and © Marvel Entertainment. Used with permission.

TWELVE

EPILOGUE

Questions without Answers

By offering role models whose heroism and transcendental qualities
would once have been haloed and clothed in floaty robes, [comic books]
nurtured in me a sense of the cosmic and ineffable that the turgid,
dogmatically stupid "dad" religions could never match.

—Grant Morrison

In 2009 the *New York Times* carried a story about a thirteen-year-old boy
who told his ex-Catholic father and nonobservant mother one day that he
wanted to go to church, and he promptly began attending a nearby Protestant chapel that "fit his idea of what a church should look like."[1] One of
his top motivations for doing so was reading fantasy literature, including
works predicting the world would end in 2013. Given that possibility, the
boy reasoned, getting acquainted with God might not be a bad idea.

This is, as we have seen, the familiar "You never know" bet-hedging
stance of a Secondary Believer trembling on the edge of Primary Belief.
In his magisterial work *A Secular Age*, Charles Taylor mentions aesthetically induced fright as the path some contemporary nonreligious Westerners choose in order to reconnect with the "enchanted world" of belief: "So
people go to movies about the uncanny in order to experience a frisson.
Our peasant ancestors would have thought us insane. You can't get a frisson from what is really in fact terrifying you."[2] Though some consumers

of the Gothick, showing greater or lesser degrees of awareness, have struggled for a very long time to do exactly this—discover Rudolf Otto's *mysterium tremendum* via a frisson of terror induced by the imaginary—in the long term Taylor's statement is profoundly true. In matters of the spirit, darkness cannot hold; sooner or later there must be light. The boy who headed for church was making just this instinctive choice.

It should be clear from the preceding pages that this is by no means the only, or even the most common, option for those so inclined, because the Gothick itself has begun altering in significant ways to accommodate the spiritual needs of its consumers. For better or for worse, religion and spirituality are vastly important in this new century and new millennium, as much so in the West as in any other part of the world. But because it has been a taboo subject for most of the First World's secular intellectuals, they have not much attended to the phenomenon of what might be called "felt spirituality" in institutional religion, in new religious movements, and especially in the shadowy realms of popular culture. In part, this oversight stems from the tendency within this same intellectual culture to conflate religion with fundamentalism and all its attendant dangers; in part, it's simply the bias of a belief system that does not acknowledge itself as such.

Arriving at the end of my journey with the Gothick strands I have been following, I find myself stymied when it comes either to drawing a conclusion or, worse, to extracting a moral from the single common theme that has emerged in a range of subgenres—a theme that, given my own biases, it was perhaps not surprising I found, but one that was unexpected nonetheless: Why human gods and not a set of new invented deities? What is there in this heterodox idea, imported to America via the sects of the Radical Reformation and propagated by their diverse descendants, that makes it so pervasive in the popular culture sub-Zeitgeist at this moment in time?

I do not have the answer to this question. What I do know is that the ascendance of alpha male superheroes on the big screen, so tied up with notions of war and the armored body, has already peaked and will soon begin its decline.[3] The superhero movies already in production will come out, and then this subgenre will begin to lose its prominence.

I do know that *Twilight* fanpires do not want to worship the vampire goddess Bella Swan. They want to *be* her. They want to have Bella's superpowers and her perfect, immortal love. That does not necessarily mean they will get fitted out with prosthetic incisors and join the Temple of the Vampire. It does mean that the notion of self-deification is somehow in the metaphysical air surrounding all these various narratives.

Is this a dangerous idea to have floating around in the sub-Zeitgeist? It's reflexive for us to think that it is, schooled as so many of us are in the belief that organized religion is a cultural atavism and heterodox religious ideas come from cults. The Lovecraft magical groups, the Church of Satan, and Zombie Walks do not provide any particular reassurance on this score. But the general shift in the imaginary worlds these practices draw from has been away from the demonic and toward human accountability, something the representation of human "divinization" in the Gothick puts heavy emphasis on. After having an apocalyptic vision of a nuclear winter, the half-human and half-demon John Constantine exclaims: "Now, if this species is going to have ANY chance of survival, we ALL have to face the demons inside us. We have to turn inwards and enter THE SIEGE PERILOUS—and WRESTLE. It's not those grotesque, tired institutions of HEAVEN AND HELL that are the problem—it's the devils we KNOW."[4]

Most of the half-human, half-god characters we have met in these pages struggle to rise above the darkness in their natures, a darkness that is linked via the Gothick with their supernatural side. Bella must conquer her vampire's addiction to human blood in order to refrain from killing. Hellboy must suppress his devilish side in order to do good. Jesse Custer must exert his human will to tame the anarchic demon-angel Genesis that has taken up residence in his soul. This is where the fright comes in. The supernatural aspect of their hybrid natures, the exact point where materiality flips over into something else, is the wild card they must gain control over or risk forfeiting their human morality.

In all cases it is their own Gothick heritage these characters are at war with. And in all cases so far, they win the battle by being humans first.

If the locus of goodness and right living in this metaphysics is the human dimension and not the transcendent one, what does that suggest about "becoming divine" as the ultimate extension of personal gnosis? In the subset of alternative spiritualities I have examined here, I think it indicates a kind of nervous ambivalence, certainly warranted given the darkness of the Gothick tradition, about the *mysterium tremendum* itself. What can happen to a person in that moment of mystical connection, judging by these stories, is anybody's guess. Based sheerly on Gothick precedent, it is likely to be unpleasant. Thus human instincts are more trustworthy than supernatural ones. This trustworthiness means something specific in the context of supernaturalism. It means that these divine humans must temper and harness the transcendental in accord with their own human values, not the other way around. Profoundly antitotalitarian, it is a metaphysics that turns the top-down religions of the past on their heads. At the same time, the universal distrust of social institutions and organized religion expressed in these works hands over a troubling amount of moral authority to the actions, or whims, of the lone visionary individual who stands apart from society.

What the new Gothick stories and the new alternative spiritual movements share with established religions of the past is their belief in realities outside our material world, realms austerely rechristened "dimensions" in the twentieth century. In his memoir *Supergods*, the graphic novelist Grant Morrison describes a mystical experience he had in Kathmandu of being "twisted off the surface of the universe into the fifth dimension," granting him a vision of all life on earth stretching from the impossibly distant past into the future as a single metaorganism. He describes this entity, in terms very close to those Garth Ennis used for his imaginary creature Genesis in *Preacher*, as "an infant god, attached to a placental support system called Earth."[5] And Morrison was given the responsibility to help this infant god be born on earth.

For some time after this experience, Morrison recounts, he could "see the shapes of things and of people as the flat plane surfaces of far more complex and elaborate processes occurring in a higher dimensional location." Everything, he writes, "was immortal and holy not as a result of some hidden supernatural essence but as a consequence of its material nature in time."[6] This kind of revelatory experience, and the sense of responsibility it instilled in its recipient, is probably the closest approximation to what being a "divine human" means in real life—not leaping tall buildings in a single bound, but communicating a startling vision of the universe and committing to living according to its dictates. Morrison states that this visionary event, which embodied the sum total of his comic book obsession and fascination with the occult, "gave me a burst of unshakable faith in a private religion that satisfactorily explained everything about how things work." Citing the fifteenth-century Italian philosopher Pico della Mirandola's *Oration on the Dignity of Man*, he exhorts us to "accept the superhuman as an undeniable fact of our nature."[7]

At a more everyday level, the Gothick low road to the transcendental can translate into the conviction, as Jeffrey Kripal writes of his own boyhood reading the superhero comics, that "anything was possible. We felt immortal, like minor gods in the making, and those superhero comics were our instruction books on how to imagine our own inner superhood into being."[8] Or as Green Lantern puts it (in a way Mary Baker Eddy would surely have applauded), "Anything I can imagine, I can create!"[9]

In this way the lowly Gothick, what Morrison dubs "the swill of twentieth-century gutter culture . . . where no one but children and illiterates were looking," has been the vehicle for the venerable strand of spirituality reflected in its narratives and their attendant Secondary and Primary Believers.[10]

Next question: Is some great beast already slouching toward Bethlehem, waiting to be born? Is a major new religion born of these fictions looming on the horizon?

When Bloom concludes that "there is a shape darkly emergent in much American Protestantism, the outline of a religion not yet fully evident among us but stretching like a long shadow beyond us," the underlying trajectory of these many small, strange sects based on popular entertainments inclines me to agree—but with qualifications.[11] It's a safe bet that a new world religion of some sort will emerge during this new century. It's not so safe a bet that this new religion will be dark. Nor will it necessarily come from North America. The Anglo-American Gothick's long imperial run is by no means over, but as a base for religion building, it is being tempered by other elements, many coming from elsewhere on the planet.

Will the doctrine of theosis I have traced through various subgenres here—Alex Owen's "immanence of the self-referential subject," in the secularized language of critical theory—figure in it?[12] Judging solely by its prevalence in the sub-Zeitgeist, my guess would be yes, probably.

What about the Gothick itself? Will this amazingly durable genre just keep on mutating and adapting to new social and cultural milieus? Or has it reached the end of its long trajectory at last?

Maybe it has. But probably it hasn't.

I do know that right now the Gothick, after 250 years, is in the midst of an extraordinary flowering. I do know that right now it is firmly entrenched in supernaturalism. I do know that right now it is giving large portions of itself back to the Romantic in an aesthetic that is spreading from below into high literary and film culture. I do know that it will always find its like-minded audience. And that's about it.

Let me close with a simple wish or two.

May the Gothick never lose its dedication to Story. May it never lose its outrageousness or its lowbrow ways. And may it never lose its ability to push us into territories that are totally unexpected.

Long live Gothick.

NOTES
ACKNOWLEDGMENTS
INDEX

NOTES

PREFACE

In John Gross, ed., *The Oxford Book of Essays* (New York and London: Oxford University Press, 1992), 372.

1. G. K. Chesterton, "A Defence of Penny Dreadfuls," ibid.

1. WHITE DOG, THE PREQUEL

"Terrorist Novel Writing," letter to the editor, *Spirit of the Public Journals for 1797* (London, 1798), 1:223–225, reprinted in E. J. Clery and Robert Miles, eds., *Gothic Documents: A Sourcebook 1700–1820* (Manchester: Manchester University Press, 2000), 184.

1. Fred Botting, "Gothic Culture," in Catherine Spooner and Emma McEvoy, eds., *The Routledge Companion to Gothic* (New York: Routledge, 2007), 199.

2. Walpole's status as the founder of a genre the majority of whose early proponents were women has been attacked as a "patriarchal creation myth" by Anne Williams in *Art of Darkness: A Poetics of Gothic* (Chicago: University of Chicago Press, 1995), 10. But in Devendra Varma's view, Walpole's bold hiccup of originality did not invent the Gothick mode; it "merely outstripped a gradual accumulation of influences," chief among them the Graveyard poetry school of the 1740s. *The Gothic Flame: Being a History of the Gothic Novel in England: Its Origins, Efflorescence, Disintegration, and Residuary Influences* (Methuen, NJ: Scarecrow Press, 1987 [1957]), 41.

3. That is, the fourteenth and fifteenth centuries. The "Gothic" style of sacred architecture actually spanned the twelfth through sixteenth centuries. The term "Middle Ages" itself was coined by the fifteenth-century Italian historian

Flavio Biondo to further downplay the thousand-year period of European history following the Roman empire as a less important cultural gray zone between two great eras. And if all this isn't confusing enough, the Tudor-Elizabethan sixteenth century in England was not dubbed a Renaissance until the nineteenth century; nowadays, coupled with the fifteenth, it goes by the plain-Jane label "premodern."

4. Radcliffe herself, curiously, was less dogmatic on the subject in her "On the Supernatural in Poetry," set up as an exchange between two travelers and first published as an essay, then as a prologue to her last novel, *Gaston de Blondville*. The more eloquent of the two, Mr. W., avers about the ghost of Hamlet's father: "I do not absolutely know that spirits are permitted to become visible on earth; yet that they may be permitted to appear for very rare and important purposes . . . cannot be impossible, and, I think, is probable." *New Monthly Magazine* 16, no. 1 (January 1826), reprinted in Clery and Miles, eds., *Gothic Documents*, 167.

5. Charlotte Dacre, *The Libertine*, in Gary Kelly, ed., *Varieties of Female Gothic*, vol. 3: *Erotic Gothic* (London: Pickering and Chatto, 2002), 264.

6. Since its inception, the Gothick is a genre that has been written by and for the very young. Matthew Lewis was nineteen when he wrote *The Monk*, as was Mary Shelley when she began *Frankenstein* (the novel was published three years later); Stephenie Meyer was twenty-four when the first novel of the *Twilight* series was published.

7. See, e.g., the last sentence of *Otranto:* "Theodore's grief was too fresh to admit the thought of another love; and it was not until after frequent discourses with Isabella of his dear Matilda, that he was persuaded he could know no happiness but in the society of one, with whom he could for ever indulge the melancholy that had taken possession of his soul." Horace Walpole, *The Castle of Otranto*, ed. Michael Gamer (London: Penguin, 2001), 123.

8. Cf. Coleridge's "Christabel," Byron's "The Giaour," and Keats's "Lamia" and "The Eve of St. Agnes," among many other examples.

9. Among the many scholars who combine the two sensibilities, see, e.g., Emma McEvoy, "Gothic and Romantic," in Catherine Spooner and Emma McEvoy, eds., *The Routledge Companion to the Gothic* (London: Routledge, 2007), 20, and Williams, *Art of Darkness*.

10. David Punter, *The Literature of Terror: A History of Gothic Fictions from 1765 to the Present Day* (London: Longman, 1980), 25.

11. Just like the terms *Gothic, medieval,* and *Renaissance,* the label *Romanticism* was applied to this aesthetic sensibility not by its proponents but by critics and historians well after it had passed its peak.

12. Punter, *Literature of Terror,* 14.

13. As Robert Bork has shown in his radical studies of cathedral ground plans in *The Geometry of Creation: Architectural Drawings and the Dynamics of Gothic Design* (Farnham, UK: Ashgate Press, 2010).

14. Leslie Fiedler, *Love and Death in the American Novel* (New York: Criterion, 1959), 47.

15. After Jane Austen's satire *Northanger Abbey* (finished by 1803; published post-humously in 1818), the definitive Victorian parody of Gothick ghosts remains Arthur Conan Doyle's *The Hound of the Baskervilles* (1901–1902), which presents a seemingly supernatural scare (killer ghost animal roaming the lonely moors) only to expose them as the props of a cunning murderer—a classic illustration of the "explained supernatural" ploy.

16. Alexandra Warwick, "Victorian Gothic," in Catherine Spooner and Emma McEvoy, eds., *The Routledge Companion to Gothic* (London: Routledge, 2007), 34. I discuss the displacement of the numinous onto the Divine Machine in detail in *The Secret Life of Puppets* (Cambridge, MA: Harvard University Press, 2002), chaps. 11 and 12.

17. *Night of the Werewolf* and *The Lazarus Plot*, respectively, both published by Grosset and Dunlap.

18. Psychoanalysis as a system, Lévy says, "can be read as a universal Gothic mechanism, inside which women *and men* [italics his] have been struggling since time immemorial: the villain is the super-ego, the victim is the ego entrapped in the psyche—an enclosed, nocturnal place, which has the dimensions and haunting quality of a castle. A very *gothic* castle, peopled with the ghosts of past traumatic experiences and the suppressed thought or desires that swarm about the subterranean shadowy regions of the unconscious." "FAQ: What Is Gothic?" *Anglophonia* 15 (2004): 24, 25.

19. Walpole, "Preface to the Second Edition," *Otranto*, 9.

20. Among any number of acknowledgments of this mainstreaming, see, e.g., Alexandra Alter, "The Season of the Supernatural," *Wall Street Journal*, May 27, 2011, http://online.wsj.com/article/SB10001424052702304520804576343310 420118894.html?KEYWORDS=summer+books (accessed May 28, 2011).

21. René Girard, *Violence and the Sacred*, trans. Patrick Gregory (Baltimore: Johns Hopkins University Press, 1977), 250.

22. In *Mimesis: The Representation of Reality in Western Literature*, trans. Willard R. Trask (Princeton: Princeton University Press, 2003).

23. Carol Clover, "The Same Thing—Sort Of," *Representations* 100 (2007): 6.

24. Michael Camille, *The Gothic Idol: Ideology and Image-Making in Medieval Art* (Cambridge: Cambridge University Press, 1989), 350.

25. Leslie J. Workman, "Medievalism," *The Year's Work in Medievalism* 10 (1995): 227.

26. For a study of the huge phenomenon of pan-European medievalism in the form of fairs, theme parks, and model villages and often linked to nationalism in the former Soviet-controlled states of eastern and central Europe, see Gábor Klaniczay, Peter Toth, and Peter Erdosi, "The Contagious Middle Ages," lecture and exhibit, Townsend Center, University of California Berkeley, November 2007.

27. Quoted in Joel Porte, "In the Hands of an Angry God: Religious Terror in Gothic Fiction," in G. R. Thompson, ed., *The Gothic Imagination: Essays in Dark Romanticism* (Pullman: Washington State University, 1974), 43.

28. Victor Sage, *Horror Fiction in the Protestant Tradition* (London: Macmillan, 1988), xxi–xxii.

29. Robert F. Geary, *The Supernatural in Gothick Fiction: Horror, Belief, and Literary Change* (Lewiston, NY: Edwin Mellen Press, 1992), 11, 16.

30. For an excellent discussion of the concept of *superstitio* from Roman times through the Enlightenment, see Wouter J. Hanegraaff, *Esotericism and the Academy: Rejected Knowledge in Western Culture* (New York: Cambridge University Press, 2012), 156–163.

31. Alex Owen, *The Place of Enchantment: British Occultism and the Modern* (Chicago: University of Chicago Press, 2004), 12.

32. Walpole, "Preface to Second Edition," *Otranto*, 40.

33. Diane Long Hoeveler, *Gothic Riffs: Secularizing the Uncanny in the European Imaginary, 1780–1820* (Columbus: Ohio State University Press, 2010), xviii, xv.

34. Keith Thomas, *Religion and the Decline of Magic: Studies of Popular Beliefs in Sixteenth and Seventeenth Century England* (New York: Charles Scribner's Sons, 1971), 587–588.

35. John L. Brooke, *The Refiner's Fire: The Making of Mormon Cosmology, 1644–1844* (Cambridge: Cambridge University Press, 1995), 27; see also D. P. Walker, "The Cessation of Miracles," in Allan Debus and Ingrid Merkel, eds., *Hermeticism and the Renaissance: Intellectual History and the Occult in Early Modern Times* (Washington, DC: Folger Shakespeare Library, 1988), 111–124.

36. Along with "Action" and "Family," the online DVD rental service Netflix offers a major category of movies called "Satanic Stories."

37. Alain Boureau, *Satan the Heretic: The Birth of Demonology in the Medieval West*, trans. Teresa Lavender Fagan (Chicago: University of Chicago Press, 2006), 3–4.

38. Nancy Caciola, *Discerning Spirits: Divine and Demonic Possession in the Middle Ages* (Ithaca, NY: Cornell University Press, 2003), 14, 19.

39. Ibid., 123–124.

40. Preface, *Daemonologie, by King James VI of Scotland, I of England, in the Form of a Dialogue, Divided into Three Books* (Oxford: Bodleian Library, 1922 [1597]).

41. Brooke notes the link between the widespread fad for occult treasure hunting after the American Revolution (the alchemical belief that metals are alive underlying the assumption that chests of money rise up in the ground in the summer from the heat; diviners had to be pure, in a state of grace) and the plates of gold that Joseph Smith discovers buried in the hills of upstate New York. Smith and his family had previously been diviners and gold seekers. *Refiner's Fire*, 30.

42. Thomas, *Religion and the Decline of Magic*, 125–126; Alexandra Walsham, "Angels and Idols in England's Long Reformation," in Peter Marshall and Alexandra Walsham, *Angels in the Early Modern World* (Cambridge: Cambridge University Press, 2006), 159. Stressing the "cautious and incomplete nature of the English Reformation," Marshall and Walsham report that "in practice . . . Protestant attitudes towards miracles were a good deal more ambiguous. . . . [There were] many reported apparitions" (18).

43. Edmund Burke, "On the Sublime," in *A Philosophical Inquiry into the Origin of Our Ideas of the Sublime and the Beautiful*, Harvard Classics, vol. 24 (New York: P. F. Collier, 1901), http://www.bartleby.com/24/2/ (accessed January 20, 2011).

44. Weiskel describes the new Romantic experience of fear in the presence of the sublime (as interpreted by Wordsworth and others) as "an exciting and apparently novel moment of heightened or intensified consciousness strangely allied to anxiety and commonly evoked by the spectacular and wild in nature or by a vivid impression of supernatural beings such as the ghosts and demons recently banished from the civilized mind." *The Romantic Sublime* (Baltimore: Johns Hopkins University Press, 1976), 13.

45. Ann Radcliffe drew a sharp distinction between terror and horror experienced aesthetically in the plays of Shakespeare. "Elevating" terror, she said, "expands the soul, and awakens the faculties to a high degree of life," whereas "circumstantial" scare-a-minute lowbrow horror "contracts, freezes and nearly annihilates them." "On the Supernatural in Poetry," 168.

46. Vijay Mishra, *The Gothic Sublime* (Albany: State University of New York Press, 1994), 17, 23, 25. This is an extension of Eve Kosofsky Sedgwick's characterization of the Gothick as the "barrier of the unspeakable" between the self and what rightfully belongs to it. *The Coherence of Gothic Conventions* (New York: Methuen, 1980), 13–19.

47. In *The Secret Life of Puppets*, 9.

48. As Peter Brooks said of this period: "Of the *mysterium tremendum*, which Otto defines as the essence of the Holy, only the *tremendum* [could] be convincingly revived." *The Melodramatic Imagination: Balzac, Henry James, Melodrama, and the Mode of Excess* (New Haven: Yale University Press, 1995 [1976]), 16.

49. The Dominicans were known as "the Lord's hounds" because of the pun resulting from the Latin *Domini-canes*. Unlike the Spinola Hours dog, who appears to be all white, the dog in Dominican tradition is black and white, like their robes, according to a tradition that links the dog to a dream by St. Dominic's mother that foretold his future. Jacobus de Voragine, *Legenda Aurea* [The Golden Legend], c. 1260, Caxton 1482 edition, reprinted in Temple Classics, ed. F. S. Ellis, vol. 4 (London, 1900), 82.

50. Ball has made many similar comments about "rooting" the supernatural in ordinary reality for this show. See, e.g., his notion of retractable vampire fangs as an expression of "our idea about the supernatural being a deeper more profound manifestation of nature," www.trueblood-online.com/category/behind -the-scenes/page/8 (accessed February 27, 2011).

51. William James, *The Varieties of Religious Experience: A Study in Human Nature* (New York: Modern Library, 1902), 53.

2 . FAUX CATHOLIC

Opening lines of Matthew G. Lewis, *The Monk: A Romance*, ed. Louis F. Peck (New York: Grove Press, 1952), 35.

1. Elizabeth Kostova, *The Historian* (New York: Little, Brown, 2005), 141.

2. *The Exorcist*, directed by William Friedkin, written by William Henry Blatty.

3. Directed by Daniel Stamm, written by Huck Botko and Andrew Gurland.

4. Directed by Mikael Håfström, written by Michael Petroni and Matt Baglio.

5. The dividing line was never absolute. In alternative strands of radical Protestantism that were also exported to America, there were Protestant exorcists, Protestant magic, and Protestant sorcerers and witches. In Alexandra Walsham's words: "Protestantism may have presented itself as a deliberate attempt to remove the magical and miraculous elements from religion, but its overall effect was surely to leave the universe saturated with supernatural forces and moral significance" in, e.g., the belief in "providences" as God's signs. *Providence in Early Modern England* (Oxford: Oxford University Press, 1999), 334.

6. Henry Bourne, quoted in Keith Thomas, *Religion and the Decline of Magic: Studies of Popular Beliefs in Sixteenth and Seventeenth Century England* (New York: Charles Scribner's Sons, 1971), 492.

7. Laurie Goodstein, "For Catholics, Interest in Exorcism Is Revived," *New York Times*, November 12, 2010.

8. Louis F. Peck, "A Note on the Text," in Lewis, *The Monk*. Monk Lewis (32) earnestly declares sources for the story of the Bleeding Nun and a few of the ballads, ending plaintively, "I have now made a full avowal of all the plagiarisms of which I am aware myself; but I doubt not, many more may be found, of which I am at present totally unconscious."

9. The discussion of the modern faux Catholic Gothick does not include the films of Luis Buñuel, which carry some strong echoes of their eighteenth-century Protestant counterparts. *The Monk* was translated into French by Antonin Artaud and became an important text for the Surrealists; Buñuel wanted to make a movie of it (and did write a script, with Jean-Claude Carrière, that was made into a 1973 movie, *Le Moine*, directed by Adonis Kyrou). A recent adaptation of the novel, also titled *Le Moine/The Monk* (2010–2011), was directed and written by Dominik Moll, whose work is discussed in chapter 9.

10. The legend of the Jewish shoemaker who reviled Jesus on the way to the crucifixion and is forced to roam the earth until Christ's second coming circulated widely in Europe during the sixteenth century and also appears as an episode in *The Monk*.

11. In a fictional foreshadowing of (or probably inspiration for) Pierre Plantard's fraudulent claims of his Merovingian ancestry that form the basis of Brown's principal source, *Holy Blood, Holy Grail*, Sue styles a French family as the direct descendants of the Wandering Jew's sister Herodias.

12. Garibaldi's *Clelia, or Of Government by Priests* (1867) and Mussolini's *The Cardinal's Mistress* (serialized 1909, published 1929). I am indebted to Massimo Introvigne for directing me to these two works.

13. The Know-Nothing sentiment lives on in some corners of the American psyche, as witness this brief excerpt from a lengthy and vituperative reader's comment on Amazon.com: "[Maria] Monk was slandered by the Catholic Church: Any born again Christian recognizes that the Catholic Church is full of pagan rituals that are evil and satanic. Read the Bible and the truth will set you free. May God bless Maria Monk for her braveness in telling her story in the face of evil." www.amazon.com/gp/product/155753134X/qid=1147716654

/sr=1–4/ref=sr_1_4/104–4488947–5855938?s=books&v=glance&n=283155, posted May 12, 2005 (accessed May 15, 2006).

14. *The Seville Communion*, for example, features computer hackers sending secret messages to the Pope, arcana of the Swiss Guard, and the negative political currents of Vatican bureaucracy under Pope John Paul, elements that are also present in Brown's *Angels and Demons*. "Our Holy Mother the church," a young priest says to the main character, a priest with no beliefs whatsoever. "So Catholic, Apostolic, and Roman that it's ended up betraying its original purpose. In the Reformation it lost half of Europe, and in the eighteenth century it excommunicated Reason. A hundred years later, it lost the workers, because they realized it was on the side of the masters and oppressors. And now, as this century draws to a close, it's losing the young and the women. Do you know how this will end? With mice running around empty pews." Arturo Pérez-Reverte, *The Seville Communion*, trans. Sonia Soto (New York: Harcourt Brace, 1998 [originally published 1995]), 133.

15. *Herushingu* (1997–2008), written and illustrated by Kouta Hirano, later an anime series.

16. Modeled after the fantasy works of Michael Moorcock and Tolkien by the venerable designer Games Workshops.

17. See J. G. Eccarius, *The Last Days of Christ the Vampire* (Gualala, CA: III Publishing, 1987) and related vampire lore at http://www.iiipublishing.com/religion/vampires.html (accessed February 1, 2011).

18. James Redfield, *The Celestine Prophecy: An Adventure* (New York: Warner Books, 1997).

19. Dan Brown, *Angels and Demons* (London: BCA, 2003), 34. Robert Langdon (and Dan Brown) seriously misdescribes the Illuminati, a Bavarian political-esoteric society founded by Adam Weishaupt and modeled after the Freemasons, which operated between the years 1776 and 1790. See Massimo Introvigne on the Center for the Study of New Religions website, www.cesnur.org/2005/mi_illuminati.htm, for a useful discussion of conspiracy theory notions about the Illuminati circulating since the mid-nineteenth century. Introvigne pinpoints the trilogy of novels collectively titled *Illuminatus* (1975), by Robert Joseph Shea and Robert Anton Wilson, as the vehicle for the more recent mainstreaming of these ideas.

20. Brown, *Angels and Demons*, 145.

21. Ibid., 35.

22. www.danbrown.com/novels/davinci_code/faqs.html (accessed 5/17/06).

23. First published as *The Holy Blood, The Holy Grail* in the United Kingdom in 1982.

24. Lewis Perdue was engaged in a long-running plagiarism suit against Brown (which he ultimately lost) for appropriating material from *The Daughter of God* (Seth Mnookin, "The Da Vinci Clone?" *Vanity Fair*, July 2006, 100ff). The novel's plot points bear little resemblance to the *Holy Blood, Holy Grail* thesis, however.

25. Dan Brown, *The Da Vinci Code* (London: BCA, 2003), 163.

26. A good summary of the hoax is found in Laura Miller, "The Last Word: The Da Vinci Con," *New York Times*, February 22, 2004 (accessed on cesnur.org, May 25, 2006). "The only thing more powerful than a worldwide conspiracy," Miller comments, "is our desire to believe in one."

27. Among widespread coverage of the case, see www.boston.com/news/local /new_hampshire/articles/2006/04/07/excerpts_from_ruling_on_the_da _vinci_code_lawsuit (accessed November 5, 2006).

28. The new wave after Brown included Kathleen McGowan, author of the initially self-published *The Expected One* (New York: Simon and Schuster, 2006), who declared herself a direct descendant of Jesus and Mary Magdalene based on personal visions and family genealogy research in France. Carol Memmot, "Is This Woman the Living Code?" *USA Today*, July 18, 2006.

29. *Da Vinci Code*, 124–125. Theodosius, not Constantine, made Christianity the official imperial religion.

30. Lisa Rogak, *The Man Behind* The Da Vinci Code: *The Unauthorized Biography of Dan Brown* (Kansas City: Andrews McMeel, 2005), 110, 138n.

31. David Van Biema, "Hail Mary," *Time*, March 14, 2005.

32. "Ruffling Religious Feathers," *Harvard Crimson*, www.thecrimson.com /article.aspx?ref=357405 (accessed April 26, 2006).

33. Brown, *Da Vinci Code*, 267, 262.

34. Rogak, *Man behind* The Da Vinci Code, 93–95.

35. Ibid., 98.

36. www.usatoday.com, April 25, 2006 (accessed April 29, 2006).

37. Vit Wagner, "10 Most Important Works of the Decade," www.thestar.com, December 30, 2009 (accessed January 1, 2010).

38. Tracy Wilkinson, "Vatican Seeks to Discredit 'The Da Vinci Code,'" *Los Angeles Times*, March 17, 2005.

39. Ian Fisher, "Vatican Official Urges Boycott of 'Da Vinci' Film," *New York Times*, April 29, 2006.

40. Thomas Doherty, "The Code before 'Da Vinci,'" *Washington Post*, May 20, 2006.

41. "Vatican Newspaper Reviews Da Vinci Code," ReligionNewsBlog.com, May 24, 2006 (accessed May 30, 2006).

42. Quoted in Anita Singh, "Angels and Demons: Vatican Breaks Silence to Review Film," *Telegraph*, May 7, 2009.

43. Peter Brooks, "Virtue and Terror: *The Monk*," *English Literary History* 40 (1973): 249–263.

44. Agence France-Presse, "'Da Vinci Code' Affects Christians in North America," www.inq7.net (accessed April 30, 2006).

45. Paul Majendie, "Reading 'Da Vinci Code' Does Alter Beliefs: Survey," Reuters, available at www.rhccsmallgroups.com/rhcc_small_groups/2006/05 /reading_da_vinc.html (accessed May 16, 2006).

46. See Christopher Partridge, *The Re-enchantment of the West*, vol. 2: *Alternative Spiritualities, Sacralization, Popular Culture, and Occulture* (New York: T. and T. Clark, 2005), which extensively documents the shift in religious thinking

to pop "occulture" drawn from esoteric tradition in the United Kingdom and United States during the later twentieth century.

47. A good example is Brown's use of England's Royal Academy. Over the centuries, he says, the scientific discoveries of the members of this "brain trust" and benign stand-in for the Illuminati of *Angels and Demons*, "including Einstein, Hawking, Bohr and Celsius . . . according to some, were the result of their exposure to ancient wisdom hidden within the Invisible College." *The Lost Symbol* (New York: Doubleday, 2009), 128.

48. Brown cites principally Lynne McTaggart's *The Intention Experiment: Using Your Thoughts to Change Your Life and the World* (New York: The Free Press, 2007) and her website, www.theintentionexperiment.com, as well as the Institute of Noetic Sciences in Petaluma, California.

49. *Lost Symbol*, 509, 359.

50. Ibid., 56, 468, 499, 507.

51. Mary Baker Eddy, "Christian Science Practice," *Science and Health and Key to All Scriptures* (Boston: First Church of Christ, Scientist, 1971), 428.

52. On the "Mind-cure" philosophy, see William James, *Varieties of the Religious Experience* (New York: Modern Library, 1902), lectures IV and V.

53. Rhonda Byrne, *The Secret* (New York: Simon & Schuster, 2006).

54. "The Making of the Secret," http://thesecret.tv/making-of.html (accessed December 7, 2010).

55. Douglas E. Cowan, *Sacred Terror: Religion and Horror on the Silver Screen* (Waco, TX: Baylor University Press, 2008), 11.

56. Maurice Lévy, *Lovecraft: A Study in the Fantastic*, trans. S. T. Joshi (Detroit: Wayne State University Press, 1988), 115.

57. Catherine L. Albanese, *A Republic of Mind and Spirit: A Cultural History of American Metaphysical Religion* (New Haven: Yale University Press, 2006), 11, 505.

58. Wouter J. Hanegraaff, *New Age Religion and Western Culture: Esotericism in the Mirror of Secular Thought* (Albany: State University of New York Press, 1998), 521.

3. GOTHICK GODS

"The Secret of the Gothick God of Darkness," http://www.trapezoid.org /thought/secret.html (accessed March 24, 2009). *GME* stands for "Grandmaster Emeritus."

1. Lovecraft seems to have borrowed the word *Aklo* from the Welsh fantasist Arthur Machen's story "The White People" (1899), "an old, old language that nobody knows now" and apparently spoken by fairies. This identification was made by James Russell, "A Tale of Two Secret Books," paper delivered at the "Knowledge to Die For" conference, Free University of Berlin and Max Planck Institute, May 2011. The sentence is rendered and translated as "In his house at R'lyeh dead Cthulhu waits dreaming" in Lovecraft's story

"The Call of Cthulhu" (1927) as part of a rite practiced by "Esquimau wizards and . . . Louisiana swamp-priests . . . to their kindred idols." *More Annotated H. P. Lovecraft*, annotations by Peter Cannon and S. T. Joshi (New York: Dell, 1999), 190.

2. The fourteenth-century term for "monster" in illuminated manuscripts was *babewyn* (Chaucer's "baboon")—not "grotesque," a later Renaissance word. Michael Camille, *Mirror in Parchment: The Luttrell Psalter and the Making of Medieval England* (London: Reaktion Books, 1998), 44. The *Oxford English Dictionary* gives thirteenth-century versions in English, Dutch, French, and Low and High German.

3. See ms 105, Walters Art Galley, Baltimore, reproduced in Michael Camille, *Image on the Edge: The Margins of Medieval Art* (Cambridge, MA: Harvard University Press, 1992), 29; Lorraine Daston and Katharine Park, *Wonders and the Order of Nature: 1150–1750* (New York: Zone Books, 1998), 28–29; and J. Paul Getty Museum ms Ludwig IX 18, fol. 260v, reproduced in Elizabeth Morrison, *Beasts Factual and Fantastic* (Los Angeles: Getty Publications, 2007), 94.

4. The quote is from his quintessential Providence story "The Case of Charles Dexter Ward," *At the Mountains of Madness and Other Stories* (Sauk City, WI: Arkham House, 1964), 112.

5. See William G. McLoughlin, *Revivals, Awakenings, and Reform: An Essay on Religion and Social Change in America, 1607–1977* (Chicago: University of Chicago Press, 1978), 24; Marshall W. Fishwick, *Great Awakenings: Popular Religion and Popular Culture* (New York: Haworth Press, 1994); and Robert Fogel, *The Fourth Great Awakening and the Future of Egalitarianism* (Chicago: University of Chicago Press, 2000).

6. See John L. Brooke, *The Refiner's Fire: The Making of Mormon Cosmology, 1644–1844* (Cambridge: Cambridge University Press, 1995), 58; Arthur Versluis, *The Esoteric Origins of the American Renaissance* (Oxford: Oxford University Press, 2001); D. Michael Quinn, *Early Mormonism and the Magic World View* (Salt Lake City: Signature Books, 1987).

7. Swedenborg's enormous influence in America by the mid-nineteenth century on major movements such as Transcendentalism, Spiritualism, mesmerism, and communalism and on notables such as Ralph Waldo Emerson and the elder Henry James is noted variously by Sidney Ahlstrom in *A Religious History of the American People* (New Haven: Yale University Press, 2004), 1:584, and by R. W. B. Lewis in *The Jameses: A Family Narrative* (New York: Anchor Doubleday, 1991), 54.

8. The phrase "American heresiarchs" is Harold Bloom's: *The American Religion: The Emergence of the Post-Christian Nation* (New York: Simon and Schuster, 1992), 141.

9. To find broad correspondences in antebellum fantastic literature—between Joseph Smith's *The Book of Mormon* (1830) and a work such as, say, Poe's *Narrative of Arthur Gordon Pym* (1837)—would be a fascinating scholarly undertaking, something like David S. Reynolds's study of the influence of sensational fiction on "high" literature in his *Beneath the American Renaissance: The*

Subversive Imagination in the Age of Emerson and Melville (Cambridge, MA: Harvard University Press, 1989). For an excellent discussion of Poe's esotericism, see Versluis, *Esoteric Origins of the American Renaissance*, 72–79.

10. Leigh Eric Schmidt, *Hearing Things: Religion, Illusion and the American Enlightenment* (Cambridge, MA: Harvard University Press, 2000), 206.

11. Hubbard produced more than 100 books plus audio and videotapes relating to Scientology, making this oeuvre the largest known scripture. Scientology is now included as a unit in college textbooks on world religions. See, e.g., Warren Matthews, *World Religions* (Belmont, CA: Wadsworth, 2010), which classes Scientology as well as the Church of Satan and Druids under the category "New Forms of Old Religions."

12. "Modern Pelagianism" is Sterling McMurrin's phrase, quoted in Bloom, *American Religion*, 126.

13. John A. Saliba, "Religious Dimensions of UFO Phenomena," in James R. Lewis, ed., *The Gods Have Landed: New Religions from Other Worlds* (Albany: State University of New York Press, 1995). In the 1920s, the Urantia Book also presented messages from extraterrestrial beings channeled through automatic writing. Helena Blavatsky's Theosophical doctrine of the Ascended Masters, supernatural entities including beings from other planets who visit the earth from time to time, may have also helped lay the groundwork for today's UFO religions.

14. Christopher Partridge, *The Re-Enchantment of the West*, vol. 2: *Alternative Spiritualities, Sacralization, Popular Culture and Occulture* (London: T. and T. Clark, 2005), 165–206.

15. See Lewis, *Gods Have Landed*, and Irving Hexham and Karla Poewe, "UFO: A Science Fiction Tradition," *Christian Century* 144, no. 15 (May 7, 1997): 489.

16. For a comprehensive survey of new religious groups of the 1960s, see Camille Paglia, "Cults and Cosmic Consciousness: Religious Vision in the American 1960s," *Arion* 10, no. 3 (Winter 2003): 57–111.

17. In the words of one Wiccan, "Just because you aren't Egyptian doesn't mean you can't work with their deities." Quoted in Douglas E. Cowan, *Cyberhenge: Modern Pagans on the Internet* (New York: Routledge, 2005), 38.

18. Ibid., 7–8. Cowan's careful study of online new religious movements punctures some of the more grandiose claims regarding the spread of new religion on the Web by showing that the most viable movements are those with a primary offline presence supplemented by an online one. The Web itself does not garner large numbers of converts to new religious movements, Cowan concludes; what it does foster is "syncretism and blending of many different traditions." For these groups, the Web remains both an essential communication tool and a somewhat overblown metaphor of connectivity (15–18, 100).

19. For a full treatment of the history of the invented "Necronomicon" in all its manifestations, see Daniel Harms and John Wisdom Gonce III, *The Necronomicon Files: The Truth Behind the Legend*, rev. ed. (Boston: Weiser Books, 2003).

20. Partly because the social marginalization of these groups makes private study desirable, as Cowan has pointed out in *Cyberhenge*, x.

21. Erik Davis, "The Remains of the Deities: Reading the Return of Paganism," www.techgnosis.com/neopaganism.html (accessed December 9, 2010).

22. Bloom, *American Religion*, 290.

23. Cowan, *Cyberhenge*, 49. According to its leader, Stephen Flowers, the Love-craftian Order of the Trapezoid "recognizes the individual Knight as the highest authority for his or her own initiation." Order of the Trapezoid, "The Methods," www.trapezoid.org/missions/methods.html (accessed December 8, 2010).

24. Cf. the word *profane*, "apart from the temple." One of H. P. Lovecraft's many deliberate archaisms was *fane* for "church."

25. From A. Ernout and A. Meillet, *Dictionnaire Etymologique de la Langue Latine* (Paris: Klinsieck, 1967), 216. I am indebted to Maurizio Bettini for this reference.

26. In a preface to *The Champion of Virtue* (1777), Gothick novelist Clara Reeve refers to Bunyan's *Pilgrim's Progress* as a "a book merely fanatical" in the sense of narrowly sectarian. "Address to the Reader," in Gary Kelly, ed., *Varieties of Female Gothic*, vol. 1: *Enlightenment Gothic and Terror Gothic* (London: Pickering and Chatto, 2002), 5.

27. Sam Moskowitz, "The Origins of Science Fiction Fandom: A Reconstruction," in Joe Sanders, ed., *Science Fiction Fandom*, Contributions to the Study of Science Fiction and Fantasy, no. 62 (Westport, CT: Greenwood Press, 1994), 27. According to Moskowitz, in 1928 the editor of the science fiction pulp magazine *Amazing Stories*, Hugo Gernsback, was the first to apply the already familiar sports and movie term *fans* to readers who wrote to the magazine.

28. Harry Warner Jr., "A History of Fanzines," in Sanders, ed., *Science Fiction Fandom*, 178. But the romance genre would later spawn fanzines, fan narrative writing, and flamboyant conventions complete with fans dressed as their favorite romance heroines. Romance fan performance art such as "Regency dancing" has also spilled over into sci-fi conventions.

29. Ibid., 180.

30. The word *fan*, of course, carries a further double-edged charge by its association with the word *fantasy*.

31. Moskowitz, "Origins," 26–27.

32. Bernadette Bosky, "Amateur Press Associations: Intellectual Society and Social Intellectualism," in Sanders, ed., *Science Fiction Fandom*, 183, 185.

33. S. T. Joshi and David E. Schutz, introduction to H. P. Lovecraft, *Lord of a Visible World: An Autobiography in Letters* (Athens: Ohio University Press, 2000), vii. About 3,000 of these letters have survived.

34. Moskowitz, "Origins," 37, 49, 52.

35. Bosky, "Amateur Press Associations," 181, and Rich Brown, "Post-Sputnik Fandom (1957–1990)," in Sanders, ed., *Science Fiction Fandom*, 77.

36. Henry Jenkins, *Textual Poachers: Television Fans and Participatory Culture* (New York: Routledge, 1992), 280. Echoing Lovecraft, Jenkins adds: "In researching this book, I spoke to many who had discovered skills and abilities that they had not recognized before entering fandom; they received there the

encouragement they had found lacking from their interactions with other institutions."

37. H. P. Lovecraft, excerpt from *United Amateur Journalism: Exponent of Amateur Journalism* (1915), in *Lord of a Visible World*, 40.

38. Milly Williamson, *The Lure of the Vampire: Gender, Fiction, and Fandom* (London: Wallflower Press, 2005), 103–110.

39. Brown, "Post-Sputnik Fandom," 78.

40. Ibid., 77.

41. In "Normal Female Interest in Men Bonking: Selections from *The Terra Nostra Underground* and *Strange Bedfellows*," Shoshanna Green, Cynthia Jenkins, and Henry Jenkins report that women fan writers say "the male hero is easier to 'feel' the adventure with." In Henry Jenkins, *Fans, Bloggers, and Gamers* (New York: New York University Press, 2006), 146. In the phenomenon of women identifying with powerful male characters we can see the flip side of the psychological reversal that Carol Clover describes in *Men, Women, and Chainsaws: Gender in the Modern Horror Film* (Princeton: Princeton University Press, 1996): the tendency of adolescent boys, the principal audience of horror movies, to identify with the "Final Girl," the powerless female protagonists of these films.

42. "Bible Slash," http://encyclopediadramatica.ch/Bible_slash (accessed July 11, 2011). A sample: "With an exasperated noise, Jesus grabbed him and pulled him into a fierce, open-mouthed kiss." There are many angry Christian posts and even a Christian woman's defense of slash fiction at www.trickster.org/symposium/symp165.htm (accessed March 2, 2009).

43. Kenneth Grant, *The Magical Revival* (London: Skoob Books, 1991 [1972]), 117.

44. In *Tree and Leaf* (Boston: Houghton Mifflin, 1989 [1964]), 36–37.

45. Quoted in an essay by Jenny Turner, "Reasons for Liking Tolkien," *London Review of Books* 23, no. 22 (November 2001): 15.

46. Ted Tschopp, quoted in Erik Davis, "Fellowship of the Ring," *Wired*, October 2001, 132.

47. Ibid., 129.

48. Tzvetan Todorov, *The Fantastic: A Structural Approach to a Literary Genre*, trans. Richard Howard (Ithaca, NY: Cornell University Press, 1973), 175. This is a late twentieth-century critical approach, and Todorov uses James's *The Turn of the Screw* as his template. See the extended discussion in *The Secret Life of Puppets*, 164, 170–173.

49. See, e.g., *Trekkies*, 1997, directed by Roger Nygard, Neo Motion Pictures/Paramount Classic. Though they are more performers than believers, the Klingon groups amount to a mild benign quasi-religion. Assuming the Klingon identity means promoting community service, racial diversity, egalitarianism, and a philosophy of optimism—like New Age Elks or Moose, but with a rather more complete adoption of the totem animal's identity than their predecessors made.

50. Davis, "Fellowship of the Ring," 132. According to Davis (personal communication, n.d.), these fans believe that the playacting "creates an experience

that is valid in itself, without the full commitment of belief." They have, he says, a strangely acute awareness of "cracks" in the Secondary World—an obsession with plot flaws that reflects this sharp awareness of the "invented construction" of their fictive world.

51. "Na'vi 'Kin Community," http://community.livejournal.com/tothehometree /492.html (accessed December 8, 2010).

52. Tirl Windtree, "What Are Otherkin?" www.otherkin.net/articles/what .html (accessed December 8, 2010).

53. The Church of All Worlds bills itself as "one of the oldest incorporated Neo-Pagan churches in the United States." See their website, www.caw.org (accessed May 5, 2009).

54. The hybrid story features a group of real-life local eminences, including ex-governor Stephen Hopkins, all four Brown brothers, and a fictitious "privateersman of phenomenal boldness," one Captain "Abraham Whipple" (a Lovecraft family name), who join forces to rid the city of the fictional warlock Joseph Curwen.

55. Amateur Lovecraftiana is an even vaster territory. Examples abound everywhere from online sites and a battery of publications both serious and whimsical to unpublished efforts by entirely respectable people such as a professor friend of mine, an Iranologist (and not the subject of this chapter's opening anecdote), who composed a story about a student who tries to buy a mysterious record in a secondhand store in Red Hook, Brooklyn (immortalized in Lovecraft's "The Horror at Red Hook"), only to meet with unexpected resistance from the Arab owner ("No, young Jewish student, you must not ask me to buy that record!" etc.).

56. Sandy Petersen, Lynn Willis, et al., *Call of Cthulhu: Horror Roleplaying in the Worlds of H. P. Lovecraft*, 5th ed. (Oakland, CA: Chaosium, 1994), 46.

57. See, e.g., G. W. Thomas, "Your Elder Sign Is in My Eye: or, Advice for Writers of Cthulhu Mythos Fiction," www.toddalan.com/~berglund/ns9nf2.htm; "The Cthulhu Lexicon," http://netherreal.de/library/lexicon/lexnfrm.htm, which gives references by story name and character or book title; Mythos-Web, www.bass.org/~cthulhu/index/.html ("your online guide to the fiction of the Cthulhu Mythos"); E. P. Berglund's *Reader's Guide to the Cthulhu Mythos*, http://www.epberglund.com/RGttCM/ (accessed October 30, 2011); and Daniel Harms's *Encyclopedia Cthulhiana: A Guide to Lovecraftian Horror (Call of Cthulhu)*(Oakland, CA: Chaosium Press, 2004). See also alt.horror.cthulhu.

58. *Alien* was written by the late Dan O'Bannon, an avowed Lovecraft fan, and Ronald Shusett. For a wide-ranging survey of Lovecraft in film, see Andrew Migliore and John Strysik, *Lurker in the Lobby: A Guide to the Cinema of H. P. Lovecraft*, rev. ed. (Portland, OR: Nightshade Books, 2006).

59. Written by Mack Carter and Jeff Blitz.

60. Erik Davis, "Pop Arcana (3)," http://hilobrow.com/2010/05/03/cthulhu-is -not-cute (accessed January 17, 2011).

61. Jason Thompson, personal communication, April 2002.

62. Brett Rutherford, personal communication, February 2002.

63. *Providence Journal*, December 4, 1997. The intruders left a hole three feet deep, not far enough to reach the grave, in a Swan Point functionary's estimation, and a single footprint. The intactness of Lovecraft's grave is a touchy issue if only because it is far and away the most visited site in that cemetery, the only one with its own map available in the front office.

64. Also Blood Ritual, a "death/black metal band," has an album called *At the Mountains of Madness*; Cradle of Filth has a track called "Cthulhu Dawn" on their album *Midian*; The Darkest of the Hillside Thickets, a "Vancouver 'punky surf' band" saturated in Lovecraftiana, has tracks such as "Yog Sothoth," on the album *Cthulhuriffomania*; there is "Shoggoths Away" and "Goin' Down to Dunwich" on *Cthulhu Strikes Back*; Forma Tadre, a German "industrial ambient" band, has a track called "Dagon"; and Shub-Niggurath, a "black/death/speed/thrash metal" band from Mexico, has an album *Evil and Darkness Prevails*. Drawn from www.hplovecraft.com/popcult/music.htm (accessed July 6, 2007).

65. See, e.g., Martin Wainwright, "Whitby Festival Draws a Black-Clad Crowd," *Guardian*, October 29, 2010. Also see Wikipedia, "Goth Subculture," http://en.wikipedia.org/wiki/Goth_subculture (accessed February 2, 2011).

66. Poppy Z. Brite, *Lost Souls* (New York: Dell, 1992), 5.

67. Mick Mercer's compendia *Hex Files: The Goth Bible* (New York: Overlook Press, 1996) and *21st Century Goth* (London: Reynolds and Hearn, 2002) are useful directories to everything from music groups to clothing stores to the scene through the early 2000s.

68. Kerry Acker, *Everything You Need to Know about the Goth Scene* (New York: Rosen Publishing Group, 2000), 19, 23.

69. Quoted in Katherine Ramsland, *Piercing the Darkness: Undercover with Vampires in America Today* (New York: Harper Prism, 1998), 91.

70. According to one former Goth, Columbine was "instrumental in dismantling the attitude and exclusivity of goth cliques," along with 9/11 and "the onset of a lighter consciousness." After these events "people became uncomfortable identifying with evil and a life driven by hate." Kristi Gansworth, personal communication, February 17, 2011.

71. See Joscelyn Godwin, *The Theosophical Enlightenment* (Albany, NY: State University of New York Press, 1994), and Alex Owen, *The Place of Enchantment: British Occultism and the Culture of the Modern* (Chicago: University of Chicago Press, 2004), for a full discussion of eighteenth- and nineteenth-century esotericism in England and North America.

72. Owen, *Place of Enchantment*, 182.

73. In another link to the Radical Reformation, Crowley was the son of devout Quakers of the Plymouth Brethren branch whose obsessive emphasis on the blood of Christ is weirdly mirrored in Crowley's own adoption of blood sacrifice in his rites. See Lawrence Sutin, *Do What Thou Wilt: A Life of Aleister Crowley* (New York: St. Martin's Press, 2000), 7, 23.

74. Did they know each other's work? S. T. Joshi, the preeminent Lovecraft scholar and biographer, does not mention Crowley in *H. P. Lovecraft: A Life*

(West Warwick, RI: Necronomicon Press, 1996). As for Crowley, his biographer Lawrence Sutin says: "Crowley did read Algernon Blackwood but deprecated him, & Crowley was not in America when Lovecraft was being published in Weird Tales. Lovecraft is Grant's enthusiasm, and the American OTO (Hymenaeus Beta) rejects Grant's work in this & most other regards." Personal communication, December 13, 2010.

75. Grant, *Magical Revival.* In "Calling Cthulhu: H. P. Lovecraft's Magickal Realism," Erik Davis correctly draws the parallel between the "fascist and racist dimensions of 20th century occultism" and Lovecraft's writing. *Nomad Codes: Adventures in Modern Esoterica* (Portland, OR: Yeti/Verse Chorus Press, 2010), 122.

76. The phrase "Lovecraft/Crowley Axis" is from Kenneth Grant, *Hecate's Fountain,* quoted in Harms and Gonce, *Necronomicon Files,* 122.

77. Discussed in Wouter J. Hanegraaff, "Fiction in the Desert of the Real: Lovecraft's Cthulhu Mythos," *Aries* 7 (2007), 85–109.

78. See Michael Aquino, *The Church of Satan,* 6th ed. (San Francisco: Michael A. Aquino, 2009), 240–241, at www.xeper.org/maquino/nm/COS.pdf (accessed February 20, 2009). Aquino states that he wrote both the ceremonies and the accompanying essay, "The Metaphysics of Satan."

79. Anton Szandor LaVey [Michael Aquino], "The Metaphysics of Lovecraft," *The Satanic Rituals* (New York, Avon Books, 1972), 177, 178. Large portions of LaVey's *Satanic Bible,* to which this book is a companion volume, were plagiarized. See "Anton LaVey: Legend and Reality," compiled by his daughter Zeena and Nikolas Schreck, February 2, 1998, www.churchofsatan.org/aslv.html (accessed September 10, 2005). This statement also asserts that the *Satanic Bible* "was conceived as a commercial vehicle by [paperback publisher] Avon Books . . . to cash in on the Satanism & witchcraft craze of the late 1960s." LaVey's presumed stature as a New Age religious thinker, as well as author of the books that bear his name, has been accepted uncritically by mainstream academic scholars.

80. A glossary is included. Umberto Eco in turn satirically cribs from the LaVey/Aquino version of Aklo *("I'a Cthulhu! I'a S'tat'n!")* in his anti-occult *Foucault's Pendulum* (New York: Ballantine Books, 1988), 493. An entry on "Yuggoth" in that compendium of sub-Zeitgeist folklore known as Wikipedia makes the following astounding statement: "Other writers claim that [Yuggoth] is actually an enormous, trans-Neptunian world that orbits perpendicular to the ecliptic of the solar system." www.en.wikipedia.org/wiki/Yuggoth (accessed April 6, 2009).

81. Michael Aquino, "Temple of Set General information and Admissions Policies," www.xeper.org/pub/org/xp_FS_pyl.htm (accessed December 10, 2010).

82. Aquino's version in his appendix 71, "The Metaphysics of Lovecraft," reads: "The time shall come when the hounds will bow before us, and apes shall speak with the tongues of hornless ones." *Church of Satan,* 681.

83. Dame Patricia Hardy, "When the Stars Come Right Again." www.trapezoid.org/thought/when.html (accessed January 19, 2009).

84. www.trapezoid.org (accessed January 19, 2009). The Shining Trapezohedron, which "translates" the primal reality of the invisible world for those who look into it, is reminiscent of Joseph Smith's magic stones Urim and Thummim. Joseph Smith testifies that he found the golden tablets and the "breastplate" lying on top of these stones. *The Book of Mormon* (Salt Lake City: Church of Jesus Christ of Latter-day Saints, 1950), chap. 9, 478, and "Origin of the Book of Mormon," n.p. In the name of the real-life "Burned-over District" of central New York State (so dubbed after the religious fervor of the Second Great Awakening that swept this area) where Joseph Smith uncovered the golden plates of Moroni, there is an unintentional but wonderful echo of Lovecraft's New England countryside, typically a ravaged landscape populated by degenerate inbred locals.

85. The appellations Knight/Dame and Frater/Soror come from the early twentieth-century occult groups, which drew them in turn from Masonic ritual.

86. www.trapezoid.org (accessed January 19, 2009).

87. Flowers, "The Secret of the Gothick God of Darkness," www.trapezoid.org /thought/secret.html (accessed March 24, 2009).

88. See the "Chaos Magick" manifesto online at www.sfmoma.org/espace/rsub /project/disinfo/cc_orgtron_chaos.html. Also see Phil Hine, *Condensed Chaos: An Introduction to Chaos Magic* (Tempe, AZ: New Falcon Publications, 1995).

89. For a genealogy that distinguishes between the Crowley line and that of the breakaways, see Gonce, "The Evolution of Sorcery: A Brief History of Modern Magick," in Harms and Gonce, *Necronomicon Files*, 80.

90. Davis maintains that Chaos magicians would insist that what they do has nothing to do with a specific set of beliefs, just whatever works to get the practitioner to the otherworldly experience or other dimension, which they do believe in. "Calling Cthulhu," 127.

91. http://w3.iac.net/~moonweb/AboutBate.html (accessed August 16, 2011). The site has not been recently updated. As with all the online groups, numbers and activity are difficult to determine.

92. Petersen, Willis, et al., *Call of Cthulhu*, 126.

93. Davis notes that *The Call of Cthulhu* role-playing game stages the clash of conscious and unconscious minds, objectivity and subjectivity, rationality and whatever, to produce the same "cognitive dissonance" evoked by the Chaos magicians and by Lovecraft's stories themselves. "Calling Cthulhu," 130.

94. Quoted in Jeffrey Kripal, *Authors of the Impossible: The Paranormal and the Sacred* (Chicago: University of Chicago Press, 2010), 67.

95. Posted in an archived statement entitled "Fungi from Yuggoth The Gnosis of Fear," http://w3.iac.net/~moonweb/archives/EOD/FungiYuggoth.htm (accessed August 16, 2011). "Fungi from Yuggoth" (1936) is a sonnet cycle composed by Lovecraft and the only specimen of the large quantity of poetry he wrote that is still widely read.

96. www.philhine.org/ick/index_mine.html (accessed March 26, 2009).

97. www.kiva.net/~julianus/staronyx.html (accessed January 19, 2009).

98. "Lovecraftian Banishing Ritual," by Phoenix and Runa Dragon. www.setii shadim.wordpress.com/2007/01/31/lovecraftian-banishing-ritual (accessed January 19, 2009).

99. See, e.g., *Lord of a Visible World*, 81.

100. http://w3.iac.net/~moonweb/archives/FT13/AeonCthulhuRising.htm (accessed September 9, 2005).

101. Grant, *Magical Revival*, 117.

102. According to Golden Dawn initiate Dion Fortune [Viola E. Firth], "Protestant Christianity threw away its occult aspect at the Reformation. All the pagan pantheons have gross aspects of divinities as well as ethereal ones. We need to search the refuse heap of history for the lost parts of our tradition if our faith is to be complete, and the most profitable line of search is in the Qaballah and the Gnostic literature." *Psychic Self-Defense* (York Beach, ME: Samuel Weiser, 1996 [1930]), 127.

103. This plaintive note of "why?" is also sounded by Gonce: "It doesn't make good sense! Why on earth would the magician want to invoke terrifying alien beings who yearn to reconquer the planet and destroy it by remaking it in their own terrifying image?" As one answer he cites Phil Hine, who sees Lovecraft's Great Old Ones not as "demonic entities to whom he must enslave himself with a Faustian pact, but as personifications of natural forces whose energies can be tapped." Harms and Gonce, *Necronomicon Files*, 120, 121.

104. Patt Morrison, "Guillermo Del Toro: Monster Mash," *Los Angeles Times*, October 30, 2010.

105. Kirk J. Schneider, *Horror and the Holy: Wisdom-Teachings of the Monster Tale* (Chicago: Open Court, 1993), xii.

4. DECOMMISSIONING SATAN

Neil Gaiman, *The Anansi Boys* (New York: HarperTorch, 2006). The novel tells the story of two half-human sons of the trickster spider god Anansi, one who uses his supernatural powers and the other who doesn't. The brothers discover by story's end that they were born as one being but were split apart by sorcery.

1. H. P. Lovecraft, "The Call of Cthulhu," in *More Annotated H. P. Lovecraft*, annotations by Peter Cannon and S. T. Joshi (New York: Dell, 1999), 188.

2. Matthew G. Lewis, *The Monk: A Romance* (New York: Grove Press, 1952), 412.

3. Christopher Partridge, *The Re-Enchantment of the West*, vol. 2: *Alternative Spiritualities, Sacralization, Popular Culture, and Occulture* (London: T. and T. Clark, 2005), 208.

4. Anton LaVey, *The Satanic Rituals* (New York: Avon Books, 1972), 177.

5. This fairy double or "co-walker" is described in the minister Robert Kirk's *The Secret Commonwealth of Elves, Fauns, and Fairies* (New York: New York Review Books, 2007), transcribed in the late seventeenth century from accounts by his Scottish Highland parishioners. In her introduction Marina

Warner notes Hogg's skillful balancing of the tension "between hallucination and truth, between diabolical possession and mental derangement" (xxix).

6. The quote is from *Bram Stoker's Notes for* Dracula: *A Facsimile Edition*, annotated and transcribed by Robert Eighteen-Bisang and Elizabeth Miller (Jefferson, NC: McFarlane, 2008), Appendix VI, 312.

7. Anne Rice, *Interview with the Vampire* (New York: Ballantine Books, 1976), 235.

8. See, e.g., P. M. Zall, ed., *A Hundred Merry Tales and Other Jestbooks of the Fifteenth and Sixteenth Centuries* (Lincoln: University of Nebraska Press, 1963).

9. This very American Devil tells his client Tom Walker: "I am he to whom the red men devoted this spot, and now and then roasted a white man by way of sweet smelling sacrifice. Since the red men have been exterminated by you white savages, I amuse myself by presiding at the persecutions of quakers and anabaptists; I am the great patron and prompter of slave dealers, and the grand master of the Salem witches." Washington Irving, "The Devil and Tom Walker," http://classiclit.about.com/od/devilandtomwalker/a/aa_devil tomwalker_2.htm (accessed June 21, 2010).

10. Stephen Vincent Benét, "The Devil and Daniel Webster," http://gutenberg .net.au/ebooks06/0602901.txt (accessed June 21, 2010).

11. In John Collier, *Fancies and Goodnights* (New York: Bantam, 1953), 140.

12. Jennifer Robison, on the results of a 2004 poll, quoted in Partridge, *Re-enchantment of the West*, 2:217.

13. Ibid.

14. *To the Devil a Daughter* (1976), aka *Child of Satan*, directed by Peter Sykes from the novel by Dennis Wheatley, is the story of a father who wants to sign his daughter over to the Devil (male pact) so that she will be the Devil's representative on earth (female possession). Roman Polanski's *The Ninth Gate* (1999), written by John Brownjohn and Enrique Urbizu, taken from a novel by Arturo Pérez-Reverte, features a man who makes a pact with the Devil by sleeping with a nicely *Monk*-like demon incarnated as a seductive female.

15. Darryl Jones, quoted in Partridge, *Re-Enchantment of the West*, 2:240.

16. Directed by Peter Hyams, written by Andrew W. Marlowe.

17. Directed by John Carpenter, written by Martin Quatermass [John Carpenter].

18. See Stephen King's comment about God as the big "juju" in pop culture, quoted in chapter 11.

19. Directed by Carl Schultz, written by Clifford Green and Ellen Green.

20. Directed by Scott Charles Stewart, written by Peter Schink and Scott Charles Stewart.

21. These same fears were voiced about Gothick novels by the anonymous writer of a letter to the editor titled "Terrorist Novel Writing" in *Spirit of the Public Journals for 1797* (London, 1798), 1:223–225, reprinted in E. J. Clery and Robert Miles, eds., *Gothic Documents: A Sourcebook 1700–1820* (Manchester: Manchester University Press, 2000), 184.

22. This quote was taken from the unedited manuscript version of Jeffrey Kripal's *Mutants and Mystics: Science Fiction, Superhero Comics, and the Paranormal* (Chicago: University of Chicago Press, 2011). Kripal's study traces a secret history of the religious imagination in the complex historical interaction

between American popular culture and paranormal-mystical experience over the twentieth century.

23. In *Our Gods Wear Spandex: The Secret History of Comic Book Heroes* (San Francisco: Red Wheel/Weiser, 2007), 45–49.

24. Laura Miller, "Chivalry and Superheroes," blog entry, September 20, 2008, lauramiller.typepad.com (accessed October 2, 2008).

25. Fredric Wertham, *Seduction of the Innocent* (New York: Rinehart, 1954). Wertham's book provoked a U.S. Senate subcommittee hearing that established a Comics Code Authority in 1955 banning certain sexual and violent content.

26. Jim Trombetta, *The Horror! The Horror! Comic Books the Government Didn't Want You to Read!* (New York: Abrams ComicArts, 2010), 32.

27. Linda Williams, "Mega-Melodrama! Vertical and Horizontal Suspensions of the 'Classical,'" 98th annual Faculty Research Lecture, University of California, Berkeley, April 4, 2011. "Vertical suspension," in contrast, is a characteristic of the single-story stand-alone feature film in which "villains fall, heroes hang by a thread, superheroes fly." See also Kristen Whissel, "Tales of Upward Mobility: The New Verticality and Digital Special Effects," *Film Quarterly* 54 (Summer 2006): 23–40.

28. Alan Moore, introduction, *Swamp Thing: The Saga of the Swamp Thing*, written by Alan Moore, artists Steve Bissette and John Totleben (New York: DC Comics/Warner Bros., 1987) [reprint of *Saga of the Swamp Thing* 21–27], n.p.

29. Ibid.

30. Frederick Strömberg, *The Comics Go to Hell: A Visual History of the Devil in Comic Books* (Seattle: Fantagraphic Books, 2005), 285.

31. Quoted in Christopher Farnsworth, "'Twilight' to 'True Blood': Why We Suck the Evil out of Vampires," *Los Angeles Times*, May 25, 2011.

32. Kripal, *Mutants and Mystics*, 244–250.

33. The comic book artists "often employed neo-medieval allegories (one reason the covers are so 'readable')," Jim Trombetta notes, "and enjoyed introducing motifs like the pietà or the deposition of Christ's body from the cross into bizarre and even sacrilegious settings." *The Horror! The Horror!*, 32.

34. Cited in Strömberg, *Comics Go to Hell*, 193. Comic book and graphic novel writers routinely use ellipses as pauses within their word balloons and so the three little dots in the passages that follow do not indicate excised material, as they do in standard text quotation. All quotes in this chapter from comics or graphic novels feature ellipses used in this way.

35. *Spawn Collection*, vol. 1, created and written by Todd McFarlane, coloring by Steve Oliff, Reuben Rude, and Olyoptics (Berkeley: Image Comics, 2006), front matter. [Originally published 1992–1993 as nos. 1–12.]

36. Reprinted in *Essential Marvel Horror*, vol. 1 (New York: Marvel, 2006). All quotes from this edition. Series writers include Steve Gerber and John Warner; principal artists were Jim Mooney and Sal Buscema. Series editor Roy Thomas, who created the story line, states that he realized later that a 1962 comic written by Bill Joe (aka Biljo) White in the fanzine *Komix Illustrated*

was probably his unconscious inspiration for the series. Thomas, personal communication, June 29, 2010.

37. Or the view of the universe the soldier Scipio is shown by his grandfather in Cicero's *Somnium Scipionis*.

38. *Hellstorm—Prince of Lies*, written by Warren Ellis, cited in Strömberg, *Comics Go to Hell*, 201.

39. In *The Secret Life of Puppets* I misidentified the *Watchmen* series as *The Night Watchmen*, to well-deserved Internet opprobrium.

40. "Rake at the Gates of Hell," *John Constantine: Hellblazer*, written by Garth Ennis, artist Steve Dillon (New York: DC Comics/Warner Bros., 2003). [Originally published as *Hellblazer* no. 78.]

41. Neil Gaiman, *The Sandman: Season of Mists*, characters created by Neil Gaiman, Sam Kieth, and Mike Dringenberg; illustrated by Kelley Jones, Mike Dringenberg, Malcolm Jones III, Matt Wagner, Dick Giordano, George Pratt, and P. Craig Russell (New York: DC Comics, 1992), panel 11. The Bowie reference was acknowledged by Gaiman in numerous interviews. See, e.g., www.bowiewonderworld.com/chats/dbchatngo601.htm (accessed March 3, 2011).

42. Alan Moore, quoted in "John Constantine," http://en.wikipedia.org/wiki /John_Constantine (accessed September 20, 2010).

43. "Newcastle: A Taste of Things to Come," *John Constantine: Hellblazer*, written by Jamie Delano, artists Richard Piers Raynor and Mark Buckingham (New York: DC Comics/Warner Bros., 2003). [Originally published as *Hellblazer* no. 11.]

44. "Sex and Death," *John Constantine: Hellblazer*, written by Jamie Delano, artists Richard Piers Raynor and Mark Buckingham (New York: DC Comics/ Warner Bros., 2003). [Originally published as *Hellblazer* no. 10.]

45. Gaiman, *Sandman: Season of Mists*, panel 11.

46. Kaz [Kazimieras G. Prapuolenis], "The Tragedy of Satan," in *Sidetrack City*, cited in Strömberg, *Comics Go to Hell*, 151.

47. Directed by Steven Brill, written by Tim Herlihy, Adam Sandler, and Steven Brill.

48. *Spawn Collection*, vol. 1, n.p.

49. "Spawn," Wikipedia, http://en.wikipedia.org/wiki/Spawn (comics) (accessed September 15, 2010). The summary (much, much longer than the extract quoted here) may not be entirely accurate to the story, but that's not really the point of Wikipedia, whose casual misinformation often assumes its own Gothick authority as it seeps into the sub-Zeitgeist.

50. As described on the official site, www.hellboy.com (accessed January 10, 2011).

51. *Hellboy: Wake the Devil*, written and drawn by Mike Mignola, colored by James Sinclair (Milwaukee, OR: Dark Horse Comics, 1997), n.p. [Originally published as nos. 1–5, 1995–1996.]

52. *Hellboy: Seed of Destruction*, by Mike Mignola, script by John Byrne, colored by Mark Chiarello (Milwaukee, OR: Dark Horse Comics, 1997), n.p. [Originally published as nos. 1–5, 1995–1996.]

53. *Hellboy: Wake the Devil*, n.p.

54. "The Time of the Preacher," in *Preacher: Gone to Texas*, written by Garth Ennis, artist Steve Dillon (New York: DC Comics/Warner Bros., 1996), n.p. [Originally published as *Preacher* nos. 1–7, 1995.]

55. "Miracle Man," in *Preacher: Until the End of the World*, written by Garth Ennis, artist Steve Dillon (New York: DC Comics/Warner Bros., 1997). [Originally published as *Preacher* nos. 8–17, 1995–1996.]

56. "Stormbringers," in *Preacher: Proud Americans*, written by Garth Ennis, artist Steve Dillon (New York: DC Comics/Warner Bros., 1997). [Originally published as *Preacher* nos. 18–26, 1996–1997.]

57. "Revelations," in *Preacher: Proud Americans*.

58. www.baptistboard.com/showthread.php?t=1497 (accessed July 30, 2010).

59. Trombetta argues that war trauma and posttraumatic stress disorder shaped a great deal of the content of the spectacularly violent 1950s American horror comics. *The Horror! The Horror!*, 140.

60. From, e.g., Tezuka Osamu's *Princess Knight* (1953), which features a Western muscular Satan in spandex briefs, cloak, and pointy goatee, to Toriyama Akira's goateed lord in *Sand Land* (2000). Strömberg, *Comics Go to Hell*, 135.

61. Ibid., 137. In Neil Gaiman's *Sandman* story line, after Satan's abdication Hell is briefly inhabited by a highly syncretic crew of gods including the Shinto god of storms and the sea, Susano-o-no-mikoto, who points out correctly that the Japanese "are expanding . . . assimilating other pantheons, later gods, new altars and icons. Marilyn Monroe is ours now, as are King Kong and Lady Liberty." Gaiman, *Sandman: Season of Mists*, panel 8.

5. GOTHICK ROMANCE

Ann Tukey Harrison, ed. and trans., *The Danse Macabre of Women* (Kent, OH: Kent State University Press, 1994), 112.

1. Thomas Carlyle, "The Diamond Necklace," *Frazier's Magazine* 85, 86 [1837], reprinted in *Critical and Miscellaneous Essays, Collected and Republished by Thomas Carlyle* (New York: Belford Clarke and Co., 1890?), 4:1.

2. Horace Walpole, "Preface to the Second Edition," *The Castle of Otranto*, ed. Michael Gamer (London: Penguin, 2001), 9.

3. At the time the terms *romance* and *novel* were often used interchangeably; then as now, their definitions have been endlessly disputed. For the origins of the debate, see the Gothick novelist Clara Reeve, *The Progress of Romance, through Times, Countries, and Manners* [1785], 1:111, quoted in E. J. Clery and Robert Miles, eds., *Gothic Documents: A Sourcebook 1700–1820* (Manchester: Manchester University Press, 2000), 179–180, and Walter Scott, "An Essay on Romance," in *Miscellaneous Prose Works* [1852] www.walterscott.lib.ed.ac.uk/etexts/prose .html (accessed November 10, 2010).

4. Northrop Frye, *The Secular Scripture: A Study of the Structure of Romance* (Cambridge, MA: Harvard University Press, 1976), 3–4, 23, 61, 28–29.

5. As noted by Maurice Lévy in "FAQ: What Is Gothic?" *Anglophonia* 15 (2004): 23.

6. Walpole, *Castle of Otranto*, 85.

7. Anna MacKenzie, *Mysteries Elucidated* (London: Minerva Press, 1795), 1:90.

8. Ann Radcliffe, *The Mysteries of Udolpho: A Romance Interspersed with Some Pieces of Poetry* (London: Oxford University Press, 2008 [1794]), 79.

9. Terry Castle, introduction to Radcliffe, *Mysteries of Udolpho*, xxii–xxiv. Castle elaborates here on Harold Bloom's idea of "internalized romance" in "The Internalization of the Quest-Romance," in Bloom, ed., *Romanticism and Consciousness* (New York: W. W. Norton, 1970), 3–24. Radcliffe's use of the word *mystery* in the title of her immensely popular novel probably helped pave the way for the emergence of the Anglo-American secular murder mystery genre in the nineteenth century, fostered by Edgar Allan Poe and Julian Hawthorne, son of Nathaniel.

10. Virginia Woolf, review of Edith Birkhead's *The Tale of Terror* (1921), quoted in Catherine Spooner, "Gothic in the Twentieth Century," in Catherine Spooner and Emma McEvoy, *The Routledge Companion to Gothic* (London: Routledge, 2007), 38.

11. Moers defines "Female Gothic" as any work of fiction "that women writers have done in the literary mode that, since the eighteenth century, we have called the 'Gothic'"; her category thus includes Mary Shelley's *Frankenstein* and Emily Brontë's *Wuthering Heights*. Ellen Moers, *Literary Women* (New York and London: Oxford University Press, 1976), 90. Gary Kelly's six-volume edition of little-known early female Gothic works, *Varieties of Female Gothic* (London: Pickering and Chatto, 2002–), has helped canonize this category in the classic Gothick.

12. Terry Castle, *The Female Thermometer: Eighteenth-Century Culture and the Invention of the Uncanny* (New York: Oxford University Press, 1995); Julia Kristeva, *Powers of Horror: An Essay on Abjection*, trans. Leon S. Roudiez (New York: Columbia University Press, 1982); Eve Kosofsky Sedgwick, *The Coherence of Gothic Conventions* (New York: Methuen, 1986).

13. Anne Williams, *Art of Darkness: A Poetics of Gothic* (Chicago: University of Chicago Press, 1995), 102–103.

14. Erich Auerbach, *Mimesis: The Representation of Reality in Western Culture*, trans. Willard R. Trask (Princeton: Princeton University Press, 2003 [1953]), 134.

15. Marina Warner has described the zombiefication of mad Bertha Rochester as the twentieth-century writer Jean Rhys beautifully reimagined this character as the heroine of her Dominica-set novel *Wide Sargasso Sea* (1966). See the discussion in chapter 7 and Warner, *Fantastic Metamorphoses, Other Worlds* (New York: Oxford University Press, 2002), 154–159. As a radical female Gothick recasting of Brontë's tale, Rhys's novel helped lay the groundwork for Sandra M. Gilbert and Susan Gubar's classic feminist rereading of Victorian literature, *The Madwoman in the Attic: The Woman Writer and the Nineteenth Century Imagination* (New Haven, CT: Yale University Press, 1979).

16. In *Wuthering Heights* the visitor Lockwood dreams of dead Cathy, and a little boy sees Heathcliff and "a woman" after he is dead, but these supernatural intrusions are smoothed over or explained by Lockwood as "mental perturbations." www
.online-literature.com/bronte/wuthering, chap. 34 (accessed August 25, 2010).

17. *Paradise Lost*, book 1, ll.589–604.

18. Mario Praz, *The Romantic Agony*, trans. Angus Davidson, 2nd ed. (London: Oxford University Press, 1951), 155–158, 61.

19. Quoted in Christopher Frayling, *Vampyres: Lord Byron to Count Dracula* (London and Boston: Faber and Faber, 1991), 6.

20. Charlotte Brontë, *Jane Eyre* (Mineola, NY: Dover, 2002), 108, 113–114.

21. Emily Brontë, *Wuthering Heights*, chap. 34. Both sisters had formed a template for their heroes in the fictional heroes and villains of their childhood writings set in the imaginary kingdom of Angria, an apt allegorical name for the womb of a character with Heathcliff's temperament.

22. Philippe Ariès, *Western Attitudes toward Death* [Essais sur l'histoire de la mort en Occident], trans. Patricia M. Ranum (Baltimore: Johns Hopkins University Press, 1975), 157. Where earlier scholars had long regarded the danse macabre as a reaction to the devastation caused by the plague, Ariès believed that the iconic image represented instead "an excessive attachment to life" (158). Denis de Rougemont likewise found it to be an expression of heterodox populist religion; the folklore of death, he observes, admits all kinds of nonorthodox beliefs, including a "nocturnal universe of demons." *Love in the Western World*, rev. ed., trans. Montgomery Belgion (Princeton: Princeton University Press, 1983), 242–243.

23. Ariès, *Western Attitudes toward Death*, 180.

24. *Romeo and Juliet* V:iii, 102–105.

25. Gábor Klaniczay links the "erotic fantasies" of the "Death and the Maiden" trope to the later sexualization of vampire folklore in Western Europe. *The Uses of Supernatural Power: The Transformation of Popular Religion in Medieval and Early-Modern Europe*, trans. Susan Singerman (Princeton: Princeton University Press, 1990), 183.

26. Ariès, *Western Attitudes toward Death*, 176.

27. Williams, *Art of Darkness*, 140–147.

28. Linda Barlow and Jayne Ann Krentz, "Beneath the Surface: The Hidden Codes of Romance," in Jayne Ann Krentz, ed., *Dangerous Men and Adventurous Women: Romance Writers on the Appeal of Romance* (Philadelphia: University of Pennsylvania Press, 1992), 19.

29. Ibid.

30. Quoted in Williams, *Art of Darkness*, 227.

31. Fred Botting, "Gothic Culture," in Spooner and McEvoy, *Routledge Companion to Gothic*, 207.

32. Jane Litte, "Dear Author," http://dearauthor.com/wordpress/2007/11/26/kindle-pricing-so-low-that-amazon-is-no-longer-discounting-paperbacks (accessed April 27, 2009).

33. Pamela Regis, *A Natural History of the Romance Novel* (Philadelphia: University of Pennsylvania Press, 2003), 206–207.

34. The Romance Writers of America recognizes nine official subgenres: contemporary series romance, contemporary single title romance, historical romance, inspirational romance, novels with strong romantic elements, paranor-

mal romance, Regency romance, romantic suspense, and young adult romance. www.rwa.org/cs/romance_literature_subgenres (accessed August 23, 2008).

35. Sarah Wendell and Candy Tan, *Beyond Heaving Bosoms: The Smart Bitches' Guide to Romance Novels* (New York: Simon and Schuster, 2009), 13.

36. See, for example, Victoria Holt, *The Demon Lover* (Garden City, NY: Doubleday, 1982) and many more from that period. The scathing reviews by post-2000 readers of this book on Amazon.com are a vivid testimony to the change of attitude over thirty years. For an excellent discussion of the rape issue in women's romance, see Wendell and Tan, *Beyond Heaving Bosoms*, 136–147.

37. www.ellorascave.com (accessed April 30, 2009). Themes on the 2011 website (each with its own icon) include "19th century, 20th century, BDSM Elements, Christmas, Comedy, Female/Female, Interracial Element, Medieval, Menage or more, Male/Male, Paranormal Elements, Regency, Rubenesque, Shapeshifter, Steampunk, Urban Fantasy, Valentine's Day, Vampire." http://www.jasminejade.com/default.aspx?skinid=11 (accessed October 29, 2011).

38. "Erotica—Fanning the Flames," *Publisher's Weekly*, www.publishersweekly.com 8/2/10 (accessed August 2, 2010).

39. See Alexandra Alter, "They're No Bodice Rippers, but Amish Romances Are Hot," *Wall Street Journal*, September 9, 2009.

40. Wendell and Tan, *Beyond Heaving Bosoms*, 148–167.

41. Stephanie Laurens, *Devil's Bride* (New York: Avon, 1998), 7.

42. Lucinda Dyer, "P Is for Paranormal—Still," *Publishers Weekly*, May 24, 2010. Among a slate of new books, the article mentions a new paranormal romance heroine in the form of a "tough-talking but vulnerable succubus."

43. Wendell and Tan, *Beyond Heaving Bosoms*, 25. The authors also cite the theory of the blogger Lilith Saintcrow "that the 'changing' or 'turning' motif of paranormal romances is the new virginity." The fact that the hero is able to see who the heroine really is, an important romance turning point, also works in the paranormal frame as another way of possessing or owning her: "That traffic of ownership and experience, be it piercing the hymen or seeing her highlights or slurping on her neck, is a constant undercurrent to the creation of any heroine, and the hero who defines her, deflowers her, or devours her" (53).

44. "Under the influence of the Calvinist Methodist preacher and missionary George Whitefield," Alexandra Walsham recounts, "the carved figures that adorned the medieval hammer-beam roof on the church of Bidleston in Suffolk were cut down by a carpenter acting on the orders of the churchwardens and burnt as abominable idols." "Angels and Idols in England's Long Reformation," in Peter Marshall and Alexandra Walsham, eds., *Angels in the Early Modern World* (Cambridge: Cambridge University Press, 2005), 167.

45. Wouter J. Hanegraaff, *Esotericism and the Academy: Rejected Knowledge in Western Culture* (Cambridge: Cambridge University Press, in press), 199n.

46. Hanegraaff makes an important caveat about alchemy as contemporary "medievalism": "The idea that alchemy is essentially a spiritual pursuit, not a scientific one, had first been proposed by Mary Atwood in 1850, from a perspective

permeated by German Romantic mesmerism and Boehmian theosophy." Popularized by Jung's alchemical metaphors for the transformation of the psyche, alchemy is often regarded now as an exclusively spiritual discipline, but in medieval times "it was both laboratory science and esoteric pursuit." Ibid., 289.

47. Hilary Mantel, *Fludd* (New York: Henry Holt, 1989), 80.
48. Ibid., 103.
49. Ibid., 173.
50. Ibid., 176.
51. Ibid., 178.

52. The Devil manifested as an invisible "spiral" among the weeds to the young Hilary, who had been, according to her own child's reasoning, looking where she had no business looking. She did not see it, she says, but rather sensed it by its "insolent motion": "It is as high as a child of two. Its depth is a foot, fifteen inches. . . . It has no edges, no mass, no dimension except the formless. . . . Within the space of a thought it is inside me, and has set up a sick resonance within my bones and in all the cavities of my body. . . . [I]t is a body inside my body, an amphibian shape, budding and malign." Hilary Mantel, *Giving Up the Ghost* (New York: Henry Holt, 2003), 93, 97.

6. THE BRIGHT GOD BECKONS

"Think of it Lover": from "If I May Have It When It's Dead," *The Complete Poems of Emily Dickinson*, ed. Thomas H. Johnson (Boston: Little Brown, 1960), J #577; whether these lines refer to the afterlife has been a subject of debate, however. "Hard though it may be": from Sarah Wendell and Candy Tan, *Beyond Heaving Bosoms: The Smart Bitches' Guide to Romance Novels* (New York: Simon & Schuster, 2009), 112.

1. From Ovid's Lycaon in the *Metamorphoses* to Marie de France's lai *Bisclavret*, featuring a man who turns into a werewolf, to accounts by the English historian William of Malmesbury to the Middle English metrical romance "William of Palerne," belief in werewolves as real entities, previously prohibited by the Church, became part of the same doctrine of demonology that revived Satan in the sixteenth century, when suspected werewolves were burned along with witches. See Carolyn Walker Bynum, "Shape and Story: Metamorphosis in the Western Tradition," Jefferson Lecture in the Humanities, March 22, 1999, www.neh.gov/new/archive/199990322b.html (accessed December 18, 2007).

2. Fernando Vidal, "Extraordinary Bodies and the Physicotheological Imagination," preprint 188 (2001), Max Planck Institute, www.mpiwg-berlin.mpg .de/Preprints/P188.PDF (accessed March 3, 2011).

3. Voltaire wrote satirically of vampires in his *Philosophical Dictionary* (1768), and the Benedictine abbot Augustin Calmet recorded more than 500 cases of vampirism in his 1746 study *Dissertations sur les apparitions des anges, des démons et des esprits, et sur les revenants et vampires de Hongrie, de Bohême, de Moravie, et de Silésie* (Isère, France: J. Millon, 1986). Though his own position was

ambivalent, Calmet's accounts of unquiet spirits became an important source-book for western European tales of the supernatural.

4. From "Visum et Repertum," the official report by Austrian physicians conducted five years after the incident, translated and quoted in Paul Barber, *Vampires, Burial and Death* (New Haven: Yale University Press, 1988), 16. This report gives his name as "Arnod Paole"; in other accounts it is rendered as Arnold Paul and Arnaut Paule.

5. Katharina M. Wilson, "The History of the Word 'Vampire,'" *Journal of the History of Ideas*, 46:4 (1985): 578. This comprehensive linguistic study corrects many misconceptions about the term and its introduction into various languages. Wilson, 579, cites first appearances of the word *vampire* in English also in the late seventeenth century.

6. This act was not repealed until 1951. Up to that year people could still be prosecuted for "fraudulently" (this is the key modernizing term) claiming the ability to cast spells, talk to spirits, and so on. Marion Gibson, *Witchcraft and Society in England and America, 1550–1750* (New York: Continuum, 2006), 6, 9.

7. Gábor Klaniczay, *The Uses of the Supernatural: The Transformation of Popular Religion in Medieval and Early-Modern Europe*, trans. Susan Singerman (Princeton: Princeton University Press, 1990), 179–180.

8. Stuart Clark, *Thinking with Demons: The Idea of Witchcraft in Early Modern Europe* (Oxford: Clarendon Press, 1997), 247.

9. Ibid., 186–187.

10. The Benedictine monk Benito Jerónimo Feijóo joked that if all the reports of vampires were true, "it would mean that more resurrections took place in Central Europe in the late seventeenth century than in the whole of Christendom since the birth of Christ." Vidal, "Extraordinary Bodies," 17.

11. For a comprehensive discussion, see Matthew Gibson, *Dracula and the Eastern Question: British and French Vampire Narratives of the Nineteenth Century* (Basingstoke, UK: Palgrave Macmillan, 2006).

12. See, e.g., William of Newburgh's blood-sucking ghost *sanguisaga* in his *Historia Rerum Anglicorum* and the "Ghost of Anant," reprinted in Andrew Jones, comp. and ed., *Medieval Ghost Stories: An Anthology of Miracles, Marvels and Prodigies* (Woodbridge: Boydell Press, 2001), 88, 100–102.

13. Keith Thomas, *Religion and the Decline of Magic: Studies of Popular Beliefs in Sixteenth and Seventeenth Century England* (New York: Scribner's, 1971), 595.

14. Christopher Frayling, *Vampyres: Lord Byron to Count Dracula* (London: Faber and Faber, 1991), 5.

15. According to Coleridge's biographer Richard Holmes, "Shelley later told Mary that the poem had conjured a vision of a woman 'who had eyes instead of nipples.'" *Coleridge: Darker Reflections, 1804–1834* (New York: Pantheon Books, 1998), 437.

16. Polidori took the name Ruthven (pronounced "Rivven") from a character based on Byron in the latter's ex-paramour Lady Caroline Lamb's novel *Glenarvon* (1816). Polidori's publisher listed Byron as the author of *The Vampyre* in its first edition; this claim even appeared in several editions of Byron's works, much to the latter's frustration. For a full account, see Franklin Charles

Bishop, introduction, in Polidori, *"The Vampyre" and Other Writings* (Manchester, UK: Carcanet, 2005).

17. Milly Williamson, *The Lure of the Vampire: Gender, Fiction and Fandom from Bram Stoker to Buffy* (London: Wallflower Press, 2006), 94.

18. For a thorough survey, see Roxana Stuart, *Stage Blood: Vampires of the 19th-Century Stage* (Bowling Green, OH: Bowling Green State University Press, 1994).

19. Robert Tracy in his introduction to Le Fanu's *In a Glass Darkly* (Oxford: Oxford University Press, 1993), xxi, suggests that Le Fanu changed the location from Ireland to Styria because his publisher didn't think Irish stories would sell.

20. I am following Frayling's comprehensive table, "A Vampire Mosaic: Vampires in Folklore, Prose, and Poetry 1687–1913," in *Vampyres*, 42–63.

21. "Dracula's Guest," a deleted portion of *Dracula* published later by his widow as a separate story, has echoes of "Carmilla" in the figure of the female vampire Countess Dollingen.

22. Gerard gives the indigenous word for "vampire" as *nosferatu*, which Stoker also adopts, but it is unknown in Romanian or any other language. Robert Eighteen-Bisang and Elizabeth Miller, *Bram Stoker's Notes for* Dracula: *A Facsimile Edition* (Jefferson, NC: McFarlane & Company, 2008), 284.

23. For ethnographic studies of the folklore of *strigoi*, see Agnes Murgoci, "The Vampire in Roumania," and Jan Louis Perkowski, "The Romanian Folkloric Vampire," both in Alan Dundes, ed., *The Vampire: A Casebook* (Madison: University of Wisconsin Press, 1998).

24. *Bram Stoker's Notes*, 245.

25. Bram Stoker, *Dracula*, ed. Nina Auerbach and David J. Skal (New York: W. W. Norton, 1997), 263.

26. In *Food for the Dead: On the Trail of New England's Vampires* (New York: Carroll and Graf, 2001), however, Michael Bell notes the first New England instance in 1793, with one or two reported in upstate New York and Chicago. Bell noted that in the local tradition the word *vampire* is not used. Lovecraft references Mercy Brown in his story "The Shunned House."

27. Reproduced in *Bram Stoker's Notes*, 186–187.

28. J. Gordon Melton itemizes a number of these innovations in his introduction to *The Vampire Book: The Encyclopedia of the Undead* (Detroit: Visible Ink Press, 1999), xiii. Frayling notes a late seventeenth-century account, Valvassor's *Ehre des Herzogstum Krains*, that reports a male peasant vampire who "likes to be invited across the threshold, after knocking on the door." "A Vampire Mosaic," in *Vampyres*, 42.

29. Stoker's widow had copies of the 1922 film confiscated on grounds of copyright infringement, resulting in the loss of all but a few prints of the German Expressionist classic. After the movie version of *Dracula* appeared, the stage adaptation it was closely taken from has stayed in "almost continuous performance" around the world in venues large and small. David J. Skal, "Theatrical Adaptations of *Dracula*," in Stoker, *Dracula*, 378–379. This adaptation was revived on Broadway in 2011.

30. Wikipedia cites a plausible if enormous figure: "more than 200 films" featuring Count Dracula and "several hundred more that have vampires as their subject . . . more than 1,000 novels . . . about Dracula or vampires along with a plethora of cartoons, comics, and television programs." http://en.wikipedia.org/wiki/Dracula_in_popular_culture (accessed May 6, 2009).

31. Milly Williamson asserts that vampires as sympathetic figures have been around since the nineteenth century, especially in their role as "bohemian outsider." *Lure of the Vampire*, 35.

32. At the same time, Rice implicitly undermines this assertion by setting the scene in a room in Paris dominated by a "medieval woodcut" of the Devil. *Interview with the Vampire* (New York: Alfred A. Knopf, 1976), 235–236, 238.

33. Bette Roberts has pointed out Rice's debt to an earlier Gothick novel in her character of Akasha, mother of vampires. "The Mother Goddess in H. Rider Haggard's *She* and Anne Rice's *The Queen of the Damned*," in James Craig Holte, ed., *The Fantastic Vampire: Studies in the Children of the Night*, Selected Essays from the 18th International Conference on the Fantastic in the Arts (Westport, CT: Greenwood Press, 2002), 103–109.

34. Rice, *Interview with the Vampire*, 239.

35. Williamson identifies the abstinence trope as starting as early as 1945, when Dracula tries to find a cure for his need to feed in the movie *House of Dracula*. *Lure of the Vampire*, 43.

36. The same Saint-Germain was dubbed a "Master of Wisdom" and a "great Theosophist" by Helena Blavatsky and other Theosophists, who declared he was still alive in Tibet as a master of the "Great White Lodge of the Himalayas," attending to the development of Western civilization. See, e.g., *The Key to Theosophy* (1887), www.theosociety.org/pasadena/key/key-hp.htm and www.blavatsky.net/magazine/theosophy/ww/setting/germain.html (both accessed March 3, 2011).

37. Colin Wilson, *The Space Vampires* (New York: Pocket Books, 1977), 17.

38. Whitley Strieber, *The Hunger* (New York: William Morrow, 1981).

39. Octavia Butler, *Fledgling* (New York: Seven Stories Press, 2005).

40. Tanya Huff, *The Blood Books, Volume I: Blood Price and Blood Trail* (New York: 2006), 406. The main character, named Victoria Nelson, is not me, though she's sufficiently well known that my ID card gave a reference librarian at a university interlibrary loan service a visible shock when I arrived to pick up a stack of vampire books.

41. Ibid., 162.

42. Ibid., 110.

43. "The Lay of the Werewolf" [Bisclavret], *Lays of Marie de France and Other French Legends*, trans. Eugene Mason (London: Dent, Everyman's Library, 1964), 85.

44. *Lara Croft, Tomb Raider*, directed by Simon West, story by Sara B. Cooper, Mike Werb, Michael Colleary, adaptation by Simon West, screenplay by Patrick Massett and John Zinman; *Xena: Warrior Princess* (1995–2001), created by John Schulian and Robert G. Tapert; *Underworld* (2003), directed by

Len Wiseman, screenplay by Danny McBride, story credited to Kevin Grevioux and Len Wiseman (also the director).

45. Joy Press, "Vampires That Don't Suck," *Salon*, www.salon.com/entertainment /tv/int/2008/09/03/ball (accessed December 14, 2010).

46. J. Gordon Melton, Massimo Introvigne, and Robert Eighteen-Bisang have compiled an ever-growing bibliography of more than 11,000 English-language vampire comic books from 1935 to 2000. www.cesnur.org/2008/vampire _comics.htm (accessed April 27, 2009).

47. Created by Mark Rein-Hagen. See www.whitewolf.com and https://vampire masquerade.webs.com (accessed October 5, 2010).

48. Directed by Patrick Lussier, written by Joel Soisson and Patrick Lussier.

49. Comic and graphic novel by various writers and illustrators; first movie (1998) directed by Stephen Norrington, written by David S. Goyer.

50. "[K.] Gelder suggests that the interviewer's desire to be a vampire at the end is a perfect representation of fandom." Williamson, *Lure of the Vampire*, 44, 63.

51. Taken from www.subgenius.com/bigfist/bulldada/X0045_VAMPIRE.TXT .html (accessed December 17, 2010). Also see the discussion in Katherine Ramsland, *Piercing the Darkness: Undercover with Vampires in America Today* (New York: HarperCollins, 1998), 125.

52. www.xeper.org/ovampyre (accessed December 17, 2010).

53. Ramsland, *Piercing the Darkness*, 21.

54. *The Black Vampyre: A Legend of St. Domingo* (New York, 1819), a self-published pamphlet by Uriah Derick D'Arcy [anagrammatic pen name of the Rev. Richard Varick Dey], went through two editions the same year that Polidori's work appeared in the United States. It's the story of a ten-year-old slave who is drowned by his master and returns for revenge as a Moorish vampire prince who turns the master, his widow, and their son into vampires. The son becomes the prince's servant boy and the prince marries the widow, producing a mulatto son "of Vampyrish propensities." Though the master and his family are turned back into humans by a magic potion, the author implies that a certain resident of Elizabethtown, New Jersey, by the name of Anthony Gibbons is the black vampire's direct descendant. Drawing the moral that dandies, embezzlers, brokers, country bank directors, plagiarists, critics, and corpse-dissecting doctors are also a kind of vampire, the author ends by confessing that he is one, too. Author identification courtesy Norbert Besch.

55. All from Alan Ball, creator of the HBO series *True Blood* (2008–). Joe Rhodes, "After All the Funerals, Prime Time Auteur Digs Up the Dead," *New York Times*, August 3, 2008.

56. P. C. Cast and Kristin Cast, the *House of Night* YA novels (2007–).

57. The Japanese anime *Karin* (1993–1994, 2005–2006).

58. Octavia Butler's novel *Fledgling* (2005).

59. Matt Haig's novel *The Radleys* (2010).

60. Meyer recounts this story at www.stepheniemeyer.com/twilight.html (accessed October 5, 2010).

61. *Twilight, New Moon, Eclipse,* and *Breaking Dawn.* Meyer wrote a fifth novel, *Midnight Sun,* from the vampire Edward's point of view, but withdrew it from

publication when a draft was leaked on a fan website in 2008. www.stephe
niemeyer.com/midnightsun.html (accessed October 22, 2011).

62. Stephenie Meyer, *Twilight* (New York: Little, Brown, 2005), 85.

63. Bella's father, Charlie, with typical naïveté, likes the Cullens because "they
    stick together the way a family should—camping trips every other weekend"
    (Meyer, *Twilight*, 23). Bella notes constantly, with admiration, the Cullens'
    "intense family binding," "the peaceful character of this life of sacrifice."
    Stephenie Meyer, *Breaking Dawn* (New York: Little, Brown, 2008), 718.

64. "I didn't relate well to people my age," Bella confesses. "Maybe the truth was
    that I didn't relate well to people, period" (Meyer, *Twilight*, 10).

65. Ibid., 92, 184.

66. Ibid., 305, 263–264, 162.

67. Ibid., 310.

68. Laura Miller, "Real Man Have Fangs," *Wall Street Journal*, October 31, 2008.

69. Meyer, *New Moon* (New York: Little, Brown, 2008), 327.

70. Laura Miller, "Touched by a Vampire," Salon.com, www.salon.com/books
    /review/2008/07/30/Twilight/index1.html (accessed August 20, 2008). One
    might note what the Victorian Gothick writer Joseph Sheridan Le Fanu has
    his hero flatly declare in the story "The Room in the Dragon Volant": "Supe-
    riority of rank is a powerful and genuine influence in love. The idea of supe-
    rior refinement is associated with it." *In a Glass Darkly* (London: Oxford
    World Classics, 1993), 121.

71. Meyer, *Twilight*, 58; Stephenie Meyer, *Eclipse* (New York: Little, Brown, 2007),
    56; *Twilight*, 280, 278.

72. Kahane sees "the spectral presence of a dead-undead mother, archaic and
    all-encompassing," filling the empty interior of the Gothick castle as well as
    haunting this father-daughter relationship. See her "Gothic Mirrors and
    Feminine Identity," *Centennial Review* 24 (1980): 43–64.

73. Meyer, *Twilight*, 210.

74. The trance states that characters such as Trilby (Svengali's victims in George
    du Maurier's *Trilby*), Lucy (in *Dracula*), and others fall into, says Auerbach,
    represent "not passivity but an ominous gathering of power as she transfig-
    ures herself from humanity to beatitude." *Our Vampires, Ourselves* (Chicago:
    University of Chicago Press, 1997), 35, 40.

75. Meyer, *Twilight*, 473–474.

76. Ibid., 260.

77. Tantric Buddhism features practices that are intended to produce "an im-
    mortal yet concrete diamond body that transcends the laws of nature." David
    Gordon White, *The Alchemical Body: Siddha Traditions in Medieval India* (Chi-
    cago: University of Chicago Press, 1996), 71. I am grateful to Maja D'aout
    for initially pointing out this association.

78. These various terms for the subtle body are not exactly synonymous, de-
    pending on the tradition.

79. John White, "Resurrection and the Body of Light," *Quest* 97, no. 1 (Fall 2009): 11.

80. Rice's vampire Louis is "utterly white and smooth, as if he were sculpted
    from bleached bone, and his face was as seemingly inanimate as a statue";

Interview with the Vampire, 2. The transsexual vampire in Whitley Strieber's *The Hunger* (New York: Morrow, 1981) has skin that at times feels "hard as stone" (188). In the White Wolf videogame *Vampire: The Masquerade* (created by Mark Rein-Hagen, first published in 1991, and billed as a "modern Gothic storytelling game"), vampire skin, though flexible, is also described as "hard as stone"; http://wiki.white-wolf.com/worldofdarkness/index.php?title=Vampire: _The_Masquerade (accessed February 3, 2010).

81. Meyer, *New Moon*, 17; *Eclipse*, 439.

82. Paull Franklin Baum, "Young Man Betrothed to a Statue," *PMLA* 34, no. 4 [n.s. 27, 4] (1919): 556. Venus was generally denounced as demonic in the Middle Ages. The tradition stretches as far back as William of Malmesbury and Vincent de Beauvais.

83. Kenneth Gross, *The Dream of the Moving Statue* (Ithaca: Cornell University Press, 1992), 115.

84. Meyer, *Breaking Dawn*, 25.

85. "Courtly love" was a Victorian label first used by Gaston Paris (1883), then taken up by C. S. Lewis and other twentieth-century critics.

86. Michael Camille, *The Gothic Idol: Ideology and Image Making in Medieval Art* (Cambridge: Cambridge University Press, 1989), 337.

87. Denis de Rougemont, *Love in the Western World*, rev. ed., trans. Montgomery Belgion (Princeton: Princeton University Press, 1983), 82, 112.

88. Ibid., 66, 105–106, 137. De Rougemont's reading of the Cathars has long since been deconstructed, but contemporary critics such as Simon Gaunt still acknowledge his perception in identifying the Cathar–*fin amor* connection and "the extraordinary power and emotional appeal of the courtly tradition over the last 800 years." Gaunt, *Love and Death in Medieval French and Occitan Courtly Literature* (Oxford: Oxford University Press, 2006), 19–20.

89. Quoted in de Rougemont, *Love in the Western World*, 67. De Rougemont glosses this as follows: "Life is indeed the terrestrial day of beings in a contingent world, in the whirl of matter; but death is the Night of Illumination . . . the Soul's Union with the Beloved, a communion with Absolute Being."

90. Baum, "Young Man Betrothed to a Statue," 565.

91. Before he stops being human himself, Jacob cries, "I'm exactly right for you, Bella. . . . I was the natural path your life would have taken . . . [if] the world was the way it was supposed to be; if there were no monsters and no magic" (*Eclipse*, 599).

92. Anne Williams, who sees the Psyche-Eros story as the prototype for women's romance generally, notes that Emily in *Mysteries of Udolpho* "performs Psyche's task and gradually discerns an orderly world." *Art of Darkness*, 170.

93. For "fairy bruising" as an outcome of human intercourse with the Devil, see Peter Marshall, *Mother Leakey and the Bishop* (Oxford: Oxford University Press, 2006), 40; with extraterrestrials, see, e.g., www.alien-ufo-pictures .com/abduction_check_list.html (accessed December 28, 2010). In the latter field, the most reliable guide is Brenda Denzler's *The Lure of the Edge: Scientific Passions, Religious Beliefs, and the Pursuit of UFOs* (Berkeley: University of California Press, 2001).

94. In *The Kingdom* (1994–1997), the TV series directed and scripted by Lars von Trier, a female doctor who is impregnated by the spirit of a serial killer swells up and delivers an enormous baby in a matter of weeks. In Dean Koontz's novel *Demon Seed* (New York: Bantam Books, 1973), which also became a film, a woman impregnated by a supercomputer gives birth in twenty-eight days.

95. Meyer, *Breaking Dawn*, 387; Rice, *Interview*, 20.

96. Meyer, *Breaking Dawn*, 753, 469. Bella's perception of "both of my faces, hideous human and glorious immortal," recalls the title of C. S. Lewis's retelling of the Cupid and Psyche story, *Till We Have Faces: A Myth Retold* (1956), which expresses the same Christian perception about drab mortal life and brilliant immortal afterlife. In Lewis's version, Psyche becomes the goddess Istra after she dies.

97. Meyer, *Breaking Dawn*, 389, 390, 395. Compare Psyche seeing her god-lover Cupid's "divine beauty" for the first time: his golden hair is "so bright that the flame of the lamp winked in the radiant light reflected from it." *The Transformations of Lucius, Otherwise Known as the Golden Ass*, trans. Robert Graves (New York: Farrar Straus Giroux, 1998), 117.

98. Meyer, *Breaking Dawn*, 388, 610, 614. Anne Rice's vampires also develop superpowers (telepathy, enhanced senses and speed, setting things on fire, immortality) after several hundred years of undead existence.

99. See especially Christina Mirabilis (1150–1224), who after being resurrected from death possessed the ability to fly through the air, survive burning and drowning, and walk on the water like Christ. See "The Life of Christina the Astonishing," trans. Margot H. King and Barbara Newman, in Thomas of Cantimpré, *The Collected Saints' Lives* (Tournhout, Belgium: Brepols, 2008), 127–157. I am indebted to Claire Fanger for pointing me to this source.

100. See, e.g., the Church of Jesus Christ of Latter-day Saints, *Doctrine and Covenants* 132:20: "Then shall they be gods, because they have no end; therefore shall they be from everlasting to everlasting, because they continue; then shall they be above all, because all things are subject unto them. Then shall they be gods, because they have all power, and the angels are subject unto them." http://scriptures.lds.org/dc/132 (accessed October 7, 2010).

101. Emanuel Swedenborg, *Heaven and Its Wonders and Hell: Drawn from Things Heard and Seen*, trans. George F. Dole (West Chester, PA: Swedenborg Foundation, 2000), 294.

102. Church of Jesus Christ of Latter-day Saints, "Gospel Principles—Exaltation," http://lds.org/ldsorg/v/index (accessed October 7, 2010).

103. Quoted in, e.g., Bill McKeever, "As God Is Man May Be?" Mormon Research Ministry, http://mrm.org/lorenzo-snow-couplet (accessed October 6, 2010). Human godhood is claimed in this article as a teaching exclusive to the Mormon faith. Other Mormon commentators stress the similarities with mainstream Christian theology across time. See, e.g., Edward T. Jones, "Mormonism and the Christian Doctrine of Deification," http://manbecomegod.blogspot.com/2009/06/mormonism-and-christian-doctrine-of.html (accessed December 20, 2010).

104. Even the Puritan Cotton Mather saw a bright angel clothed in white "whose face shone like the noonday sun." Diary of Cotton Mather, quoted in Elizabeth

Reis, "Angels in Elite and Popular Magic," in Peter Marshall and Alexandra Walsham, eds., *Angels in the Early Modern World* (Cambridge: Cambridge University Press, 2006), 285.

105. Meyer, *Breaking Dawn*, 534.

106. See Arthur Versluis, "Sexual Mysticisms in Nineteenth-Century America," and Cathy Gutierrez, "Deadly Dates: Bodies and Sex in Spiritualist Heavens," both in Wouter J. Hanegraaff and Jeffrey J. Kripal, eds., *Hidden Intercourse: Eros and Sexuality in the History of Western Esotericism* (Leiden: Brill, 2008), 309–332, 331–354. John L. Brooke maintains that Mormon celestial marriage, after Swedenborg, is likewise an alchemical union to regain lost perfection, creating a dual-gendered being that is one entity. *The Refiner's Fire: The Making of Mormon Cosmology, 1644–1844* (Cambridge: Cambridge University Press, 1996), 257.

107. Meyer, *Breaking Dawn*, 754.

108. Ibid., 465.

109. Beth McDonald, *The Vampire as Numinous Experience: Spiritual Journeys with the Undead in British and American Literature* (Jefferson, NC: McFarland, 2004), 2, 36.

110. Alexandra Walsham, *Providence in Early Modern England* (Oxford: Oxford University Press, 1999), 331. Within the shells of the old churches, "traditional attitudes were gradually invested with different values until the original framework for understanding was shattered" and the new, more austere religion of ideas prevailed. "Beliefs, by this means," she adds, "were slowly but thoroughly transformed."

111. *Dracula 3: The Path of the Dragon* (Kheops Studio, 2008).

112. McDonald, *Vampire as Numinous Experience*, 10, 182.

113. Meyer, *Breaking Dawn*, 479.

7. POSTAPOCALYPTIC GOTHICK

"*Zombie* remains a devastating word": Max Brooks, *World War Z: An Oral History of the Zombie War* (New York: Crown, 2006), 10; "isn't 'zombie' a silly name": Isaac Marion, *Warm Bodies* (New York: Atria Books, 2011), 127.

1. Brooks, *World War Z*, 188.

2. In *Fantastic Metamorphoses, Other Worlds* (New York: Oxford University Press, 2002), 118–160, Marina Warner traces the history of the word in English, from its first mention in the poet Robert Southey's *History of Brazil*, where he advances the "Deity" meaning over a Portuguese historian's "Devil," and his brother-in-law Samuel Taylor Coleridge's glossing of this word in his copy of the book with the notation that the entity was "a" god or devil in a pantheon, not "the" God and Devil of Western monotheistic religion.

3. Ibid., 142–145.

4. The best seller was W. B. Seacliff's *Magic Island* (1929); see the comprehensive discussion of the historical background in Gary D. Rhodes's *White Zombie:*

Anatomy of a Horror Film (Jefferson, NC: McFarlane, 2001). *White Zombie* was directed by Victor Halperin and written by Garnett Weston; it was probably inspired by the U.S. occupation of Haiti from 1915 to 1934 as well as by Seacliff's travel memoir. See Rhodes, *White Zombie,* and Shawn McIntosh, "The Evolution of the Zombie: The Monster That Keeps Coming Back," in Shawn McIntosh and Marc Leverette, eds., *Zombie Culture: Autopsies of the Living Dead* (Lanham, MD: Scarecrow Press, 2008), 4–5.

5. Halperin was later successfully sued by the movie's financiers, Amusement Securities Corporation, because he had signed over rights to the word *zombie.* See Rhodes, *White Zombie,* 171–174.

6. A motif probably drawn from Seacliff, according to Rhodes, *White Zombie,* 32.

7. Murder Legendre has also turned various of his white enemies into a zombie retinue. Beaumont, the white plantation owner, enters into a classic male pact with the satanic Legendre and dies for his sins after having almost been turned into a zombie himself. Rhodes, *White Zombie,* 48, notes that the interiors of Murder's castle were leftover sets from *Dracula.*

8. Written by Curt Siodmak and Ardel Wray and remade in 2011 in the wake of the zombie craze. Michael Koven describes Siodmak's script, in contrast to almost every other U.S.-made work on the zombie, fiction or nonfiction, as a "strong anticolonial discourse about the white presence and exploitation of Haiti." "The Folklore of the Zombie Film," in McIntosh and Leverette, eds., *Zombie Culture,* 29.

9. Marina Warner, *Fantastic Metamorphoses, Other Worlds* (New York: Oxford University Press, 2002), 156.

10. *King of the Zombies* (1941), directed by Jean Yarbrough, story by Edmond Kelso.

11. *Revenge of the Zombies* (1943), directed by Steve Sekely, written by Edmond Kelso and Van Norcross.

12. Victor Halperin's follow-up zombie film *Revolt of the Zombies* (1936).

13. E.g., in *King of the Zombies* and *Revenge of the Zombies.* See McIntosh, "Evolution," 6–7.

14. In *Dark Mysteries,* no. 20 (October 1954), writer unknown, reproduced in Jim Trombetta, *The Horror! The Horror! Comic Books the Government Didn't Want You to Read* (New York: Abrams ComicArts, 2010), 178–183.

15. *Voodoo,* no. 14 (March-April 1954), writer unknown, reproduced in Trombetta, *The Horror! The Horror!,* 192–199.

16. Most notably *Dawn of the Dead* (1978) and *Day of the Dead* (1985), though he has directed three more in the wake of the post-2000 zombie craze. Wes Craven's 1985 *The Serpent and the Rainbow,* based on another sensationalistic ethnographic study by Wade Davis, was a throwback to the subgenre's earlier colonial roots.

17. McIntosh notes that zombies were first represented as decomposing corpses in the 1966 Hammer film *Plague of the Zombies.* "Evolution," 8. But the rotting ghouls of the 1950s comics almost certainly helped lay the foundations for this new filmic image.

18. *Resident Evil* (2002), *Resident Evil: Apocalypse* (2004), *Resident Evil: Extinction* (2007), and *Resident Evil: Afterlife* (2010), all directed and written by Paul W. S. Anderson.

19. For an in-depth discussion of this effect, see Ron Scott, "'Now I'm Feeling Zombified': Playing the Zombie Online," in McIntosh and Leverette, eds., *Zombie Culture*, 169–184.

20. *Stake Land*, written by Mickle and Nick Damici.

21. One of innumerable posts can be found at http://thisorthat.com/fast-zombies-vs-slow-zombies (accessed August 13, 2011) and "The Federal Vampire and Zombie Agency," www.fvza.org/vandz.html (accessed August 13, 2011), which states: "In ancient times zombies and vampires were frequently pitted against each other for the enjoyment of bloodthirsty spectators. So which is more formidable? It's a question I'm frequently asked."

22. The U.S. president says the zombies "have robbed us of our confidence as the dominant life form." Brooks, *World War Z*, 260, 267.

23. Directed by Danny Boyle, written by Alex Garland.

24. Directed by Juan Carlos Fresnadillo, written by Rowan Joffe and Juan Carlos Fresnadillo.

25. *The Walking Dead*, vol. 2: *Miles Behind Us*, created, written. and lettered by Robert Kirkland, penciler/inker Charlie Adlard, gray tones by Cliff Rathburn (Berkeley, CA: Image Comics, 2006). [Originally published as nos. 7–12, n.d.]

26. *Dawn of the Dead* was remade in 2004 by Zack Snyder, written by James Gunn from Romero's screenplay. The quote is from Kim Paffenroth, *Gospel of the Living Dead: George Romero's Visions of Hell on Earth* (Waco, TX: Baylor University Press, 2006), 10.

27. Quoted in Alex Pappademas, "Dead Reckoning: Robert Kirkman Brings Zombies to Don Draper's Backyard," *GQ*, August 2, 2010.

28. Kyle Stephens, "American Nightmare: Reconciling Post 9/11 Anxieties within the New Zombie Aesthetic," thesis proposal, University of California, Berkeley, Department of Film Studies, personal communication, May 25, 2011.

29. *Shaun of the Dead*, directed by Edgar Wright, written by Simon Pegg and Edgar Wright; *Zombieland*, directed by Ruben Fleischer, written by Rhett Reese and Paul Wernick.

30. Max Brooks's best-selling *The Zombie Survival Guide: Complete Protection from the Living Dead* (New York: Three Rivers Press, 2003) is the gold standard here, but see also, e.g., Steven C. Schlozman's copiously illustrated *The Zombie Autopsies: Secret Notebooks from the Apocalypse* (New York: Grand Central Publishing, 2011).

31. The first Zombie Walk is listed by Wikipedia as occurring in Sacramento, California, in 2001. "Zombie Walk," http://en.wikipedia.org/wiki/Zombie_walk (accessed May 31, 2011).

32. "What Is Zombie Squad?" http://zombiehunters.org/whatiszs.php (accessed August 13, 2011).

33. Ali S. Khan, "Preparedness 101: Zombie Apocalypse," Public Health Matters blog, Centers for Disease Control, May 16, 2011, http://blogs.cdc.gov

/publichealthmatters/2011/05/preparedness-101-zombie-apocalypse (accessed May 19, 2011).

34. Including Wellington, New Zealand; Bristol, United Kingdom; and Okeechobee County, Florida, among many others.

35. Daniel Levy, personal communication, February 15, 2011.

36. Brooks, *Zombie Survival Guide*, 82.

37. "Services," http://zombiehunters.org/services/consult.php (accessed August 13, 2011).

38. It was followed in turn by a graphic novel, illustrated by Ibraim Roberson, called *Zombie Survival Guide: Recorded Attacks* (New York: Three Rivers Press, 2009), a faux history in which zombies are traced through key periods all the way back to prehistoric times.

39. Brooks, *World War Z*, 52.

40. Ibid., 340.

41. *The Walking Dead*, Book 2, Chapter 3, "Safety Behind Bars"; Robert Kirkman, creator, writer, letterer, and Charlie Adlard, penciler, inker (Berkeley, CA: Image Comics, 2009).

42. Paffenroth, *Gospel of the Living Dead*, 13. So far the Christian-centric Gothick has not introduced *shava-sadhana*, Tantric necrophilia or "practice with corpses."

43. See, e.g., http://www.buyzombie.com/2010/10/13/zombie-clothing/zombie-hats/cute-zombie-hat/ (accessed February 24, 2011).

44. Stacey Jay, *You Are So Undead to Me* (New York: Razorbill/Penguin Group, 2009).

45. Cf. *Awakening*, a projected TV series in which two sisters, one a lawyer, deal with the legal and social ramifications of the zombiefication of America.

46. Stacey Jay, *My So-Called Death* (Woodbury, MN: Flux, 2010), 207. This author's forthcoming novel *Juliet Immortal* follows closely the arc set by Meyer: "Juliet Capulet didn't take her own life. She was murdered by the person she trusted most, her new husband, Romeo Montague, a sacrifice made to ensure his own immortality. But Romeo didn't anticipate that Juliet would be granted eternal life, as well, and would become an agent for the Ambassadors of Light. For 700 years, Juliet has struggled to preserve romantic love and the lives of the innocent, while Romeo has fought for the dark side, seeking to destroy the human heart. Until now. Now Juliet has found her own forbidden love, and Romeo, oh Romeo, will do everything in his power to destroy their happiness." http://www.staceyjay.com/juliet-immortal (accessed May 31, 2011).

47. Scott Kenemore, *Zombie, Ohio: A Tale of the Undead* (New York: Skyhorse Publishing, 2011).

48. *I, Zombie*, vol. 1: *Dead to the World*, written by Chris Roberson, illustrated by Michael Allred, colorist Laura Allred (New York; Vertigo, 2010).

49. Marion, *Warm Bodies*, 223.

50. Ibid.

51. Ibid., 236.

52. Directed by David Fincher, written by Vincent Ward (story), David Giler, Walter Hill, and Larry Ferguson.

53. Directed by Jean-Pierre Jeunot, written by Joss Whedon.

54. http://wiki.urbandead.com/index.php/Church_of_the_Resurrection (accessed August 17, 2011).

55. See, e.g., http://answers.yahoo.com/question/index?qid=20080921050007 AAt5iww (accessed June 23, 2011).

56. As noted in chapter 4, comic book illustrators often skillfully and deliberately imitated medieval Christian iconography.

8. THE GOTHICK THEATER OF HALLOWEEN

"Goth is Death": Interview in *True Blood* promotional trailer, season 1 (HBO Productions, 2006).

1. Sir James Frazer's classic work of social anthropology *The Golden Bough* (1890) was the template for the widespread late nineteenth-century reinterpretation of folk custom as pagan survival.

2. See, e.g., Jack Santino, ed., *Halloween* (Knoxville: University of Tennessee Press, 1994), cited in Noel Carroll, "The Fear of Fear Itself: The Philosophy of Halloween," in Richard Greene and K. Silem Mohammad, eds., *Zombies, Vampires and Philosophy: New Life for the Undead*, Popular Culture and Philosophy, vol. 49 (Chicago: Open Court, 2010), 234.

3. See Jason Zinoman, "Haunted Houses Profit by Going to Extremes," *New York Times*, October 21, 2010. More than five of these productions were being staged in Manhattan during October 2010.

4. Quoted in Hester Lynch Piozzi, *Anecdotes of the Late Samuel Johnson, LL.D., during the Last Twenty Years of His Life* (London: T. Alman, 1822 [1786]), n.p. As a demonstration of how utterly allegory has faded from mainstream consciousness, this thinly veiled insult to dogs is proudly posted on literally scores of animal lovers' sites on the Web.

5. See especially *Death: The Time of Your Life* (New York: DC/Time Warner, 1997). [Originally published as issues no. 1–3, 1993, 1994, 1996.]

6. Peter Kingsley, *In the Dark Places of Wisdom* (Inverness, CA: Golden Sufi Center, 1999), 33. Modernist and postmodern commentators on allegory—from Walter Benjamin and Gershom Scholem to Paul de Man and Eve Kosofsky Sedgwick—reinterpret allegory essentially on their own terms, outside its original metaphysical context. Even the Romantic critique of allegory (Coleridge's "counterfeit product of the mechanical understanding") does not take into account its talismanic dependence on a two-worlds cosmogony. But as David Williams has said of medieval allegory, "the integrity of the literal level is seen as the guarantee of the meaningfulness of the more abstract levels." *Deformed Discourse: The Function of the Monster in Mediaeval Thought and Literature* (Exeter: University of Exeter Press, 1996), 73.

7. Angus Fletcher, "Allegory without Ideas," *boundary* 2 33, no. 1 (2006), 88.

8. Guillaume de Lorris and Jean de Meun, *The Romance of the Rose*, trans. Harry W. Robbins (New York: Dutton, 1962), 22, 11, 4–5.

9. Jody Enders, *Death by Drama and Other Medieval Urban Legends* (Chicago: University of Chicago Press, 2002), 11.

10. In the dour words of A. C. Cawley, "[Everyman's] lenten austerity can hardly fail to impress any but the most spiritually torpid." *Everyman and Medieval Miracle Plays* (New York: Dutton, 1965), xxvi.

11. William Howard Engel, "Theurgic Elements and the Memory Arts in Later Medieval Drama," lecture, Modern Language Association, New York, December 28, 2002.

12. C. S. Lewis, *The Discarded Image* (Cambridge: Cambridge University Press, 1964), 214.

13. Written by Grant Morrison, illustrated by Jon J. Muth (New York: Vertigo/DC Comics, 1994).

14. This information comes from *Hell House*, dir. George Ratliff. 2001. DVD © Plexigroup, 2003.

15. Cited in *Hell House*.

16. Quoted in ibid.

17. For an excellent historical overview, see Harold B. Segel, *Pinocchio's Progeny: Puppets, Marionettes, Automatons, and Robots in Modernist and Avant-Garde Drama* (Baltimore: Johns Hopkins University Press, 1995).

18. In Peter Arnott's 1955 staging of *Everyman*, the character Worldly Goods was portrayed by an ironbound chest whose lid opened to ventriloquize the character's lines. When Everyman makes his last-ditch appeal in the face of death, the lid snaps definitively shut. Peter Arnott, *Plays Without People: Puppetry and Serious Drama* (Bloomington: Indiana University Press, 1964), 71.

19. Edward Gordon Craig, "The Actor and the Uber-Marionette," in *On the Art of the Theater* (Chicago: Browne's Bookstore, 1913), 84–85.

20. See *The Secret Life of Puppets* for the full discussion of this topic.

21. Chris Hardman, personal communication, March 24, 2003. An important and immediate influence on Hardman's ecumenical religiosity and his populist political advocacy was the famous Bread and Puppets theater company of Vermont. Hardman worked briefly with its founder, the sculptor Peter Schumann, on various productions, including a *Totentanz* inspired by the etchings of Hans Holbein as well as this artist's depictions of the Seven Deadly Sins.

22. Program notes, "A Body of Water," Antenna Theater, June 6–25, 2005. "Walkmanology" has remained intact through the twenty-first century. Chris Hardman, personal communication, January 28, 2011.

23. Iain Chambers, quoted in Anne Allison, *Millennial Monsters: Japanese Toys and the Global Imagination* (Berkeley: University of California Press, 2006), 89.

24. Steven Connor, *Dumbstruck: A Cultural History of Ventriloquism* (Oxford: Oxford University Press, 2000), 4.

25. See chapter 11 for a discussion of the same, equally paradoxical result of combining digital and analogue special effects to create a single holistic on-screen monster.

Epigraph from Luis Buñuel, *My Last Breath*, trans. Abigail Israel (London: Flamingo, 1984).

1. Laura M. Hobson, "Hollywood's Road Trip: The Search for Hits at a Foreign Box Office," *New York Times*, April 3, 2006.

2. Buñuel, *My Last Breath*, 222.

3. As Patrick Goldstein, the movie columnist for the *Los Angeles Times*, states, "The epic scope of [Hollywood's] Big Event movies can't be achieved in other countries, which is why some of the most striking overseas box-office successes have been achieved by 3-D movies or special-effects driven animated films." "The Strange Trajectory of Hollywood Movies," LATimes.com, http://lat imesblogs.latimes.com/the_big_picture/2011/01/the-strange-trajectory -of-hollywood-movies-fizzling-in-us-but-skyrocketing-overseas.html (accessed January 25, 2011).

4. Douglas Cowan, *Sacred Terror: Religion and Horror on the Silver Screen* (Waco: Baylor University Press, 2008), 9.

5. *La Monja* (The Nun, 2009), directed by Luis de la Madrid, written by Manu Diez and Julio Fernández.

6. Written by Balagueró, Luis Berdejo, and Paco Plaza.

7. Directed by Kobayashi Masaki, written by Mizuki Yoko.

8. Anne Allison, *Millennial Monsters: Japanese Toys and the Global Imagination* (Berkeley: University of California Press, 2006), 39.

9. Japanese animators and their audiences alike insist that the time-honored tradition of round eyes for all anime characters, so suggestive of assimilation to Western norms of beauty, is a device that only suggests a fantasy or unreal world to the Japanese viewer.

10. Thomas LaMarre, "Otaku: Kiyoka [Gothic] Activism and Fan Media in Japan," lecture, University of California, Berkeley, April 28, 2009.

11. Allison reports that the *kawaii* sensibility extends even to such merchandise as the "Kitty-chan" dildo; *Millennial Monsters*, 18. Erik Davis argues that the "cute Cthulhu" phenomenon demonstrates that "the very cutification of Cthulhu renders the monster truly horrible. Why? . . . Having exhausted the vectors of conventional horror fandom, perhaps Cute Cthulhu has become [*the Great Old Ones'*] *ultimate strategy*, a self-replicating code of gibbering madness from the depths of space genetically implanted in a cuddly retrovirus." In "Pop Arcana (3)," http://hilobrow.com/2010/05/03/cthulhu-is-not -cute (accessed January 17, 2011).

12. http://www.otakureview.net/?p=8321 (accessed January 17, 2011).

13. "Dimensional Beasts," episodes 1–9, as described on http://www.supersentai .com/database/1991_jetman/vi-dbeasts.html (accessed March 17, 2011).

14. Miyazuki Mayao, endnote, "On Nausicaä," *Nausicaä of the Valley of Wind* (San Francisco: Viz Communications, 1995), n.p.

15. Directed by Nakata Hideo, screenplay by Takahashi Hiroshi and Suzuki Koji from the novel by Suzuki.

16. Directed and written by Kurosawa Kiyoshi.

17. Directed and written by Takashi Shimizu, who also directed the 2004 American remake.

18. To the question, "Is there such a thing as C- (as in China) horror?" East Asian film scholar Dan Cuong O'Neill replies that the short answer is no. "This is not because there hasn't been interesting horror. But 'Chinese' cinema is such a big and unwieldy category as it encompasses: Hong Kong cinema, Taiwan cinema, films coming out of China, Singapore, and other diasporic iterations of Chinese cinema. So the category of C-Horror would be difficult to sustain without any attention to regional inflections of the term. That being said, lots of interesting stuff coming out of Hong Kong and some from Taiwan that directly deal with horror borrow from the iconography of J-Horror. Not much from China because of the stronghold of social realism in film/literature, though we might detect cracks in the socialist and post-socialist cinema of China where the uncanny can be made legible." Personal communication, October 10, 2011.

19. In *The Soul Guardians* (1998), directed by Park Kwang-chun and written by Park from a novel series by Lee Woo-hyuck, Korean Catholic priests try to stop a young woman born in a satanic cult from delivering the Devil's baby.

20. Directed by Gore Verbinski, written by Ehren Kruger.

21. A. O. Scott, "A Golden Age of Foreign Films, Mostly Unseen," *The New York Times,* January 25, 2011.

22. Think, for example, of the fiendish witch of Mario Bava's 1960 *Black Sunday* (original title *La maschera del demonio*), from a story by Nikolai Gogol.

23. The anime *Rasuto burrado* (2001) was directed by Kitakubo Hiroyoki, screenplay by Maeda Shigeji. (*Burrado* is the loanword for English *blood*.) *Blood: The Last Vampire* (2009) was directed by Chris Nahon and written by Kamiyama Kenji. A manga series and videogame were spun off the original movie.

24. I would argue that graphic novel female characters of the 1990s, such as Angela, the scary warrior angel created by Neil Gaiman for the *Spawn* series, are already showing the influence of Asian anime, manga, and videogame story lines and characters, drawn in turn from American comic book female superheroes such as Wonder Woman and Supergirl.

25. Carol Clover, *Men, Women, and Chainsaws: Gender in the Modern Horror Film* (Princeton: Princeton University Press, 1992), 35.

26. In a blog post on *Asian Correspondent* titled "Why Do Korean Horror Movies Only Have Female Ghosts?" (June 21, 2009), Nathan Schwartzman quotes an unnamed figure in the Korean movie world: "In the past women were systematically repre[ss]ed and invisible. . . . I think that as that insurmountable repression continued on and on and on, they entered a freakish state and the result was for them to take care of their grudge through vengeance. The preval[e]nce of women ghosts in so many horror movies so far can be seen as due to that freakish state brought on by repression." http://asiancorrespon

dent.com/23554/why-do-korean-horror-movies-have-only-female-ghosts (accessed January 10, 2011).

27. V. Propp, *Morphology of the Folktale*, 2nd ed., trans. Laurence Scott, ed. Louis A. Wagner (Austin: University of Texas Press, 1968).

28. See also Julia George, "The Horror Film: An Investigation of Traditional Narrative Elements," *Folklore Forum* 15 (1980): 159–179, which situates the genre within Stith Thompson's structural classification of folklore types.

29. Quoted in Catherine Velay-Vallantin, "From 'Little Red Riding Hood' to 'The Beast of Gevaudan': The Tale in the Long-Term Continuum," trans. Binita Mehta, in Francesca Canade Sautman, Diana Conchado, and Giuseppe Carlo Di Scipio, eds., *Telling Tales: Medieval Narratives and the Folk Tradition* (New York: St. Martin's, 1998), 269.

30. In terms of the Gothick, Douglas Cowan calls this effect the "metataxis" of modern horror genres. *Sacred Terror*, 7.

31. Joseph Campbell, *The Hero with a Thousand Faces* (Cleveland: World Publishing Company, 1956).

32. Directed by Spike Jonze, screenplay by Charlie Kaufman.

33. Robert McKee, *Story: Substance, Structure, Style, and the Principles of Screenwriting* (New York: HarperCollins, 1997), 196–197.

34. Buñuel, *My Last Breath*, 131–132.

35. Ibid., 133.

36. See full discussion in *The Secret Life of Puppets*, chap. 5, 131–137.

37. See Carroll, "Fear of Fear Itself," 234–237, but especially his full treatment found in *The Philosophy of Horror* (New York: Routledge, 1990); Clover, *Men, Women, and Chainsaws*, 35 and passim.

38. David Edelstein, "Now Playing at Your Local Cineplex: Torture Porn," *New York Magazine*, January 28, 2006.

39. Alan Jones, a British horror festival director, attributes the rise in new European horror to the declining fortunes of Euro art films and the ready avenues of international distribution for horror films ("with horror a European director can reach an international audience. A horror fan doesn't mind reading subtitles"). Scott Roxborough, "Sicker, Darker, and More Twisted: The New European Horror Film at Berlin," *The Hollywood Reporter*, February 8, 2011, www.hollywoodreporter.com/news/human-centipede-director-film-pony-95389 (accessed February 8, 2011).

40. The quote is from Maximilian Forte, "The Revenge of the Local, the Horror of the Provincial, and Western Cosmopolitanism at Risk," Open Anthropology blog, December 1, 2008, http://zeroanthropology.net/2008/12/01/the-revenge-of-the-local-the-horror-of-the-provincial-and-western-cosmopolitanism-at-risk/ (accessed December 16, 2008).

41. Ibid.

42. "A movie is always a manipulation, regardless of whether it's a biopic or a romantic comedy, and 'Funny Games' takes this manipulation as its primary subject," Haneke told a *New York Times* interviewer. John Wray, "Minister of Fear," *New York Times*, September 23, 2007.

43. Written by Stephen Massicotte from a novel by Simon McGinn.

44. McKee, *Story Structure*, 104–105.

45. These three films were first thematically linked by Marina Warner in "Dark Arts," *Guardian*, October 14, 2005. *Piano Tuner* was written by the Quays and Alan Passes; *The Corpse Bride* was directed by Burton and Mike Johnson, written by Burton and Carlos Rangel (characters), screenplay by John August, Caroline Thompson, and Pamela Pettler; *Brothers Grimm* was written by Ehren Kruger.

46. Constructed by the Quays when budgetary problems prevented them from shooting in a real villa in Portugal.

47. Directed by James Wan and written by Leigh Whanell, cocreators of the *Saw* series.

48. Elizabeth Miller refutes the widespread story that Bram Stoker got the idea for *Dracula* from a nightmare. "Coitus Interruptus: Sex, Bram Stoker, and *Dracula*," in *The Gothic: From Ann Radcliffe to Anne Rice*, no. 44 (November 2006), www.erudit.org/revue/ron/2006/v/n44/014002ar.html (accessed October 4, 2010). In her introduction to the 1831 edition of *Frankenstein*, Mary Shelley testifies that her inspirational vision, though it came to her at night while she was in bed, was a "waking dream." www.rc.umd.edu/editions/frankenstein/1831v1/intro.html (accessed October 30, 2011).

49. Directed by Joseph Ruben, written by David Loughery, Chuck Russell, and Joseph Ruben.

50. Screenplay by Seishi Minakami and Satoshi Kon.

51. Luis Buñuel, "Cinema as an Instrument of Poetry," in *An Unspeakable Betrayal: Selected Writings of Luis Buñuel*, trans. Garrett White (Berkeley: University of California Press, 2000), 139.

52. See the full discussion of New Expressionism in chapter 9 of *The Secret Life of Puppets*.

53. See the discussion in chapters 8 and 9 of *The Secret Life of Puppets*.

54. The title of an exhibition held at the San Jose Museum of Art in December 2002, curated by Michael Duncan. Artists included were Ed Ruscha, John Baldessari, John McCracken, Robert Irwin, and James Hayward. Duncan says: "This is art that suggests routes back to direct expression and away from buzzwords and ironic art-about-art." www.sjmusart.org/content/about Us/press/press_info.phtml?itemID=39 (accessed March 4, 2003).

55. Peter Brooks, *The Melodramatic Imagination: Balzac, Henry James, Melodrama, and the Mode of Excess* (New Haven: Yale University Press, 1995 [1976]), 20. Brooks adds that melodrama "tends to diverge from the Gothic novel in its optimism, its claim that the moral imagination can open up the angelic spheres as well as the demonic depths and can allay the threat of moral chaos."

56. Guy Maddin, lecture, October 9, 2004, Berkeley, California, Pacific Film Archive premiere of *Cowards Bend the Knee*. See also Maddin's *From the Atelier Tovar: Selected Writings* (Toronto: Coach House Books, 2003).

57. Brooks, *Melodramatic Imagination*, 56.

Guillermo del Toro, interviewed by Terry Gross on *Fresh Air*, National Public Radio, January 24, 2007.

1. Guillermo del Toro, "How I Made Hellboy in My Image," *Observer*, www.guardian.co.uk, July 27, 2008.

2. Lloyd Levin, quoted in John Horn, "Thinking Small to Dream Big on 'Hellboy,'" *Los Angeles Times*, May 4, 2008.

3. Del Toro interview by Terry Gross, *Fresh Air*.

4. Director's commentary, *The Devil's Backbone*, special edition DVD (Sony Pictures Classics, 2003).

5. Del Toro, "How I Made Hellboy in My Image."

6. David S. Cohen, "Del Toro's 'Golden Army' of Creatures," *Variety*, July 10, 2008.

7. David Williams, *Deformed Discourse: The Function of the Monster in Mediaeval Thought and Literature* (Exeter: University of Exeter Press, 1996), 16.

8. David Williams, "Wilgefortis, Patron Saint of Monsters," in Robert A. Collins and Howard D. Pearce, eds., *Scope of the Fantastic* (Westport, CT: Greenwood Press, 1985), 176–177. She was also known as Uncumber, Liberata, and Viergeforte, among other names.

9. Ibid., 176.

10. Leah DeVun, "The Jesus Hermaphrodite: Science and Sex Difference in Premodern Europe," *Journal of the History of Ideas* 69, no. 2 (2008): 193–219.

11. Robert Mills, "Jesus as Monster," in Bettina Bildhauer and Robert Mills, eds., *The Monstrous Middle Ages* (Toronto: University of Toronto Press, 2003), 31, 37, 48.

12. See Williams, *Deformed Discourse*, 322, 329.

13. These five productions were quickly followed by fourteen more, all different, in England, France, and the United States. Richard Holmes, *The Age of Wonder: How the Romantic Generation Discovered the Beauty and Terror of Science* (New York: Pantheon, 2008), 334.

14. From the children's story by William Steig; directed by Andrew Adamson and Vicky Jenson, screenplay by Ted Elliott and others.

15. Kristen Whissel, "Vital Figures: The Life and Death of Digital Creatures," *Digital Effects Cinema* (Durham, NC: Duke University Press, in press), chap. 3. In the stories where they appear, Whissel notes, these hybrid digital-analog monsters are typically extremely difficult to kill, suggesting that technological hybridity itself lends them extra powers of "lethal vitality" in the minds of both their creators and their audiences.

16. See Michael Camille's *Image on the Edge: The Margins of Medieval Art* (Cambridge, MA: Harvard University Press, 1992), 21, 55, 114, 148.

17. Rick Bentley, "Hellboy Director Guillermo del Toro Credits Mexican Heritage for His Artistic Vision," *Fresno Bee*, July 8, 2008.

18. Del Toro, "How I Made Hellboy in My Image."

19. Robert Bly, "My Father's Wedding," ll. 25–30 (New York: HarperCollins, 1981).

20. Of Jung's theory of synchronicity, Wouter Hanegraaff says: "Presented explicitly as an alternative to instrumental 'causality,' it questioned the most fundamental assumptions of post-Cartesian philosophy and Newtonian physics, replacing them by a psychological re-formulation of analogy and 'correspondences': the very thing that positivist anthropology had rejected as the epitome of 'magical superstition.'" *Esotericism and the Academy: Rejected Knowledge in Western Culture* (Cambridge: Cambridge University Press, 2012), 294.

21. Director's commentary, *The Devil's Backbone*.

22. In a London interview with Mark Kermode, del Toro discusses both *Devil's Backbone* and *Pan's Labyrinth* as "microcosms" of the Spanish Civil War, which he describes as "a household war. People that shared beds, shared dining tables and shared lives ultimately killed each other." He deliberately paired them structurally: "*Devil's Backbone* is the boy's movie. It's the brother movie. But *Pan's Labyrinth* is the sister movie, the female energy to that other one. I wanted to make it because fascism is definitely a male concern and a boy's game, so I wanted to oppose that with an 11-year-old girl's universe." "Guillermo del Toro," http://www.guardian.co.uk/film/2006/nov/21/guardianinterviewsatbfisouthbank, November 21, 2006 (accessed January 27, 2007).

23. Denis Faye, "In the Garden of Good and Evil," http://www.wga.org/content/default.aspx?id=3076 (accessed January 18, 2007).

24. See Marie Louise von Franz's Jungian commentary on this and the archetype of the miller's daughter in *Problems of the Feminine in Fairy Tales* (New York: Spring Publications, 1972), 113–115, 70–78. Von Franz believes the meaninglessness of the repeating motion that never quite reaches its goal "express[es] the idea of not having been redeemed" and for this reason is traditionally "attributed to demons or cursed beings."

25. Commentary on *Vampyr*, Criterion 2008 British edition, quoted in www.davidbordwell.net/blog/2009/11/19/i-am-not-carl-dreyer-and-I-should-shut-up/ (accessed November 19, 2009).

26. Del Toro has consistently described the *Pan's Labyrinth* underworld as a womb. In the *Guardian* interview he says: "I very deliberately designed the idea of the fantasy world to be extremely uterine. We used a fallopian palette of colours: we used crimsons and golds, and everything in the fantasy world is very rounded while everything the real world is cold and straight. . . . This girl's idea of heaven, ultimately is to go back into her mother's belly."

27. Cowritten with Matthew Robbins from a story by Donald Wolheim, a film removed from the director's full control in its released form.

28. After centuries of inflation and deflation by opposing sides in the scholarly debate about alchemy, the most trustworthy definition to date belongs to Hanegraaff: "Alchemy is a complex historical and cultural phenomenon that does *not* have a conceptual core or essence (whether scientific, rational, religious, spiritual or psychological) but is characterized by basic procedures of transmutation that can be pursued in laboratory settings and function as narratives in religious or philosophical discourse." *Esotericism and the Academy*, 197.

29. Philippa Hawker, "Unraveling the Entrails of the Mind," *The Age*, www.theage .com.au, April 4, 2005 (accessed April 8, 2007). Another example of child mutilation from the Hugo novel was cutting smiles into the mouths of children. This in effect happens to Captain Vidal when the servant Mercedes slashes his face with a knife. The captain sews up the slit himself with a needle and thread.

30. Director's commentary, *Pan's Labyrinth*, special edition DVD (Sony Pictures Classics, 2004).

31. Faye, "Garden of Good and Evil."

32. "Pan's Labyrinth," August 25, 2007, http://rogerebert.suntimes.com/apps /pbcs.dll/article?AID=/20070825/REVIEWS08/70825002/1023 December 29, 2006 (accessed May 5, 2008).

33. Commentary to *Pan's Labyrinth* DVD.

34. Williams, *Deformed Discourse*, 174, 311.

35. Over the years an alternative religion has formed around Gaudi's Gothick fantasia, the Temple Expiatori de la Sagrada Familia, in Barcelona.

36. Del Toro interview by Terry Gross, *Fresh Air*.

37. Early interpretations of this tale as a straightforward ghost story (echoing James's own view) gave way, in deference to its author's high literary reputation and in keeping with the predilections of the twentieth century, to revisionist readings as a case study in female hysteria. See the extended discussion of the real-versus-crazy debate in *The Secret Life of Puppets*, chap. 7.

38. Michael Chabon, "Dark Adventure: On Cormac McCarthy's *The Road*," in *Maps and Legends: Reading and Writing Along the Borderlands* (San Francisco: McSweeney's Books, 2008), 108.

39. Currently on hold after production was abruptly canceled in 2011.

40. For a full discussion, see *TheSecret Life of Puppets*, chap. 5.

41. "Madness Tops Del Toro's List," Sci Fi Wire, http://www.cinemablend.com /new/Del-Toro-Eyes-The-Mountains-Of-Madness-7282.html (accessed December 24, 2007).

42. Luis Buñuel, "Pessimism," in *An Unspeakable Betrayal: Selected Writings of Luis Buñuel*, trans. Garrett White (Berkeley: University of California Press, 2000), 263.

11. THE NEW CHRISTIAN GOTHICK

William P. Young in collaboration with Wayne Jacobsen and Brad Cummings, *The Shack* (Los Angeles: Windblown Media, 2007), 237. Young credits his publishers as cowriters in his revision of the novel.

1. As interpreted by Georges Duby, *The Age of the Cathedrals: Art and Society 980–1420*, trans. Eleanor Levieux (Chicago: University of Chicago Press, 1981), 99–102.

2. Maurice Lévy, "Mountains, Mezzotints, and Gothic Imagery," in Francoise Besson, ed., *Mountains Figured and Disfigured in the English-Speaking World* (Newcastle upon Tyne: Cambridge Scholars Publishing, 2010), 303.

3. Anne Rice, *Christ the Lord: Out of Egypt* (New York: Random House, 2005), *Christ the Lord: The Road to Cana* (New York: Random House, 2008).

4. Anne Rice, "Essay on Earlier Works," August 15, 2007, www.annerice.com /Bookshelf-EarlierWorks.html (accessed August 4, 2008).

5. Northrop Frye, *The Secular Scripture: A Study of the Structure of Romance* (Cambridge: Harvard University Press, 1976), 13–14.

6. Anne Rice, *Angel Time: The Song of the Seraphim* (New York: Alfred A. Knopf, 2009), 8.

7. Anne Rice, *Of Love and Evil: Songs of the Seraphim* (New York: Alfred A. Knopf, 2010), 168–169.

8. Quoted by Huysmans scholar and translator Brendan King on his website, http://homepage.mac.com/brendanking/huysmans.org/en/biog.htm (accessed December 23, 2010).

9. On her Facebook page: www.facebook.com/annericefanpage?v=wall&story _fbid=113868381998571&ref=mf (accessed July 30, 2010).

10. Cf. Tim LaHaye and Jerry B. Jenkins, *Nicolae: The Rise of the Antichrist* (Wheaton, IL: Tyndale House, 1997), 380.

11. As reported on the series' official website, www.leftbehind.com (accessed December 22, 2010).

12. LaHaye and Jenkins, *Nicolae*, 358.

13. Inspired Media Entertainment, www.leftbehindgames.com/index.php (accessed December 22, 2010).

14. Stephen King, "A Preface in Two Parts," *The Stand: The Complete Uncut Edition* (New York: Signet, 1991), xi.

15. Quoted in John Marks, "Stephen King's God Trip," Salon.com, www.salon .com/books/int/2008/10/23/stephen_king/index1.html (accessed April 28, 2009).

16. All page references to Stephen King, *The Stand: The Complete and Uncut Edition* (New York: Signet, 1991), 504. Mother Abagail herself is the token black woman in this 1970s Euro-American vision of a United States consisting of 99 percent white people with strangely fabricated WASP names (Alberta Edmonton, etc.), no Asians, and no Latinos.

17. Ibid., 503–504.

18. Ibid., 569, 573.

19. Ibid., 730–731.

20. King himself has stated that his original intention was to write a "fantasy epic like *Lord of the Rings*, only with an American setting." www.stephenking .com/library/novel/stand:_the_complete__uncut_edition_the_inspiration .html (accessed February 11, 2011).

21. See Max Blumenthal, "Kill or Convert, Brought to You By the Pentagon," *Nation*, August 7, 2007, www.thenation.com/blog/kill-or-convert-brought -you-pentagon (accessed December 23, 2010).

22. http://windblownmedia.com/news/html (accessed December 22, 2010). According to the book's website, it is currently being translated into thirty languages; www.theshackbook.com/news.html (accessed October 31, 2009).

23. First quote from William P. Young, lecture sponsored by North Valley Calvary Chapel, Riverton School, Yuba City, California, September 19, 2008; second phrase quoted in Motoko Rich, "Christian Novel Is Surprise Best Seller," *New York Times*, June 24, 2008.

24. Young, *The Shack*, 64–65.

25. Ibid., 73, 81.

26. Ibid., 73, 111.

27. Ibid., 106, 82, 93.

28. Ibid., 146.

29. Ibid., 185.

30. Ibid., 128.

31. As parsed by Kathleen Raine in "The Human Face of God," in *Testimony to the Invisible: Essays on Swedenborg* (West Chester, PA: Chrysalis Books, 1995), 63, 67.

32. See the discussion of David Bohm's theory of the "holographic paradigm" in Wouter J. Hanegraaff, *New Age Religion and Western Culture: Esotericism in the Mirror of Secular Thought* (Albany: State University of New York Press, 1998), 67–68: "Holography has the peculiar characteristic that each fragment of intermediate frequency pattern contains the information of the whole object. Bohm's theory suggests that, in a similar way, the whole of the universe is implicit in each of its parts."

33. See the work of Robert Bork in *The Geometry of Creation: Architectural Drawings and the Dynamics of Gothic Design* (Farnham, UK: Ashgate Press, 2010).

34. Ibid., 158.

35. Arthur Versluis has traced the Sophia/Wisdom tradition in America in *Wisdom's Children: A Christian Esoteric Tradition* (Albany: State University of New York, 1999) and *Wisdom's Book: The Sophia Anthology* (St. Paul, MN: Paragon House, 2000). Also see Arthur Versluis, "Sexual Mysticisms in Nineteenth-Century America: John Humphrey Noyes, Thomas Lake Harris, and Alice Bunker Stockham," in Wouter J. Hanegraaff and Jeffrey J. Kripal, eds., *Hidden Intercourse: Eros and Sexuality in the History of Western Esotericism* (Leiden: Brill, 2008), 339.

36. In private diaries dated 1675, later disseminated by Pordage's followers. Versluis, *Wisdom's Children*, 19, 51.

37. Ibid., 103–111. See also Versluis's *Esoteric Origins of the American Renaissance* (New York: Oxford University Press, 2001) for the influence of these groups on nineteenth-century American literature.

38. Ibid., 271.

39. Jean M. Humez, *Mother's Firstborn Daughters: Early Shaker Writings on Women and Religion* (Bloomington: Indiana University Press, 1993), 47; Mary Baker Eddy, *Science and Health with Key to the Scriptures* (Boston: First Church of Christ, Scientist, 1971), "Christian Science Practice," 372 and "Genesis," 517.

40. Young, *Shack*, 172, 177.

41. Ibid., 210.

42. Ibid., 218.

43. Ibid., 233–234.

44. The fact that this ending is inserted on top of the dream frame suggests that it may have been an afterthought. Essentially it serves as a double qualifier of the "reality" of the story.

45. Young, *Shack*, 237, 240.

46. Ibid., 182.

47. Ibid., 181. In his public lecture in Yuba City, Young remarked, "I'm a Canadian, not a Republican."

48. Ibid., 198.

49. "The Shack: Helpful or Heretical? A Critical Review by Norman L. Geisler and Bill Roach," www.normangeisler.net/theshack.html (accessed December 4, 2009). The *New York Times* also notes that some conservative Christian leaders, including the president of Southern Baptist Theological Seminary, have found the novel heretical. Rich, "Christian Novel."

50. Raine, "Human Face of God," 53.

51. Harold Bloom, *The American Religion: The Emergence of the Post-Christian Nation* (New York: Simon and Schuster, 1992), 32, 40, 15.

52. Young, *Shack*, 99.

53. Ibid., 248.

12. EPILOGUE

Grant Morrison, *Supergods: What Masked Vigilantes, Miraculous Mutants, and a Sun God from Smallvile Can Teach Us about Being Human* (New York: Spiegel and Grau, 2011), 416.

1. Michael Winerip, "A Child Turns to the Fold," *New York Times*, June 14, 2009.

2. Charles Taylor, *A Secular Age* (Cambridge, MA: Belknap Press, 2007), 38.

3. Trade journals indicate sharply falling ticket sales for this subgenre. See, e.g., Brian Lowry, "Second-Tier Heroes Face a Dose of Reality," *Variety*, June 22, 2011, http://www.variety.com/article/VR1118038916?refCatId=13 (accessed August 17, 2011).

4. "Newcastle: A Taste of Things to Come," *John Constantine: Hellblazer*, written by Jamie Delano, artist Richard Piers Raynor and Mark Buckingham (New York: DC Comics/Warner Bros., 2003). [Originally published as *Hellblazer* no. 11.]

5. Morrison, *Supergods*, 272–273.

6. Ibid., 273.

7. Ibid., 276.

8. Jeffrey Kripal, "How We Got to Super: Grant Morrison's Visionary Gnosticism," *Religion Dispatches*, August 20, 2011, http://www.religiondispatches.org/books/culture/4883/how_we_got_to_super:_grant_morrison's_visionary_gnosticism/ (accessed August 22, 2011). I'm indebted to Kripal's review for first steering me to Morrison's book.

9. From the movie *Green Lantern* (2011), directed by Martin Campbell, written by Greg Berlanti, Michael Green, Marc Guggenheim, and Michael Goldenberg, from the DC comic book.

10. Morrison, *Supergods*, 29.
11. Harold Bloom, *The American Religion: The Emergence of the Post-Christian Nation* (New York: Simon and Schuster, 1992), 35.
12. Alex Owen, *The Place of Enchantment: British Occultism and the Culture of the Modern* (Chicago: University of Chicago Press, 2004), 147.

ACKNOWLEDGMENTS

Knowledge transmission, for me, comes through friendships as much as books, and much of the direction my ideas have taken I owe to colleagues and friends who have generously shared their ideas me, along with an ever-growing matrix of institutions that have supported my work. First on the list must be the amazing Lindsay Waters, everything an editor and loyal friend should be, along with his assistant Shanshan Wang and everyone at Harvard University Press responsible for producing this book. Special thanks to my copyeditor, Sue Warga, for her outstanding work on a challenging project, to my proofreader, Megan Roberts, and to Melody Negron, for her fine oversight on the project. I am also grateful to my four peer reviewers for their insightful comments and their extended engagement with the book's premises.

I wish to thank the institutions and private individuals who provided both support and venues for presenting papers on which portions of this book were based: the American Council of Learned Societies for a fellowship taken in 2008–2009; Joyce Botelho and the John Nicholas Brown Center for the Humanities, Brown University; Arthur Versluis and the Association for the Study of Esotericism; Aura Satz and the Association of Art Historians; Angus Fletcher and the Getty Museum; Michael Murphy and the Esalen Institute; Rosalie Basten and the Château de Taurenne; Gauri Viswanathan and Columbia University; and finally the University of

California, Berkeley, Rhetoric Department and the exceptional students of my Rhetoric 178 class at UC Berkeley in fall 2009.

Librarians and libraries vital to my research included Arevig Caprielian, for assistance above and beyond the call of duty, and also Laura O'Keefe at the New York Society Library; Elizabeth Denzinger and Charles Carter at the Pforzheimer Collection of the New York Public Library; the British Library; and the University of California, Berkeley, Doe Library. Last but not least, I am indebted to the Berkeley and Albany, California, public libraries, with their extensive collections of graphic novels and many other popular fictions beneath the radar of university collections.

I am further indebted to the following friends, colleagues, and students: Maurizio Bettini, Harold Bloom, Simon Ditchfield, Claire Fanger, Kristi Gansworth, Robert Geary, Gayle Greene, Robert and Ted Grudin, Wouter Hanegraaff, Diane Hoeveler, Jay Hyatt, Bruce Ingram, Massimo Introvigne, Claire Kahane, Gábor Klaniczay, Cariel and Tadea Klein, Danielle Klenak, Christopher Knowles, Jeffrey Kripal, Daniel Levy, Maurice Lévy, David and Mary Alice Lowenthal, Michael Mascuch, J. Gordon Melton, Frank Muniz, Dan Cuong O'Neill, Theodore and Betty Roszak, Paul Selig, Kyle Stephens, Paul Strohm, Lawrence Sutin, Gary Ungar, and Marina Warner.

Special thanks to Erik Davis for his trailblazing work on the Lovecraft cults and to the indefatigable Roy Thomas and his comicologist colleagues Mike Conroy, Ofer Berenstein, Jim Van Dore, Stephen Rowe, Juan Gonzalez, Brian Saner Lamkin, Bruce Mason, and Bill Schelly for sharing with me their deep knowledge of comic book lore.

All errors in this and other areas of discussion are solely mine.

Portions of Chapter 2 first appeared as part of "Faux Catholic: A Gothic Subgenre from Monk Lewis to Dan Brown" in *boundary 2*; some parts of Chapter 8 as part of "A Postcool *Everywoman*" in *Articulate Objects: Voice, Sculpture, and Performance* (Peter Lang, 2009), edited by Aura Satz and Jon Wood; portions of Chapter 9 as part of "The Ten Rules of Sitges" in *Raritan*; and portions of Chapter 10 as part of "Cathedral Head: The Gothick Cosmos of Guillermo del Toro" in *The Believer*; all are reprinted here with permission.

INDEX

INDEX